A woman in history tells the fascinating story of the life and work of Eileen Power, a major British historian who once ranked in fame alongside Tawney, Trevelyan and Toynbee. Drawing on Eileen Power's personal correspondence and diaries, as well as the vivid memories of the many people who knew her, Maxine Berg recreates the life of this charismatic personality whose interests were a potent and exotic mixture of medieval history and literature, the new social sciences and China.

Eileen Power was the best-known medieval historian of the interwar years. She wrote one of the classic medieval histories, *Medieval people*, which is still in print today. An active participant in the campaign for women's suffrage, she became one of the first writers and teachers of women's history. She made her career as lecturer then as professor at the London School of Economics and, together with R. H. Tawney, turned a frontier subject, economic and social history, into a prominent part of the historical disciplines. She defined her subject as comparative and international in her passionate engagement with the forces of nationalism and militarism. Her major works on trade, merchants and comparative economic history were conveyed in writing that was individual and human, rich in narrative and ranging widely over time and place. In her evangelism for the subject on the lecture platform, on the radio, through the press and in the school-book, she made her subject glamorous, and her history became compelling reading and listening to a whole generation. Yet when she died prematurely at the age of fifty-one, her legacy to history was lost, and now we have largely forgotten her and the passions that drove her to write history.

A WOMAN IN HISTORY
EILEEN POWER, 1889–1940

A WOMAN IN HISTORY
EILEEN POWER, 1889–1940

MAXINE BERG

University of Warwick

CAMBRIDGE
UNIVERSITY PRESS

Published by the Press Syndicate of the University of Cambridge
The Pitt Building, Trumpington Street, Cambridge CB2 IRP
40 West 20th Street, New York, NY 10011–4211, USA
10 Stamford Road, Oakleigh, Melbourne 3166, Australia

First published 1996

Printed in Great Britain at the University Press, Cambridge

A catalogue record for this book is available from the British Library

Library of Congress cataloguing in publication data
Berg, Maxine, 1950–
A woman in history – Eileen Power, 1889–1940 / Maxine Berg.
p.   cm.
Includes bibliographical references and index.
ISBN 0 521 40278 6. – ISBN 0 521 56852 8 (pbk.)
1. Power, Eileen Edna, 1889–1940.
2. London School of Economics and Political Science – Faculty – Biography.
3. Women historians – Great Britain – Biography.
4. Medievalists – Great Britain – Biography.
5. Great Britain – Historiography.   6. Middle Ages – Historiography.
7. Europe – Historiography.   I. Title.
DA3.P69B47   1996
940.1′092–dc20   95–34779   CIP
[B]

ISBN 0 521 40278 6 hardback
ISBN 0 521 56852 8 paperback

For my daughters
Frances, Gabriel and Jessie

Contents

Illustrations

Preface

Like many economic historians of my generation, I first read *Medieval People* and *The Medieval Wool Trade* when I was an undergraduate, but reflected little on the historian who wrote them. *Medieval Women*, first published during the 1970s, was a founding text and inspiration of the new women's history. Passed among graduate students and young lecturers, it was a bond among female historians. But I only discovered Eileen Power as a historical figure in her own right during the early 1980s when I was writing my book *The Age of Manufactures*. This was a study of industries and work during the eighteenth century, emphasising the place of family and women's labour. My secondary sources were limited, and I was drawn back to books written by Alice Clark, Dorothy George, Joyce Dunlop, Dorothy Marshall and Lilian Knowles. The prefaces to their books established their connections with each other through the LSE, and in some cases also through Girton College, Cambridge. Eileen Power's name appeared frequently in these prefaces and in many others of the period as my net spread wider. A search for material on the eighteenth-century economy thus opened my eyes to the existence to a whole group of female economic historians writing in the interwar years, and to the central place played in this group by a medieval historian. I told the story of these 'first women economic historians' at a launching session of the Women's Committee of the Economic History Society at the annual conference of the Society in 1988. I decided thereafter to focus on Eileen Power. Not a biographer by experience or inclination, I owe this change in my approach to a suggestion made by Sir Keith Thomas after a seminar presentation of an early version of the paper in 1989.

I have not written this biography as a professional and official biographer with access to a large body of family papers. Indeed, I was told at an early stage that Eileen Power's personal papers had been destroyed by her sisters after her death. My concerns are not those of the political biographers, 'valets to the famous', now in a state of anxiety over the literary merit of their enterprises.[1] Nor are they those of the medieval historian. But I am an economic historian and a female historian. As a biography this book makes no claims to be definitive; new material and new perspectives in future will, no doubt, recast some of what I have written. I have tried to set Eileen Power in the intellectual and cultural history of her generation, to analyse her work and the contribution she made, and with this to uncover what I could from fragmentary evidence the details of her personal life, the longings and disappointments as well as the successes and pleasures she experienced as a woman. I hope the picture that emerges of her provides the combination of serious analysis of her work and reconstruction of the personality that made her so much more than the books and articles she wrote.

I am grateful to the Women's Committee for support, and for the new focus of interest it gave me in the historical association founded seventy years ago by Eileen Power, R. H. Tawney and Ephraim Lipson. Many members of the Society have been very generous with ideas and suggestions, and sometimes recollections. Negley Harte and Theo Barker, guardians of the Society's memory, had not thought much about the women before, but they then told me many stories and put me on to many connections. John Hatcher helped me with the medievalists and with some key sources. Maurice Beresford and the late William Ashworth gave me their memories. I have interviewed and spoken to many others: Marjorie Chibnall, Elizabeth Crittall, Sir Raymond Firth, Sir John and Lady Habakkuk, Christopher and Bridget Hill, Joan Thirsk, Sir Isaiah Berlin, Lord Briggs, A. F. Thompson, Professor Chimen Abramsky, Jean Floud, Marjorie Durbin, Nadine Marshall, Sir Michael and Lady Clapham, Martin Robertson and Eleanor Robertson. I have corresponded with and talked to many others too numerous to list, but their names appear in various footnotes.

Two key articles helped me during the early stages of my writing – Joan Thirsk's foreword to *Women in English Society 1500–1800* edited by Mary Prior, and Natalie Zemon Davis' 'History's two bodies'.[2] I have been grateful for suggestions and information at an early stage

---

[1] See Ben Pimlott, *Frustrate Their Knavish Tricks: Writings on Biography, History and Politics* (London, 1994); short version in *The Independent on Sunday*, 14 August 1994, 24–6.

[2] Joan Thirsk, 'Foreword', in Mary Prior (ed.), *Women in English Society 1500–1800* (London, 1985), pp. 1–21; Natalie Zemon Davis, 'History's two bodies', *American Historical Review*, 93

to Peter Linebaugh, Ludmilla Jordanova, Jay Winter and Fernanda Perrone. Kate Perry, the archivist of Girton College, Cambridge and Lois Reynolds, research assistant on the History of the School Project at the London School of Economics (and also my indexer), gave me more support and information than anyone could expect. The Simm Fellowship at the University of Manchester gave me a year's teaching leave to research and to write. Eileen Power recognised the significance of female friends to her life, her career and her writing. Ruth Pearson, Phyllis Mack and Pat Hudson have played that part in my life. John Robertson, Elspeth Robertson and Phyllis Mack read my early drafts, and pressed me for more information, better organisation and better writing. Sir John Habakkuk, Joan Thirsk and Claire Tomalin all read the book. Sir John Habakkuk pointed me towards important aspects of Eileen Power's family background, and provided helpful information on a number of interwar historians. Joan Thirsk was not only a most careful reader: her own commitment to the 'History Women' has been a constant support. Claire Tomalin's interest, advice and above all encouragement came at a crucial stage. I am grateful to Richard Fisher and expecially Ruth Parr at the Cambridge University Press for their advice on the book, and to Ruth Parr herself for all her hard work in pushing the book through the process of publication.

This book could not have happened without the papers and information provided by Lady Cynthia Postan. She has not given me access to everything she knows and all the papers she has, for some of these things are entwined with her own life. But she has provided me with all that she could. She has kept careful guardianship over the memory of a woman she never knew, the first wife of her husband. It is to her that we owe the publication of *Medieval Women*, and I am deeply indebted to her for her insight into the personality, indulgences and frivolities that were part of the making of this scholarly woman.

The Robertson sisters, to whom this book is dedicated, have grown from babies to young girls during the making of this book, and they think it is time to stop sharing their mother with the Power sisters. John Robertson, my husband and fellow historian, has been not just a husband but 'a historic friend'. He has read my typescripts and demanded that I write better, and he has listened with sympathy and understanding as I have tried to be an economic historian.

(1988), 1–30; Maxine Berg, 'Introduction', in Maxine Berg, *The Age of Manufactures: Industry, Innovation and Work in Britain 1700–1820* (1st edn, London, 1985), pp. 15–20.

CHAPTER I

Introduction

Women's writing has been a subject of enduring interest, but it is only recently that women's historical writing has attracted attention. This is despite the place history was accorded among the arts during the eighteenth and early nineteenth centuries, when history represented the highest form of literature after poetry. Clio, the muse of history, was represented as a woman. As a woman she inspired the prophets and bards of history. The muses were appealed to during the Renaissance as presiding over the high disciplines where intelligence, memory and inspiration were required. Natalie Davis has written that the muse 'embodied in her female form the arts that men practiced ... she favoured them from without and represented their activities and the qualities to which they must aspire.'[1]

Did the muse write history herself, or were any of her prophets women? It is at first sight difficult to answer this question, for the great historians who are remembered, Thucydides, Gibbon, Hume, Macaulay, Ranke, Maitland and others, were men, and the historical profession, progressing through various schools of history – the German historical school, the Annales school, the students of Croce, and English social history – seemed to be masculine. Biographies of Toynbee, Namier, Bloch and Trevelyan have appeared in recent years. The History Men dominate our view of the profession.

My book stands apart from – and challenges – this tradition of historiography. It is the story of one woman's quest to write history and to make an impact on her discipline and on the culture of her time. I might have chosen to write a general history of female historians, to resurrect the memory of the women lost to the historical profession, and thus to redress the condescension of the History Men. There are now a number of articles in learned journals

---

[1] Natalie Zemon Davis, 'History's two bodies', *American Historical Review*, 93 (1988), 1–30.

which 'reinstate' the careers of interesting female historians.[2] But
among these, and among historians generally in the years before the
Second World War, there was one whose character along with the
appeal of her historical writing brought her a high popular and
international reputation. Eileen Power during her lifetime was just as
well known as were R. H. Tawney, G. M. Trevelyan and Marc
Bloch. Her story stands alongside theirs in the making of history as a
part of the culture of the day. But her struggle to do this was different
because she was a woman. However much she may have wished it,
or even at times have imagined it, she was not a 'genderless soul'[3]
before the court of history. Her historical writing should be so
judged, but her making as a historian and a public figure was also
her own personal story of becoming a woman. I was thus drawn to
write about Eileen Power herself. Her individuality mattered to her,
and it was clearly this that created her impact. But writing her
biography was also a way to bring much more immediately to life the
contemporary impact of the new economic and social historical
writing, the academic and literary circles in which she lived, and
finally her experiences as a woman finding her way in the historical
professions at the time.

Eileen Power was the best-known medieval historian of the
interwar years, and brought medieval history into general culture.
She was the author of one of the most popular medieval histories,
Medieval People, which went into ten editions, and is still in print
seventy years later. She was one of the first writers and teachers of
women's history. Together with R. H. Tawney she made a frontier
subject, economic and social history, into a prominent part of the
historical disciplines. She created a cosmopolitan and comparative

<hr/>

2   See Bonnie Smith, 'The contribution of women to modern historiography in Great
    Britain, France, and the United States, 1750–1940', *American Historical Review*, 89 (1984),
    709–32; Billie Melman, 'Gender, history and memory: the invention of women's past in
    the nineteenth and early twentieth centuries', *History and Memory*, 5 (1993), 5–41; Susan
    Mosher Stuard, 'A new dimension? North American scholars contribute their perspective',
    in Bernard Rosenthal and Paul Szarmach (eds.), *Medievalism in American Culture*
    (Binghampton, NY, 1984), pp. 67–84; Joan Scott, 'American women historians, 1884–
    1984', in J. W. Scott, *Gender and the Politics of History* (New York, 1988), pp. 178–231; Judith
    Bennett, 'Medievalism and feminism', *Speculum*, 68 (1993), 308–31; Joan Thirsk, 'The
    history women', in Mary O'Dowd and Sabine Wichert (eds.), *Chattel, Servant or Citizen.
    Women's Status in Church and State* (Belfast, 1995), pp. 1–11; and Mary O'Dowd, 'Irish
    historiography and women historians in Ireland', unpublished paper presented to the
    Warwick Regional Seminar on Gender, History and Historiography, 28 February 1994.
3   This phrase is Phyllis Mack's. See her *Visionary Women: Ecstatic Prophecy in Seventeenth-Century
    England* (Berkeley, 1992), p. 10.

economic history which departed from nationalist and Eurocentric historical traditions. She was famous in her time, and achieved accordingly. She had a career of mainstream scholarly success – she was the first woman to hold the Kahn Travelling Fellowship, in 1920, and she was the first woman to give the Ford lectures in Oxford, in 1939. She taught first in Cambridge, then made her career at the London School of Economics (LSE), and though she was not the first female professor in economic history in Britain (Lilian Knowles was), she was the second, and also achieved this at the age of forty-two. She received an honorary D.Litt. in 1933 from Manchester University, and one from Mount Holyoke in the USA in 1937, and she was made a corresponding member of the Medieval Academy of America in 1936. But Eileen Power's fame and significance reached far beyond the academic enclosure. She also participated actively in the life of literary London; she reviewed frequently in the weeklies, and was a popular lecturer and pioneer radio broadcaster. She combined her work as a historian with journalism and lecturing on contemporary politics from a progressive liberal and socialist stance.

Even more than this, Eileen Power stood for a new kind of history; she organised her discipline and in her own personal style she acted as its ambassador. Most of Power's own generation of medievalists sought such professionalism through the study of institutions and politics as against what they perceived as a past legacy of 'romantic antiquarianism'.[4] Power sought her professionalism in developing the new discipline of economic history. Together with R. H. Tawney she lifted the subject out of its former framework in economic policy and constitutional development. The social history they both introduced in different ways was integrated with economic history, but was individual and human, as well as wide ranging in its scope and chronology. It was a history that could be conveyed to ordinary people in village lecture halls, in newspapers and over the radio, and to schoolchildren as well as to academic colleagues and university audiences. Alongside Tawney's moral commitment and socialism Power brought to her subject an aesthetic as well as a political perspective. This was something that also set her apart from other female medievalists and economic and social historians. She not only wrote and taught, but she shaped the character of her discipline. In

---

[4]   Scott, 'American women historians,' p. 181.

her evangelism for the subject on the platform, radio, the press and the school book, she made the subject glamorous.

Eileen Power's independent stance in bringing together her scholarship and her identity as a woman produced in this way a very attractive alternative public face for academic life. Part of the glamour was made by her own personality, and the kind of woman she represented. Eileen Power stood out from most other academic women of her generation, especially in the historical disciplines where there were virtually no precedents for the kind of mainstream recognition she achieved. For she was no bluestocking, and combined the feminine and the scholarly in a way that few other women of her generation did. Scholarship was set apart for most women from the spheres of gender that defined the place of women – femininity, physical beauty, sex and family life. Eileen Power did not marry until late in life, and she did not have children, but in other ways she crossed this divide. She was a charismatic figure to those men and women who came into contact with her. She was scholarly and beautiful, with a mysterious family background and a progressive, cosmopolitan reputation. Her interests were a potent and exotic mixture of medieval history and literature, the new social sciences and China. She indulged herself in travelling, dancing and fine clothes. Men and women loved her: she had close and intense female friendships, she was engaged for a time to Reginald Johnston, the tutor to Pu Yi, the last emperor of China (the subject of Bertolucci's recent film, with Peter O'Toole playing Johnston), and eventually married her former research assistant, Michael Moissey Postan, who was some ten years her junior and a dazzling figure in his own right, only three years before she died. This personal charisma was combined with a literary and aesthetic presentation of her innovative historical work, lending it a broad appeal.

Eileen Power achieved all this by the age of fifty-one, when she died suddenly. Despite her fame while she lived, she appeared to leave no legacy. Soon after her death she was remembered only as one of the colourful personalities of the early days of the LSE, and for a time as the author of *Medieval People*. In recent years this legacy has extended to a mention in the annals of feminist history. Now we know little of her, and we have forgotten the passions that drove her to write history.

I wrote this book to discover more than the achievement. I wanted to know how this woman came to write history, how she played a prominent part in reshaping her field, and why she has since slipped into relative obscurity. When I started to read about her I became fascinated by the emotions that drove her as a young historian to write to a friend: 'You don't know how I long to be able to research & write books all the time ... I want to write books. Oh dear, Oh dear!' and 'I ache for a historic friend at times.'[5] I wondered about the constraints placed on her career by her gender, constraints she tried to deny: 'The difference is between good books and bad books, straight-thinking books and sentimental books, not between male books and female books', but was forced to confront: 'These silly remarks would not be made to male candidates.' I was inspired by the open, expansive and comparative history she mapped out, through which she expressed her political commitment to the peace movement. Her medieval history provided a 'peculiarly suitable basis' for the comparative method. 'It is so far removed from the present that neither contrasts nor similarities are blurred; each problem appears small and clear; it is

> like a little book
> Full of a thousand tales,
> Like the gilt page the good monks pen
> That is all smaller than a wren,
> Yet has high towers, meteors and men
> And suns and spouting whales.[6]

Finally, I was saddened by the loss of her project which followed fast upon her death. The broadly based comparative economic history informed by sociological and anthropological concepts became a lost byway. Economic history narrowed to the economists' plaything; social history split off and went its separate way. The historians' memory of Eileen Power 'withered like grass'.

To tell Eileen Power's story is not to reinstate a female intellectual against the 'patriarchal silences of the past'. Important as it is to reveal the reasons for those patriarchal silences, this is not the story of a victim of the exclusivity of the male academic hierarchy. Nor is it the case that her achievement was unique among women. In the first place, it was clear that Eileen Power was not alone as a woman in her field. In part, her achievement was based on the prior place

---

[5] Eileen Power to Margery Garrett, Power–Postan Papers, in the possession of Lady Cynthia Postan, 17 May 1911 and 10 July 1912.
[6] Eileen Power, 'On medieval history as a social study', inaugural lecture, LSE, 1933 and *Economica*, 12 (1934), 13–29, at 23.

that women had created for themselves in medieval history and in economic history.

A number of women, long before they had access to the universities, had clearly achieved prominence in the use of archives and primary sources, going back to the example set in the eighteenth century by Catharine Macaulay.[7] The opening up of higher education for women from the 1860s created the framework within which women could study history academically. The Middle Ages was also a popular and controversial period at a time of transition from the Victorian cult of medievalism to the new 'scientific' document-based history. History itself was still a relatively young discipline, and medieval history dominated in the universities.[8] The late nineteenth-century fascination with archives, documents and manuscripts brought with it a turning to more legal and constitutional history on the one hand, and a new religious history on the other. Pioneers in the new women's colleges excelled at this history; their work was notably encouraged by innovators in their fields. Mary Bateson went to Newnham College, Cambridge in 1884, and was taught by Mandell Creighton, the professor of ecclesiastical history. She was an ardent suffragist and liberal supporter, but he 'checked a tendency to dissipate her energy in public agitation on the platform or in the press', and persuaded her that her vocation in life was to 'write true history, and to pursue a scholar's career'. Her work was later encouraged by the legal historian F. W. Maitland, and she left studies of enduring importance on women's monastic lives and on municipal history.[9] Female medievalists played a prominent part in the *Victoria History of the Counties of England*; in the first volumes published between 1905 and 1911 78 per cent of the social and economic essays were written by women. A number of these had probably been taught by Sir Paul Vinogradoff, the great legal and social historian, and they made extensive use of contemporary records to uncover the lives of the medieval peasantry.[10] Another of

[7] See Bridget Hill, *The Republican Virago. The Life and Times of Catharine Macaulay, Historian* (Oxford, 1992). Cf. Thirsk, 'The history women'.

[8] Rosemary Jann, 'From amateur to professional: the case of the Oxbridge historians', *Journal of British Studies*, 22 (1983), 122–47, at 139; G. Kitson Clark, 'A hundred years of the teaching of history at Cambridge, 1873–1973', *The Historical Journal*, 16 (1973), 535–53, at 541.

[9] T. F. T. (T. F. Tout), 'Mary Bateson (1865–1906)', in Sir Sidney Lee et al. (eds.), *Twentieth Century DNB* (Oxford, 1901–60).

[10] Zvi Razi, 'The historiography of manorial court rolls before World War II', in Zvi Razi and R. M. Smith (eds.), *Medieval and Small Town Society* (Oxford, forthcoming 1996), chap. 1.

Vinogradoff's students, Ada Elizabeth Levett, wrote a famous study of the the impact of the Black Death, and conducted pioneering work on the manorial courts of St Albans. She was eventually recognised with a University of London chair in history, but she died before her major work on St Albans was finished and she did not build up a following of research students.[11] Elizabeth Levett said of Vinogradoff's influence upon her: 'He taught me to unify my varied interests ... into the great framework of Economics and Jurisprudence, and to bring it to bear on practical social history.'[12] Yet other female medievalists left important books, among them Rose Graham, who wrote about the 'double monasteries' (those Benedictine abbeys with joint houses, but led by an abbess) and Bertha Phillpotts, who wrote on women's legal position, but failed to gain significant academic recognition in their own time.[13]

In the United States too women came to the new colleges opened for them, and studied history initially under men trained abroad in the German methods of historical analysis, based on archival research on documents with findings discussed in the format of the research seminar. One of these medievalists, Herbert Baxter Adams, taught for four years between Johns Hopkins University and Smith College when this was founded in 1870. Among the women he taught at Smith, two were recommended for Ph.D.s, and went on to teach other women in turn.[14] At Bryn Mawr and Mount Holyoke in the United States, 'generations of young women were inspired to take up careers in medieval studies'.[15] A number came to find their way as medieval historians and scholars in the North American university system during the interwar years.[16]

The women who had contributed such vitality to their fields of medieval history and economic and social history were soon written out of the chronicles of the historical profession. J. P. Kenyon's *The History Men* tells us how medieval history dominated in the Universities before the Second World War, but he mentions only the men who occupied major positions. In Oxford these were William Stubbs,

[11] Ada Elizabeth Levett, 'The Black Death on the estates of the See of Winchester', in Paul Vinogradoff (ed.), *Oxford Studies in Social and Legal History*, vol. v (Oxford, 1916), pp. 1–180; Ada Elizabeth Levett (ed.), *Studies in Manorial History* (Oxford, 1938).

[12] E. R. Jamison, 'Memoir', in Levett (ed.), *Studies in Manorial History*, pp. i–xix.

[13] Rose Graham, *S. Gilbert of Sempringham and the Gilbertines* (London, 1901); Bertha Phillpotts, *Kindred and Clan* (London, 1913).

[14] Stuard, 'A new dimension?', p. 68.

[15] Bennett, 'Medievalism and feminism', 312.

[16] See Stuard, 'A new dimension?', p. 73.

Paul Vinogradoff, R. L. Poole and F. M. Powicke. In Cambridge
after Acton there was F. W. Maitland and J. B. Bury, C. W. Previté-
Orton and G. G. Coulton. There were those who dominated the
Manchester History School – T. F. Tout and James Tait.[17] There
was a similar deletion of women from among the founders of
medieval studies in America.[18] Kenyon also examined the origins of
economic history in Oxford, Cambridge and the LSE, but confined
his list of economic historians to Cunningham, Clapham, Tawney
and the Hammonds. Clapham and the Hammonds are credited with
the legacy of the standard of living debate, and Tawney with leaving
major historical debates in the wake of his *Religion and the Rise of
Capitalism* (1926) and his *Economic History Review* article, 'The rise of
the gentry 1558–1640' (1941).[19]

   Yet economic history likewise provided important opportunities
for women; this was because it really was a new subject, and it soon
became firmly entrenched in the historical and social sciences
syllabuses at Cambridge, the LSE and Manchester. It was developed
in Oxford by those with a background in classics, political and
constitutional history, among them J. R. Green, Thorold Rogers,
Arnold Toynbee and A. L. Smith.[20] In Cambridge William
Cunningham, who lectured in economic history, and F. W. Maitland, the reader in English law, helped to shape the school of history:
a paper in political economy and economic history was part of the
early tripos; in 1885 this became a separate paper in English economic
history.[21] Both men encouraged students at the new women's
colleges to take up research in the subject, and Cunningham in
particular was a champion of women's education in Cambridge.

   Economic history achieved its greatest popular impact as a frontier
subject in the initiatives for workers' education in the University
Extension Movement, and later the Workers' Educational Association (WEA). A number of its leading writers, such as Arnold
Toynbee, Cunningham, R. H. Tawney and many others, taught the

[17] John Kenyon, *The History Men* (London, 1983), pp. 177–83.
[18] Judith Bennett argues that medieval studies adopted a pluralistic model: 'Men have
     tolerated women in the field, but women have been kept segregated from and
     subordinated to the mainstream.' Bennett recounts a number of histories of medieval
     studies by F. N. Robinson, S. Harrison Thomson, William J. Courtenay and Norman
     Cantor which ignore the feminine constituency of the discipline. See Bennett, 'Mediev-
     alism and feminism', 313.
[19] Cited in Kenyon, *The History Men*, pp. 247–8.
[20] Alon Kadish, *Historians, Economists and Economic History* (London, 1989), chaps. 1, 2.
[21] Clark, 'A hundred years of the teaching of history at Cambridge', 537, 546.

subject extensively in these forums outside the universities. Eileen Power was to follow in their footsteps, and to combine her university teaching with WEA and extension classes. Economic history was also one of the new and exciting social science disciplines that formed a major core of the syllabus at the London School of Economics, opened in 1895. There men and women studied together; women were brought into the LSE by its first lecturers, and were given scholarships and academic posts. They were an important presence in a new and exciting institution, and a number of them helped to create an academic discipline still in its infancy. Institutional links were also forged from early on between the women of Girton College, Cambridge and the LSE. William Cunningham taught Ellen McArthur and Lilian Knowles in Cambridge; he also taught as an external lecturer at the LSE. Both women were to follow in his footsteps, Lilian Knowles to a lectureship then chair in economic history at the LSE. At Girton McArthur and Knowles, then Eileen Power herself, taught their students economic history, and opened routes for training and jobs between Cambridge and the LSE.[22]

The LSE had a buzz about it; it was somewhere that engagement with the issues of the day mattered, and where all kinds of intellectual initiatives were afoot. The economic history courses brought together all kinds of unconventional teachers and students. Alice Clark was a case in point. For her, historical research was an interlude in a life that contained several other strands. She came to the LSE at the age of thirty-eight without formal educational qualifications, but the LSE and her subject, economic history, were still sufficiently open to accommodate vocation alongside profession. While she was there she took a major part in the suffrage campaign, and after this the Quaker War Relief Campaign, and wrote her great classic, *Working Life of Women in the Seventeenth Century*. Then she returned home to the family shoe firm to become the first British female director in what was to become one of Britain's major private companies.

Intellectual issues were just as important as the institutional framework in attracting women and giving them the opportunity for scholarly achievement. Feminist ideas certainly provided one impetus. There was a series of studies on medieval women by female scholars at the turn of the twentieth century: Elizabeth Dixon on craftswomen in Paris; Lina Eckenstein on female monasticism, Mary

---

[22] This story is told in Maxine Berg, 'The first women economic historians', *Economic History Review*, 45 (1992), 308–29.

Bateson on women in English towns and Annie Abram on working women in London.[23] Eckenstein dedicated her book to Karl and Maria Pearson, campaigners for the 'new woman', and later eugenists. Her book argued that in losing the possibility of religious profession with the Reformation, women lost the last chance that remained to them of an activity outside the home circle. 'The subjection of women to a round of domestic duties became more complete when nunneries were dissolved and marriage for generations afterwards was women's only recognised vocation.'[24] Other studies were not so directly feminist in their approach, but Eileen Power's first book, *Medieval English Nunneries*, had its roots in the questions about women's history raised at the LSE.

A perception at the time of the practical and moral role of economic history was another factor that attracted women to study the subject at the LSE. This was a time when social policy was central, not marginal, to British intellectual life.[25] Concern for contemporary social issues was to suggest the opening up of whole areas of the economy and society to historical enquiry. Social issues helped to create the discipline of economic and social history and attracted reform-minded intellectuals. The writing of a number of these female historians was inspired by these political and social issues, and it too has been forgotten by the annalists of the profession. A good example of this, and of the reasons for such amnesia, is provided by David Cannadine's 'The past and the present in the English industrial revolution, 1880–1980'.[26]

Cannadine's survey of changing perceptions of the industrial revolution by economic historians raises the question of whether successive generations of historians rewrote their history in accordance with the preoccupations of the present. He argues that early cataclysmic and pessimistic interpretations of the Industrial Revolution were influenced by contemporary fears over national decline or

---

[23] Bennett, 'Medievalism and feminism', 315; E. Dixon, 'Craftswomen in the Livre des Métiers', *Economic Journal*, 5 (1895), 209–28; Lina Eckenstein, *Women under Monasticism: Chapters on Saint-Lore and Convent Life between AD 500 and AD 1500* (Cambridge, 1896); Mary Bateson (ed.), *Borough Customs*, Selden Society 18 and 21 (London, 1904 and 1906), vol. i, pp. 222–30, vol. ii, pp. c–cxv and 102–29; Annie Abram, 'Women traders in medieval London', *Economic Journal*, 26 (1916), 276–85.

[24] Eckenstein, *Women under Monasticism*, p. viii.

[25] José Harris, *William Beveridge: A Biography* (Oxford, 1977); Jay Winter, 'Introduction', in J. M. Winter (ed.), *History and Society: Essays by R. H. Tawney* (London, 1978), pp. 1–35.

[26] David Cannadine, 'The past and the present in the English industrial revolution', *Past and Present*, 103 (1984), 149–58.

concern for current social problems. Later gradualist, growth-oriented and optimistic accounts were written against the backdrop of the post-war boom. His account, however, is devoid alike of politics and of female historians, apart from brief mentions of Beatrice Webb and Barbara Hammond. Two political issues that stood out in the formative years of the discipline, women's suffrage and the political response to the First World War, are completely bypassed. Women's suffrage campaigners frequently addressed the subject of women's work, and many were interested in the extent to which industrialisation had restricted or expanded women's opportunities. The impact of industrialisation upon women's work was thus a standard subject for comment by Eileen Power's predecessors, B. L. Hutchins and Lilian Knowles, and by her students and contemporaries, Alice Clark, Ivy Pinchbeck, Dorothy George and Mabel Buer. The First World War was above all the major influence on economic history and much political history as well. Eileen Power and a substantial number of other women, along with a number of male historians, belonged to the League of Nations Union or other internationalist organisations. The connections between their pioneering campaigns for higher education and votes for women and their attitudes to war were passionately expressed in Virginia Woolf's *Three Guineas*:

Sir, if you want us to help you to prevent the war ... we must help to rebuild the college ... we must hope that in time education may be altered. That guinea must be given before we give you the guinea that you ask for your own society. But it is contributing to the same cause – the prevention of war.[27]

Comparative and world history, along with economic and social history, developed as they did in response to the military, political and nationalist histories that predominated in the years before and during the war. These two examples of the way in which issues of gender mattered were sufficient to bring large numbers of women into the discipline, and several exercised an original influence on the profession. Eileen Power was the leading figure among these women. It was in the years following the Second World War that women fell away from the discipline, and the consequent decline in their influence coincided with the exclusion of the earlier generation of women from the annals of historical writing.[28]

[27] Virginia Woolf, *Three Guineas* (1938; London, 1991), p. 46.
[28] See Berg, 'The first women economic historians'.

This then was the world of medieval history and economic history which Eileen Power entered and came herself to shape when she started her graduate studies in 1910. Eileen Power by 1940 stood at the pinnacle of a new kind of history, economic and social history, which precisely because it was so new included more women than other more established historical disciplines.[29] A higher proportion of women made academic careers in the interwar years than at any time since the Second World War up to the present, and they made up a substantial constituency of economic and social history. Eileen Power was one of these women, and it is important that female historians today know that in the formative stages of the discipline there was not one isolated Catharine Macaulay or later one Eileen Power, the exceptions that proved the rule that history is a man's job. The large numbers of women in the field, however marginalised the careers of many of them may have been, did provide the examples, the inspiration, and the networks that made the successes of some of them possible. The issues that mattered to these women at the time, women's suffrage, social reform and the peace movement, also made a difference to the subjects given intellectual priority in the field – wages, welfare, women's employment and consumption. These subjects disappeared from the field after the Second World War; the numbers of female historians in academic positions fell sharply, and their intellectual legacy was lost.

Eileen Power does not feature in Kenyon's accounts of either medieval history or economic history. She is little more than a footnote in David Cannadine's biography of Trevelyan. She is not there with her friends the Hammonds among Peter Clarke's *Liberals and Social Democrats*. Donald Coleman's history of the new discipline of economic history dismissed her for her popularisation of the subject which 'identified her with a cosy sort of social history, short on the analytical and strong on the picturesque'.[30] There is now little recollection of Eileen Power, and indeed of any other woman who wrote history, in standard accounts of both economic history and of history more broadly.

I have written this book for Eileen Power, historian, because she deserves to be remembered as an economic historian, a medieval historian and a historian who made a major cultural impact. I have written it for other historians whose own perception of the past and

[29]   *Ibid.*
[30]   D. C. Coleman, *History and the Economic Past* (Oxford, 1987), p. 90.

their intellectual heritage has been greatly impoverished by a loss of knowledge of her work and the issues which excited her. Finally, I have written for all those curious to know how one woman became an intellectual and a scholar, established a successful career beyond the glass ceiling, enjoyed being a woman and yet was so quickly lost as a historical figure in her own right.

CHAPTER 2

Family, friends and college

The lives and writing of many of the major historians of the first half of the twentieth century were shaped by the privileges and expectations to which they were born. G. M. Trevelyan was perhaps the most privileged of all, born to the aristocracies of both birth and talent. But others were born into the substantial bourgeois classes or into established academic families with a way clear to the material support and educational opportunities that shaped their early careers. Sir Paul Vinogradoff was born in Russia, the grandson of a general and the son of a director of a school in Moscow. He studied at the Universities of Moscow and Berlin. Henri Pirenne was the son of a prosperous woollen manufacturer from Vervier; he was destined for the law, but encouraged by his father when he turned to history. Marc Bloch was the son of the ancient historian Gustave Bloch, and one of a remarkable group of Jewish savants of the Third Republic. His historical interests were fostered by his father; he was sent to elite schools, then to the Ecole Normale Supérieure.

The route to scholarship and an academic career for a woman born in the last decade of the nineteenth century was much less predictable. For Eileen Power, as for a number of other women of her generation, higher education was still a novelty. That women should pursue this, and beyond it an academic career, was still associated with a choice against marriage and family life. Men no longer had to make such a choice. For women, family backgrounds shaped their educational opportunities in much more complicated ways. Their friendships with other women were vital to their self-development. In the years before the First World War, the experience of the campaign for women's suffrage, reinforced by the recognition of new female aspirations and possible new directions for any educated woman, altered the fixed expectations of marriage and motherhood. It was thus family, friends and college that shaped

Eileen Power's early life and career, as they did those of many literary and academic women of her generation.

I

Eileen Edna le Poer Power was born on 9 January 1889 in the village of Dunham Massey, Bowdon, Altrincham in Cheshire. Her two sisters were born in the years immediately following; Rhoda in 1890 and Beryl in 1891.[1] They were the daughters of Philip Ernest Le Poer Power, a stockbroker, and Mabel Grindley Clegg. The Power family had Irish roots in Waterford, and the Cleggs were an English middle-class family.

This much has long been almost all that was known of her family background and her childhood.[2] The rest was quickly blanked out of Eileen Power's accounts of herself, leaving her origins shrouded in mystery. With some searching, however, we can find some of the peculiarities of her antecedents which shaped her view of herself.

Eileen's grandfather was the Reverend Philip Bennett Power (1822–99), a prolific writer of evangelical tracts. Philip Bennett Power was born in Waterford in Ireland and educated at Trinity College Dublin, then ordained. He moved to England, and began a career as a clergyman first in Leicester, then in London with two years at Holloway followed by seven as the incumbent of Woburn Chapel. From there he moved to Worthing in Sussex, where he lived for the rest of his life. He was the vicar of Christ Church for ten years, before in his mid forties his 'health broke down', and he never worked as a clergyman again. This may well have been a mental breakdown, for he lived for another thirty-five years. He turned during this time to writing religious tracts, and he was very good at it. He published over a hundred collections of short tracts and individual longer tracts between 1864 and 1894. These tracts were all vividly written, centred on a story or parable concerning a historical or contemporary figure which immediately personalised the point of the tract. He was ranked among the most popular of tract writers of his time – 'Mr Power wrote tracts which compelled men to read'. His

[1] Beryl Power to M. M. Postan, 1 December 1972, Power–Postan Papers, in the possession of Lady Cynthia Postan. These papers will be referred to in subsequent notes as Power–Postan Papers.

[2] 'Postan, Eileen Edna le Poer Power' (1889–1940), in *Dictionary of National Biography Twentieth Century DNB 1901–1960* (Oxford, 1975).

2.1 Beryl, Eileen and Rhoda Power, aged approximately four, seven and five

tracts were either lucrative or he had an independent income, for he lived in his later years in a 'delightful home on the cliff at East-bourne'.[3]

His son Philip Ernest le Poer Power was born in Worthing in Sussex 1860, and educated at Oxford. He moved to Manchester, and became a stockbroker. He married Mabel Clegg and went into business with his brother-in-law, Henry Clegg. He was a member of the Manchester Stock Exchange which, alongside those of Glasgow and Liverpool, was one of the three big provincial exchanges. These exchanges traded mainly in local stocks and shares. But they were profitable enough for the partnership, with its offices in St Ann's Street, to be trading on a scale of over £100,000 by the time Philip Power was thirty. The partnership acted as stockbroker to some of Manchester's banks, and Philip Power had a reputation as an energetic and trustworthy man of business. He was attractive and charming, with all the finesse of the Edwardian gentleman and the

---

[3]   I owe this information to Sir John Habakkuk. Information on Phillip Bennett Power can be found in C. H. Unwin, 'Introduction' to P. B. Power, *Breviates or Short Texts and their Teachings* (London, 1916).

security of membership of the establishment. By the time his children were born he was already well off, and lived with his wife in the best of Manchester's suburbs. Altrincham was a small market town of less than 10,000 people, eight miles to the south of Manchester. The town was a neat, clean place known for its healthy climate, and was surrounded by the villas of the Manchester merchants and manufacturers.[4]

Philip Power was given the middle name 'le Poer', a name belonging to a medieval barony, and claimed by other Power families with origins in Waterford. There is no evidence that the name belonged to Philip Power's family, since neither his father, nor his grandfather, John Power,[5] had used it. It was probably an affectation with some deep distant gleam of truth to it. But the family had no close connections to the other county families from Waterford who claimed the name. Philip Power passed the 'le Poer' name on to all his daughters. Along with his house, and his name, he had also accumulated an art collection by his later twenties. An exhibition was mounted in 1887 in London of his collection of some 300 engravings and their plates by Samuel Cousins.[6]

Eileen's mother, Mabel Grindley Clegg, was born in Kingston in Surrey in 1866. Her father, Benson Clegg, was a silk and woollen merchant who was probably descended from an old Lancashire family, whose most notable member was Samuel Clegg, an inventor and engineer of the classic days of the Industrial Revolution.[7] She appears to have been a tall, rather severe woman with a long angular face, and was always photographed in black, as most of her peers of the time would have been. She doted on her beautiful children, dressing them, unlike herself, in long curls and lace. Eileen and her sisters seemed to have the good fortune to be born into a family that offered not only financial and social security, but a close and loving environment.

In 1891, when Eileen was only three, these expectations of happy and contented family life came to a bitter end. Her father, for seemingly inexplicable reasons, committed a large fraud on the Manchester Stock Exchange. He forged a client's signature on a

[4] *Encyclopaedia Britannica* (9th edn, Edinburgh, 1875), vol. 1, p. 643.
[5] John Power was given the title 'Generosus', which refers to 'gentle' rank.
[6] P. Ernest Power, *Catalogue of a Complete Collection of the Works of the late Samuel Cousins, RA (1801–1887)*, collected by and the property of P. Ernest Power Esq. of Manchester. On view during June and July 1887 at Messrs Henry Graves & Co. Galleries, 6 Pall Mall, SW.
[7] Birth certificate of Mabel Grindley Clegg, 29 December 1866, General Register Office.

bank guarantee to raise loans to himself of £28,000. When accused he admitted to other forgeries going back nearly six months. His case was heard first at hearings over several days at the end of June in the Manchester police court, then held over to the Manchester assizes in November.[8] He was pronounced guilty, and was sent to prison for five years. While his case was first being heard in the police courts, a petition of bankruptcy was made against Philip Power's partner, Henry Clegg.[9] Philip Power was adjudicated bankrupt in 1893 while he was in Parkhurst Prison on the Isle of Wight. He owed £134,000[10] – a massive bankruptcy by the standards of the time, parallel today in actual value to several millions of pounds, but in the scale of its impact to far more.

By this time bankrupts and debtors were no longer sent to prison, and debt was not a criminal offence. Cases were heard in the local county courts, and proceedings were begun by a petition from one or more creditors. Cases then went to a court of bankruptcy, consisting of a chief judge, registrars and other officers. If a case was appealed in the county courts, it went to the chief judge, and from there to the Court of Appeal in Chancery. If someone was adjudicated a bankrupt, their property was taken over by the court until a trustee was appointed. All their property was confiscated apart from the 'tools of his trade' and the 'necessary clothing and bedding of his family to the extent in all of £20'. A bankrupt could only be discharged if his estate had paid ten shillings in the pound, or if a majority of the creditors declared that he was not responsible for his debts. The bankrupt also had three years in which to pay his creditors the ten shillings in the pound, and any property he accumulated in the meantime was protected from them. If he had not paid his creditors this amount within the three years, then his creditors could take whatever wealth he had acquired since up to the amount of the debts owed them.

Philip Power went to prison not for his bankruptcy, but for his forgery, and his bankruptcy was not discharged. By 1905, when his daughters were in their teens, he had still not redeemed himself, nor it seems reformed his character. That year he was indicted again for

[8] *Manchester Evening News*, 15 June 1891, 3; 29 June 1891, 3; *Manchester Examiner and Times*, 30 June 1891, 7; *Altrincham Guardian*, 17 June 1891, 4 and 24 June 1891, 5; *The Times*, 30 June 1891.

[9] *Altrincham Guardian*, 24 June 1891, 5.

[10] *The Times*, 25 February 1893.

2.2   Rhoda, Beryl and Eileen Power with their mother, Mabel Grindley Clegg
Power (*c.* 1896–7)

obtaining a cheque for £100 by false pretences. It was reported then that since his release from prison in 1895 he had been to South Africa and to New York. Since his return to England he had been living at different boarding houses in Bloomsbury, where he made his living by inducing his fellow boarders to speculate in stocks and shares. Even in these conditions he seemed easily to pass off his gentlemanly status, for he went into a leading furniture store, chose and ordered £1,500 worth of furnishings on credit, and talked the managing director into lending him £100 on the security of two debentures which turned out to be fakes. He was sentenced to five years again, to be followed by three years police supervision.[11]

The girls and their mother endured the impact of a full-scale Victorian scandal. They were left with nothing, and moved to London, under the care of Mabel's father, Benson William Clegg, and her three unmarried sisters. During this time they were said to have changed their name from Power to Raymond. The three children resumed the name of Power by their own choice when they were older schoolgirls and had moved to Oxford.[12] This dramatic change in family life, combined with the loss of her father in what her family perceived to be deeply shameful circumstances, made a lasting impression on Eileen. Though so young when it happened, the dislocation to her home life and the feelings of her aunts towards her father cannot have escaped her during these early years of childhood. She had lost her trust in and was abandoned by one of the two key adults fundamental to the formation of her own identity. Mabel Power became ill shortly afterwards with consumption and they moved to Bournemouth for her to take the open-air therapy. When Eileen was nine, Mabel was sent with her daughters to Switzerland so that she could attend a clinic. The therapy did not arrest the disease, and Mabel Power died when Eileen was fourteen.

After their mother's death the Power children were cared for by their maternal grandfather and their spinster aunts. They moved to Oxford with their grandfather and their Aunt Lilian, and they were joined later by their Aunt Ivy. Henry Clegg, now discharged of his bankruptcy, was already living in Oxford at 30 Marlborough Road, and the rest of the family probably came to live with him. From 1907 their grandfather took out a lease on a new house on part of the Woodstock estate, 'Newlands', far out on the Woodstock Road (no. 305), some way from the main centres of academic and middle-class Oxford.[13] He kept up the lease until his death in 1910.[14] The house was small and ensconced among those of lower-middle-class tradesmen.

Eileen Power's father was responsible for this fall from grace, and

11 *The Times*, 29 April 1905.
12 Mary Danvers Stocks, *My Commonplace Book* (London, 1970), pp. 93–4.
13 *Oxford Directory*, 1904; 1907.
14 *Oxford Directory*, 1910.

he was rarely spoken of outside the immediate family. She never told more than a very few of her closest friends about this shadowy part of her past. Eileen and Rhoda Power were said never to have seen their father after their infancy; they never forgave him. Their youngest sister, Beryl, did not mind so much, and did visit him from time to time. The sisters had been left dependent on their mother's side of the family, and the Cleggs were clearly much less well off than the Powers, some of whom moved in county circles. But Ernest Power's relatives had also lost money on his fraudulent shares, and in their anger they refused to help his wife and daughters.[15] The only communication from the Power side of the family was through the girls' paternal grandmother, who provided a little money for a time in the form of a dress allowance. Eileen later wrote to her friend Margery Garrett about the visit of a policeman to the house after a burglary. 'One comic incident occurred when the Inspector told us that the burglar (who held a position of trust at our milk company) had a daughter who was cashier in the same firm still. "O I shouldn't like that" ejaculated my aunt, "The daughter of such a man! I should be afraid! One never knows ..." then to her horror she recollected me, smiling urbanely on the sofa. She clutched at safety ... "one never knows how they've been brought up", said she, "But of course the poor girl is all right." Not a bad effort. I nearly split the sides of a new evening dress, through suppressed mirth.'[16]

Eileen had a very close relationship with her two sisters, and they too developed into gifted independent personalities. All three sisters grew to be tall, slim dark-haired and physically attractive women. All were well educated and chose to pursue careers rather than marriage, though marriage was not necessarily ruled out. With no resources left after their grandfather's death, they clearly had to earn their own livings and expected to do so. Eileen was very close to her nearest sister, Rhoda (1890–1957). Rhoda lacked self-confidence as a child. She was the emotionally needy child of the trio, and was mothered by Eileen from the time they were small children. She had some difficulty in making her way after she finished school, and even as an adult was much protected by Eileen. After school and some

15 Recollections of Lady Cynthia Postan, September 1993.
16 Power to Margery Garrett, 10 January 1912, Power–Postan Papers. The correspondence between Eileen Power and Margery Garrett (later Spring Rice) is all in the Power–Postan Papers held by Lady Cynthia Postan. These letters will be referred to as 'Power to MLG' in future notes.

time out, she went to St Andrews University in 1911, and in 1913
gained first- and second-class certificates there in languages, political
economy and in economic history, where she ranked first.[17] She then
taught for a year in America, and took up freelance journalism. Her
great formative experience was a trip to Russia during the middle of
the war. She arrived in Southern Russia at Rostov on the River Don
at Christmas in 1916; she had a position there as a nanny to a minor
noble family. Soon caught up in the Revolution, she kept a diary of
her experiences, describing bloodshed in the village as white and red
factions overran it.[18] She eventually tried to leave, travelling across
Russia. She picked up a troop train in Moscow, spent seven weeks in
a cattle shed, and eventually caught the last boat to go out across the
North Sea to Bergen. After this she wrote her book *Under Cossack and
Bolshevik*.[19] She continued to travel and to write, taking on contracts
periodically for travel-book series and travel guides. She started a
career in broadcasting in 1927 and in children's book writing, both in
close collaboration with her protective older sister.

Beryl Power (1891–1974) was the great feisty character of the trio,
full of self-confidence and panache. She followed Eileen to Girton in
1910, where she too studied history. She gained a second-class degree
in parts I and II of the tripos in 1912 and 1913. From then she entered
wholeheartedly into the suffrage campaign, and for two years was an
organiser and speaker for the National Union of Women's Suffrage
Societies. Following the war, she entered the Civil Service, where she
held several important posts in the Board of Trade and the Ministry
of Labour. These were followed by membership of the Royal
Commission on Labour in India (1929–31), the post of Assistant
Secretary in the Ministry of Supply during the war, and secondment
to the China National Relief and Rehabilitation Administration after
the war.[20]

Beryl was opinionated, brash and self-important, and the subject
of much family amusement. Rhoda in 1915 wrote to Eileen of Beryl
that she was 'temporarily off eugenics (which she's been studying
with passion)'. While in the kitchen one day making soup, 'Beryl,
who had an orange-backed tome propped up in front of her,

---

[17] BBC written archives, Rhoda Power, certificates and photograph, 1912–18, special
collections. Also see *Adelaide Advertiser*, 28 February 1961.
[18] Rhoda Power, diary, Power Papers, Girton College archives.
[19] Rhoda Power, *Under Cossack and Bolshevik* (London, 1919).
[20] *Adelaide Advertiser*, 28 February 1961.

suddenly announced that she had "no use for virginity as such". Now I ask you! I grappled with the first part of the statement & vaguely realised with inward qualms, that perhaps Beryl *wouldn't* have any use for it. But my dear, the "as such" stumped me. What does she mean?' [21]

There was more amusement when some months later Beryl tried to tell Eileen all about the Cafe Royal: 'It's the French place where all the homosexuals go – and Lord Alfred Douglas & people – all the women talking & smoking & drinking absinth . . . It's just an ordinary French cafe – the only place in London where you can see life as you do in a French one.' Eileen commented dryly: 'I judged it wiser to permit myself to be instructed on what goes on at a French cafe (to which I have been dozens of times in France) by my superior sister who has never set foot out of England since she was seven!'[22]

'Family' for the sisters after their mother died comprised their grandfather, Benson William Clegg, and their aunts. The aunts played out the classic family role of Victorian or Edwardian spinster aunts, providing close nurturing of their family charges. Though there were three aunts, the sisters' main care was provided by Ivy and Lilian Clegg. These were not considered by Eileen to be role models or mother figures, though she told others in later years how much she owed to their support and encouragement. It was her grandfather who provided the stability in the family during these difficult years. Then he died during Eileen's last year at Girton. She wrote to Margery Garrett when he died of how fond she had been of him, and how much she would miss him. Her aunts were struck down with terrible grief at his death, 'especially Aunt Ivy . . . who is morbid and exceedingly hysterical by nature'. She 'has been living strung up to highest possible pitch for two months, – & has collapsed completely'. Eileen wished she would go away somewhere, for she only upset the other aunts. She found the funeral a distressing but distant affair, for it caused great agitation to her aunts, but she could find within herself no affinity for their religion. A number of uncles who had not been much seen by the girls beforehand appeared for the funeral, and Eileen reported having some amusing arguments with them. They were clearly not used to dealing with educated women.[23]

[21] Power to MLG, 16 March 1915.
[22] Power to MLG, 22 September 1916.
[23] Power to MLG, 7 April 1910.

Ultimately, the financial difficulties of the family may well have entailed some benefits, for education for the three sisters became a priority. When the girls were small during those first years after the family left Manchester they were sent to a small private school in Kensington. Then in Bournemouth they went to the Bournemouth Church High School, and after this closed down to the Bournemouth High School. This school was a member of the Girls' Public Day School Trust group, and Eileen attended it until the death of her mother in 1903.[24] During the last years before her death, Eileen's mother had set her heart on the move to Oxford so that her daughters could attend the Oxford High School for Girls, one of the best-known of the PDST schools. They attended the school from 1904;[25] Eileen was at the school between 1904 and 1907.[26] At the time the PDST schools charged minimal fees, and were known to provide good academic schooling and a way to university scholarships. Mabel Power had felt so strongly about the school that on her death her father and sisters made the move to Oxford to provide what she had wanted for her daughters. All the sisters succeeded at the school, and went on to take scholarships to university. Without the scholarships their further education would have been in doubt.[27]

From their modest house far up the Woodstock Road, the sisters passed daily from the dwelling that spoke of their 'fallen' status and their straitened circumstances across to streets lined with substantial bourgeois residences, academic residences and their school in Banbury Road which was also perceived as part of academic Oxford. They began that existence split between the cultural and class aspirations of the upper middle class and the financial insecurity of women from lower down the social scale of the middle class. With no independent means and a tainted family background, future prospects for the sisters, including marriage within the social circles once taken for granted by their parents, looked difficult. All three girls acquired early on the self-sufficiency that drove them to achieve at school, to go to university and to seek full-time careers in the professions.

---

[24] Beryl Power to C. K. Webster, 21 September 1940, Webster Papers, British Library of Political and Economic Science (hereafter BLPES).
[25] Beryl Power to M. M. Postan, 1 December 1972, Power–Postan Papers.
[26] R. M. Haig-Brown to M. G. Jones, 23 September 1940, Power–Postan Papers.
[27] Power to MLG, 15 March 1910.

At a time when the daughters of upper-middle-class and professional families were educated, often rather badly, at home by governesses or in boarding schools, academic day schools for girls were attended by those whose families could not afford the other options, or who believed in the value of education and even of higher education for women.[28] The reformed girls' boarding schools including Cheltenham Ladies' College, St Leonards School in St Andrews in Scotland, Wycombe Abbey School and Roedean were sending students to Oxford and Cambridge by the beginning of the twentieth century, but the number of these was small. Even among the educated classes who did believe in educating girls, the formal teaching was frequently carried out in home schoolrooms by governesses, interspersed with periods abroad to learn languages, or sometimes with time in small private boarding schools which had a greater concern for social graces than for scholarship. The famous daughters of the intellectual aristocracy succeeded despite this haphazard education, but they succeeded as writers. The Stephen family did not provide Virginia Woolf or her sister or half-sister with any form of systematic education.[29] Gwen Raverat was educated within the Darwin family by governesses at home until she was sixteen, then in a small girls' boarding school with few academic pretensions.[30] Naomi Mitchison, a Haldane, attended the Dragon School in Oxford with her older brother, but when he went to Eton she was brought home to be taught by governesses.[31]

Women of the intellectual classes were educated, especially in literature and foreign languages, but only more rarely in the classical education required for entry to Oxford and Cambridge.[32] The lack of such an education was not regarded as an impediment to a literary career. When Vera Brittain met the mother, a novelist, of her first love, Roland, and told her of her plans to go to Oxford, the response she had was ' "Why does she want to go to Oxford? It's no use to a writer – except of treatises." ' I was, therefore pleased and relieved

---

[28] See Gwen Raverat, *Period Piece. A Cambridge Childhood* (London, 1952), pp. 60–75; Carol Dyhouse, *Feminism and the Family in England 1880–1939* (Oxford, 1989), pp. 28–33; Leonore Davidoff, *The Best Circles* (London, 1973), pp. 71–84.

[29] Quentin Bell, 'Introduction', in Anne Olivier Bell (ed.), *The Diary of Virginia Woolf Vol. 1 1915–19* (Harmondsworth, 1979), p. xix.

[30] Raverat, *Period Piece*, pp. 60–74.

[31] Naomi Mitchison, *Small Talk: Memories of an Edwardian Childhood* (London, 1973); Naomi Mitchison, *All Change Here, Girlhood and Marriage* (London, 1975).

[32] See Noel Annan, 'The intellectual aristocracy', in J. H. Plumb (ed.), *Studies in Social History: A Tribute to G. M. Trevelyan* (London, 1955), pp. 243–87, at p. 249.

when she turned to him and remarked: "Why, she's quite human, after all! I thought she might be very academic and learned." '[33]

There were, of course, many cases where women from established intellectual families were well educated, and increasingly so by the time Eileen Power went to university. Margery Garrett, the niece of Millicent Fawcett and Elizabeth Garrett Anderson, was sent to Girton, but even she had been educated earlier by governesses, small private schools and time abroad. Rosalind Smith, one of the seven beautiful daughters of A. L. Smith, the fellow and later Master of Balliol went to the Oxford High School for Girls, then on to Girton. She was not considered conventional, however; the Haldanes viewed the Smiths as radical, and the children did not associate.[34]

Broader access to higher education for women and men without such a background had only recently appeared with the founding of the London School of Economics in 1895. The daughters of commercial and industrial families such as Eileen Power's might be well educated especially if they came from religious minorities such as the Quakers.[35] More frequently, however, they were prepared for marriage, with only the personal whim of father, mother, or spinster aunts providing some special pressure for systematic education.[36]

Eileen worked hard at school. By the age of eleven she was so attached to her study of Latin and Greek that her mother decided that suitable punishment for being unpunctual for weeks would be 'stopping the Greek'.[37] She took to literature early, and from the time she was twelve she was collecting her own anthologies of verse in sixpenny notebooks; she had some dozen volumes of these by the

---

[33] Vera Brittain, *Testament of Youth* (1933; London, 1978), p. 115.

[34] 'Garrett, Margaret Lois (Mrs Spring Rice), 1907–1910'; 'Smith, Rosalind Grace (Mrs Wrong) 1911–1914' *Girton College Register 1869–1948* (Cambridge, 1948), pp. 184, 230; Mitchison, *Small Talk.*

[35] All the daughters of the shoe manufacturer W. S. Clark were sent to the Mount, the Quaker boarding school in York, and from there all but Alice Clark went to Oxford and Cambridge colleges. The sons and Alice were educated at school, but from then were brought up and trained within the firm. Alice Clark took time out from the firm to study at the LSE where she wrote her classic study, *The Working Life of Women in the Seventeenth Century* (London, 1919). See Margaret Gillett Clark, *Alice Clark of C & J Clark Ltd., Street Somerset* (Oxford, 1934); interview with the Clark family (21 November 1988).

[36] Power's contemporary Dorothy George is a good example. Her father declared when she was nine that she was to go to St Leonards and then to Girton after he saw the *Punch* cartoon in 1887 celebrating Agnata Ramsay's first in the classical tripos. Though he died shortly afterwards, his widow made sure his plans were carried out. See 'George, Mary Dorothy', *Who Was Who*, vol. VII (London, 1980); 'George, Mary Dorothy', obituary, *The Times*, 14 September 1971.

[37] Beryl Power to C. K. Webster, 21 September 1940, Webster Papers.

age of fourteen. The Oxford High School fostered these literary interests: her favourite reading during the years she was there was Elizabethan followed by French medieval poetry, and she started seriously to write her own verse from this time, publishing in the school magazine. She kept booklets of her own poetry, mainly romantic verses, from the age of fourteen, and she continued to write verse throughout her life, publishing her pieces occasionally in the weeklies. It was through literature that she came to history.[38] But she liked acting and drawing just as much, and years afterwards her schoolteachers really remembered her as an all-rounder, though with a special affinity for literature, language and history.[39]

II

Eileen went off to Cambridge in 1907 to study history; she was funded by a Clothworkers Scholarship to Girton College. Girton was the first of the Cambridge women's colleges, founded in 1869. From its beginning under Emily Davies' leadership it had a high academic reputation, and its students took the same course of examinations, the tripos, as did the men, though they were not accepted as part of Cambridge University, and were not given Cambridge degrees after their tripos. The college was on a large site a mile-and-a-quarter outside the centre of Cambridge; it had only recently been built, on seventeen acres of land bought after Girton's first big bequest left by Jane Catherine Gamble. The red-brick buildings were arranged in a large rectangle around a central courtyard with long corridors stretching to half a mile. With a 'lopsided tower over the main gate', they were 'not beautiful'.[40] A key distinguishing feature which marked it out as a women's college were the long corridors, instead of the staircases and sets of rooms of the men's colleges. Eileen's first experiences must have been of trying to find her way along dark-panelled silent corridors, lit in the evenings by gas lamps with few distinguishing marks to set out one side of the college from the other. There were extensive college grounds and woodlands for walks alone or with friends if the corridors became too forbidding.

---

[38] C. K. Webster, 'Eileen Power (1889–1940)', *The Economic Journal*, 50 (1940), 561–72, at 562.
[39] R. M. Haig-Brown to M. G. Jones, 23 September 1940, Power–Postan Papers.
[40] Margaret Cole, *Growing up into Revolution* (London, 1949), pp. 36–7.

Girton before the First World War had the reputation common to
all women's colleges at the time for plain, badly cooked food, poor
cold rooms, and a joyless existence among deprived sexless female
dons. The picture was set in 1928 in Virginia Woolf's *A Room of One's
Own* of an assembly in a big dining room eating bad food. She told of
the enormous effort of raising £30,000 to build Girton's buildings
sixty years before. 'And it was only after a long struggle and with the
utmost difficulty that they got thirty thousand pounds together. So
obviously we cannot have wine and partridges and servants carrying
tin dishes on their heads ... We cannot have sofas and separate
rooms. "The amenities ... will have to wait." '[41] Vera Brittain
described her college room in Somerville as 'old and dingy, with oak
beams, a crooked floor, and innumerable dark corners and crevices
partially concealed by fatigued draperies suggestive of spiders, black-
beetles, and similar abominations'.[42]

By the time Eileen came to the college there were about 170
students. Each had a bed-sitting room; a scholar would have a
bedroom and a sitting room to herself, and each bedroom had a little
bath in it.[43] The sitting rooms were lit by gas, and the bedrooms by
candles. This separate quiet place to study in spaces the students
could call their own had been very important to Emily Davies' idea
of the college. The domestic needs of the students were met by the
college servants, called 'gyps'. 'Each morning the gyp left a can of
hot water outside your bedroom door and "knocked" you up. She
then cleaned and relaid the fire and dusted and swept the sitting
room.'[44]

The freedom and independence to study without the constant
social and domestic interruptions of their parents' homes, rooms they
could beautify and furnish themselves and call their own – this is
what the college meant to the first generation of students. To the
generation of students coming up in the decade before the First
World War there was still the excitement of leaving home for the first
time to make their own lives, make new friends and to gain the
qualifications for independent careers or for jobs that they would
hold for a time at least before marriage. A student's room was her

[41] Virginia Woolf, *A Room of One's Own* (London, 1928), p. 22.
[42] Brittain, *Testament of Youth*, p. 147.
[43] Barbara Stephen, *Girton College, 1869–1932* (Cambridge, 1933), p. 161.
[44] Lily Baron, 'Girton in the First World War', *Girton Review* (Cambridge, Easter Term,
      1965), 10.

'private domain'. Helena Swanwick, one of the leaders of the women's suffrage movement, was a student at the college twenty years before Eileen Power's time. She described her own and her mother's feelings on their first visit to Girton. 'When the door of my study was opened, and I saw my own fire, my own desk, my own easy chair and reading lamp – nay, even my own kettle – I was speechless with delight. Imagine ... when my mother turned to me with open arms and tears in her eyes, saying, "You can come home again with me Nell, if you like!" It was horrible. That which had enraptured me had struck her as so unutterably dismal that she was prepared to rescue me at all costs.'[45]

Margaret Postgate, who later became a socialist and historian and married G. D. H. Cole, wrote how she felt when she came to Girton in 1911: 'My first impression of College was one of freedom – freedom to work when you liked; to stop when you liked; to cut even lectures which turned out unhelpful or uninteresting; to be *where* you liked *when* you liked, with *whom* you liked ... to get up and go to bed when you pleased and if desirable to go on reading, writing, or talking till dawn.'[46] Vera Brittain in her first few weeks at Somerville was 'in a state of exhilaration, "half-delightful, half-disturbing, wholly exciting." I have never known anything so consistently stimulating as that urgent, hectic atmosphere, in which a number of highly strung young women became more neurotic and exalted than ever through over-work and insufficient sleep ... It is a delightful change to me to be in surroundings where work is expected of you, instead of where you are thought a fool for wanting to do it.'[47]

The student body was also still a mixed age group. Substantial numbers were now entering straight from school, but there were many too who were in their twenties, starting university later because they had been doing other things, or simply because family pressures had kept them at home. They made friends along the corridors, visiting each others' rooms in the evenings, following the college custom of 'jug'. The gyps left a small jug of milk in each student's room after dinner. Students would issue written invitations to each other to 'jug'. They would take their jugs of milk along to whoever

---

[45] H. M. Swanwick, *I Have Been Young* (London 1935), pp. 117–18.
[46] Cole, *Growing up into Revolution*, p. 37.
[47] Vera Brittain, *Testament of Friendship: The Story of Winifred Holtby* (London, 1940), pp. 108, 110.

had asked them to come, and find others gathered there before a fire. They would all make hot chocolate and eat toasted crumpets together while they discussed sex, religion, philosophy and gossiped furiously until 'Silence Hours' was called, and they had to grope their way back to their rooms with candle or torch along the darkened corridors.[48] Social lives revolved around getting invitations to these 'jug' parties, especially those held by the most desirable and popular students, and thus gaining access to favoured inner circles. The character of the student body changed during the early years of the twentieth century; the missionary tone of high seriousness among the pioneers was lightening, and Eileen Power's own attitudes reflected this. Friendships, intimate discussion during the evening 'jug', breaking rules and choosing lenient chaperones, singing the college songs, and participating in the ritual charades in the years just before and just after the First World War brought students together in a new irreverence for their serious-minded predecessors.[49] They chafed at the limitations of their surroundings, but they wanted to be a part of the wider university. They aspired to have not just their education, but their femininity and flirtations, careers afterwards and marriages.

Social class was still a big divide among the students; clothes and personal contacts were all-important. Some who could afford it did not care about their personal appearance and dressed badly. Others on scholarships and small allowances did feel the deprivation keenly. Winifred Howard Hodgkins, who was at Girton during the war, described a time of little spending-money and few gay clothes: 'Rosamund Lehmann, who was two years my junior, described the "romance" that came her way; she was attractive, but through her family she had social contacts that were denied to me, and the money to make the most of them. In "Memories", Frances Partridge of Newnham, later one of the Bloomsbury set, tells how her father settled £2,000 on her for her three years' expenses – I had to make do with £5 a term.'[50] Eileen Power and her sisters had £45 a year to share for their clothes. They received this from their paternal grandmother, until she declared in 1911 that she could no longer afford it.

---

[48] Baron, 'Girton in the First World War', p. 9.
[49] Martha Vicinus, *Independent Women: Work and Community for Single Women 1850–1920* (London, 1985), pp. 142, 147; Dorothy Marshall, diary extracts 1918–21, sent to the author by the late Dorothy Marshall.
[50] Winifred Howard Hodgkins, *Two Lives* (Leeds, 1983), p. 39.

This sum was small in comparison with the levels then being spent on women's dress among some at least of the academic families in Oxford and Cambridge. Gwen Raverat, born four years before Eileen Power, recalled being given a dress allowance of £60 a year when she turned eighteen. This was to cover her clothes and private expenses, but she found that much of it went quickly on the requisite few evening dresses, some pairs of long white kid gloves and silk stockings.[51] Naomi Mitchison, nine years younger than Eileen Power, had little interest in fashion, but brought with her assumptions about clothes that placed her in leagues of spending far beyond what the Power sisters could afford. She always slept in silk pyjamas, bought arty dresses from a boutique, and had embroidered silk evening dresses designed and hand-made by the Swedish wife of a distinguished lawyer.[52]

Clothes for Eileen became a symbol of family disgrace. She was desperately upset at the prospect of losing the small amount she had to spend. She wrote an anguished letter to Margery Garrett:

O if *only* I were rich and could throw her confounded cheque in her confounded face, and have done with the whole confounded lot of them. What with being dependent on her for a dress allowance, and being convinced that my father will be pirouetting in the daily press at any moment, & coming up against one reminder or another of his beastly forgeries and abscondings and this and that & the other every year, I sometimes wish the whole of the Power family at the bottom of the sea & myself on the top of them.[53]

Eileen did not want to be seen as part of that deprived group in the student body, scrimping their way through college and destined for schoolteaching. The clothes allowance rankled; Eileen acquired instead the sensibility to style and the ingenuity to put together outfits that made her look as if she belonged to the wealthier classes. Clothes, style and spending what she had on these were to become one of the key elements of her personal identity.[54]

The teaching was made up of lectures, usually held outside the college in Cambridge, and individual supervisions and small classes usually held in the college. The Girton students attended university

51 Raverat, *Period Piece*, pp. 60–75.
52 Naomi Mitchison, *You May Well Ask. A Memoir 1920–1940* (London, 1979), pp. 45–7.
53 Power to MLG, 6 October 1911.
54 Sally Alexander, *Becoming a Woman and Other Essays in Nineteenth and Twentieth Century Feminist History* (London, 1994), pp. 215–24 describes a similar significance placed by young working-class women in interwar London on their clothes.

lectures on sufferance, for they were not members of the university. Some lecturers refused to lecture to women; others created special spaces for them, by leaving the front two rows of the lecture theatres free for them. Getting into and out of Cambridge to attend these lectures was another trial. In the early days Girton had supplied special 'flys' or horse-drawn carriages to take the students. These were hired from Moore's then later Coxe's livery stables in Cambridge.[55] There were no buses until 1914, and Coxe's cabs were said to be decrepit: 'There was a legend that the bottom of one of them had once dropped out en route, leaving the students to run along inside keeping pace with the horse.'[56] A better alternative was a bicycle, and women's clothes were getting looser and their skirts slightly shorter to allow them to cycle. The college also had a building in the town, the Girton Waiting Rooms, where the students could have lunch and work between lectures.

The college was a female society; men (apart from designated relatives) were not allowed into the women's sitting rooms without a chaperone present. Nor could female students go to parties or the theatre in the evenings without taking a chaperone; the younger dons were usually prevailed upon for this task. Girton did not relax these rules until after the war, and it was considered to be 'Victorian' in comparison to Newnham College. Newnham was anyway only a quarter of a mile from King's Parade, and was believed by the Girton students to be much more accessible than geographically isolated Girton.[57] But in fact the Newnham students were equally restricted by the attitude of college authorities that there should be 'total separation from the masculine undergraduate population'.[58] Most of the students made their friendships within the college or with the women at Newnham; they were much more likely to meet men during their term breaks back at home and by visiting their friends' families.

The older dons at Girton were among the pioneers of the campaign for women's higher education, and they were part of the older generation of suffrage campaigners. The Girton history tutors while Eileen was there were two well-known suffragists, Ellen McArthur (1862–1927) and Winifred Mercier (1878–1925). They were

[55] Stephen, *Girton College*, p. 151.
[56] Cole, *Growing up into Revolution*, p. 36.
[57] *Ibid.*, p. 44; Barbara Wootton, *In a World I Never Made* (London, 1967), p. 43; Hodgkins, *Two Lives*, p. 39; Baron, 'Girton in the First World War', 10.
[58] Mary Agnes Hamilton, *Remembering My Good Friends* (London, 1944), p. 38.

both part of Girton's feminist tradition, and contributed to the foundation of economic history through the connection being forged between Cambridge and the LSE. Mercier was a suffragist and educationist, and McArthur a suffragist and economic historian.

McArthur was a direct descendant of the pioneers of women's suffrage and women's higher education. She had been educated at St Leonards school under Louisa Lumsden. She lectured in economic history in Cambridge between 1902 and 1912, and collaborated with William Cunningham in his *Outlines of English Industrial History* (1895).[59] But although still director of studies in history when Eileen came up to Girton, McArthur was away from Cambridge a great deal from then and for the next four years while she also supervised the history department at Westfield College during the illness of its supervisor, Caroline Skeel. Mercier was trained for schoolteaching, then taught for five years in Scotland. From here she went on to Somerville College in Oxford in 1904, and completed a degree in modern history. She returned to teaching at Manchester High School, and in 1909 went to Girton as director of studies in history. She stayed at Girton until 1913, then went into teacher training at Leeds City Training College. She trained welfare workers there during the early years of the war, and in 1916 became principal of Whitelands Training College, pursuing educational reform until she died in 1925.[60]

Girton's Mistress while Eileen was a student was Emily E. C. Jones. She was well known for her success in economics and philosophy. Her first in the tripos and the quality of her economics papers in particular challenged Alfred Marshall, who had fought against the participation of women in teaching and in the wider university life of Cambridge. He conceded after Jones's tripos that women were good at examinations, but this, he argued, was because they were naturally diligent, and they lacked the ability to go further. Jones had been taught by V. H. Stanton, J. N. Keynes and Henry Sidgwick, all of whom were known for their part in forwarding women's higher education.[61] Their support for women, however, was not enough to induce them to provide equal treatment. Jones reported that no examiner needed to look over the paper of a female student unless he

[59] M. B. Curran, 'Ellen Annette McArthur, 1862–1927', *Girton Review*, 75 (1927), 83–103.
[60] 'Winifred Mercier', *Time and Tide* (17 July 1925), pp. 695–6; Lynda Grier, *The Life of Winifred Mercier* (Oxford, 1937).
[61] Kadish, *Historians, Economists and Economic History*, p. 149; Rita McWilliams Tullberg, *Women at Cambridge* (London, 1975), p. 88.

chose to do so, and that the women's marks were not announced with the men's. 'So to us out at Girton, remote & anxious and uninformed, it seemed there was some delay in letting us know our fate.' A messenger was sent to Sidgwick who was found at the examiners' dinner, and the note sent with the messenger 'came back with our results pencilled on the outside page'.[62] Miss Jones was known as 'Jonah' to the undergraduates, and was later described by Dora Russell as 'fragile and exceedingly ladylike'.[63] Margaret Postgate described the dons of her day as 'funny old things, and not the least funny was the mistress, Miss Constance Jones, a woolly lady with a lisp who professed philosophy and was said to be tolerated by the administrators because she was so distinguished a philosopher and by the philosophers because she was so good an administrator'.[64]

Katherine Jex-Blake was vice-mistress, then mistress from 1916. She was a classics don and a direct descendant of the intellectual aristocracy. She was seen by the time Power was a student as a severe character, much in the mould of Rosamund Lehmann's picture of Girton. Lehmann, in *Dusty Answer*, wrote of the college as claustrophobic, its dons, remote figures in 'black garments, grey, close-brushed intellectual heads, serious thin faces, looking down the room, one young one, drooping a little: piles of chestnut hair and a white Peter Pan collar'.[65] The students called her 'Kits'; unlike Miss Jones she was 'thoroughly robust and rather like a horse'.[66] The students treated Jex-Blake as a figure of fun, the remnant of a bygone era, as Eileen wrote of her to Margery Garrett in 1910: 'Miss Jex-Blake's latest: 'What *is* a camisole?''[67]

The impact of these pathbreaking educationists and intrepid feminists on Eileen's outlook was not at first very strong. There was then a marked difference between the older and younger generations of dons. The older ones belonged to or identified with the pioneers; they were Victorian in dress and hairstyle, feminist and single-mindedly academic. The younger generation was closer to the students who now looked on their education as a part of, not an alternative to, futures which might include marriage and family life.

[62] 'Jones, Emily E. C.', *Girton College Register*, p. 628; E. E. C. Jones, *As I Remember. An Autobiographical Ramble* (London, 1922), p. 55.
[63] Dora Russell, *The Tamarisk Tree: My Quest for Liberty and Love* (London, 1975), p. 35.
[64] Cole, *Growing up into Revolution*, pp. 36–7.
[65] Rosamund Lehmann, *Dusty Answer* (London, 1927; Harmondsworth, 1936), p. 107.
[66] Russell, *The Tamarisk Tree*, p. 35.
[67] Power to MLG, n.d., 1910; cf. Cole, *Growing up into Revolution*, pp. 36–7.

Dances, clothes and love affairs were for them as much a part of university life as they had not been for their elders. Eileen was, however, fond of both McArthur, referred to as Mac, and Mercier, and continued to visit them and to write in the years immediately after she left Girton.[68]

Eileen Power left very little evidence of what courses she studied and who taught her as an undergraduate. The Cambridge history tripos had been reformed in 1897; but even in its reformed state the course still reflected the tension between those who thought its purpose was the practical training of citizens and those who saw it as the first grounding in the new research-based 'scientific' history. All the students still had to do a politics course, either political science, comparative politics or analytical and deductive politics. All had to choose either political economy or international law. All had to do three English history courses, including constitutional history, economic history and an English special period. Then there was European history covered by an outline paper in medieval European history and another in modern European history.[69]

Eileen was taught economic history by Ellen McArthur, who then left after Eileen's first year. College supervision after this was haphazard. Winifred Mercier did not come to Girton until Eileen was in her third year, and then she did not teach her. Eileen later said of her: 'I believe she was a most stimulating teacher, and I wish I'd had her, but she let me off all essays in my last year, so I never coached with her. But I remember that I was always discussing things with her and always impressed with her wisdom and humour. She was a perfect revelation as a don in fact, and formed all my own subsequent notions about what a don ought to be like.'[70] Eileen attended lectures and some supervisions outside the college for most of her courses. For her politics paper she chose analytical and deductive politics, and was most probably taught this by Goldsworthy Lowes Dickinson at King's College. He was already famous for his *Greek View of Life* (1896) and his *Letters from John Chinaman* (1901). He had an unconventional way of teaching, so Eileen would have come to know him as supervisor and tutor rather than just as a distant lecturer. He taught in small classes and used a conversational

---

[68] Power to MLG, 6 January 1911; 27 February 1911; Power, diary, March 1911, Power–Postan Papers.
[69] Clark, 'A hundred years of the teaching of history at Cambridge', 543–6.
[70] Grier, *Life of Winifred Mercier*, p. 81.

method, putting questions and problems to the students. 'He looked, even then, although it was long before he actually went to China, slightly Oriental, with his parchment pale face, inscrutable eyes, and the delightful, sudden smile that revealed an intensely human being. We wrote papers for him, and went to his room to talk them over with him.'[71]

There is no evidence of who else taught Eileen Power outside her college. The medieval historians who became well known in Cambridge, Z. N. Brooke, C. W. Previté-Orton and G. G. Coulton, were not appointed to college fellowships or lectureships until after she had finished the tripos. She kept a few of her undergraduate essays from courses in general European history, modern European history, and analytical and deductive politics. She wrote essays easily, integrating literary imagery with historical reconstruction of personality. One tutor set her the pedestrian question 'Describe the chief forces at work which made for change in Europe towards the end of the Fifteenth Century'. He was clearly surprised by what this elicited, for he commented: 'You show a tendency to deal in a priori imaginative reconstruction which (though in your case very convincingly done) is somewhat dangerous today.' Eileen Power wrote her own comment back: 'My good man, how else do you expect me to treat the Renaissance?'[72] Some of her time while she was in her final year was also diverted to coaching Newnham students in that subject: 'a great "honuah" for EEP to say nothing of some £25 per annum in her pocket – 18 freshers to coach, and I get 2/6 per paper and 10/6 per hour's coaching once a fortnight'. The money looked good, but she found getting up the material a heavy chore.[73] She was paid the standard rate for lecturers as established by the education committee at Newnham – classes with less than three Newnham students were paid ten shillings and sixpence whatever their nature.[74]

During one of her term breaks back in Oxford Eileen met Edward Armstrong (1846–1928), bursar and history tutor at Queen's College, Oxford, and she visited him frequently in Oxford during holidays. He was known for his book on Charles V, and his interests in the Renaissance, languages and travel attracted her. He later also

[71]   See Power, diary, 4 October 1911. Hamilton, *Remembering My Good Friends*, pp. 40–1.
[72]   Postan Papers, Cambridge University Library archives (CUL).
[73]   Power to MLG, n.d., 1910.
[74]   Newnham College, education committee minutes, 28 April 1910, Newnham College archives.

contributed to the *Cambridge Medieval History* on 'The Papacy and Naples in the Fifteenth Century' and on 'Italy in the Time of Dante'. Armstrong offered historical advice, lent her books, wrote to her while she was in Paris, and asked her out to Greek plays at Bradfield, where he was warden.[75] She soon found there was a mutual attraction, and wrote to Margery Garrett about it.

You will be pleased to hear that Mr. Armstrong (you know, the historian) has been seized by an unconquerable affection for me & is now 'spoiling' me within an inch of my life. If my career is in his influential hands it seems assured! I wrote him a very witty letter on the subject of Altrincham (sorry, but it was!) which has finally sealed his devotion, and I'm going to a tête-à-tête lunch with him in his rooms at Queens. Why oh why is it that old men always like me & young men never? And why oh, why do I so infinitely prefer old men? Anyhow we get on like a house on fire, and he really is most helpful over my work and full of books and hints.[76]

She discounted any suggestion from Margery that she had been deploying feminine wiles on him. 'No one could expect your jaded palate and obscene mind to appreciate freshness and innocence when you met it. Wily indeed!'[77] No doubt Armstrong was touched by Eileen's attentiveness, but it is hard to discern what influence he may have had on her intellectually.

When Eileen's grandfather died during the Easter vacation before her finals, she spent the break trying to study while coping with grieving relations. Like so many students before and after she worried about her looming examinations, especially constitutional history. She thought she had done too little work during the year to produce very good results.[78]

During this time of anxiety over work and teaching, Eileen talked through what she should do after her exams with Winifred Mercier. Mercier was tremendously helpful at this point. 'I hadn't the foggiest idea what it would be possible for me to do, but she said "You must get a scholarship and go to the Ecole des Chartes (of which I had never heard) to train for historical research." And she organized

[75] Power to MLG, Paris, 7 February 1911; various diary entries, diary, 1911. Cf. Edward Armstrong, 'Italy in the time of Dante', in J. R. Tanner, C. W. Previté-Orton and Z. N. Brooke (eds.), *Cambridge Medieval History*, vol. vii (Cambridge, 1932), pp. 1–48; Edward Armstrong, 'The papacy and Naples in the fifteenth century', in Tanner et al. (eds.), *Cambridge Medieval History*, vol. viii (1936), pp. 158–201; 'Armstrong, Edward', *Twentieth Century DNB*.
[76] Power to MLG, 20 September 1910. Altrincham was where Eileen Power was born.
[77] Power to MLG, 23 September 1910.
[78] Power to MLG, 7 and 10 April 1910.

everything so that I did.'[79] When Eileen Power sat her exams she
was awarded a first in both parts of the history tripos, one of two
women to do so. With this she also won the Gilchrist scholarship to
study in Paris at the Ecole des Chartes.[80]

III

Cambridge was about independence and personal space; it was
about studying and intellectual life. But for most of the young
women there at the time it was about making new friends outside the
framework of family life. Friends brought intimacy, self-confidence,
fun, and glimpses and even chances of joining other ways of living.
Girton was the place where Eileen formed her closest lifelong friendships – Margery Garrett, later Jones then Spring Rice, her contemporary at Girton, and Mary Gwladys Jones, who was in her third
year at the college when Eileen joined it. Other close friendships
developed with Margaret Coursolles Jones and Karin Costelloe.
Later friendships were with Elizabeth Downs, whom she called
'Pico', with M. G. (Barbula) Beard, when they were all young Girton
tutors, and with Petica Jones, Margaret Jones' sister.

In the relatively isolated academic environment of Girton, most of
Eileen's contemporaries and friends were women. She easily attracted others, who were drawn to the impressive-looking scholarship girl
who also deflated the serious environment with wit and irreverence.
She was also fiercely committed on political issues, taking up the
suffrage cause with others and defending proposals for social legislation. She read Tolstoy at Girton, and not only became a pacifist, but
pushed most of her friends into becoming so as well.[81]

These were the passionate schoolgirl-like friendships of a single-
sex college with all their intimacies and jealousies, but they were also
the more long-term relationships of academic women. These women
had a new self-confidence about their independence and their
sexuality and they indulged in their friendships as love affairs. In the
case of Eileen Power and her friends, these were not exclusive
friendships; they ran alongside relationships with men. But the

[79]   Grier, *Life of Winifred Mercier*, p. 81.
[80]   C. W. Previté-Orton, *Index to Tripos Lists 1748–1910 Contained in the History Register of the
       University of Cambridge to the Year 1910* (Cambridge, 1923); J. R. Tanner (ed.), *History Register of
       the University of Cambridge, 1910* (Cambridge, 1917), pp. 934, 937.
[81]   M. G. Jones, 'Memories of Eileen Power', *Girton Review*, 114 (1940), 3–13, at 3–4.

special intimacy and emotional attachments among these women could accommodate and transcend their relationships with the opposite sex and their marriages.

Writing about the place of Eileen Power's female friends in her life raises all manner of problems of identifying aspects of friendship and sexuality, and the boundaries between the two. The intimacy of friendship and its significance to these early generations of academic women has rarely been written of. Friendships have generally been discussed only within the framework of homoerotic relationships. The homoerotic friendships of young men in Cambridge during these years have become part of the intellectual glamour of the Apostles and Bloomsbury. This celebration of male homosexuality as a 'higher form of love' than that between men and women went with an assumption that such love was more in tune with intellectual pursuits.[82] With this discussion of male homosexuality at Cambridge, however, has gone a suppression of contemporary female homoerotic relationships, and with this, in addition, the significance of close female friendships to female intellectual life.

Eileen Power's friendships with women played a prominent part in the rest of her life. Uncovering their formation during her student years also brings us close to her perceptions of herself as a scholar, a historian, and a woman. She married late in life, and while she had numbers of close male friends, she appears to have had only a few romantic attachments with men. Much of her emotional life was taken up with her female friends. These friendships were a continuation of a long tradition of close friendships among women, friendships frequently deploying the language of romantic heterosexuality. They were an important part of the framework of feminist and suffragist politics in the nineteenth and early twentieth centuries.[83] They were also part of the experience of Victorian literary women whose friendships were much written about.[84] In a similar way close

[82] Robert Skidelsky, *John Maynard Keynes*, vol. 1: *Hopes Betrayed* (London, 1983), pp. 128–9.

[83] Philippa Levine, 'Love, friendship and feminism in later 19th-century England', *Women's Studies International Forum*, 13 (1990), 63–78, at 72–4.

[84] Janet Todd, *Women's Friendships in Literature* (New York, 1980); for other references on women's friendship, see Caroll Smith-Rosenberg, 'The female world of love and ritual: relations between women in nineteenth century America', *Signs*, 1 (1975),1–29; Lillian Faderman, *Surpassing the Love of Men: Romantic Friendship and Love between Women from the Renaissance to the Present* (New York, 1981); Janice Raymond, *A Passion for Friends: Towards a Philosophy of Female Affection* (London, 1986); Martha Vicinus, 'Distance and desire: English boarding-school friendships', *Signs*, 9 (1984), 600–22.

emotional friendships among female tutors, and among tutors or teachers and students, were as much a part of the story of the making of women's higher education and academic schooling as are the scholarship and professional standards.[85] There was little fear at this time over such close attachments among women; they were not associated with bohemianism, alternative lifestyles, or a rejection of marriage and the family. They were conceived in Victorian and Edwardian middle-class circles as a step in growing up, and as a valuable alternative to flirtations with the opposite sex. As Vicinus has argued, these friendships were seen to socialise girls into the world of women; they were a means of reinforcing a girl's identity with her mother; good friendships could be kept within the family and helped to defuse adolescent conflict.[86]

These ideas were in process of change, however, during the 1910s and 1920s. There was both greater access to birth control and to companionship in marriage, but also a new psychological discourse which stigmatised the love between women.[87] Female friendships especially in single-sex educational institutions came under new public criticism; a new conflict was seen between the mother and the female celibate pedagogue.[88]

Eileen Power was one woman living through these times of changing mores over single women. Others were Winifred Holtby and Vera Brittain who, though contemporaries, were not part of Eileen Power's circle. Their friendship was celebrated in Brittain's *Testament of Friendship*, and has been analysed in Jean Kennard's *Vera Brittain & Winifred Holtby: A Working Partnership*. Brittain wrote in *Testament of Friendship*:

From the days of Homer the friendships of men have enjoyed glory and acclamation, but the friendships of women ... have usually been not merely unsung, but mocked, belittled and falsely interpreted. I hope that Winifred's story may do something to destroy these tarnished interpretations, and show its reader that loyalty and affection between women is a noble relationship.[89]

---

[85] Vicinus, *Independent Women*, pp. 150–62, 187–210.

[86] *Ibid.*, p. 188.

[87] Deborah Gorham, 'Have we really rounded seraglio point? Vera Brittain and inter-war feminism,' in Harold L. Smith (ed.), *British Feminism in the Twentieth Century* (Aldershot, 1990), pp. 84–103, at p. 87.

[88] Vicinus, *Independent Women*, p. 206.

[89] Brittain, *Testament of Friendship*, p. 2; See Jean E. Kennard, *Vera Brittain & Winifred Holtby: A Working Partnership* (Hanover and London, 1989).

What we know about Eileen Power's friendships must be reconstructed from the letters she wrote to her close friend Margery Garrett. Any correspondence with Gwladys Jones and her other friends, Margaret Jones and Karin Costelloe, was not kept. Eileen's letters to Margery bring us into this world of the real closeness of good friends expressed in a way very different to that we know now. She courted her friends, experienced infatuations; and they enjoyed the intimacy of closest thoughts, shared jokes, hugging and touching each other and sometimes sharing beds. But Eileen never perceived these relationships as exclusive; they accommodated her friends' boyfriends and husbands, and she fantasised with her friends over the various merits of the men they met.

Eileen met Margery Garrett (1887–1970), nicknamed Margie, at Girton. They were exact contemporaries, though Margery was studying for the moral sciences tripos. Margery's background was both privileged and progressive. She came from a family of East Anglian maltsters, and they lived in the Maltings at Snape, now headquarters of the Aldeburgh Festival.[90] They had strong liberal and suffragist traditions. Margery had been educated before Girton by private governesses, in her case some rather eminent ones: Isabel Fry the daughter of Sir Edward Fry, a judge, and sister of Roger Fry, the artist and art critic, followed by Constance Crommelin, who later married John Masefield. She also studied in Paris and at Bedford College.[91] Her famous cousin Philippa Fawcett had done as well as it was possible to do at Cambridge by coming out above the senior wrangler in 1887. Philippa had gone on to become an active suffrage campaigner, then pursued a career in the Civil Service.[92] This was a hard act to follow, even a generation on. Margery had already decided by the time she came to Cambridge that life had more to offer than academic achievement. Beside Eileen Power's slender five foot seven inches, she was very small, hardly five foot, with a curvaceous figure that became stout in old age. When young she was blonde and pretty; she was said to have looked rather like a dairy maid, and she was very attractive to men. She was instantly likeable and jolly, and was like Eileen in her passion for causes. She took up crusades, and dominated and bullied her friends into matching her

[90] The origins of the family business and the house at Snape are described in Millicent Garrett Fawcett, *What I Remember* (London, 1924), pp. 30–3.
[91] 'Garrett, Margaret Lois', *Girton College Register*, p. 184.
[92] Barbara Caine, *Victorian Feminists* (Oxford, 1992), p. 208.

own energy in pursuing them. She was also cosmopolitan, irreverent and sexually adventurous.[93]

Eileen's other close friend, Mary Gwladys Jones (1880–1950), known as Gwladys, was very different. She was much older than Eileen Power, and started her higher education as a mature student. Her family was Welsh; her father was an architect, and her mother had died when she was at school. As she was the eldest of a large family, she had to take time out to care for them. She was an international hockey player before she came to Girton, but gave up playing to study. She valued what Girton had to offer probably much more than many students, because she had to wait for the opportunity to go there. She was already twenty-seven when she started at Girton, probably regarded by some of the students as of an age with some of the dons. She was a woman of medium height with a stocky build and a face with large features. She was serious and studious, but never saw herself as one with intellectual flair.

She was very much a college woman concerned to fulfil her duty, and devoting herself to integrating newcomers into the college, joining and leading a number of college societies and playing the part of the senior student who helped to take charge when the history tutor, Ellen McArthur, suddenly took on supervising at Westfield College during the autumn term of 1907. Gwladys Jones was at Girton between 1905 and 1908, and did the history tripos in 1907 and 1908, achieving a second class. She was part of that group in the college clearly set on earning their livings and destined for schoolteaching. She left for a post at Cheltenham Ladies' College immediately on finishing at Girton; then spent six years as the head of the Training Department for Women Teachers in Dublin. She returned to Girton as a tutor much later when Eileen Power resigned her Girton fellowship to take up a lecturership at the LSE.[94]

Gwladys Jones followed college custom, and as a senior called on Eileen when she first came up to Girton. She was immediately attracted to the grace and charm of the younger woman, who was also scholarly and marked like herself with family misfortune. Eileen had the physical beauty and style that Gwladys Jones admired, but

[93] Recollections of Mrs Nancy Raphael, 5 April 1995.
[94] Jean Lindsay, 'M. G. Jones', *Girton Review* (1955), 28–33; 'Jones, Mary Gwladys', *Girton College Register*, p. 653. The seriousness of M. G. Jones was emphasised by Marjorie Chibnall, interview, 15 March 1990 and Lady Cynthia Postan, June 1988.

lacked in herself, as well as the intelligent scholarly side she could also appreciate, but more easily connect with.

Eileen was devoted to both women, and saw them as the bedrock of her emotional life, but she also took up other more short-term flirtations and other friendships which she never saw in quite the same way. Margery Garrett was her true confidante, to whom she could tell anything, and to whom she turned for worldly advice. Margery was her 'wicked lady'; she made Eileen laugh, entertained her with a constant flow of gossip, and shocked her with a series of affairs and sexual entanglements with the fiancés and husbands of friends. Margery was also her friend in need. Eileen, in turn, offered her support in later years when Margery faced the death of a child, the early death of her first husband in the war, and a later unhappy marriage. Gwladys Jones, on the other hand, was Eileen's intellectual friend, to whom she turned for discussion of history, teaching and careers, and the companion with whom she frequently shared her holidays and term breaks throughout much of her career. Eileen was also the object of intense emotional attachment on Gwladys Jones' part; Gwladys loved Eileen uniquely and possessively.

Absences from both during term endings in Oxford, and afterwards during her year in Paris, generated a great flow of letters, and Eileen assiduously kept a small diary while in Paris, recording their visits and letters. She wrote to Margery in 1911 about their friendship: 'You have no idea how immensely valuable your friendship is to me: you are the only person to whom I can ever talk absolutely openly on any subject under the sun (because there are heaps of things I instinctively don't talk even to Gwladys about), and I do think that absolutely straight, equal, free and sympathetic intercourse is the best thing in the world. Also I really am rather fond of you.'[95]

Eileen's friendships with both were developed in new ways over the course of 1910 and 1911, with the entry of another friend, Margaret Jones, and with it a triangular relationship between Eileen, Margery Garrett and Margaret Jones. Gwladys Jones was never part of this circle. Margaret Jones (1887–1972), nicknamed Pikey by her family, but called Puppy by Eileen, was another contemporary, though studying history at Newnham.[96] She came

[95] Power to MLG, Paris, 6 January 1911.
[96] 'Margaret Gwendoline Coursolles Jones', *Newnham College Register 1871–1923*, 1 (Cambridge, 1979). Margaret Jones studied for the history tripos at Newnham 1907–10. She taught at Fulham Secondary School for a year, then became an organiser and an honorary secretary

2.3   EEP (Eileen Power), KmSR (Catriona Marion Stewart Robertson (later Lady
Garrett)), MLG (Margery Garrett (later Spring Rice)), Puppy Jones (Margaret Jones
(later Game))

from a large family, of six sisters and two brothers. Her family was
Canadian and Protestant, from Montreal, but they were all convent
educated in Canada, England and France. Like Margery Garrett,
Margaret Jones had been educated privately and in Paris before
going to Cambridge. Her family lived in Southwold, not far from
Aldeburgh where Margery Garrett's family had a house and, like
Margery's family, it was firmly suffragist. Margaret was a great wit,
and fun to be with, but highly unstable, emotionally demanding,
constantly going on and off her friends and causing rifts between
the other friends.[97]

Margaret Jones immediately attracted Eileen then Margery.
There were soon stories of vast sums spent on taxi fares between

for the National Union of Women's Suffrage Societies. She married Arthur Kingsley
Game in 1919.

[97]   Letters to the author from Mrs Giles Robertson, 19 and 24 November 1992; interview with
Professor Martin Robertson, 17 February 1993. The family became characters in the novel
by Romer Wilson, *If All These Young Men* (London, 1919).

Newnham and Girton.[98] Eileen enjoyed long walks, and intense discussions with her, 'billing and cooing', indulged her inconsistency and shared her with Margery.[99] She spent chunks of her holidays in Suffolk visiting one then the other. Eileen wrote to Margery in early April 1910 about her grandfather's death, and went on to comment in fun on her friends:

I wish to inform you and the pestilential pup that if you both get fonder of each other than each other is of me, you will both wish you were each dead, because I shall inflict you each with all the furies of a jealous woman who adores you both.[100]

A few days later she was praising their friendship. She copied out constitutional history notes for Margaret, and advised Margery to make her do some work, fearing she was heading for a third.[101]

Eileen's friendship with Margaret Jones continued through 1911 and 1912; there were letters and visits in Paris and Southwold. Eileen was taken into the broader family when she befriended Margaret's younger sister, Emilia Beatrice, nicknamed Topsy, who was then a schoolgirl in Paris.[102] She also drew close to Petica, another of Margaret's sisters.[103] Margery Garrett's connection to the family was cemented in the autumn by a love affair and engagement to Margaret's brother Edward, a bill broker, followed by her marriage in April 1911.[104]

Eileen and Margery wrote back and forth about their career plans as they finished at Girton. Eileen won her scholarship to the Ecole des Chartes, so her course seemed set for the next year at least. Margery's plans, however, were a subject of much discussion and managing counsel from Eileen. To her latest suggestion of a career in art, Eileen wrote back:

[98] Recollections of Martin Robertson.
[99] Power to MLG, 23 March 1910.
[100] Power to MLG, 7 April 1910.
[101] Power to MLG, 10 April 1910; Power to MLG, n.d. She did in fact achieve a second-class degree. *Newnham College Register*.
[102] Power, diary, 12, 14, 15, 16, 18, 19, 20, 22, 23, 25, 27 April 1911. Topsy did not go to university, but became a novelist, writing as E. B. C. Jones. She was married for ten years to Peter Lucas, a fellow of King's College, Cambridge. Later divorced, she continued to live in Cambridge. Interview with Professor Martin Robertson, 17 February 1993.
[103] Petica Jones never went to university, and later married Donald Robertson, and went to live in Cambridge. She was a founder and treasurer of the Cambridge birth control clinic after the First World War, and her house was a popular gathering place for academics, writers and supporters of liberal left causes. Letter from Eleanor Robertson, 11 November 1992.
[104] Power to MLG, Paris, 6 November 1910; Power to MLG, Paris, 23 April 1911.

I had my heart on your doing Factory Inspectorship: I think you are one of
the few people who are cut out for that kind of great, thankless, all-
demanding social work ... I cannot pretend to you that I think art is your
vocation in life because I don't. I think it lies between marriage and social
work! I really see you in my dreams as a kind of Mrs. Russell (as far as
public work goes) embellished with a moderately sized family.[105]

Margery's engagement then marriage shortly after this prompted
Eileen to take stock of their friendship and of her own attitudes to
family life. She liked Margery's fiancé, Edward, and seemed quite
happy that her friendship would not be set aside by the marriage; for
he was their other best friend's brother. Indeed she was sure that
Margery would carry on just as she liked with her old friends and
interests, and pompously offered her general views on love.

You are one of the few girls I know whose marriage I can look forward to
with equanimity, because I don't think what you refer to as your 'brilliant
career' will be cut short by it ... the abstract cause which I care for more
than anything else is the cause of women, and it seems to me that until
women learn to keep their individuality after marriage and to recognise
that love is not the only thing in the world and its satisfaction with all that
that entails, their only function, we shall never get anywhere or be
anything.[106]

Margery visited Eileen in Paris a few months before her marriage.
They talked out the forthcoming event, and Eileen wrote in her diary
on 2 January that she 'stayed in bed with MLG all morning'.
Margery returned to England later that day, and Eileen went off
shopping, bought her a baby's bib for her trousseau, and wrote to
her that night.[107] She did not go to England herself for the wedding
of her best friend, and there was no sign that this was expected.
Margery wrote her later with intimate details of her wedding
night,[108] and Eileen interrupted the honeymoon with letters de-
claring her love: 'Oh Margie *dear*, I do love you so ... please do not
forget that you mean a very great deal to me & if you were chopped
out of my life I should lose some of the things which I value the most
in it. I don't think I ever "make love" to you, because somehow we
did not begin being friends on that basis & we've been particularly
"masculine" (can't think of an expressive word, but you know what I
mean) about it dès le commençement. So I never seem able to find

[105]   Power to MLG, 15 August 1910.
[106]   Power to MLG, 6 November 1910; Power to MLG, 26 March 1911.
[107]   Diary, 2 January 1911.
[108]   Power to MLG, 23 April, 4 May 1911.

any words at all to express what I feel about you ... I do want you to understand that the two things I value most in this world are your friendship and Gwladys.'[109]

Marriage, however, did make a difference to friendship, for Margery soon had a baby on the way. Her son Charles meant the end of impromptu holidays with Eileen, who wrote in high-handed tones with advice on motherhood and independence:

What earthly harm does it do Charles if you go away for a holiday? He isn't old enough to derive any advantage from your personal presence & anyone who looks after him is just as good as you at this stage of his career ... It is far more important to be your child's friend when he is old enough to want friends than to be his nurse when he is so young that anyone can fill that post ... the crunch comes when the child can discriminate between people & then the woman who has her own life behind her scores. You might publish this under the title of 'Letters from a Spinster'.[110]

Eileen's friendship would, however, be much needed by Margery Garrett in later years. In 1914 Margery's baby daughter died;[111] and by 1915 she had two sons and her husband had been killed at the front. Margery had an affair in 1915 with her friend Margaret Jones' fiancé, Kingsley Game, and Margaret Jones never spoke to her again.[112] By 1917 Margery had not only played at a relationship with her friend Margaret's fiancé, she now also 'snatched' the boyfriend of Margaret's young sister, Topsy, Dominick Spring Rice.[113] They were soon married, but within ten years Margery went through a very acrimonious separation from him. Eileen was dismayed to hear what she had been through, and wrote:

You deserve to be happy all the time without stopping & it is a shame. I do hope it will be possible to fix up something which will allow you to do your political work & live apart from Dominick & keep the children. But if he *does* turn nasty about it, do remember that he can only create a scandal among the Kensingtonians, & that he can't make a scrap of difference among your friends – it will only make us all fonder of you than we were before ... Anyhow, darling Margie, I love you devotedly & always have, and anything I can do to help I will do with the utmost joy, from spitting in the eye of Kensington, to having you here as much as you want. [114]

[109] Power to MLG, 23 April 1911.
[110] Power to MLG, n.d. (July or August 1912).
[111] Power to MLG, 21 July 1914.
[112] Power to MLG, 29 September 1915; letter from Eleanor Robertson to the author, 24 November 1992.
[113] Letter to author from Mrs Giles Robertson, 19 November 1992.
[114] Power to MLG, 22 October 1927.

2.4   (Mary) Gwladys Jones D. Litt as director of studies in history at Girton and
vice-mistress

During these ten years, Eileen had clearly seen less of Margery, who
with her family now spent much of her free time with Naomi and
Dick Mitchison. Margery took family holidays during the 1920s in
France and Greece with the Mitchisons, and bought a cottage with
them on Bledlow Ridge.[115] Eileen sometimes joined them, and was
later recalled by Naomi Mitchison as the 'most delightful of medieval
historians'.[116] The Mitchison–Spring Rice friendship clearly turned
into something of a ménage by the later 1920s, complicated by
Margery's affair with Dick Mitchison. Eileen offered her unstinting
support during the breakdown of Margery's marriage and difficulties
with the Mitchisons.[117]

Eileen's friendship with Gwladys Jones took a different course.
Gwladys was not part of the triangle with Margaret Jones, nor part
of Eileen's broader group of Cambridge friends. Gwladys lacked the

[115]   Mitchison, *You May Well Ask*, pp. 64–7, 79–80.
[116]   *Ibid.*, p. 65.
[117]   Power to MLG, 22 October 1927, 25 December 1930.

frivolity and class assurance of the others. She was an outsider in that world of the comfortably-off liberal middle-class establishment to which Eileen easily gravitated as her heritage and birthright. Eileen found in her someone who could really understand her own family afflictions, financial insecurity and need to earn her living. Eileen's attraction to Margaret Jones caused a rift with Gwladys who felt she'd been dropped, but Eileen protested to Margery, 'I never cared two pence for Puppy or anyone compared with Gwladys (besides I detest comparison of affections)'.[118] She could not leave her friendship in question, and made a special visit to Gwladys and her family in Cardiff during the summer.[119]

Eileen's feelings for Gwladys were very special; as she wrote to Margery: 'I believe that you and Gwladys are the only people in the world I ever really miss ... I miss Gwladys so violently sometimes that I am positively unhappy.'[120] In the summer of 1911 Gwladys spent a week in Oxford with Eileen: 'We talked history all afternoon & ourselves all evening.' They walked by the river and in the parks, talked in bed together, planned a historical novel on Perkin Warbeck, and discussed Eileen's research plans.[121] They were just as close in the summer of 1912. Eileen wrote then of an 'epic' five days with her: 'I love her so violently that I feel as if I should explode sometimes ... it was too wonderful altogether. We talked a lot of history too, which was very nice: I ache for a historic friend at times.'[122] Eileen and Gwladys spent another weekend together in Cambridge in August, writing: 'We are well into a Sonata Apassionata now: very wonderful and a revelation to me!'[123]

Eileen Power's friendship with Gwladys Jones was a long and loving relationship. Through the rest of Eileen's life they visited each other frequently, went on holiday together, and discussed their work. Gwladys had difficulty facing up to Eileen's marriage in her late forties,[124] but her sudden death in 1940 was a devastating blow to Jones, poignantly expressed in her letter to Helen Cam: 'There is nothing I can say. My darling has gone & I do not know how I can

---

[118] Power to MLG, 10, 15 August 1910.
[119] Diary, 28 August 1910.
[120] Power to MLG, 23 September 1910.
[121] Diary, 4–10 August 1911.
[122] Power to MLG, 9 July 1912.
[123] Power to MLG, n.d. August 1912.
[124] Interview with Miss Barbara Clapham, 21 July 1993.

get through the next few years without her. You knew better than most what she has meant to me & you loved her too.'[125]

Eileen met another new friend in the summer of 1910. She went to Alys Russell for German lessons in August, and there met Karin Costelloe (1889–1953), who was staying with her aunt Alys. Karin was Mary Berenson's daughter and Ray Costelloe's sister. Karin Costelloe was studying moral sciences at Newnham, but had interrupted her degree with a year at Bryn Mawr in 1909–10. She was very bright, but quiet and shy. She was plagued by constant hearing difficulties, and had undergone a number of ear operations in previous years. During the summer of 1910 she was preparing for her final year at Newnham, when she would do the final tripos in one year. She was being coached by Bertrand Russell, who thought 'she had more philosophical capacity than I have ever before seen in a woman'.[126] Karin Costelloe took a first in her tripos, then followed this with training in medicine and psychiatry, and later ran a clinic with her husband.[127]

Mary Berenson was Alys Russell's sister; her daughters from her first marriage to the Fabian lawyer Frank Costelloe were Ray and Karin Costelloe. But she was by this time married to the art connoisseur Bernard Berenson. She had run away to Florence with him while she was still married to Costelloe, and was scandalous, vital and extravagant.[128] Both her daughters went to Newnham, and married into the Bloomsbury circle – Ray to Oliver Strachey, brother of Lytton, and Karin to Adrian Stephen, brother of Virginia Woolf.

Eileen and Karin worked during this summer and other holidays on their German, and forged a new friendship. Eileen wrote to Margery: 'I have been progressing like prairie fire with Karin, very carefully though, remembering past lessons ... I said to Karin: I wish I were coming up to Cambridge next year. We could have had such a jolly time! "Yes" said Karin "I think we are going to fit in with each other pretty well don't you?" ... I hadn't expected Karin to

[125] M. G. Jones to Helen Cam, n.d., Girton College archives.
[126] Cited in Skidelsky, *Keynes*, p. 428.
[127] She wrote *The Misuse of the Mind: A Study of Bergson's Attack on Intellectualism* (London, 1922) and *Psychoanalysis and Medicine: A Study of the Wish to Fall Ill* (Cambridge, 1933); 'Costelloe, Karin', *Newnham College Register*.
[128] See Barbara Strachey, *Remarkable Relations. The Story of the Pearsall Smith Family* (London, 1980).

express liking even if she felt it.'[129] Karin and Eileen had something else in common – they both liked clothes. Karin's sister Ray never thought about them, and Margery Garrett didn't care what she looked like. So here at last were two kindred spirits, the one devoted to elegance and style, the other indulging in garish and extraordinary colours.[130] This was a friendship that opened up whole new vistas for Eileen. She was frequently swept away from her small cramped environment at Newlands, her Oxford family house, by car and taken off to Bertrand Russell's expansive household at Court Place. This was the house that Bertrand and Alys Russell had had built for themselves in Iffley in 1906. It was described as a pleasant house on the banks of the Thames at Iffley, just across the river from Bagley Wood, but was in fact a huge rambling place. Hannah Pearsall Smith, Karin's grandmother, and her brother Logan lived there with the Russells.[131] Mary Berenson dominated the whole household during her visits; she loved to organise parties, and bought a car during that summer. She taught Ray how to drive, and rushed out and bought her all the right clothes including 'a real motor cap with the eyes sewed in and a false nose, and all the rest of it ... What Ray really liked, though, was lying in the muddy road underneath the machine trying to get it going again when it stopped.'[132]

Eileen went on motor expeditions with Ray, Karin, Mrs Berenson and various young men. On one expedition in it, 'our tyre burst, and we had to spend ages putting on a new one, during which process the two men & Ray remained stretched at full length beneath the car. Finally one emerged covered from head to foot with dust & remarked ruefully to EEP, "Behold what a son of toil I am." Quoth EEP "You look more like a ton of soil." '[133]

Eileen was overawed by Court Place 'because everyone who has been staying there seems to have been so clever, and directly they begin to talk I become as silent as an oyster'.[134] She wrote to Margery for books on philosophy and ethics. She found the Berensons amusing, and was greatly attracted to Alys Russell, who took her up and mothered her, taking her for walks, asking her sisters out,

---

[129] Power to MLG, 8 August 1910.
[130] Strachey, *Remarkable Relations*, p. 250.
[131] *Ibid.*, p. 235.
[132] *Ibid.*, p. 232.
[133] Power to MLG, 8 August 1910.
[134] Power to MLG, 18 August 1910.

talking to her about her friends and marriage and careers. 'She is also going to "push" me when I return from Paris in order to try & save me from the fate of high school teaching.'[135]

Alys Russell took her to a memorable suffrage meeting in the summer of 1910, and Eileen described it to Margery:

I went to Court Place for the night & we bicycled 8 miles to a lovely Elizabethan house owned by a rich American artist – a charming woman. We had dinner (prepared by a French chef. Lor!) & then Mrs. Russell addressed a meeting from the Terrace. She speaks excellently. I had to speak too, which rather disconcerted me, as you know what an atrocious speaker I am at the best of times & it was too dark for me even to use notes. Moreover a crowd of shy bucolic yokels fill me with more awe than the academic audiences of Girton. However desperation probably carried me through ... our bicycles punctured five miles from Court Place ... We walked back on a deliciously balmy night & talked about everything under the sun, but chiefly me! ... Mrs. Russell (who liked you) gave vent to the banal opinion that you were pretty & would probably get married![136]

Karin visited Eileen in Paris, and Eileen spent much of the summer of 1911 at Court Place, doing more German, reading some philosophy, and enjoying motor cars, dancing, smoking by the river and generally idling away time. Later, when they both lived in London, Eileen shared Karin's flat for a time, and also stayed there frequently in the years after this. Eileen's friendship with Karin quickly took her into the fringes of Bloomsbury, for in 1914 Karin married Adrian Stephen. This was shortly after the marriage of another Girton friend, Ruth Fox, to Hugh Dalton. Eileen wrote ruefully after this: 'It is perfectly awful the way all one's friends rush off and get married: I seem to spend my life writing congratulatory letters on engagements, buying wedding presents or embroidering babies' frocks.' When she heard of Karin's engagement, she was 'plumbed to the depths of atrocious misery, because I had taken a dislike to Adrian sixty times greater than my dislike to Hugh Dalton & considered all those Bloomsberries as unsatisfactory folk with whom to have permanent relationships. I am a perfect idiot about Gwladys & you & Karin; you were always more important than other people ... & I very seldom do like men.'[137] But by the following day she had reconsid-

[135]   Power to MLG, 18 August 1910.
[136]   Power to MLG, 18 August 1910.
[137]   Power to MLG, 24 September 1914. Hugh Dalton (1887–1962) was an economist and later Labour politician. He was a reader in economics at the LSE 1923–36.

ered, writing that Adrian was 'a dear' because 'heaven be praised he won't interfere with the philosophy'.[138]

Eileen loved her friends, but quite clearly rejected any suggestion that her friendships were homoerotic relationships. She rebuffed a younger woman who fell in love with her, and was angry when she was accused by her of sexual encounters with other women. She was annoyed with Margaret Jones who caused more trouble when 'she tried to spoil all her harmless girl-friendships by goggling her eyes and seeing something mysterious and sexual in them'.[139]

Her friends were also political – a new generation of suffrage campaigners. Eileen's views on women's social and political rights had been shaped long before university by her own upbringing by three self-reliant aunts who believed in education for women. These views were now integrated into the broader pacifist and socialist outlooks she developed at university, and cemented by her friendships among other suffrage campaigners. Margery Garrett and Margaret Jones were involved as a matter of course through their families; Catriona Robertson, Irene Snelling, Eileen's sister Beryl, and a number of others she knew at Girton became organisers for a time, after leaving college, for the National Union of Women's Suffrage Societies (NUWSS), the moderate wing of the suffrage movement, led at the time by Millicent Garrett Fawcett.[140] Karin Costelloe's sister, Ray Strachey, made her career in the suffrage campaigns and other women's issues later.[141] While still an undergraduate Eileen was attending National Union Council meetings, and advising Margery Garrett on how to vote.[142] Alys Russell took her campaigning in Oxfordshire in 1910 and 1911, and while she was in Paris she wrote many times to Margery Garrett on her political and feminist commitment. 'I'm not a bit "anti man" really & of course I don't think all men are like that. But I honestly can't help thinking that the majority are. What is to be done ... Education and eugenics and the inculcating of proper ideas into women's heads I suppose.' In reply to a request for information about herself from

---

[138] Power to MLG, 24 September 1914.
[139] Power to MLG, 10 April 1910, 27 February 1911, 27 May 1912.
[140] All were NUWSS organisers after leaving college. See *Girton College Register* and *Newnham College Register*.
[141] See Ray Strachey, *The Cause: A Short History of the Women's Movement in Great Britain* (London, 1928).
[142] Power to MLG, 15 March 1910.

someone writing about Girton students for the *Girls' Realm* she said to put in that she was a strong feminist.[143]

When Eileen returned to Cambridge in 1914, she was heavily involved in organising for the NUWSS. By this time the organisation had 50,000 members. Eileen expressed pent-up frustrations over poor organisation and bad meetings,[144] and spoke on a platform with Mrs Fawcett twice in 1914–15.[145] She shared rooms in London with Irene Snelling in 1911–12, and with Karin Costelloe in 1912–14, and her sister Beryl was frequently with her in between bouts of organising for the Eastern region between 1913 and 1914.[146]

The family disaster that had forced Eileen Power into social and financial insecurity and the father who could not be trusted were compensated for by supportive aunts and female tutors and friends. Going to college created another life for Eileen, one of careers and independence, but also a rich and cosmopolitan world which she entered vicariously through the lives and families of her close friends. She acquired the style and social ease that gave her access to any social circle. As she finished her tripos in the summer of 1910, even greater vistas seemed about to open for her. She went on to the Ecole des Chartes in Paris, and aimed to become a historian. This is exactly what she did in the following years spent in Paris, London and back in Cambridge.

[143] Power to MLG, 7 February 1911.
[144] Power to MLG, 24 September 1914.
[145] Power to MLG, 24 September 1914, 16 March 1915.
[146] Power to MLG, 21 July 1914.

CHAPTER 3

Becoming a historian: Paris, London and Cambridge 1910–1920

Eileen Power only seriously considered continuing academic work while she was in her final year at Girton. She had no set direction at this stage, and only knew she had to earn her living in some way. Continuing meant reliance on scholarships, and there were few of these to be had. She was encouraged by Alys Russell to have high expectations. With the end of her undergraduate years looming, she was in the same state as most young women then, as now, of not knowing what she wanted to do. Winifred Mercier's timely suggestion of Paris and the Ecole des Chartes provided something to aim for. Most of Eileen's friends went back home to their families for a time, got married, or became suffrage organisers or teachers. The only one with similar abilities and the determination to pursue these further was Karin Costelloe, and she still had a year to go before her tripos. Eileen had no expectations that she would get the scholarship to take her to Paris, and once she was there she still viewed it as an interlude, and fully expected, much as she hoped she would not, that she would soon have to slot into some kind of teaching job in a school. The graduate work she pursued was not, therefore, a step along a well-trodden career path taken by medievalists before her. There was little long-term planning either in personal terms or for an institutional framework for these next crucial stages of her life that were to make her into a historian.

I

Eileen's year in Paris in 1910–11 was a great new experience. She had not been abroad since the age of nine, the time she went with her mother and sisters to the tuberculosis clinic in Switzerland. Paris represented to Eileen at the age of twenty-one what it did to generations of young women before and after her – the outside, 'grown-up' world, cosmopolitan, avant-garde and romantic. Before she even crossed the Channel she was planning ways of extending her scholarship money so that she could spend two years there, and looking forward to 'living la vie Bohème in an atmosphere of much cigarette smoke, conversation and respectability!'[1]

She left for Paris in mid-October, travelling with her sister Rhoda, who came for a short visit. She came with introductions into French academic life. This was the Paris of the Third Republic which for the years between 1875 and 1914 provided a vibrant intellectual and cultural life. The universities were at the centre of debates on science, education and democracy. The arts were alive with new movements – symbolism in painting and in poetry, and the music of Debussy and Ravel. The two sisters were met by Mme Huillard-Breholles, an old widow of a French medievalist,[2] who introduced Eileen to the ways of studying in Paris, and took her to meet her supervisor, C. V. Langlois.[3] She lodged in Mme Breholles' house, along with a Swedish student, in the Rue de l'Estrapade, Paris V. Here she was on the left bank, in the heart of the university quarter, living next to the Panthéon and only a short walk away from the Sorbonne and the Collège de France on one side and the Ecole Normale Supérieure on the other. She delighted in her large room with three comfortable chairs and a chesterfield.[4] Eileen spent her first months in Paris alternating between a frenzy of activity and homesickness. Most of her days were filled with work in the Bibliothèque Nationale, lectures, and long hours in the Louvre. She also managed to cram in visits to other galleries, shopping and lunch, tea, dinner and concerts with a wide range of friends, new acquaintances and visitors. Soon after she arrived, and while Rhoda was still with her, she described a visit by some rich American friends of

---

[1] Power to MLG, 15 August 1910.

[2] Her husband was Jean Louis A. Huillard-Breholles (1817–71), an archivist at the Archives Nationales, and author of a number of major works of medieval history including *Grande chronique de Mathieu*, 9 vols. (Paris, 1840–1) and *L'Histoire générale du moyen âge*, 2 vols. (Paris, 1842). See M. Prévost, R. D'Amat and H. Tribout de Movembert, *Dictionnaire de biographie française*, vol. XVII (Paris, 1989), p. 1511 (hereafter *DBF*).

[3] C. V. Langlois was a social historian of the later Middle Ages and author with Charles Seignobos of *Introduction aux études historiques* (Paris, 1898), a pathbreaking work of historical method. This book was later to become the subject of extensive critique by Marc Bloch and Lucien Febvre. Langlois was professor of paleography at the Faculté des Lettres, and also well known for his books *Le règne de Philippe III le Hardi* (Paris, 1887) and *Histoire du moyen-âge (395–1270)* (Paris, 1890).

[4] Power to MLG, 6 November 1910.

Rhoda. '[They] take us about in the most heavenly way. Motor cars galore, tea at Rumpelmayers, boxes at the opera – haw! haw!'[5]

The Paris that Eileen came to was in political and intellectual ferment. The effects of the Dreyfus Affair were still being felt. The Dreyfus Affair had stirred political passions over anti-Semitism. The Dreyfusards had successfully defended the full citizenship of French Jews, but it was only in 1906 that the judgment on Dreyfus was overturned by the Court of Appeals, and he was reinstated in the army. The radical ascendancy in the elections of 1906 yielded a government of the left under Clemenceau. But the left was split; the government put down strikes with increasing harshness over the next three years. Clemenceau had been replaced by Briand who did not belong to any particular group, and whose government followed similar policies to Clemenceau's. French politics entered a phase of instability where prime ministers changed many times even in the brief period before the First World War, and parties fragmented into parliamentary groups. The radical government still contained radicals, but was not led by radicals or even dominated by a radical majority. Briand had once been a militant advocate of the general strike, but became a staunch defender of republican order against strikes. He presided for the next few years over a general malaise and decay of political life.[6]

Eileen Power arrived in Paris during the railwaymen's strike of the autumn of 1910 which Briand was soon to put down by calling up the reservists and forcing the strikers back to work under martial law.[7] Eileen described the city as 'under siege – nothing is allowed in or out except by motor car'. She wrote home at length about the strike, keen to convey the strong sense of sympathy she felt all around her for the strikers. She thought their demands moderate and just, 'rest every ten days, and a rise of 1 franc 50 centimes in their wages'. She reported the political turmoil caused by the strike, with Briand denounced by the socialist journal *L'Humanité*, for his treachery in abandoning the ardent socialism and support of the strike weapon of his earlier years.

Eileen wrote of her reactions:

---

5   Power to MLG, 1910–11; 16 October 1910; Power, diary, 1911.
6   Maurice Agulhon, *The French Republic 1879–1992* (Oxford, 1993), pp. 129–34; Jean-Marie Mayeur and Madeleine Rébérioux, *The Third Republic from its Origins to the Great War 1871–1914* (Cambridge, 1984), pp. 278–85.
7   Mayeur and Rébérioux, *The Third Republic*, p. 281.

I could not help feeling wildly socialistic and revolutionary over this strike, partly because I think the men's demands were moderate & partly because the method which Briand took of putting it down was one of the most disgraceful things I have ever read of ... to make the cause of national defence a means of turning free workmen into public slaves, liable to military discipline seems to me almost inconceivable ... with a precedent like that no one's liberties are safe, and the working classes are deprived of practically the only weapon they have for bettering their conditions ... you can stop any strike if you suddenly deprive the strikers of their liberty & of all their rights as free citizens in a civilized & peaceful state. At any rate here is a quite new & original argument against conscription, next time Girton gathers to debate that well worn theme!'

Eileen went on to explain that the railway workers could have stayed out another two weeks without punishment, but they did not know their legal rights on this. Instead they went back to work, and 'their resentment found expression in acts of sabotage – bombs, attempts to wreck the line etc. – which only injured their cause in public opinion. It is all horribly depressing. Why didn't I study economics?'[8]

The political decay of this phase of the *belle époque* was paralleled by a turn in French cultural and intellectual life to intuition and the irrational and against the positivism of the previous generation. The Sorbonne was reeling in a torrent of debate on positivism and the principles of education. It had so recently reformed itself, moving away from an elite style of education towards the sciences and social sciences and the democratic cultivation of talent. The Sorbonne was identified with the radicals and the Dreyfusards.[9] Across the road at the Collège de France the new philosophical challenge of Henri Bergson (1859–1941) attracted audiences of students from many disciplines, as well as scholars and writers, to crowded lectures, and journalists gave his views wide currency. His impact was described at the time as 'a return to metaphysics in the world'.[10] His ideas on free will and intuition were a revelation. The critique of the old intellectual certainties was taken in different directions by the students who were attracted to the new methodologies. For some it meant a critique of the application of mathematical and scientific methods to

[8]   Power to MLG, 17 October 1910.
[9]   Fritz Ringer, *Fields of Knowledge. French Academic Culture in Comparative Perspective 1890–1920* (Cambridge, 1992), pp. 234–40.
[10]   Mayeur and Rébérioux, *The Third Republic*, p. 289; Eugen Weber, *The Nationalist Revival in France 1905–1914* (Berkeley, 1968), pp. 80–3; H. Stuart Hughes, *Consciousness and Society. The Reorientation of European Social Thought 1890–1930* (New York, 1958), pp. 113–25.

the study of human society, the reduction of literary and historical study to the techniques of the laboratory.[11] For others it also justified a political turn to the right. There was a conservative, Catholic and nationalist revival among students after 1905, against the prevailing secular republicanism at the Sorbonne. This included a resurgence of anti-Semitism. Such a position was taken by the writers of *Agathon*, who surveyed student opinion as preferring action to doctrinal speculation, and praised qualities of endurance, virility and self-control with references to Stendhal and Nietzsche. They turned their backs on the intellectual citizens, Bohemians and free-thinkers of the Sorbonne of the 1890s. That was the world of their fathers, now sober old gentlemen with official status. In contrast the return of a moral order and a nationalism of action was seen as the new cultural system of the young against the values of the left.[12]

As Eileen Power entered the Sorbonne, the big issue of the day was *Agathon*'s attacks on the university's leading scholars, C. V. Langlois (who would supervise her), Charles Seignobos and Emile Durkheim for their scientism.[13] French historical writing was under attack for being overly influenced by German ideas of scientific history. In their defence Langlois, Ernest Lavisse and Seignobos argued that positive history only meant scholarly rigour and research on political and institutional history, and they saw themselves as heirs to the republican tradition. How much this conflict of attitudes impinged on Eileen Power is difficult to assess. She was an outsider, attending lectures and occasional supervisions, working in the Bibliothèque Nationale, indeed still trying to improve her French. She probably found it very difficult to meet other students, and wrote home only rarely of such encounters. She spent most of her free time with friends or acquaintances visiting Paris, or with a few academic families to whom she had introductions. Among these were Elie Halévy the liberal philosopher and political historian of England, and his wife Florence.[14] She established a firm friendship with them,

---

11 Phyllis H. Stock, 'Students vs. the university in pre-world war Paris', *French Historical Studies*, 7 (1971–2), 93–110, at 97–100; Ringer, *Fields of Knowledge*, p. 240.
12 Agulhon, *The French Republic*, p. 140.
13 Carole Fink, *Marc Bloch. A Life in History* (Cambridge, 1989), p. 39.
14 Elie Halévy (1870–1937) was lecturer then professor of philosophy at the Ecole Libre des Sciences Politiques from 1892. He wrote *La formation du radicalism philosophique*, 3 vols. (1901–4) and *Histoire du peuple anglais aux XIX siècle*, 6 vols. (1912–31). His wife, Florence, helped a great deal in the drafting of his work, and was herself known for her translation of Goethe's *La vocation théâtrale de Wilhelm Meister* (1924). Halévy came from a distinguished Jewish intellectual family. *DBF*, vol. XVII, pp. 506–7.

but this was the only lasting connection she made in France. The visits from her friends at home were intermittent, and most of her French acquaintances did not become friends. Margery Garrett, Karin Costelloe, Margaret Jones and Gwladys Jones each visited once. By early December she had tired of her landlady and her room-mate.[15] She wrote long letters home to her friends, and frequently took her friend Margaret Jones' young sister Topsy, now a schoolgirl in Paris, out on excursions. She also read widely – Dostoyevsky, Wilde, Meredith, Flaubert, Anatole France.

Eileen's image of French student life was bohemian, political and feminist. Soon after she arrived, the other lodger in her house introduced her to Mme Gastellier, 'a very interesting well-read woman whose friends are all feminists, radicals and poets. She is very poor, & supports herself & a three year old child by sewing and some French lessons.' Eileen gave her English lessons and books by Olive Schreiner and Oscar Wilde.[16] The Paris of Eileen Power's preconceptions was partly made up of the celebrated anti-establishment bourgeois women of the generation before such as Marguerite Durand, the advocate of women's rights who had founded *La Fronde*, a newspaper edited entirely by women and which lasted from 1897 to 1905. Eileen's letters and diaries during the year only rarely referred to her spending time with any younger French people. One occasion she did record showed the nature of her preconceptions. At 'a soirée at Georges' she discussed feminism, internationalism and peace with three young French men. They argued over the suffrage, and she despaired at their views, but wrote in her diary: 'Great gift of tongues for once & stumped 'em – even in French, but it is discouraging – lord!'[17] She wrote to Margery afterwards: 'I am getting more and more "cranked" over this woman movement. If only one could do something. It is so dreadful to come up against an immoveable case of conviction such as that young man's & to feel that one lives in a state of society where he & his like really rule ... Please don't think me absurdly bitter & hard & intolerant.'[18] This argument was not the only episode to challenge her progressive assumptions. She soon noticed the extent of anti-Semitism around her, and read up the Dreyfus case as well as Anatole France's *L'Ile*

---

[15] Power to MLG, 4 December 1910.
[16] Power to MLG, 6 November 1910.
[17] Power, diary, 4 February 1911.
[18] Power to MLG, 7 February 1911.

des Pingouins, a satire of the Dreyfus case. She wrote home: 'There's been another burst of anti-semitism here: ... it is incredible how strong it is.'[19]

Eileen felt her position as an outsider, an English student in Paris, even more in her lack of connection with the debates then going on among French historians. She was sent to the traditionalist Ecole des Chartes which was perceived in England as providing the historical training in the use of documents and the paleography that would form the basis for historical research. Many of the great medievalists had studied at the Ecole des Chartes, where document-based history and professional training of archivists were offered in the Benedictine tradition of medieval textual studies. The training the Ecole offered historians was famous during the 1880s when Henri Pirenne, the great Belgian medievalist, studied there. It was now under attack. Its position was represented during the years before the First World War by Seignobos, a historian of modern France, and Langlois, a medievalist, who together had published a manual of historiography in 1898. They insisted on the primacy of gathering facts from documents, and also emphasised the significance of individual events.[20] Their approach was challenged by the sociologists on the one hand, who found this kind of history overly occupied with politics, with the actions of individuals and with chronology, and on the other by the students of the new right who condemned its positivism. The Ecole was to come under scathing criticism from Lucien Febvre much later during the 1930s for training 'chartistes', who were good at the 'impeccable presentation of studies of all kinds of medieval institutions,' but without any serious analysis.[21]

Langlois, who supervised Eileen Power while she was in Paris, had taught Marc Bloch a few years before. He was identified then with the close reading of historical documents, the use of literary sources and narrative history. In his own work on fourteenth-century France he built up a kind of social history constructed around vignettes of life taken from the documents and literature.[22] Langlois was part of the world of the traditional historians now confronting the demands

[19] Power to MLG, 23 February 1911.
[20] Langlois and Seignobos, *Introduction aux études historiques*.
[21] This paragraph is based on material in Fink, *Marc Bloch*, pp. 20–33, 158–9. On Seignobos see Stuart L. Campbell, *The Second Empire Revisited. A Study in French Historiography* (New Brunswick, NJ, 1978), pp. 96–108, 150.
[22] See for example his later work, *La vie en France au moyen âge d'après quelques moralistes du temps* (Paris, 1926).

of the new social sciences. Marc Bloch was working at the time on his
doctoral thesis, and was to be one of those students whose perspectives would be framed by the debates then taking place among
French historians. Oppositions between prescientific and scientific
history, between 'culture' and specialisation and between popular-
isers and learned scholars were a challenge to the young historian
seeking his own approach. But Bloch's response to the idealist
sceptical attack on history was to change his conception of his
profession. It became a 'craft', and the task of the historian was to
reconstruct the past from tangible realities such as archaeological
evidence, languages and folklore.[23]

These debates made little impression at the time on Eileen Power.
For a foreign student at the beginning of her graduate work, Langlois
did not represent any school of history. He was simply a major and
'illustrious' French medievalist who had just published 'a rather
important book'.[24] He directed her to follow a number of courses,
provided a small number of supervisions, and eventually produced a
thesis topic for her. Langlois directed her to attend lecture courses at
the Ecole des Chartes on romance philology, paleography, and
methods of historical research. She also chose herself to attend
lectures on the sources of French history at the Ecole des Chartes,
and lectures on the sources of English history of the Tudor period at
the Ecole des Hautes Etudes. She planned to attend lectures later at
the Collège de France by Bédier on the legends of the Middle Ages,
lectures on art in the Italian republics, and another set on intellectual
civilisation during the Renaissance.[25]

By February she was desperate for a thesis topic, and longing to
tackle something seriously. Langlois was remote and unobtainable.
'One can't read poems in old French and look through odd mss.
indefinitely ... If I cannot pluck up enough courage to assail my man
after a lecture and ask him if he thinks I can begin soon ... I know he
is very busy – he has just published a rather important book, but I
am afraid of putting his illustrious back up ... Oh for one of my kind
and interested Cambridge men!'[26] But finally after some toing and
froing with Langlois, Eileen had settled on a topic by the end of

[23]   Ringer, *Fields of Knowledge*, pp. 257–76; Hughes, *Consciousness and Society*, pp. 105–25, 337–58;
       H. Stuart Hughes, *History as Art and as Science* (New York, 1964), pp. 15–17.
[24]   Power to MLG, 23 February 1911.
[25]   Power to MLG, 6 November 1910.
[26]   Power to MLG, 23 February 1911. The book she referred to was *La connaissance de la nature et
       du monde au moyen âge, d'après quelques écrits français a l'usage des laïcs* (Paris, 1911).

March. This was to be Isabella of France, wife of Edward II, popularly known as the 'she-wolf'. Eileen thought the period a bit late, and the subject less theoretical than she would have liked, but viewed it as good training and a clear field with enormous amounts of research to do. She also thought her subject could certainly hold her interest, for Isabella was 'the most disreputable woman of her day – her young life was a perfect hotch potch of lovers and murders & plots – & I am afraid my thesis will be like somebody or others definition of a savoury, "a little bit of much on toast.!" '[27]

Langlois directed Eileen Power to a standard 'women's topic', focused as it was on biography, queens and documents. She appeared to be set to join a long line of female social and popular historians, most of them working outside the university.[28] Power's undergraduate studies and the Girton traditions in economic history were all set aside in favour of direction to the biographical approach. Langlois was not inexperienced in supervising female medievalists with some background in economic history. Only a few years before, he had directed Ada Elizabeth Levett, who took the more conventional and 'male' route of medieval scholarship in constitutional, ecclesiastical and manorial history. But her work in these areas did not start until some time after her year in Paris and, unlike Eileen Power, she left little information in letters or memoirs of what she studied in Paris.

Eileen was initially inspired by her subject, despite her reservations on being shunted into biography. The prospect of writing about an independent, 'evil' woman clearly appealed. A month later, however, she was depressed and complaining of a wasted year, working alone with no good seminars, and only two brief interviews with Langlois.[29] Things soon picked up, with Langlois offering more help, and Eileen making plans to find the money to stay in Paris another year to pursue a doctorate there.

All her plans were thrown into disarray, however, when she was asked to apply for a job at Royal Holloway. She knew she had to go in for it; she had to get a job at some point to support herself, and for a time her sisters too, and she had to pursue what openings her tutors saw for her. She wrote in anguish to Margery: 'You don't know how I long to be able to research & write books all the time. I

27 Power to MLG, 26 March 1911.
28 See Thirsk, 'The history women' for details of these other historians.
29 Power to MLG, 23 April 1911.

am so infinitely more cut out for that than for stumbling along the
dull path of dondom, & I could weep sometimes when I think that
sooner or later I shall have to start earning my living & only be able
to get in fitful research work, in odd moments ... I'm *dead* keen on
work at present & I will not hurry Isabella & do her badly ... O
Margie, I don't really think I feel like a don. I want to write books.
Oh dear, Oh dear!'[30] In the event, she didn't get the job; it went to
someone with teaching experience, but the prospects of her finding
the money to stay on in Paris for another year also withered.[31] She
returned home to Oxford in mid-June.

Eileen Power's year in Paris was financed on a fellowship from
Girton, and she worked out that when she returned in June she
would have spent £140 over the whole year. Her fellowship did not
come to this; she had managed to make up the shortfall with tutoring
in English and French. Money worries and shopping were her twin
bêtes noires – portions of her scholarship intended for books and
tuition went on hats and skirts: 'I fear they did not mean tuition in
the art of life, for which I have used it. I fear I have a large dose of
the nature of my respectable maternal great grandfather, who was
more beautiful than the sun, and ran through three fortunes!'[32]
When her paternal grandmother finally did cut off her dress
allowance, she immediately went out and spent three guineas on a
dress and another guinea on a hat.[33] Despite her straitened finances,
Eileen took great delight in occasional shopping trips in Paris:
'Shopped all day: ordered coat & skirt & bought two TRE-
MENDOUS hats. Can't afford them, mais enfin ... ?'[34] She got
depressed about her clothes, went to her tailor, quarrelled with her
tailor,[35] all interspersed with marathon days working in the Bibliothèque Nationale and the Sorbonne library.

What impact did the Ecole des Chartes, lectures at the Ecoles des
Hautes Etudes and the Collège de France, Langlois, and research on
Isabella have on Eileen Power's history writing? This is difficult to
establish. She was a foreign student who took what she could out of
an assortment of lecture courses, and worked for a good part of the
time she was there without much direction. She did not participate

30   Power to MLG, 17 May 1911.
31   Diary, 29 May 1911; Power to MLG, 23 April 1911.
32   Power to MLG, 28 August 1910.
33   Power to MLG, 20 September 1910.
34   Diary, 15, 17 February, 28 March, 11 April 1911.
35   Diary, 18, 21 April, 10 June 1911.

in the debates in French history then going on, nor did she particularly identify herself with any school of French history. She did, however, see herself as having spent a year with the masters of medieval paleography. The lectures, along with regular long days in the Bibliothèque Nationale, had provided her with a close knowledge of French medieval literature and printed and manuscript historical documents. She was to draw on the knowledge and material she had accumulated for books and articles she would write over much of the rest of her career. Langlois' narrative style, construction of individual vignettes of medieval life, and juxtaposition of literary and historical sources were absorbed into her early history writing, but along with other influences she would come under back in England and her own personal proclivities. The legacy of the work on Isabella is unclear. Eileen Power amassed a large amount of material during her last five months in Paris as well as her summer back home in Oxford, but then she was to jettison the topic. She did, however, continue to work on medieval women, though in a very different way. She kept a large collection of carefully assembled research notes on Isabella all her life, but never afterwards wrote anything about her or directly drew on this material for more general books and papers.

II

During her summer back in Oxford, there was a short time in limbo before Eileen heard about and applied for the Shaw studentship at the LSE. While she was back in Oxford she carried on with her work, assuming that she would spend the next year doing research by some means. The week she returned from Paris she went up to a great suffrage meeting in London on 17 June, 'a splendid show', where she reported seeing a great group of her Girton friends, as well as Ellen McArthur and H. G. Wells.[36] She read Ibsen and Strindberg, discussed Wells' *The New Machiavelli* with Margery, and spent a lot of time at Court Place working on her German and discussing philosophy.[37] She spent time picnicking, punting and going to plays with a friend, Neville Gorton.[38] She also renewed her visits to Edward Armstrong.[39]

[36]   Diary, 17 June 1911.   [37] Power to MLG, 8 September 1911.
[38]   Diary, 14–21 June 1911. Eileen Power kept in touch with Gorton in later years. He became a chaplain at Blundells School in Devon. See Eileen Power, address book, Power–Postan Papers.
[39]   Diary, 17 June, 11, 14, 17, 25 July 1911.

Eileen heard about the Shaw studentship on 27 June, and applied immediately. She wrote to Margery to say she wished she could get it. 'It would be almost too good to be true to have a reasonable number of one's friends gathered together in the same place.'[40] She was interviewed for it on 18 July and heard of her success on 20 July.[41]

The 'Shaw' was a scholarship of £105 a year for two years, set up in 1904 by Charlotte Payne Townshend Shaw at the London School of Economics. Charlotte Shaw was a leading member of the Fabian Women's Group which conducted a series of debates and produced a number of papers on women's economic position.[42] She was also the wife of George Bernard Shaw. The studentship had not initially been set up exclusively either for women or for women's history. The first recipient was Marion Phillips, one of the active members of the Fabian Women's Group,[43] and later a Labour Party activist. The next five awards, between 1906 and 1910, however, went to men. Among the unsuccessful female candidates were Mabel Atkinson, author of a remarkable Fabian tract on the history of women's work, and Helen Cam, who was to become a fellow of Girton and a leading legal historian of Medieval England.[44] Five men in a row were enough for Charlotte Shaw; she decided to limit the scholarship to women, and to define the topics they were to research.

An open scholarship was thus turned into one for women only, and for research on women's history. When the Shaw research studentship was advertised in 1911, it now stated: 'Henceforth this studentship will be open to women only ... the subject of research will be specified ... the holder of the scholarship will be expected to prepare an original monograph. The subject this year is "The social

---

[40] Power to MLG, n.d. June 1911.

[41] Diary, 28, 20 July 1911.

[42] On the Fabian Women's Group see S. Alexander (ed.), *Women's Fabian Tracts* (London, 1988), pp. 1–17. See Fabian Women's Group, 'Summary of six papers and discussion upon the disabilities of women as workers', *Fabian Tracts* (London, 1909), reprinted in Alexander (ed.), *Women's Fabian Tracts*, pp. 105–28; Fabian Women's Group, 'Summary of eight papers and discussion upon the disabilities of mothers as workers', *Fabian Tracts* (London, 1910); B. L. Hutchins, 'The working life of women', Fabian Women's Group Series, *Fabian Tracts*, 157 (1911); Mabel Atkinson, 'The economic foundations of the women's movement', Fabian Women's Group Series, *Fabian Tracts*, 175 (1914), both reprinted in Alexander (ed.), *Women's Fabian Tracts*, pp. 164–78; 256–82.

[43] Marion Phillips gained a D.Sc. Econ. in 1908, and later in 1912 became organising secretary of the Women's Trade Union League and, in 1913, the general secretary of the Women's Labour League. See *The London School of Economics Register*, ed. Mildred Bulkley and Amy Harrison, intro. by William Beveridge (London, 1934).

[44] Shaw research studentship file 835, LSE CF LSE archives BLPES.

and economic position of women in England at some period before the Industrial Revolution".' Charlotte Shaw presented a list of six questions, and expected the recipient of the award to pursue them. She was, she later said, 'looking for a series of monographs on the position of women in England (or Britain) from early days down to the present'.[45]

When Charlotte Shaw set out to direct her studentship so prominently to women working on women's history, this was not so extraordinary a step as it may appear to us now, looking back with hindsight. Female research students formed a significant group at the LSE at the time, and a number of these held LSE research awards, then later the Russell and Ratan Tata Foundation studentships. B. L. (Bessie) Hutchins followed Charlotte Shaw's initiative in 1925. She too had been active in the Fabian Women's Group. She was a research assistant to the Webbs, then later an independent scholar who, with Amy Harrison, wrote a history of factory legislation, followed by her well-known book, *Women in Modern Industry* (1915). She gave the LSE £2,000 in 1925 to start a two-year studentship at £150 a year for a female student studying economic history.[46]

Eileen Power was the first to receive a Shaw fellowship under the new rubric. Her subject was 'The social and economic position of women in England during the thirteenth or perhaps the fourteenth century'. Her success was followed by Alice Clark, who held the fellowship in 1913 to pursue research on women's work in the seventeenth century, and later by Alice Meyer, who studied Anglo-Saxon women.[47] Thus Charlotte Shaw managed effectively to carve up the study of women's history.

The timing of the Shaw fellowship in 1911 coincided with the Fabian Women's Group discussions on women's economic situation and its historical background. The group included Charlotte Shaw,

[45] I owe this point about the change in the specifications of the Shaw research fellowship to Carol Dyhouse, who also directed me to two files on women's studentships in the BPLES archives. See Carol Dyhouse, *No Distinction of Sex? Women in British Universities 1870–1939* (London, 1995), pp. 142–3. See Shaw research studentship CF file 835, LSE archives BLPES: printed advertisement and six subjects, May 1911; Shaw to Miss MacTaggart, secretary, 22 July 1915.

[46] See Studentships for women file CF 46/45E 1926–38, LSE archives BLPES; *LSE Register*, pp. 217–18.

[47] Alice Clark worked as Shaw research student under the supervision of Lilian Knowles 1913–15 and later published her book, *The Working Life of Women in the Seventeenth Century* (1919). Alice Meyer did research on 'The influence of Roman civilization on the national position and characteristics of Anglo-Saxon womankind'. See Shaw research studentship file CF 835, LSE archives BLPES.

Marion Phillips, Mabel Atkinson and B. L. Hutchins, and at the time
they were all addressing the issues raised in Olive Schreiner's *Woman
and Labour*. Lilian Knowles, who had taught economic history at
Girton just before Eileen went there, was now lecturer in economic
history at the LSE, and she took up this debate on women's work in
her lectures, and later in her textbook.[48]

We learn a little more about the fellowship in Eileen Power's
graphic report of her interview to Margery Garrett. 'The Committee
meeting was not very alarming. The only people there were Pember
Reeves (I struggled with a temptation to address him: "good
morning, have you read The New Machiavelli?") & Hubert Hall.[49]
They were quite nice.'[50] *The New Machiavelli*'s author, H. G. Wells,
had recently caused scandal and pain to William Pember Reeves, the
LSE's director, by openly conducting an affair with Reeves'
daughter, Amber. He had added to the humiliation by writing a
thinly veiled novel, *Ann Veronica*, about the affair.

The LSE was a new world in comparison with the Oxford and
Cambridge of Eileen Power's earlier education. It was also a very
different prospect from that of the learned traditions of the Paris of
the Sorbonne and the Ecole des Chartes. This was a new university,
hardly fifteen years old, pushing the boundaries of knowledge into
new subject areas in the social sciences. In a ten-year-old building
with a new refectory, but no student accommodation, located in
Clare Market, midway between the City and Westminster, this was a
new concept in a university. It had an emphatically practical outlook,
one of involvement in the heart of metropolitan and political life.
And it attracted students from a wide range of ages and social and
cultural backgrounds. The newness of the LSE and the Fabian
background of its leading founders, the Webbs, still lent the School a
radical, reforming image.

Eileen Power was a little sceptical, if not snooty, on her first
encounter – all too much the sophisticated twenty-two-year-old
stepping in from Cambridge and Paris: 'Do you know, I do dislike

---

[48]   See the debate in Fabian Women's Group, 'Summary of six papers', and Fabian Women's
       Group, 'Summary of eight papers'; Olive Schreiner, *Woman and Labour* (London, 1911);
       Lilian Knowles, *The Industrial and Commercial Revolutions in Great Britain during the Nineteenth
       Century* (London, 1921), pp. 93, 100.
[49]   William Pember Reeves was director of the LSE 1908–19. Hubert Hall was London
       University reader in history 1908–25 and an LSE occasional lecturer. *LSE Register*, pp. 228,
       235.
[50]   Power to MLG, 22 July 1911.

the London School of Economics! I don't know why, but it was borne upon me while I was there. I don't think I much love the type of person who goes there – dewdabblers, pretentious socialists & frothy Fabians & unconscionably earnest young people generally! However I am landed there for two years now, so I suppose I shall have to develop a taste for it.' The difference that studying there would make to her work was, however, daunting, and not what she wanted. She was faced with economics rather than literature, and a change in her thesis topic.

I am extremely perturbed because the whole thing has turned out very much more economic than I expected, and I sometimes have doubts whether I am doing the wisest thing ... I am bound to enter my name for the degree of D.Sc. (Econ) at London. I don't want that degree: I simply detest Economics and always have, and besides I'm a perfect fool at them – the literary and purely historic side is my line. I want a D.Litt., but the School of Economics will never allow me to work for that instead, and I shall have to take this undesired degree.[51]

The research proposal for this particular Shaw fellowship was not open; it was clearly directed to women's social and economic history. Women's history was thus given a clear prominence in the form of a special research fellowship. The subject was even more clearly constrained, as Power was to discover to her discomfort.

The chief thing which attracted me about the Shaw was the subject, and I had intended to take 'The Social and Economic Position of Women in England during the XIII or perhaps XIV Century' ... rather a wide subject, but it would be fascinating and would give plenty of scope not only for real, hard research, but for good writing. Beside the purely economic part – like the position of women in the trades and guilds – one could do the wider social position, as gleaned from the literature of the period, something about women in the nunneries and so forth.

Imagine my horror when the School of Economics sent me a list of six perfectly disgusting and exclusively narrowly economic subjects for research and tells me to choose from them ... the very sight of them makes me weep with boredom and numbers 3 & 4 are the only ones which I would touch with the end of a barge pole!

1. Women's position in agriculture during the Middle Ages in England 2. The influence of the break up of the National System on the economic position of women in England 3. British women in their relation to the Guilds 4. Trades partly or entirely carried on by women in the Middle Ages in England 5. Women's position in agriculture and other industries

[51] Power to MLG, 22 July 1911.

during the tribal period and early middle ages in Great Britain. 6. The effect upon the economic position of the married woman in South Britain of the transition from tribal custom which placed her, in part at least, under the protection of her own kindred even during married life, to the theory developed by English Common Law during the Middle Ages, that a wife was entirely subordinate to and dependent on her husband.[52]

The topics were set out by Charlotte Shaw, but Shaw had a disagreement over them with Lilian Knowles. Knowles presided over economic history at the LSE from 1904 when she became the first full-time lecturer in economic history, and was professor from 1921 and dean of the faculty of economics from 1920 to 1924. She was a county tory, a patriot and imperialist – very much a direct product of the German historical school which had also inspired her own mentor, William Cunningham, and the other early economic historian at Manchester, George Unwin. At first sight there was little in her background or her own historical interests to indicate a great championing of women's history. She wrote and lectured on commerce, trade, transport and especially the empire. She carried over Cunningham's interest in the state and economic policy and moved forward from his work on the mercantile system to her own work on the nineteenth century. She was 'fascinated by the romance of pioneering, of man's triumph over the wilderness and over disease in the tropics and elsewhere'.[53] Her big book, *The Industrial and Commercial Revolutions in Great Britain during the Nineteenth Century* was published after she died.

Knowles was not narrow in her interests, however, and she supervised over a broad range, including the work of number of women who completed major theses: Alice Clark, Joyce Dunlop and Ivy Pinchbeck on women's and children's labour; Mabel Buer on population; Dorothy George on Stuart finances; Julia Mann on the cotton industry, Alice Murray on Anglo-Irish trade, and Vera Anstey on Indian economic history. In her general textbook, she addressed at some length the issue of the impact of industrialisation on women's employment and working conditions. She showed a famili-

[52]   Power to MLG, 22 July 1911.
[53]   See W. H. Beveridge, 'Professor Lilian Knowles', *LSE Register*; W. H. Beveridge and Graham Wallas, 'Lilian Knowles 1870–1926', *Economica*, 6 (1926), 119–22; 'Knowles, Lilian Charlotte Anne', *Who Was Who*, vol. II (1916–28), p. 595; Eileen Power, 'Professor Lilian Knowles', *Girton Review*, 72 (1926), pp. 3–6; C. M. Knowles, 'Professor Lilian Knowles', in L. S. A. Knowles and C. M. Knowles, *The Economic Development of the British Overseas Empire*, vol. I (1930), pp. vii–xxii, p. xv.

arity with the German debate on the issue as well as with the historical work pursued by the Fabian Women's Group, and especially that by B. L. Hutchins.[54] She was astute enough to see that women's economic history was a major historical issue, and one which the LSE should support. Though she was a tory, Knowles was also a feisty, no-nonsense character who took on the administration at the LSE over her own working conditions and salary. She gave enormous support to her female students, and was proud of the fact that she had managed to combine marriage and motherhood with an academic career.[55]

Charlotte Shaw wrote to the director, Pember Reeves, about her dispute with Knowles over the research topics for her fellowship: 'I beg you to influence Mrs. Knowles to stick to the subjects I proposed and sent to you. She wants to go in for rather easier and simpler subjects, and especially to drag in the *Church*. I rely on you to stand up for me.' Shaw received assurances, and Eileen Power was appointed to the first women-only research studentship.[56] Lilian Knowles did not interview Power for the scholarship, nor did she supervise her thesis. She did, however, see her several times during her first two terms, and took part in the early supervision of her general programme.[57] Eileen attended Hubert Hall's seminar, and made up the inevitable shortfall between her grant and her living expenses by doing some research assistance for him. Hall, a close friend of the Webbs, was one of the founding spirits of the LSE. He taught paleography, and diplomatic and economic history. He was above all an archivist who had turned from work on modern departmental records to medieval history. He was best known for his pioneering work on medieval documents, especially the Pipe Rolls.

[54] See Knowles, *Industrial and Commercial Revolutions*, pp. 93, 100. See work by the German feminists Lily Braun, *Die Frauenfrage, ihr geschichtliche Entwicklung und Wirtschaftliche Seite* (Leipzig, 1901); and Elizabeth Gnauck-Kühne, *Warum organiseren wir die Arbeiterinnen?* (Leipzig, 1905), as well as the debate conducted within German Marxism and social democracy, as set out by Alys Russell, 'Appendix on social democracy and the woman question in Germany', in Bertrand Russell (ed.), *German Social Democracy* (London, 1896), pp. 175–95. See Martha Howell, Suzanne Wemple and Denise Kaiser, 'A documented presence: medieval women in Germanic historiography', in Susan Stuard (ed.), *Women in Medieval History and Historiography* (Philadelphia, 1987), pp. 101–31. Cf. Hutchins, 'Working life' and Schreiner, *Woman and Labour*.

[55] 'Personalities and powers: Lilian Charlotte Anne Knowles', *Time and Tide*, 5 February 1926, 126–7. Cf. W. H. Beveridge, *The London School of Economics and its Problems* (London, 1960), p. 49.

[56] Shaw research studentship file: Shaw to Pember Reeves, 18 June 1911; secretary to Shaw, 19 June 1911.

[57] Shaw research studentship file: secretary (MacTaggart) to Shaw, 3 April 1912.

He also took an active part in the Selden Society which published editions of medieval records. When Eileen Power came to the LSE he had recently been appointed secretary to the Royal Commission on Public Records, and he was also working on a bibliography of sources for English medieval history.[58] While Hall's focus on medieval documents and paleography was similar to that of Langlois, there the resemblance stopped. Hall was the dry, dull archivist of legal and diplomatic documents, while Langlois had been a witty lecturer with literary sensibilities and with interests in romance philology, epic and court culture.

Eileen discovered at her interview for the Shaw fellowship that Hall 'showed an inclination to insist that I should do all over again the paleographical training I have received in Paris ... It amused me rather, since I really have slaved for a year in the best school in Europe where English attempts at training are not regarded as first rate, to say the least of it! I wish they could hear M. Langlois on the subject of Hubert Hall (who is to direct my studies – I loathe being directed).' She attended his seminar which he was using to organise his students to collect material for his medieval bibliography. She like the others was paid two shillings an hour for doing the work.[59] She hoped for some light relief when she discovered that Goldsworthy Lowes Dickinson was an occasional lecturer at the LSE, and hoped to do some course work under him, but she had already covered the material he would teach while she was at Cambridge.[60]

During her Shaw fellowship, which she held from 1911 to 1913, Eileen Power abandoned her research on Isabella for broader work on medieval women, but soon narrowed down to a manageable research topic on medieval nunneries. She saw her subject as a compromise between the literary and cultural history she had pursued in Paris and the economic and social history then being developed at the LSE. This intellectual background together with the priorities of her fellowship and her own suffragist background played a part in the direction of her interests towards women's history. Power worked on the subject during the two years she was to spend at the LSE. The first four chapters of the book she was

[58]   Hubert Hall, *Bibliography for the Study, Sources and Literature of English Medieval Economic History* (London, 1914). See 'Hubert Hall 1857–1944', *Twentieth Century DNB*.
[59]   Power to MLG, 22 July 1911, 10 January 1912.
[60]   Power to MLG, 6 October 1911; diary, 4 October 1911.

eventually to write out of this research were submitted for a London MA.

During this time Eileen Power saw Charlotte Shaw a number of times, and during the final year of her fellowship, Shaw was sufficiently impressed to promise an extension of her fellowship. Shaw wrote of her in 1913: 'I think she takes her work really seriously, and is rather an exceptional person herself.'[61] Living in London presented new problems. The lease on the Oxford house had been given up when Eileen went to London and her sisters returned to university, and Eileen's Aunt Ivy was already working as a secretary in London. Rooms were found which Eileen intended to share with her Girton friend Irene Snelling. Eileen's fellowship was small, much less than the sum she had spent in Paris in eight months.[62] She supplemented it with some research assistance for Hubert Hall. These small funds had to provide not only for herself but for her sisters, who needed access to a room or the flats of friends during the holidays.[63]

As it happened, however, Eileen stayed at the LSE for only two years; and she spent the intervening summer of 1912 back in Girton working and teaching. After the constant worries over money while in London, she now had free rooms and meals in college, and earned £27 6s. over the summer. Despite the rapid descent of 'dondom', she was clearly pleased to be back, and was teased by the dons about her clothes.[64] Then in 1913 she returned to replace Winifred Mercier as director of studies in history.

Coming back to Cambridge brought Eileen into close contact with the two historians who were to have the greatest influence on her early approach to history – Alexander Hamilton Thompson (1873–1952) and George Gordon Coulton (1858–1947). Both were in marginal positions in Cambridge. Thompson had been appointed an extra-mural teacher by Cambridge in 1897, and over the next twelve years travelled about lecturing, though still living in Cambridge. He left Cambridge in 1919 for Newcastle, and from there soon after for Leeds. At the time that Eileen came back to Cambridge he was working on fifteenth-century monastic records, and had a reputation for his knowledge of primary sources in English medieval church

[61] Shaw research studentship file: Shaw to Reeves, 20 January 1913.
[62] It barely covered the £100 then commonly charged in London colleges for fees and residence.
[63] Power to MLG, 22 July 1911.
[64] Power to MLG, 9 July 1912; Power to MLG, n.d. August 1912.

history. Eileen drew on his extensive knowledge of the monasteries, his ideas as to how to extend this work to the relatively unexplored area of women's religious houses, and the sources he was compiling for his influential *Visitations of Religious Houses in the Diocese of Lincoln*.[65] She would follow Thompson's example in writing on the convents as institutions rather than focusing on religious ideas.

G. G. Coulton, one of the major historians of medieval monasticism, was also in Cambridge at the time Eileen returned. He was a colourful character who enlarged her interests in social history, and with whom she established an easy though critical rapport. She wrote frankly to him over the early part of her career, sought his advice on jobs and research, and exchanged references to archive sources with him. After years of teaching in a public school Coulton had, in 1910, been given the title of Birkbeck lecturer in ecclesiastical history by Trinity College, and he lived in Cambridge, putting together an income with freelance lecturing and coaching. Coulton was already a famous anti-Roman Catholic controversialist. His reputation was largely founded on the long controversy he initiated with Cardinal Gasquet,[66] the Catholic chronicler of monastic life, over the dissolution of the monasteries. Coulton was an irascible character, with a mission for revealing the dark underside of medieval 'golden ages'. The spirit of controversy around his name had become so marked that his own daughters were dismayed at the prospect of his autobiography.[67] Coulton was a classic anti-cleric, and wrote of Gasquet's monkish scholarship in much the same tone as that used later by another anti-cleric, Hugh Trevor-Roper: 'The Cardinal and his pretentious historiography are now dead ... Four great volumes and a few lapidary sentences make for their final tombstone.'[68] Coulton was in many ways an old-style Whig historian. He believed in progress, and saw this in enlightened rationalism and the greater use of reason in religion, as well as in improved morality. He thought that some institutions such as monasticism were bound to fail because they possessed a built-in capacity for becoming

---

[65]   A. Hamilton Thompson (ed.), *Visitations of Religious Houses in the Diocese of Lincoln*, Lincoln Record Society, vol. vii (Lincoln, 1914).

[66]   F. A. Cardinal Gasquet, *English Monastic Life* (London, 1904); F. A. Cardinal Gasquet, *The Eve of the Reformation* (London, 1900).

[67]   See G. G. Coulton, 'Introduction', in his *Fourscore Years. An Autobiography* (Cambridge, 1943). For more information on Coulton see Gerald Christianson, 'G. G. Coulton: the medievalist as controversialist', *Catholic Historical Review*, 57 (1971), 421–41.

[68]   H. R. Trevor-Roper, 'The twilight of the monks,' in H. R. Trevor-Roper, *Historical Essays* (New York, 1975), p. 73.

outdated and degenerate. He liked to regard the Middle Ages as a period of convalescence, that is, neither a grim litany of darkness nor a golden age. His overemphasis on the iniquities of monasticism, however, affected his readers' perception of his meaning. What they saw was a one-sided emphasis on clerical immorality, popular ignorance and crude dogmas, which made a new Dark Ages of the later Middle Ages.[69] Eileen Power later put the perception well in one of her reviews of his work: 'The public seeking his honey is disturbed by the bee which buzzes in his bonnet.'[70]

Coulton's approach to medieval history was also expressed in *The Medieval Village*. This book was first and foremost a plea for social history, and a turning away from constitutional history. He wrote in his preface:

Sooner or later, we must outgrow what may almost be called the present monopoly of constitutional theory and social theory; sooner or later, we must struggle to discover not only what men were organized to do six centuries ago, and not only what the academic publicists of that age prescribed for them to do, but what they actually did and suffered; and, by the way, what they themselves actually thought of the civil and ecclesiastical constitutions, or the social theories, under which they had to live.[71]

Eileen Power certainly internalised Coulton's unromantic approach to the past, and he served as her mentor for much of the time she spent in Cambridge. She admired his ability to write synthetic history effectively, unlike so many of 'our best historians who content themselves with producing learned monographs for each other, like the community in the political economy book who earned a precarious livelihood by taking in one another's washing'.[72] Ultimately, however, Power was very critical of him as a historian. His trenchant critique of other historians deflected him from a sympathy for the complexities of the past. She chastised him for his propagandist style, putting it diplomatically: 'I believe a treatment less overtly referring to the opposing thesis would have been more effective.'[73] She was less diplomatic in print:

The one effect of Dr. Coulton's work is familiar to his readers, and increases rather than decreases with his successive books. It is the tone of controversy which pervades them. The reason for this controversial tone and for his

---

[69] For a discussion of Coulton and his history see Christianson, 'G. G. Coulton'.
[70] Cited in Coulton, *Fourscore Years*, 'Introduction'.
[71] G. G. Coulton, *The Medieval Village* (Cambridge, 1925), p. ix.
[72] Eileen Power, 'The problem of the friars', *The Nation and Athenaeum*, 18 January 1928, 753.
[73] Power to Coulton, 17 January 1926, Power Papers, Girton College archives.

concentration upon the dark side of medieval civilization is a perfectly understandable anger at the uncritical and tendentious writings of certain Catholic and Anglican historians, who stress only the bright side. Yet it is doubtful whether the business of controverting them is worth the fire and energy which convert Dr. Coulton's books into shell-strewn battlefields.[74]

Although Power's research on women's religious communities was started at the LSE, it was at Cambridge, under the influence of Hamilton Thompson, and especially Coulton, that it acquired its distinctive shape. It was to be social history, and like Coulton's work, it would eschew the study of monastic ideals and religious thought. Instead, it would be a study of nunneries as social institutions and economic organisations.

Over the next two years, 1913 and 1914, Eileen combined a directorship of history at Girton with some lectures at the LSE, and lived between Girton and a flat in London she shared with Karin Costelloe. The flat also provided a place during the vacations for her sisters, her friends and the occasional hunger striker or refugee. She felt particularly responsible for Rhoda: 'Her delicacy makes her a great responsibility & as I upheld giving up the Oxford house & am moreover the only monied woman (lord!) of the three, the family looks to me to see after her, naturally.'[75] In the spring of 1915 she applied for and got the Pfeiffer fellowship at Girton with the backing of Lilian Knowles, but continued to do some teaching at the LSE. The fellowship allowed for a reduction of her tutorial teaching, and gave her more opportunity for writing. The Pfeiffer paid £150 per year and was tenable for three years. In 1917 she was awarded the Gamble prize for an essay, 'The enclosure movement in English nunneries'.[76] Both the fellowship and the prize were a part of Girton's initiatives for encouraging postgraduate research. The prize was named after Jane Catherine Gamble, whose original bequest had funded the college buildings; the Pfeiffer was named after another benefactor, Mrs Emily Pfeiffer,[77] a poet and feminist who had died in 1890, leaving a substantial trust for the promotion of higher education for women.

Teaching during these years was dominated by the war and suffrage work. Wartime Cambridge had the reputation of a bleak

---

[74]   Power, 'The problem of the friars', 753.
[75]   Power to MLG, 13 September 1912, 13 November 1913, 21 July 1914, 16 March 1915.
[76]   Power Papers, Girton College archives.
[77]   Stephen, *Girton College*, pp. 80–99.

place of women and old men. But it also opened up some opportunities for female tutors in the university. Eileen Power was soon
doing most of the mainstream lecturing for the university in
economic history, as well as some occasional lecturing for the LSE,
and the research time her fellowship was meant to provide was soon
eaten into by teaching. In practical terms, the early days of the war
meant only some disruption to teaching and the presence of soldiers
about the place. The war disrupted classes, and by late September
1914 Eileen heard that nearly all the young men at the LSE had
enlisted. She wrote to the director offering to postpone her lectures.
'After all it would be horrid to come up weekly for an audience of
two or three',[78] Eileen wrote to Margery in January 1915:

We are having what the Daily News calls Cambridge in the Grip of War.
The War Office at one blow struck our light out and our bells silent on the
eve of his Imperial Majesty's birthday ... And there is a picket of soldiers at
the bottom of Woodlands & a barricade of carts & a sentry across
Huntingdon Rd. & any cars going in & out are stopped & searched & the
name of the occupant taken. The Director of Studies in History much
enjoys being saluted & questioned by romantic young officers on her way
back from her Thursday lecture.[79]

But a few months later the killing had affected her own family, when
her youngest uncle died in Egypt.[80] Her sense of the anguish of war
was vividly expressed in her description of a family parting from a
son:

At Barnstable I saw a most painful farewell between a boy off to the front &
his family, farmer-folk. His mother lost her control & sobbed at the top of
her voice in a funny deep tone, like a man shouting, & clung to him. I was
sorry for the poor boy. When the train steamed out we passed her on the
platform, rocking herself up & down with her arms lifted to the sky & tears
rolling off her cheeks & screaming 'Oh my boy, oh my boy': we heard her
for ages, getting fainter & fainter. She was like one of the Trojan women.
What a damned shame it is. I would rather see a German ticket-collector
on the platform than her any day.[81]

Eileen was feeling much the same sense of the irrelevance of her
existence as was expressed by Vera Brittain at the time in Oxford.
Brittain wrote, 'I returned for the last term of my first year to an
Oxford that now seemed infinitely remote from everything that

[78] Power to MLG, 25 September 1914.
[79] Power to MLG, 21 January 1915.
[80] Power to MLG, 16 March 1915.
[81] Power to MLG, 5 September 1915.

counted ... .Oxford was now almost empty of undergraduates'.[82]
Another student at Girton wrote of the loss of what university life
should be. 'There is always a lurking feeling of uneasiness, sub-
conscious perhaps ... that never allows us quite to forget the happen-
ings of world-wide importance that are taking place not so far
away.'[83]

Eileen found life in Cambridge very tedious by the later stages of
the war, and complained after visiting Margery:

I get the most ghastly blues over the contrast between you & this. I don't
believe I was ever cut out for this sort of life: I die within me month by
month ... the war makes it worse, for Cambridge is an awful place to be in
just now – no one under forty! ... It seems such a short life for all the best
years of it to be spent here ... I really think the deadliness is chiefly due to
abnormal war conditions – there *isn't* anyone to talk to even in Cambridge.

By 1918 she was entertaining hopes of a job coming up eventually in
London, and in the meantime wished that she could go half-time at
Girton, and have the rest of the week in London.[84]

She survived the time, however, by frequent trips to London,
doing some work for the National Union, and some lecturing for the
WEA and the League of Nations. She gave one with Mrs Fawcett in
1915 at a suffrage meeting, and spoke on the Congress of Vienna[85]
(and followed the topic up a few years later for the WEA):

I'll do something I'm very keen on & have just lectured on here – to wit the
Congress of Vienna & the attempt at government by a confederation of
Europe 1815–23. The parallel with the present is simply amazing ... it is
exceedingly important as propaganda because it broke down for reasons
which will wreck the League of Nations after the Congress at the end of this
war, if its mistakes aren't avoided.[86]

Eileen was also sustained by her friends among the younger tutors at
Girton, especially Elizabeth Downs and M. G. Beard, the German
tutor, and teaching. When Dora Russell was a student she often saw
Barbula Beard and Eileen together, Beard 'a tall elegant Irish
woman with a slight stoop and a lorgnette and a very agreeable
brogue' and Eileen, 'We always found it a pleasure to watch her, tall
and placid and very much a personality, as she came in to take her

[82]   Brittain, *Testament of Youth*, p. 145.
[83]   Stephen, *Girton College*, p. 105.
[84]   Power to MLG, 25 September 1918.
[85]   Power to MLG, 16 March 1915.
[86]   Power to MLG, 7 July 1917.

3.1   Eileen Power as a young don in her rooms at Girton

place for dinner at high table. She had very beautiful candid blue-grey eyes.'[87]

Eileen Power's youth made her a popular and favoured tutor and chaperone, and she was well aware of this. 'I wish it made no difference to the students to have people like me & Pico [Elizabeth Downs] here. And yet when I look at some of them after I've put three years of my best effort – moral & intellectual – into them I cannot conceal from myself that they've started life better equipped than they would have been without us.'[88] Her students, especially the

[87]   Russell, *The Tamarisk Tree*, p. 36.
[88]   Power to MLG, 10 June 1917.

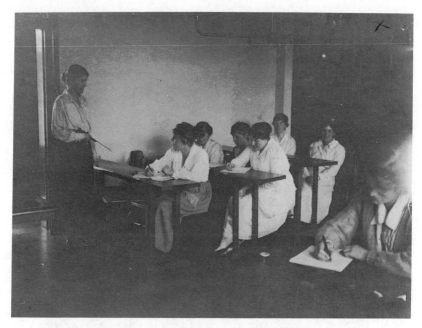

3.2   Eileen Power teaching in Girton, *c.* 1919

senior inner circle, clearly idolised her. She was a good lecturer,
though not immediately spontaneous or charismatic. She prepared
her lectures carefully, building up an analysis illustrated with vignettes and passages from literature to hold her audience and bring
them into her confidence, then to engage them with a storyteller's
gift. She provided the style, intelligence and wit they all aspired to.
She was their 'princess out of a medieval story book' who 'sat at the
edge of her chair, offering chocolates'.[89] She had a room with a
black carpet and ran poetry and musical evenings, reading avant-
garde poets such as Rupert Brooke, Ralph Hodgson and W. H.
Davies. Vera Brittain also recalled her English tutor inviting her and
a friend to her room where she read from the just-published first
edition of Rupert Brooke's *1914*. 'For the young to whom Rupert
Brooke's poems are now familiar as classics, it must be impossible to
imagine how it felt to hear them for the first time just after they were
written.'[90]

[89]   Dorothy Marshall, diaries.
[90]   Brittain, *Testament of Youth*, p. 155.

Eileen's Sunday poetry readings were an institution: 'We looked forward to them all week and wore our best white or pink crêpe de chine blouses in honour of the occasion.'[91] Mary and Theodora Llewelyn Davies, students at Girton between 1914 and 1920, wrote: 'We were a generation of young women starved at a sensitive age of most of the normal poetry of life. Our imaginations were caught and our affections held by Eileen's dazzling personality, by her brilliance, her beauty and her goodness.'[92] The students found themselves somewhat in awe of an intellectual superiority and a social poise that kept them at a distance. Winifred Hodgkins, who studied history at Girton during the later years of the war, clearly found the beauty and brilliance a bit too much to cope with: 'She was always kind and accessible but I was too diffident to dare to get on very close terms with her.'[93] Interspersed with these performances, however, were more down-to-earth confessions to Margery Garrett: 'I am feeling dreadfully depressed owing to dowdiness. My new coat & skirt which I got at the end of the summer (a silly thing to do anyhow) looks hopeless and I cannot see in the whole of London a hat that looks decent. Also I want a coat dress more than words can say.'[94]

The war ended, and with it the old enclosed order of the college. The men returned to the university, and Dora Russell was a fellow in Girton on the occasion when

just after the First World War ended a horde of undergraduates stormed out from Cambridge, ... yelling 'where are the women we have been fighting for?' Hanging out of every window and preparing to descend were, needless to say, the women in question. Miss Jex-Blake, like an Abbess, in her plain alpaca bodice and full long skirt, followed by a retinue of senior dons, received the invaders at the doorway under the arch ... Then she invited them to a dance at the College on the following Saturday. Such a function would not have been thought of only a few years previously.[95]

Lily Baron, a medical student at Girton at the time, found that when the armistice was signed, smoking was suddenly allowed in their rooms after dinner. It was a sign of a new emancipation, and she rushed out to buy her first packet of Turkish cigarettes. At lectures in

[91] Mary Llewelyn Davies and Theodora Calvert, 'Memories of Eileen Power at Girton', Girton College archives.
[92] *Ibid.*
[93] Hodgkins, *Two Lives*, p. 38.
[94] Power to MLG, 22 September 1916.
[95] Russell, *The Tamarisk Tree*, pp. 35–6.

the anatomy theatre during the day when the armistice was announced a 'wild stampeding broke out'. She went back to Girton with some other students later in the evening, but they found themselves locked out and the men rushing around the bonfire they had built in the courtyard. After Miss Jex-Blake's dance, the students thanked her, and she replied: 'In Cambridge, I understand, I am considered a sport.'[96]

Dances at Girton were one thing, but integration into the Cambridge academic community was still some way off for women. Eileen was clearly unhappy with the new 'double standards' of post-war university life. When she was asked to write a women's column for *The Old Cambridge*, she used the space to denounce the idea.

Let the women of Cambridge speak out in 'The Old Cambridge,' but let it be side by side with the men under any of the headings which interest them, and not snugly tucked into their own column, cheek by jowl with the fashions ... Editors and reviewers are all the same: they think they know a woman's work when they see it ... But they have no real criterion, because there is no real difference. The difference is between good books and bad books, straight-thinking books and sentimental books, not between male books and female books.[97]

If Cambridge had not yet moved on sufficiently enough even after the war to accept an academic woman such as Eileen Power, her own life and those of her friends had. Eileen continued work on *Medieval Nunneries*, and spent part of the winter and summer of 1917 and 1918 in Coggeshall living in the Paycocke House while she worked on papers there for her *Paycockes of Coggeshall* (1920).[98] She supported Margery over these years in her pregnancies, the death of a child, and the death of her husband Edward at the Somme. She watched her friends Ruth Fox Dalton, Mary Brinton Stocks and Karin Costelloe Stephen marry,[99] but had herself formed no serious liaisons. The great event of her life was to come with an interview in 1920 for the Kahn Travelling Fellowship.

---

[96]   Baron, 'Girton in the First World War', 11.
[97]   Eileen Power, 'Women of Cambridge', *The Old Cambridge*, 14 February 1920, 11.
[98]   Power to MLG, 26 February 1917, 25 September 1918.
[99]   Power to MLG, 24 September 1914, n.d. August 1912.

CHAPTER 4

Travelling east

In April 1920 Eileen Power went for an interview with Sir Cooper Perry, principal of the University of London. This was for the Kahn Travelling Fellowship, a prized fellowship providing funding for a year's travel around the world. It had been held in 1912 by Goldsworthy Lowes Dickinson, who used it to travel with E. M. Forster.[1] It had never before been held by a woman. Eileen wrote immediately after her interview to G. G. Coulton to thank him for his testimonial, and reported that there were two other women being interviewed for it.

But I rather doubt their giving it to a woman. Sir Cooper Perry obviously did not take women's work very seriously (or perhaps it was me he didn't take seriously!) One of his obiter dicta was 'I have often been amused at women historians; so many of the springs of human action must be hidden from them.' He also suggested that I might defeat the objects of the trust (sic) by subsequently committing matrimony, so I suppose he keeps his wife in purdah: anyhow these silly remarks would not be made to male candidates. However he obviously can't help being made like that, so I possessed my soul in patience and without argument.[2]

Perry, who was vice-chancellor of London University from 1917 to 1919, and principal between 1920 and 1926, was a man of whom it was said: 'He published practically nothing; his life's work is embodied in minutes, memoranda and charters.'[3] Much to her surprise, however, Power was successful, and set off on her journey in the autumn of that year.

[1] E. M. Forster, *Goldsworthy Lowes Dickinson* (London, 1934). Dickinson (1862–1932) was a fellow of King's College, Cambridge and a Cambridge Apostle. He wrote *A Greek View of Life* (1896), *Letters from John Chinaman and Other Essays* (London, 1901) and *International Anarchy* (1926).
[2] Power to Coulton, 27 April 1920, Power Papers, Girton College archives.
[3] Negley B. Harte and J. North, *The World of University College London, 1828–1978* (London, 1978), p. 198.

4.1   Eileen Power in the year of the Albert Kahn Travelling Fellowship, 1920–1

This world journey came at a crucial stage in Eileen Power's development as a historian. Apart from her year in Paris after her undergraduate work at Girton she had scarcely been abroad. Now she was to travel through India, Malaysia, China, Japan and North America. Her early research had followed in the paths set out by others, though she developed her own focus on medieval women. Her travels through a range of very different underdeveloped countries were now to shape her historical writing in altogether new directions.

Just before she left Eileen finished *Medieval English Nunneries*, all but the appendix and the revision of three chapters. She wrote to Coulton from Rome with all the unfinished business over the book: the chapters to be sent to Margaret Clapham, who would send the whole manuscript to the press, the illustrations to be chosen by him, and worries over her index.[4] The index was written by another of Coulton's students, H. S. Bennett. But at last the book was done, after over eight years work garnered in the intervals of teaching.

Eileen Power owed a lot during the final stages of the book to Margaret Clapham, the wife of John Clapham, a fellow of King's College, Cambridge and the major economic historian in Cambridge from 1908 to 1938. Clapham was elected to the newly created chair of economic history in 1923. Eileen Power became a good friend of the Clapham family during the years she taught at Girton, and she stayed with them frequently later when she visited Cambridge. Margaret Clapham, like the wives of several other distinguished historians, helped her husband with research, editorial work, and writing his indexes.[5] She also provided extensive help to Eileen Power at this point, collecting all the final parts of the book together for her publisher, Cambridge University Press, and effectively seeing it through the press while Eileen Power was travelling.

Eileen set off for Paris on 15 September 1920. She spent a few days trying to rekindle memories of her year there ten years before, and again spent time shopping, this time for a hat to wear to Indian garden parties.[6] In Rome a few days later she watched a procession of soldiers, civilians and red shirts celebrate the anniversary of 1870, 'a most moving sight, in spite of my sound pacifist principles and my detestation of nationalism'.[7] She continued her search for hats in Rome, and started on the social rounds that would characterise much of the rest of her journey. Though she complained to Coulton that nearly all the people to whom she had introductions were away,[8] she still managed lunch, tea and dinner with several English expatriates. One of these was Oscar Browning,[9] 'the great old boy of Eton and Kings, hero of a hundred stories'. He had lived in Rome

4   Power to Coulton, 23 September 1920, Girton College archives.
5   J. H. Clapham, *An Economic History of Modern Britain*, vol. 1, *The Early Railway Age 1820–1850* (Cambridge, 1926), p. x.
6   Travel diary (hereafter TD), vol. 1, 15–18 September 1920, Power–Postan Papers.
7   TD, vol. 1, 20 September 1920.
8   Power to Coulton, 23 September 1920, Power Papers.
9   Oscar Browning (1837–1923) was a former assistant master at Eton, then a college lecturer and university lecturer in history at King's College, Cambridge. He had lived in Rome since 1908. He was a famous Cambridge character and, with Dickinson, responsible for setting the social atmosphere at King's, and cultivating the close relationship between dons and undergraduates. This included the homoerotic values, clever intellectualism and eccentricity associated with the college during the decade before the First World War and the interwar years. See Skidelsky, *Keynes*, pp. 107–11.

since 1908. He was the 'most supreme egotist' she had ever met, but he still impressed her with his thousand words a day of a *History of the World*, at the age of eighty-three. When she asked him what he thought of H. G. Wells' *An Outline of History*,[10] he denounced the treatment of Napoleon, whom he considered 'the greatest man who has ever lived except Julius Caesar, and the best, except Jesus Christ'.[11]

As a historian Browning was known for his views that the study of history was to prepare citizens, not to aspire to any research ideal. As a training in citizenship, it should be organised around subjects that could contribute to politics, and he was the main supporter for compulsory courses in politics in the Cambridge history tripos. During his later years in Cambridge he had become a ridiculous, obese figure, 'his scholarship always superficial, became flatulent ... his snobbery ... a by-word'.[12]

I

By 5 October Eileen Power was in Alexandria, the beginning of her mythical 'Orient'. Like so many others who made these journeys, she carried with her all the baggage of orientalist preconceptions and ideas of 'otherness' that affected what she saw and her responses. For her the 'Orient' was 'medieval' in Egypt, in India, in Burma and China. And her own medievalism became in turn 'orientalism', for the images of medieval society she was subsequently to summon up in her writing took on the outlines, often mixed indiscriminately, of the bazaars of Cairo, the villages of Mandalay, the caravans of Peshawar and the monasteries of T'an Cho Ssu and Chieh T'ai Ssu. Power's perceptions bound together Europe's medieval past with the 'closed system' of an unchanging 'Orient'; they fitted easily into the set of European ideas that Edward Said later defined as 'orientalism'.

In Alexandria, Eileen Power first encountered the medieval societies she had for so long imaginatively reconstructed. She went round a bazaar, 'exactly like a medieval town, open workshops in

---

[10] H. G. Wells, *An Outline of History* (London, 1920).
[11] TD, vol. 1, 27 September 1920. Browning's thousand words a day on his history of the world had occupied him at least since early 1918. See Skidelsky, *Keynes*, p. 110.
[12] Clark, 'A hundred years of the teaching of history at Cambridge', 543; Jann, 'From amateur to professional', 140.

narrow little streets, arranged by trades; and men sitting there welding fine gold chains, weaving by hand the coloured edges to common twill scarves from Manchester, dying cloths in small dye tubs ... and everywhere women in black'.[13] Many times again, in India, Malaysia and China she was to experience the same 'flashbacks' to medieval scenarios. The re-enactment of such scenes before her eyes, as part of the everyday life of contemporary underdeveloped countries, gave her the insight to write later in such graphic detail on the economic and cultural characteristics of medieval societies. The contrasts and similarities between the countries she visited also stimulated a new interest in comparative history.

Later in the month Eileen joined her ship the *SS Orontes* at Port Said, and spent the next four weeks at sea on the way to Ceylon. She soon impressed herself on the ship's company, and was placed at the captain's table, where she met Sir Matthew Nathan on his way to the governorship of Queensland. He was a former career soldier who had administered the colonies of Sierra Leone, the Gold Coast, Hong Kong and Natal, and had been a civil servant since 1909. During the war he was under secretary for Ireland, and had been in charge at Dublin Castle when the Easter Rebellion broke out in 1916. He had been relieved of his duties there, and spent the next three years in England as secretary at the Ministry of Pensions. In 1920 he was appointed to the governorship of Queensland, where he stayed for the next five years.[14]

Eileen Power and Sir Matthew became lifelong friends from this time; she was later to make him one of that inner circle of close male friends of herself and her sisters, 'the Honorary Powers'. She also became a close observer of shipboard personalities and relationships, with a special interest in the ship's pursar and the doctor. They were suffering what she saw as the same discontent and ennui as medieval monks.[15] For them, she was an attractive woman travelling alone, a good dancing partner and, despite being a don, diverting company for the next month on board ship.

By the beginning of December, Eileen was in South India contemplating her Western rationalist perceptions of Hindu temples and deities. She found the temple at Madura oppressive and horrible: 'Everywhere was dirt and ornament ... Here the gods are

[13] TD, vol. 1, 5 October 1920.
[14] 'Nathan, Sir Matthew (1862–1939)', *Twentieth Century DNB*.
[15] TD, vol. 1, 28 October–9 November 1920.

monstrous and outlandish and yet never, and that is the horrible part
of it, inhuman ... they seem to represent the principle of life ... life
without the animating force of reason, order, restraint, rejoicing in
the crass fact of its teeming fertility.'[16] In India she found an
unbridgeable gulf between Europe and the perceived mystery and
irrationality of the East.

Going to India, however, was going to a territory of the East
under Britain's direct colonial dominion. The meeting point between
European superiority and a subject race was directed by the whole
apparatus of colonial officialdom and missionary societies through
which any European first coming to India would pass. Eileen Power
came to India with introductions to take her to the heart of British
India, and there she gathered more introductions to take her into
Indian political debate and into some contact with Indian society. At
every point in her journey her colonial hosts provided her with a
filter of assumptions and political attitudes that she was ill equipped
to tackle and confront. As a newcomer to India who would pass
through the country in a matter of months, she was given the respect
due a well-educated woman, but was also treated as one who needed
to be initiated into the ways of thinking about colonial India. Her
own curiosity and the ill-defined left–liberal inclination in favour of
independence she brought with her were soon reshaped in a context
now expressed as 'political realities'.

Eileen Power spent her first week in India at the Women's
Christian College in Madras. While there she was taken by the
bishop to visit a Brahmin and his family; the absurdity of this
'cultural contact' did not seem to have occurred to her. But she was
struck by the extent to which the Brahmin's way of life showed the
effect of the encounter between Western colonialism and indigenous
culture. There was a world of contrast between his legal profession,
his Western style of education and his European dress on the one
hand, and his private life of Hindu devotions and culture on the
other.

Eileen stayed during her time in Bombay with Sir Stanley and
Lady Reed, and tried to immerse herself in Indian politics, especially
the debates over recent events at Amritsar and the non-co-operation
movement. Reed was a widely respected journalist and the editor of
the *Times of India* from 1907 to 1923. She was taken to Government

---

[16]   TD, vol. 1, 1–2 December 1920.

House and introduced to Sir George Lloyd, governor of the Bombay presidency, but she chafed against the constraints of her sex in gaining access to Indian labour leaders and other political reformers. 'The fact is that being a woman, looking rather nicely dressed & quite incapable of clever conversation (how I wish I were Beryl), I do not seem the sort of person who would be worth politicians wasting time over.' Instead she was taken to a purdah party, to visit crèches, and to a seminar given by Patrick Geddes, the Scottish biologist, sociologist and town planner.[17] Geddes was then professor of civics and sociology at the University of Bombay, and after his seminar in this subject, she listened to his long monologue over lunch which rambled in vague generalisations from one topic to the next. But what really irritated her was his latest obsession with his theory of the evolution of sex, and the generalisations he drew from this on the respective contributions of men and women to civilisation.

While in Bombay, however, Eileen Power did manage to arrange an entry pass to the National Congress at Nagpur, and a half-hour's discussion with Sir George Lloyd. During the latter, she

enjoyed the novel experience of hearing problems of government discussed in terms of 'I'. To someone only just emerged from the groves of Academe, where nationalism and democracy are words employed in the study of political science, and where the British Empire is a subject variously of the historical textbook or the debating society, it is exceedingly entertaining to sit upon a sofa in a place called Government House & to hear a short man with an emphatic manner saying 'I had to dethrone one of our native princes for torture today ... ', or 'Gandhi has stood here and begged me to put him in prison & I said "I very likely shall, Mr. Gandhi, but at my own time, not yours."'[18]

Lloyd was a Conservative, and a firm believer in Britain's imperial destiny. He achieved a reputation in India for controlling the agitation for self-government. He guided the inauguration of the Montagu–Chelmsford constitution, and in his own time did imprison Gandhi.

Eileen Power had arrived in India at a momentous time. The process of reform had started with a new constitution set to bring co-operation between the Indians and the British. The Montagu–Chelmsford reforms of 1919 had passed some legislative powers over to enlarged provincial and central legislative councils. But military

[17] TD, vol. I, 15–18 December 1920.
[18] TD, vol. I, 24 December 1920.

and foreign affairs, income tax, currency, communications and criminal law remained the preserve of the government of India exercised through the viceroy and the colonial governors.[19] Along with the reforms came new political elements. Gandhi had just made his breakthrough into all-India politics, and was emerging as a major political leader with few challengers. The Amritsar Massacre was less than a year old. During a period of martial law in the Punjab city of Amritsar in 1919, the British General Dyer had ordered his troops to fire on the crowd. They killed 379 people, and injured 1,000 others. The official investigation in London had recently condemned the action, but failed to punish General Dyer. The 'Dyer episode' was a major topic of debate at most of the social gatherings she attended. Non-co-operation was the other great issue. Gandhi had taken over as president of the All-India Home Rule League from Annie Besant[20] in April 1920. He succeeded at the Calcutta Congress in August 1920 and later at the Nagpur Congress in December in gaining Congress support for his programme of non-co-operation. The policy lasted from August 1920 to February 1922.

Eileen Power may have appeared at first a typical European female traveller to the raj, young and attractive, dressed in loose-fitting white muslin dresses, her long dark hair coiled under broad-brimmed straw hats. But unlike most of these young women, she was not content with socialising and tourism. She had her own career and independence, and saw this as her entrée to the centre of political debate. She also saw it as her job, as holder of the Kahn Fellowship, to witness and report on the politics of the countries she visited, and she sent back a number of pieces of political journalism to weeklies in Britain. She therefore used her contacts among the British in India to make other contacts in the colonial administration, and both to gain access to the events she wanted to attend and the politicians she wanted to meet. Being a woman made this easier, if anything. She cultivated her easy sociability with the women, and

---

[19]   The manner in which these reforms were actually introduced and skewed in such a way as to prevent urban centres and educated Indians from gaining too much legislative power are discussed in Clive Dewey, *Anglo-Indian Attitudes. The Mind of the Indian Civil Service* (London, 1993), pp. 58–60, 217–18.

[20]   Annie Besant (1847–1933) was an English theosophist, journalist and politician. Theosophy gained popularity in India, and Besant went out there as a religious leader. She soon became involved in politics, and became leader of the All-India League, with the aim of reuniting and revitalising Congress. She also ran the widely circulated newspaper *New India*. See J. M. Brown, *Modern India: The Origins of an Asian Democracy* (Oxford, 1985), pp. 191–5.

her attractiveness and intelligence for the men. Thus she got what she wanted.

She pursued all the contacts she had, especially among the 'memsahibs', to discover the means to get a pass to the Nagpur Congress. She was eventually introduced to an inspector of schools who arranged a pass for her. Eileen went on to Nagpur at the end of December, but missed the opening address to Congress. She was one of six European spectators at the Congress, and watched the debates as the policy of the Indian National Congress was changed. She wrote about her reactions to the theory and practice of non-co-operation just before the Nagpur Congress:

This is a thrilling moment in which to be in India & I wish extremely that I could stay longer, or could succeed in seeing more of Indian life & opinions ... when I ask but – *how* could India attain complete swaraj, (could she bear it if she did), are not the new reforms the next step, is not the programme of non-cooperation based on an extraordinary lack of political *realism.*[21]

In Delhi in mid-January 1921, and again in early and mid-February, she stayed with Sir William Vincent, the Home Member of Council in the government of India. Her entry was an introduction from his daughter, a friend in England. From him, as from Lloyd and Reed, she got the government point of view, and was candid enought to admit, as against her left-wing preferences, 'that I left India with a great deal more sympathy for the Government than I had when I entered it'. Her perspectives on Indian politics were heavily influenced by Vincent; he took her seriously, discussing Indian politics with her over the course of several evenings. She in turn regarded him as the voice of the government of India, 'a man who is engaged in the actual work of government', and a person 'of integrity and justice'.[22]

During her early weeks in India her sympathies with the non-co-operation party stopped short at the many instances of violent intimidation behind the boycotts and strikes. She thought Gandhi's doctrines, for 'all his talk of the Vedas & of returning to primeval India', were 'pure western anarchism'. 'He has not a single doctrine which he did not learn from Tolstoy, Thoreau or Edward Carpenter.' She recognised that his sway over the masses lay in his appeal as the Mahatma, but she could not really understand this.[23]

[21] TD, vol. I, 21 December 1920.
[22] TD, vol. II, Delhi, 13–19 January 1921.
[23] TD, vol. II, 30 January–3 February 1921.

Her views grew more in tune, as her time in India went on, with those of her colonial hosts, and she virtually abandoned her belief in self-government, opting instead for what she saw as the gradual route under British guidance. She preferred the Moderate Party, and was impressed at Nagpur by their 'desire ... to let bygones be bygones & work for the future'. She thought the only practical route to self-government lay in an alliance between the government and the moderate party in a new assembly and councils.[24] But she also recognised that the Amritsar Massacre, and its aftermath, especially English responses to it, had destroyed any chances of reconciliation.[25]

Later, some time after the congress and in reaction to the violence that accompanied non-co-operation, she grew much more critical of the movement. 'Even the methods by which non-cooperation is spread among the Indians themselves are often conspicuously lacking in non-hatred & self restraint.'[26] She took on the Anglo-Indian dislike of the Khilafat movement among the Muslims, and denounced the alliance between the two movements: 'stranger partners for the saintly Mr. Gandhi it is impossible to imagine'. Eileen Power's support for the Moderate Party at this stage placed her completely in line with colonial opinion. The British, by the time of the Nagpur Congress, had been virtually forced to hope for the resurgence of the Moderate alliance as against the 'Extremists'. Though both alliances were home-rulers, the Moderates at least maintained a policy of co-operation with the raj, and through them the government vainly hoped to save the Montagu–Chelmsford reforms.[27]

Eileen Power had made great progress in gaining access to political circles since her time in Bombay, and was very happy with a series of intense political discussions during her week in Delhi: 'Somehow I seem to have been a success here. People seem to like me! Sir William laughed & says the whole Government of India seems to be taken up with assisting me!'[28]

She went on to Lahore, where she met Lal Rajpat Rai and other

[24] Power to Coulton, 20 March 1921, Girton College archives; Eileen Power, unpublished essay, 'Mahatma Gandhi's boycott: another view' (6 July 1921), Power–Postan Papers.
[25] TD, vol. II, 13–19 January 1921.
[26] Power, 'Mahatma Gandhi's Boycott'.
[27] Judith M. Brown, *Gandhi's Rise to Power. Indian Politics 1915–1922* (Cambridge, 1992), pp. 130–5, 288–90.
[28] TD, vol. II, 13–19 January 1921.

leaders of the non-co-operation movement, and 'had a terrific argument' over the prospects of immediate self-government for India as against the moderate route through the councils. By now she was fairly confident in what she regarded as the moderate course; her views had been filtered through the viewpoint of the colonial administration, and she had acquired the ammunition to debate the road to self-government. She took on a voice of authority as an educationist herself, and condemned the policy of the student movement, sending students out to spread propaganda in the villages, with their studies confined to learning Hindustani and spinning so as to promote Gandhi's crusade against western civilisation. She conveyed the government line, and argued over the prospects of a Bolshevik advance on the North-West Frontier with Afghanistan if it were not defended by the English.[29] From Lahore she went on to Gwalior, and further debate on Gandhi with the maharajah's political secretary.[30]

Back in Delhi in early February, Eileen met Annie Besant, the former English radical who had helped to lead the matchgirls' strike in 1886, and had been a member of the Fabian Society and the Social Democratic Federation. She had lived in India since 1893 as a theosophist, and was famous for the important part she had played in the home rule campaign. She was president of the Indian National Congress in 1918. The riots of April 1919 following the Amritsar Massacre had shocked her into calling for support for the colonial government in restoring order. She had thereafter lost the support of her nationalist followers; her home rule initiatives had been overtaken by non-co-operation, and by now she was regarded by some as a 'tiresome old lady'.[31] Eileen described Besant as 'an amazing old woman ... dressed in a beautiful white gold saree ... she was rather bitter about the Ali brothers, & amusing, too, about Mahomet Ali, whom she described as arguing with her in favour of violence, asserting "God kills – why should not I?".'[32]

In Delhi Eileen heard the debates on the Repressive Legislation, the Rowlatt Bills and the Punjab.[33] She had a brief meeting with Gandhi, 'who sat on the floor looking very frail and ascetic, while I

[29] TD, vol. ii, 26–8 January 1921.
[30] TD, vol. ii, 30 January–3 February 1921.
[31] 'Besant, Annie (1847–1933)', *Twentieth Century DNB*; Brown, *Modern India*, p. 215.
[32] TD, vol. ii, 3–5 February 1921.
[33] These Bills were a continuation of the 1916 wartime emergency powers on detention and freedom of speech. They were not repealed after the Montagu–Chelmsford reforms.

sat on a string bed'. Gandhi was surrounded by Motilal Nehru, the Ali brothers and Rajpat Rai, 'who kept butting in, so that I did not hear as much of Mr. G. himself as I wished'. Of Gandhi she said his 'manner is the perfection of quiet & gentle courtesy. He is an attractive creature. I left them almost in tears, for they are clearly intransigent & there can be no common ground with them.'[34]

She spent several days attending the debates. Her sympathies lay with the Moderates, who showed a spirit of co-operation with the English. 'This debate will have little reverberation outside the house, but as an indication of the temper of the moderate party it seems to me highly significant. There is a real desire to co-operate with the English, & to concentrate not on vengeance for the past, but on a creative policy for the future.'[35]

Power was pleased by the extent to which she had crossed the gender divide in Indian politics. She was not treated like the typical memsahib, and in her short time in India had been able to debate with leading members of the colonial administration and India's nationalist leaders. Whether she was prepared to admit it or not, however, it was colonial officials who had given her these opportunities. She, in turn, had great difficulty understanding the position of most of the other women she came across in India. She wrote about the memsahib who has 'no interest except in household, tennis, club – no work and no ideas'. Such women were faced when they had children with the cruel choice between staying with their husbands in India and sending their children back to boarding school and relatives, or of returning to England themselves with their children when they reached school age. But they also lacked the more serious occupations, especially in voluntary and social work, which the average middle-class woman took up in England. There were few unmarried women or women who earned their living in this class in India, and the wives appeared to her to be 'of the type which makes a good sofa cushion for a tired man in the evening, rather than an interested and equal companion'.[36] She put the racial antagonism between the English and the Indians down largely to the English wives who would not socialise with the Indians. She thought there had been much greater understanding between Indian and Englishman in the eighteenth and early nineteenth centuries, when

[34] TD, vol. II, Delhi, 12–26 February 1921.
[35] TD, vol. II, Delhi, 15 February 1921.
[36] TD, vol. II, 5–12 February 1921.

women did not go out to India.[37] Eileen's attitudes to the women of British India were similar to those of other educated women with progressive views who met for the first time the lack of purpose and cultural apartheid such women appeared to cultivate in India. There was more than a hint of social and intellectual snobbery in this tendency to compartmentalise women from a wide variety of class and educational backgrounds forced by circumstance to live together in a relatively small colonial expatriate community.[38]

The rest of Eileen's time in India was spent experiencing the 'East', on a number of short trips to Bhopal, Peshawar, Agra and Bihar. These were areas outside the 'Western' debate on politics and modern nationhood. They were, for her, the ancient India, properly oriental, at one with her imaginative picture of medieval Europe, yet in an important sense unknowable. All she said about them was a part of 'Europe's collective day-dream of the Orient'.[39]

In Bhopal at the end of December 1920, she found the 'otherness' of the East, an otherness she felt was the way it ought to be, uncomplicated by either westernisation or modernisation. Bhopal was a native state, which she described as 'a homogeneous society, eastern and self sufficient', where 'western improvements have somehow taken on an Eastern guise'. It was a relief from the congress she had been attending in Nagpur, 'westernised Indians discontented with westernization ... I crawled along in my carriage through the narrow streets, with open shops on each side, trade by trade, the owners sitting cross-legged within, for all the world like the middle ages.'[40]

In late January 1921 she found a similar historical empathy on a tour of Rajputana and through the Punjab to Peshawar. In Peshawar she met quantities of English soldiers and government officials, and encountered an entirely different political debate over the frontier and the Khilafat question. But it was India's 'medieval' echoes that struck her once again; 'timelessness and otherness' were more comprehensible to her than the political and social turmoil of India's encounter with modernisation and self-government. She was fascinated by the frontier tribesmen, describing them as like 'one's own

[37] TD, vol. II, 5–12 February 1921.
[38] For a revealing picture of these attitudes of social superiority among educated women of liberal–left circles see Dewey's portrait of Josie Darling in *Anglo-Indian Attitudes*, pp. 148–59.
[39] Edward Said, *Orientalism: Western Conceptions of the Orient* (1978; Harmondsworth, 1991), p. 52.
[40] TD, vol. I, 31 December 1920.

medieval ancestors'. The road to the Khyber had caravans coming in

from Afghanistan and beyond: interminable lines of shaggy camels ... roped to each other & laden with great bales of carpets and skins, tiny little donkeys ambling along under loads which almost hide them; & there were wild men, riding here & there, but mostly walking by their beasts with the long slouching stride, which has carried them day after day out of the rocky hills & valleys of Afghanistan & beyond, thro' the Khyber & into the crowded streeets of Peshawar, where central Asia & India meet.[41]

Eileen looked forward to going over the Khyber Pass, only to discover it was closed to women. Undaunted she went anyway, disguised as a man. On returning she described the end of the pass: 'There spread out the vale of Peshawar, ringed by blue hills behind, the same sight which burst upon Alexander's soldiers, upon the Han, upon the Pathan, upon the Moghul, upon all the conquerors from the North who have poured into India ... I have never – I think – been in a place where I felt so strongly the continuity of history.'[42] The word went out among the guides, however, that a woman had crossed the pass, and Eileen returned to a reprimand by British officials.

From Agra in mid-February Eileen visited the Red Fort and Fatehpur Sikri, and wrote at length of the impressions of a beautiful but dead city which had lived a mere twenty years:

The great king prayed in the mosque, communed with his ministers in the council chamber, visited his wives in their carved houses, shot the antelope from the Hirian Minor. For less than twenty years money was coined in the mint, merchants in their booths under striped awnings set out tables of silken broideries & shot gold scarves from Benares, ivories from Delhi, inlaid knives from Rajpatana, carpets from Bagdad & Bokhara, jewels from Ceylon and myriad coloured needlework upon stiff brocade from the distant East ... For less than twenty years this crowded, splendid life moved in & out of the palaces & streets of Fatehpur Sikri, city with the strength of stone & the colour of a rose.[43]

Here in a dead city she found the mystery of India and the imaginative reconstruction of lost worlds.

In the Bihar a week later, she immersed herself in culture; she listened to Indian music, watched performances of nautch dance,

[41] TD, vol. II, 21–5 January 1921.
[42] TD, vol. II, 21–5 January 1921.
[43] TD, vol II, 5–12 February 1921; also Eileen Power, 'Fatehpur Sikri', unpublished essay, Power–Postan Papers.

and heard a recitation of an epic about an ancient feud, performed in much the same manner as Beowulf, the Odyssey and the Mahabharata would have been. 'I felt, as I have so often felt in India, as though I had for a moment outwitted time, stolen back through forbidden gates and caught a glimpse of the far, far distant morning of the world.'[44] Her perception of this cultural experience was of a kind of eastern medievalism.

In mid-March Eileen moved on to Burma. In Mandalay she wrote several letters home, and the sections of her Kahn report setting out the parallels she saw between medieval Europe and India. In the Kahn report she wrote: 'It was not until I spent nearly two months in India that there suddenly flashed upon me one day the solution of the mystery; I *had* "been there before"; I [was] familiar with this way of life and these ideals of civilisation; for I had spent the greater part of the last twelve years in studying the European Middle Ages – and India was the Middle Ages.' She wrote in her diary: 'Today I have seen Doomsday Book in the making. It called itself the Settlement Officer's Enquiry for the new assessment of land revenue – but it was clearly Doomsday Book for all that.'[45] The settlement officer was her Norman; the village elders being interrogated, her Saxons.

And the questions – how familiar they were. What is the name of the village? How many families are there? How is the land divided up? how much is good land and how much poor? how many horses, how many oxen? what was it assessed at in the time of King Edward? what is it worth now? After five minutes of this I said to the Norman, who translated the uncouth Saxon tongue to me: 'If you like I can make the questions and returns of this *Inquisitio* in the best abbreviated Latin of the eleventh century for you.'[46]

Eileen Power saw in India the whole mentality of Western Europe in the Middle Ages, the basic ideas upon which medieval civilisation were built. Between India and modern Europe were dichotomies of static and progressive civilisations; of religious as opposed to secular and scientific civilisations; and the seclusion and subjection of women in India as opposed to the increasing freedom and growing part in public life played by women in the West. These dichotomies were just like those that existed between medieval and modern

44 TD, vol. II, 17–20 February 1921.
45 TD, vol. II, 12 March 1921.
46 Eileen Power, *Report to the Trustees September 1920–September 1921, Alfred Kahn Travelling Fellowship* (London, 1921), p. 16.

Europe.[47] But as Said has suggested, in this system of 'synchronic essentialism' which prevailed in European ways of thinking about the East, Europe had a history, a narrative, whereas the Orient was synonymous with stability and unchanging eternality.[48] Indian and Burmese villages, caravans, bazaars and cultural festivals provided the standard by which Power depicted and analysed Europe's medieval institutions, rather than – as she thought at the time – her knowledge of medieval history allowing her better insight into these cultural artefacts of the Orient.

These ideas of India's medievalism blended with Eileen's political perspectives on India. Her engagement with Indian politics was, to be sure, brief and superficial. Four months was no great time to grasp the complexities of provincial and national, Muslim and Hindu, nationalist and government politics. But through contacts and perseverance she did gain far greater access than many such visitors to key political figures and major assemblies. The 'otherness' of India's culture did not penetrate her assumptions about politics; her judgements were made from secular rather than spiritual values. India's present, in her view, was like Western Europe's past, but complicated now by the impact of current westernisation. She therefore took the liberal view of the nationalist movements, preferring moderate reform incorporating Western institutions and a continued British presence. This was the world of E. M. Forster's *A Passage to India*: she hoped that the moment of closeness between Asia and the West that might exist in the moderate movement would bridge the great distance she also perceived between the West and the 'foreignness' or estrangement of so much of India.[49]

Eileen Power's time in Burma was overshadowed by political antagonism between the Burmese and the British. She was to miss out entirely on political debate and cultural contact with the Burmese. She was staying with British officials whom she found reactionary and unsympathetic to the self-government movement in Burma. The Burmese had passed a law banning Europeans wearing shoes in the pagodas, and the British had reacted by boycotting the pagodas. The result was that Eileen met no Burmese while in

---

[47]   *Ibid.*, p. 20. Also see Eileen Power, 'The place of women in modern society', lecture to the
        Indian Students' Hostel, 27 April 1924, Postan Papers.
[48]   Said, *Orientalism*, p. 240.
[49]   *Ibid.*, p. 244.

Burma, and did not get into any of the pagodas because she could not offend her hosts.[50]

She did not stay long, and had moved on to Java by early April. There she visited Batavia, was entertained at the court of the sultan of Jogjakarta by the srimpi dancers in their dance 'which gave me so strong an impression that it was the climax of a great & old civilisation ... it has in it the whole of a civilisation; the body is in it the vehicle of the mind & of a mind, which for centuries has brooded upon mysteries & been possessed by thought.'[51] Eileen travelled on by way of Singapore, and reached Hong Kong in May.

II

Eileen Power spent the next two months in China. Of all the countries she visited it was China that was to have the greatest impact upon her ideas, her sensibilities and subsequently her personal life. China was a rather different 'Orient' from India. First, while the Chinese treaty ports were regarded by the British as an extension of the empire, the only British colonies in China were Weihaiwei and Hong Kong. The largest British settlement was in Shanghai, and for most European settlers in China, this was a socially more open Orient than was the institutionalised and hierarchically stuffy empire of India. Most of the British settlers there were missionaries or businessmen; few had been attracted to China for its culture and civilisation. The missionaries went to change the culture; the businessmen for the profit of their firms and for the easy living. The values among the British there were isolation from the Chinese and insularity among the small British communities spread over China.[52]

Eileen Power's entry into China as a traveller was much the same as that of an English expatriate going out there for a longer period of time. She travelled first on her own from Singapore to Hong Kong, stayed there for one night, then travelled on to Canton, where she was met by a British businessman who was a friend of a friend. He

---

[50] Power to Coulton, 20 March 1921, Power Papers; TD, vol. II, 16–21 March 1921.

[51] TD, vol. II, 3, 25 April 1921.

[52] See Robert Bickers, 'Changing British attitudes to China and the Chinese, 1928–1931' (University of London Ph.D. thesis, 1992), chap. 3, pp. 77–122.

told her about China and Canton, in much the same manner as others had told him.[53]

Whatever he told her, it did not inhibit her, for she was immediately overwhelmed by what she saw in China. She abandoned her diary for a time, and took instead to writing several imaginative pieces and poetry. She did not record any impressions of Peking, despite spending most of her time in China there. Canton she described in detail. It was a scene 'which is as old as Marco Polo & older yet: these narrow streets, these sweating crowds, these oval eyed junks & these flower boats'. But she also found 'much that is modern in Canton' – it had become a centre of political resistance to the Peking government and to British interests, and a focal point of international power politics. 'Canton, you see is the centre of a very modern situation. There is a maelstrom of modern politics, whirling beneath its medieval surface. Gigantic western rivalries are creating more & more problems in the East.'[54] Her time in Peking and Canton was filled out with visits to Hong Kong and Shanghai, and a trip up the Yangtse to Hankow.

The China that most profoundly affected her was to be found during Eileen's trip to the Western Hills. During the latter part of June she went on a walking tour with British friends among the temples in the Western Hills. This was to be her true entry into the blending of medievalism with the romanticised orientalism already deeply embedded in her cultural heritage. She wrote 'The Way to Miao Feng Shan' on 21 June:

Someone brings you out a cup of tea, clear amber-coloured chinese tea in a blue grey handle-less cup; a dim gong sounds from the hidden temple above & a sudden puff of wind, the last breath of the expiring day, rustles the roseleaves on their mats. The dimming shadows, the scents & the faint sounds are like the dreams which escape still fragrant from the ivory gate. Rise, traveller, throw off this delicious madness of the spirit; your goal is no valley of roses, but the high rock, the temple & the keen upper air. The last lovely home of the senses lies in this village. There is another vision in the height above, – clear self-possession strange to rosy valleys, intellectual ardours here unknown.[55]

At T'an Cho Ssu she identified medieval parallels with the largest and richest monastery of the neighbourhood. 'I always look at

[53]   TD, vol. III, 10–12 May 1921.
[54]   TD, vol. III, Canton, 10–12 May 1921.
[55]   Eileen Power, 'The Way to Miao Feng Shan', TD, vol. III, 21 June 1921.

monasteries with an eye trained in the English middle ages and T'an Cho Ssu struck me as having much the same atmosphere as a lax & worldly house towards the close of the 15th Century. I hear that the abbot is an opium fiend, which is another illustration of the almost invariable rule in the middle ages that a bad abbot meant a bad house.' She found the monks there cadging for tips and gambling. The next monastery, at Chieh T'ai Ssu, was a great contrast with the worldliness of T'an Cho Ssu: 'It might have stood for the good monastery of medieval documents & true to analogy, it had a saintly abbot.'[56]

While she was at this monastery she wrote of 'Mr. Johnston's place'. Sir Reginald Johnston was then the tutor to the young Manchu emperor, Pu Yi, and he had built a house and temple in the Western Hills.[57] Reginald Johnston was everything that most of the British expatriates in China were not. He had a good command of Chinese and a deep appreciation of Chinese literature and culture. He had travelled widely in China, and was an authority on Chinese folklore, chronicles and religion. To the other expatriates he was an example of the eccentricity of 'going native'. He was suspected of being a Buddhist, but was actually a Confucianist. His house in the Western Hills became a stopping-off place for a select number of writers, academics and sinologists visiting China; he played both the recluse and the poseur. Johnston may have been dropped from the expatriate community for 'going over to the Chinese', but he did not much care what others in that community at least thought of him.[58] He clearly fascinated Eileen Power – he had the knowledge of an ancient China which she yearned for, and he in turn responded to a beautiful and intellectual woman with common literary interests with

[56]   TD, vol. III, 19, 20 June 1921.
[57]   Reginald Fleming Johnston (1874–1938) was born in Scotland and educated in Oxford, where he studied history. He went into the Hong Kong Civil Service in 1898, and had postings in the government of Weihaiwei at various times between 1904 and 1930. He was known as a scholar and a traveller, and an authority on the interior of China. He was tutor to the boy emperor of China between 1919 and 1925, during the time when Power visited. While he was in China he published anonymously a collection of his poetry, *The Last Days of Theodoric and Other Verses* (Oxford, 1904). He also published many studies on China, Buddhism and Confucianism, including *From Peking to Mandalay* (1908) and *Lion and Dragon in Northern China* (1910). His best-known book was *Twilight in the Forbidden City* (London, 1934). Johnston returned to England in 1930, and was knighted. He was professor of Chinese in the School of Oriental Studies, University of London, 1931–7. See also *Who Was Who 1929–1940*, p. 720; 'Johnston, Sir Reginald Fleming', *Twentieth Century DNB*.
[58]   Robert Bickers, '"Coolie work": Sir Reginald Johnston at the School of Oriental Studies, 1931–1937', *Journal of the Royal Asiastic Society*, 5 (1995), [12].

his own. He made an effort to put on a good show for her, and entertained her at his retreat in the Western Hills, Cherry Glen.

An account of her visit there became her imaginative essay, 'The haunted valley', later published in *The Raven*. This described a scholar's life in a valley between two small villages in the mountains. The scholar was one who had 'escaped from the man-built walls of the city' to the 'protection and peace' of the hills. He had built his house on a mound in a valley between two villages. In this place the scholar had sought and found a succession of those landscapes painted by the great artists of the long ages of Chinese civilisation. The scholar she wrote of was Reginald Johnston. 'Life slips away here in the haunted valley, haunted indeed by peace. Sometimes the scholar sits alone, reading old poems by T'ao Yuan-ming and Po Chu-I & Li Po, or pondering old philosophies. Sometimes he bids other scholars to be his guests, old men so learned and so reverend that they must be borne in swaying chairs along his paths.'[59]

Eileen's fascination with this place and the scholarly Scotsman within it were conveyed only indirectly here through this imaginative piece. A later entry in her diary referred to writing a piece about 'Mr. Johnston's place', and she wrote to Coulton after her return to England for his address:

I stayed for a weekend with him at his house in the Western hills outside Peking – it was when Miss Harding & I were on our walking tour: afterwards I did a thing about it which was printed in *The Raven* ... He is English tutor to the little Manchu emperor. I remember him with pleasure because he was soaked in Chinese things & because he was so amusing & because he lent me a horse.[60]

The image of this scholarly man in his haunted valley stayed with Eileen. Nine years later she was back in China on a sabbatical year, then became engaged to the scholar in the haunted valley.

After this trip in the Western Hills, Eileen wrote the two other imaginative pieces which she published in English journals: the piece of verse 'I wish I were a mandarin', and the short story 'The little god'. She concluded her diary entries on China, 'Here ended a holiday as near perfect as any holiday can well be.' In her Kahn Travelling Fellowship report, Eileen Power wrote of the quite different impressions that China made upon her from those of India. The great contrast for her, as it had been for Lowes Dickinson on his

59   Eileen Power, 'The haunted valley', TD, vol. III.
60   Power to Coulton, 23 December 1921, Power Papers.

Kahn Fellowship ten years before, was religion. In China she found a rationalistic and scientific outlook, as opposed to the religious habit of mind in India. In this she found China to be 'western' or 'modern' in its outlook. But as a country it was 'oriental (or medieval)' in its 'carelessness of all that we mean by progress'. China was a great trading nation, but still 'fundamentally an agricultural country'. Its 'extraordinary imperviousness to progress', however, was partly explained by social reasons; its social system was moulded by Confucianism which stressed the wisdom of the past, and by a patriarchal family system cemented by ancestor worship. But China exuded an enormous attraction to the West. There was the attraction of Chinese orientalism in the eighteenth century; and the recent cultural attraction once again based on translations of Chinese poetry and Lowes Dickinson's popular *Letters from John Chinaman*.[61] Eileen Power was aware of the impact of Lowes Dickinson's book on herself. This together with 'Mr. Waley's admirable translations of Chinese poetry displayed ... a culture modern in all its attributes, and as it were an expression of everything that a war-ridden Europe found most desirable and most unattainable'.[62]

In China in 1921 what Eileen Power saw was the possibility of a great modern power and the 'immense potentialities of this race'. 'China has not yet adapted herself to modern life, but one has the strong impression that she will do so, and that in doing so she may avoid some of the evils which progress has brought to the West, since a profoundly rational people is more capable of learning from experience than others less reasonable.'[63]

In Peking Eileen met Bertrand Russell and Dora Black, the first recovering from double pneumonia, and the second pregnant. They had been in China for several months, for Russell had nearly died in Peking from his bout of pneumonia. Eileen travelled with them to Japan, and on to Canada, in order to be useful to them 'as they are both rather crocks'.[64] They found her a welcome entertainer, 'full of amusing gossip about Cambridge where nasty rumours about Dora Black were going about'. Eileen's reply to the gossip had been that 'she was staying with the nasty rumours'.[65] In spite of the illness, they

[61] Power, *Kahn Report*, pp. 49–55. See Dickinson, *Letters from John Chinaman*; G. L. Dickinson, *Albert Kahn Travelling Fellowships. Report to the Trustees October 1913* (London, 1913).
[62] Power, *Kahn Report*, p. 55.   [63] *Ibid.*
[64] TD, vol. IV, 11–30 July 1921; Power to MLG, 21 July 1921; cf. Russell, *The Tamarisk Tree*, pp. 135, 143.
[65] Russell, *The Tamarisk Tree*, p. 131.

proved good travelling companions. Later, on the boat from Japan to Canada, among uncongenial company, Eileen enjoyed Russell's wit, and 'discussion of politics, books & the position of women raged furiously'.[66]

Russell's own response to China bears some comparison with her own. He too visited towns just like medieval towns, with narrow streets, sedan chairs and rickshaws. But he associated China with rational hedonism, as an eighteenth-century European society, 'what Europe would have become if the eighteenth century had gone on till now without industrialism or the French Revolution'. People differ 'from Europeans through the fact that they prefer enjoyment to power. People laugh a great deal in all classes, even the lowest.'[67]

Eileen's visit to Japan with Russell and Dora Black was spoiled by swarms of journalists, constantly trying to interview Russell. 'We lived in a perpetual fire of flash light photographs, cameras, cinemas & what not.' Of the dozens of Japanese they met, the only ones they really liked were three socialist labour leaders, one a woman.[68]

Despite the press, there were some advantages to being with Russell, for through him she met numerous Japanese professors and labour leaders. She visited the slums of Kobe with a saintly socialist, Kagaura, and Osaka, 'a hideous manufacturing town for all the world like Manchester':

The whole thing, smoke & chimneys & canals, westernised municipal buildings, clank of machinery, dismal piece of common, were painfully familiar. I suddenly longed for Peking, carved shop fronts, pink walls, shining yellow roofs, droves of packmules & camels along the roads ... All manufacturing cities are the same. They make a desert & call it industry.[69]

After following in the shadow of Russell through Nara and Kyoto, Eileen and Dora organised their own meeting with feminists in Tokyo. Eileen visited cotton mills and the licensed quarter where the brothels were collected. She said of the painted girls of the quarter:

Candour compels me to admit that they look a great deal healthier and happier than the wretched little girls of twelve years & upward in the cotton mills, working from 10 to 14 hours & herded in dormitories. But I do not know which is the more painful sight – love profaned by buying an hour or two of animals in cages; or life profaned to a slavery in the roar of machines

[66] TD, vol. IV, 11–30 July 1921.
[67] Bertrand Russell, *The Autobiography of Bertrand Russell 1914–1944*, vol. II (London, 1968), p. 138.
[68] Power to MLG, 21 July 1921.
[69] TD, vol. IV, 11–30 July 1921.

and the lung-destroying cotton fluff, which is drawn in with every breath. The human individual is not allowed for in either of these manifestations of civilisation, old & new.[70]

Eileen felt Japan to be alien after China, responding to the beauties and delights of the old temples, gardens and tea ceremonies of pre-western Japan, but hating the westernised ports and factories, 'their horrible efficiency'. She found the Japanese to be essentially 'an imitative race' which had 'borrowed from China, borrowed from India, and from Europe'. She found the people 'had adopted the Western idea of civilisation as material progress while clinging to the Eastern idea of religion in the shape of a blind patriotism'. She always found herself 'being asked to admire Japan for the things I most dislike in Europe'.[71] 'One knows where one was born, but one does not know where one's lares and penates are; & having travelled all round the world in search of mine I have arrived at the conclusion that they are irremoveably settled in Peking.' With this, Power left the East.[72]

Eileen Power's Kahn report and her reaction to China and Japan tell us much about her ambivalence to Western economic and social change. She saw herself as an exponent of modernism in literature and art and in labour and socialist politics. But what she found to admire in China was an idealisation of the past, a medievalism in land, family life and ways of thinking. Japan offended her because westernisation brought factories, industrial cities and admiration of those Western values she was trying to escape. Her Kahn report and her diaries are suffused with the orientalism and rejection of modern industrial societies of Lowes Dickinson's *Letters from John Chinaman*, written twenty years earlier in the wake of the Boxer Rebellions.[73] In Dickinson's view China still offered the possibilities of the civilisation, aesthetics and intellectual life that the West had given up for economic growth. It lacked good government, and needed to learn this from the West in order to provide more 'opportunities and rights for her toiling masses' and the 'emancipation of the individual from the tyranny of the family'.[74]

---

[70] TD, vol. IV, 11–30 July 1921.   [71] Power, *Kahn Report*, p. 56.
[72] TD, vol. IV, 11–30 July 1921.
[73] On the images of China conveyed by Western intellectuals see J. A. G. Roberts, *China through Western Eyes. The Nineteenth Century* (London, 1991); Colin Mackerras, *Western Images of China* (Oxford, 1991).
[74] G. L. Dickinson, 'An essay on the civilisations of India, China and Japan (1914)', in his *Letters from John Chinaman*, pp. 66–7.

Yet Eileen Power might have taken another position. Sidney and Beatrice Webb had visited Asia ten years earlier. They had come down on the side of the Japanese, describing their social divisions as transitional developmental problems. In their view Japan was the land of hopefulness, the land of the rising sun in Asia. Of China, by contrast, they had the confidence to pronounce (after only three weeks) that it had no capacity for adopting Western learning, indeed, 'no capacity for anything'. They summed up the Chinese achievement as mere endurance, and denounced the country for 'lower[ing] the tone and coarsen[ing] the fibre of the European in the Far East'.[75]

Eileen Power unhesitatingly chose Lowes Dickinson over the Webbs. Her experience of China was of elite culture and aesthetics; she wrote about the peasants and the land, describing tiny plots and underfed peasants, but in a remote way: 'They had neither the time nor the opportunity to absorb the culture of the aristocracy who created the wonderful lotus-flower, which we call Chinese civilisation.'[76] There was not much in her views to divide her from Lowes Dickinson's indictment of the West for its invasion of high Chinese culture. Lowes Dickinson's image of China was of a community of peasants, a casting back to the England of yeoman farmers before the enclosures.[77] Much of the point of his tract was an attack on modern technology and economic growth in the West, along with the 'mass culture' this entailed. He argued that the success of the West in mechanical arts accompanied a failure in spiritual insight.

Machinery of every kind you can make and use to perfection; but you cannot build a house, or write a poem, or paint a picture; still less can you worship or aspire. Look at your streets! Row upon row of little boxes, one like another, lacking in all that is essential, loaded with all that is superfluous.[78]

What Lowes Dickinson really objected to in the West was the 'brute and overwhelming force of the Mass' and what he really despised were businessmen:

When I look at your business men, the men whom you most admire; when I see them hour after hour, day after day, year after year, toiling in the mill

---

[75]   Sidney and Beatrice Webb, 'The social crisis in Japan', 'China in revolution', *The Crusade*, 3 (January 1912); both repr. in George Feaver (ed.), *The Webbs in Asia, the 1911–12 Travel Diary* (London, 1992), pp. 359–74.

[76]   Power, *Kahn Report*, p. 51.

[77]   Dickinson, *Letters from John Chinaman*, p. 21.

[78]   *Ibid.*, p. 23.

of their forced and undelighted labours; when I see them importing the anxieties of the day into their scant and grudging leisure ... I reflect, I confess, with satisfaction on the simpler routine of our ancient industry ... and prize ... the beaten track so familiar to our accustomed feet.[79]

Lowes Dickinson's indictment of Western economies and culture was echoed in Eileen's attitudes to her fellow travellers on the boat from Japan to Canada. Like him, she despised the

rich Americans and business Jews from Shanghai, Hong Kong & Kobe ... There was hardly a man who was not gross & fat ... There was hardly a woman ... who was not dressed and powdered & painted & scented for the one & only purpose of attracting or retaining the attentions of men. Looking at their faces I thought that there was not one of them who had ever had a real emotion in the whole of their money-grubbing, man-hunting lives.[80]

After this, Canada was a relief. 'The beauty of [Victoria] had that piercing & almost intolerable quality. It was a salute from the west, unique, individual & suddenly welcome after all the landscapes of the East.' The Vancouver traders looked at the Pacific 'with the eye of Cortez', and the people still suggested 'some of the strength & simplicity of the pioneers'.[81]

Eileen Power's trip had come to an end, but it only whetted her appetite for more travel, and she planned a return to China. She wrote to Margery Garrett of her feelings:

But the place I really loved & to which I shall never be happy unless I can return is Peking. I like the Chinese immensely & of all the cities I have ever seen, Peking is miles the most fascinating. Paris & Cairo are the only other that come near it & they are far behind.

She sent a packing case of presents to Margery, and added:

I've done this journey comfortable: that's to say I've blewed most of my capital as well as the Kahn on it & I've spent about £300 on beautiful things, mostly stuffs. But I've seen enough to be certain that on journalism & odd jobs one could very easily pay one's way out east, if one started out with a small nucleus. I'm coming out to China after I've been three years in London: I shall get a summer term off, have from April to September inclusive & come across the Trans Siberian. You'd better come too![82]

[79]   *Ibid.*, p. 31.
[80]   TD, vol. IV, 30 July–11 August 1921.
[81]   TD, vol. IV, 11–30 July 1921.
[82]   Power to MLG, 21 July 1921.

She went to visit the Claphams, and announced: 'You know, I've been all round the world, and I haven't had a single proposal of marriage.'[83]

The Kahn Fellowship was also to change the focus of Eileen Power's research interests. She wrote to Coulton some years after her trip: 'The A.K. fellowship has been my ruin, for my heart will stray outside its clime & period. I think I shall have to compromise by working at the trade between Europe and the East in the middle ages – if Heyd has left any little nook or cranny unworked, into which I can put my nose.'[84]

While Eileen was in India and China letters arrived which promised another big change in her life. Shortly after she had arrived in Madras, Eileen received a letter from Lilian Knowles, telling her she was to be offered a post in economic history at the LSE. The prospect then had both attracted and alarmed her, and she had debated her feelings on it.

I would go unhesitatingly in October, 1922, but I simply quail from rooting myself out in the brief three weeks which will elapse between my return to England and the beginning of term; also I frankly desire to leave Girton deliberately and in the midst of savouring friends and not in this hole and corner way![85]

In Bombay she heard that Cambridge had just turned down the proposal for women's degrees, something she added to the arguments for going. By the time she wrote to Coulton, she still feared being swamped by hack teaching with very little time for research, and 'the L.S.E. is so very utilitarian, whereas I am hopelessly humanistic & have a mortal distaste for the pure economist!' She was going, however, because she had been advised it would be a new experience to stand her in good stead for future posts. 'I do it very reluctantly, because though I often chafed at being cooped up in Girton, I love the college & I love Cambridge & I shall never feel the same towards London as a university. If we had won the degree fight in December, I think I should have refused London.' She wrote too, however, that she had ambitions for the headship of one of the women's colleges one day, and that Miss Jex-Blake, Girton's Mistress, and her friend M. G. Jones had advised her to take the post for

[83] Clapham family recollection, interview 21 July 1993.
[84] Power to Coulton, 5 September 1925, Power Papers. See W. Heyd, *Histoire du commerce du Levant au moyen-âge*, trans. F. Raynaud, 2 vols. (Leipzig and Paris, 1885–6; repr. 1923).
[85] TD, vol. I, 10 December 1920.

the broader experience it would give her. In the end, it was probably this rather than feminist arguments about the failure of Cambridge University to pass the proposal to grant degrees to women that persuaded her to accept the LSE post.[86]

While Eileen was in China the serious letters about her new job at the LSE went back and forth. She had received Lilian Knowles' letter about the post while in Madras, asking for an indication of whether she would accept the job if offered. She wrote to Knowles from Rangoon in early April, telling her she had wired to accept the post, but had as yet had no communication from the director. She complained about the salary she was offered, and worried about the amount of teaching she would do, for Girton had recently given her much more time for research, 'which is the thing which I *really* care about'. She had a contract for two books with Collins and Methuen, and wrote of wanting to finish the book on medieval women, which she described at this point as 'half done'.[87]

Letters between Eileen and Beveridge, the director of the London School of Economics, were lost in Rangoon and Shanghai, but she eventually heard about her teaching conditions and courses. Beveridge assured her there would be some provision for research time, but she would be asked to teach some modern political history.[88] And she wrote about the job to Margery Garrett while on board ship between Japan and Canada:

I want to be in London for a bit & I'm tired of community life. It is the wrong moment to leave Cambridge, just as things look more hopeful & the Chairman of the Economics Board wrote & said he'd announce me as a lecturer in Economic History if I'd reconsider my decision & wire him. But I think it is best to come to London & I shall be able to see a lot of people I want to see more often: I'm damned tired of being played fast & loose with by Cambridge University.[89]

[86] Power to Coulton, 20 March 1921. Girton College archives.
[87] Power to Knowles, LSE personal file, 3 April 1921.
[88] Beveridge to Power, 21 May 1921; Power to Beveridge, 26 June 1921; 26 July 1921, Power personal file, LSE Personnel Office.
[89] Power to MLG, 21 July 1921.

CHAPTER 5

Women, peace and medieval people

Eileen Power's responses to India, China and Japan were refracted through her only knowledge of underdeveloped societies, that of medieval Europe. She visited the East self-conscious of her position as a medieval social historian. What she experienced there, however, was to have a very significant impact on her choice of subjects and her ways of writing about these. To understand this, we must turn back to the kinds of medieval social history and women's history with which she had become firmly identified in the years just before her journey.

We must first ask how the Middle Ages were viewed and studied during the time Eileen Power started to write history. How did this differ from the medievalism of the Victorians? What distinctive approaches did she bring to the subject in her early and enduring work on medieval social and women's history? She was a woman who was trained in the highest scholarly traditions of her discipline, but at the formative stages of her education and career, she was also a committed suffragist, and after this a passionate peace campaigner. Both these enthusiasms drove her to cut through the scholarly and methodological apparatus and even complacent assumptions of the contemporary historical paradigms. She chose to write about those previously excluded from historical accounts – women and ordinary people, and she set out to write this social history as an account of international connection and community. What did medieval history mean to her predecessors and contemporaries, and what set her on her quest for a new framework and a new way of writing history?

The writing of medieval history during the two decades before the First World War became professionalised and specialised in a way that the medievalism of the Victorians had never been. Where writing about the medieval period was once a part of the Gothic revival, this had all changed by the end of the century. The broad-scale narrative syntheses, literary history and picturesque detail were, for the Victorians, part of the turning back to a medieval ideal as an escape from the atomised, divided society created by industrialism. Many different groups turned to medieval society to frame their protests against their own society. For Carlyle and Froude the Middle Ages offered a chivalric antidote to *laissez-faire* capitalism. For William Stubbs, Edward Freeman and J. R. Green the study of the Middle Ages vindicated the gradual triumph of constitutional democracy. The Middle Ages provided examples of what might be – the face-to-face democracy of the village commun-ity, the municipal values and institutions of medieval towns. These were the proof to Edward Freeman that 'freedom is older than bondage'. The Young Englanders around Disraeli looked to the feudal ideals of social hierarchy and communal responsibility. Radicals found in the medieval past an ideal society of rural yeoman and smallholders. Complementing these historical and political interests were the literary and aesthetic attractions of the Middle Ages. There were the Arthurian romances of Tennyson, Swinburne and Morris and the medieval romanticism of the Pre-Raphaelites. Pugin, Carlyle, Ruskin and Morris held up the medi-eval ideal in their social and aesthetic criticism. The theologians of the Oxford Movement and the Catholic Revival identified with the medieval church.[1]

This close emotional identity that the Victorians found in medieval history was pushed aside towards the end of the nineteenth century in favour of professional specialised research on voluminous medi-eval records, which were collected and published by antiquarian societies and individual historians. The growth of nationalism and liberalism in the nineteenth century had fostered an interest in collecting medieval records to demonstrate national origins. In England there was the Rolls Series, the best of which were edited by William Stubbs. Historical societies were founded in London and the

---

[1] Jann, 'From amateur to professional', 125; Florence S. Boos, 'Alternative Victorian futures: "Historicism", *Past and Present* and *A Dream of John Ball*', in F. S. Boos (ed.), *History and Community: Essays in Victorian Medievalism* (New York, 1992), pp. 3–37, at pp. xii, 8; Charles Delheim, 'Interpreting Victorian medievalism', in Boos (ed.), *History and Community*, pp. 39–58, at pp. 40–5; Marc Baer, 'The memory of the Middle Ages: from history of culture to cultural history', in Leslie J. Workman (ed.), *Medievalism in England* (Cambridge, 1992); R. J. Smith, *The Gothic Bequest: Medieval Institutions in British Thought, 1688–1863* (Cambridge, 1987).

provinces to publish historical records. There was the Camden Society in London in the 1830s, and the Surtees Society set up at the same time to publish English chronicles.[2]

Soon the great influence of the literary historians was treated as a rival authority that the new professions felt they had to discredit. Medieval history provided the principal terrain for the exercise of 'scientific history' – the minute documentation of facts and figures to provide a positive accumulation of evidence. But evidence for what? The questions that drove this new research and new methodology were still the same Victorian concerns with the role of the medieval church, with the constitution and administration, and with the medieval village. The positivist historians with their rigorous research on a growing body of medieval documentation confined themselves to exposing the romantic misconceptions of their predecessors.

The methodology of medieval history changed during the Edwardian period. The influence of F. W. Maitland's reaction to Victorian teleologies was widespread. He took a modernist approach to medieval law, seeking to understand its structure and function as would a Durkheimian sociologist. The study of the law became for him the route to medieval social behaviour and the intellectual perspectives that shaped it.[3] The work of Maitland and of his contemporary Sir Paul Vinogradoff was to take the forefront of medieval history into legal, constitutional and manorial history; another direction was provided by the administrative history of the Manchester School of Medieval History led by T. F. Tout.[4] The original political inspiration for this legal–constitutional history may have been contemporary European debates on the peasantry and land policy, but the heirs of Maitland and Vinogradoff were also engaged in a now highly specialised debate on the questions of medieval corporatism and communalism thrown up by their Victorian predecessors. The impact of the legal–constitutional tradition was enormous in the early twentieth century. Eileen Power's friend and Girton successor Helen Cam was later part of this world, and

---

[2]   Clare A. Simmons, *Reversing the Conquest. History and Nineteenth-Century British Literature* (New Brunswick, 1990), pp. 48–9.

[3]   Norman F. Cantor, *Inventing the Middle Ages* (Cambridge, 1991), p. 57.

[4]   On T. F. Tout see F. M. Powicke, *Modern Historians and the Study of History* (London, 1955), pp. 19–44. His major work in administrative history was his *Chapters in the Administrative History of England*, 6 vols. (1920–31).

she described its impact: 'We are all pupils of Maitland, of Vino-gradoff and of Tout.'[5]

Where does Eileen Power's writing fit in this trajectory of historical writing? First she avoided the traditions of legal and constitutional history as a graduate and followed instead her inclination towards literary history and the history of religious life. This, together with the background she acquired at Girton in economic and social history, led her to develop her own route towards the social history of the Middle Ages. She saw the significance of the legal-manorial history to ideas on international co-operation in the years after the First World War, and was also to draw on this in the development of comparative economic history in her later work. This particular influence will, therefore, be discussed at a later point in this book. But Eileen Power's earlier historical writing grew out of her revival of the older literary traditions of history which she put together with the study of previously neglected social groups, especially women and the bourgeois and labouring classes. She sought to write about the lives of these groups directly, and not as reflected through the evolution of legal codes. Her inspiration lay, as we have seen, in her own sympathies with suffrage and socialist values, but more signifi-cantly with the influence of Langlois, Coulton and the LSE. During Eileen Power's year abroad her book, *Medieval English Nunneries*, was in press. Several of the seminal essays on women which she published or delivered as major lectures during the early to mid-1920s were also started in her later years at Girton. Eileen Power's reputation as one of the first women's historians, and the special area she carved out for herself as the historian of medieval women, were based on the research she did for her thesis and first book, as well as her first major lectures and articles. She was also to extend the work she did on women's history during these years to the broader social history that appeared in her most famous book, *Medieval People*.

Power's research moved from the study of a queen, to women in medieval religious life, and from there to the broader study of medieval women and social history. She appeared to start out with a very traditional kind of history, but turned this into a new kind of social history which she saw as an alternative approach to the dominant legal-constitutional tradition. What histories of medieval

---

[5] Helen M. Cam, *The Hundred and the Hundred Rolls. An Outline of Local Government in Medieval England* (London, 1930), p. vii.

women had been written before Eileen Power's work, and what
traditions of religious history did she develop?

I

The subject area Eileen Power set out for herself was a new one. Such
women's history as had been written was largely non-academic, for
few women had access to higher education and the historical profession before the twentieth century. Memoirs of queens and families,
histories of fashion and domesticity, editions of letters and diaries
were the staple fare of popular female historians during the nineteenth century. But these, with rare exceptions, were not academics.

Prior to Eileen Power's work, there were a few German and
Austrian studies by men – Karl Weinhold's *Deutsche Frauen in dem
Mittelalter*, published in Vienna in 1897 and Karl Bücher's *Die
Frauenfrage im Mittelalter*, published in Tübingen in 1910. Both were set
within the framework of the German historical school. Bücher's book
was for some time the main scholarly work available on women's
work in medieval society, and it was widely cited in English historical
writing.[6] The book closest to Power's work was Lina Eckenstein's
Woman under Monasticism, published in Cambridge in 1896. This was
an overtly feminist work, dedicated to Karl and Maria Pearson. It
was a wide-ranging book, not based on archive sources. Its purpose
was to correct the bad light in which nuns had been depicted since
the Reformation. The book was a celebration of female communities;
it looked back to the cult of female saints and analysed the general
position of women under monasticism in a positive light. Eckenstein
saw the dissolution of the nunneries as the end of an alternative
which had previously existed for women to marriage and domesticity. She argued that standards of scholarship and intellectual
attainment fell in the convents in comparison with the monasteries
after centres of education shifted to the universities, and women
could not secure houses there. This led to a lack of interest in the
intellectual attainments of nuns, 'and it was accompanied by a
growing indifference in the outside world to the intellectual capacity
of women generally'.[7] 'The right to self-development and social

---

6   For a discussion of Bücher's demographic arguments for the relatively egalitarian position
    of women in the trades and crafts of late medieval German cities see Howell et al., 'A
    documented presence', 116–18.
7   Eckenstein, *Woman under Monasticism*, p. 481.

responsibility which the woman of today so persistently asks for, is in many ways analogous to the right which the convent secured to womankind a thousand years ago.'[8] Eileen Power's agenda was not primarily this feminist project. Her book, a much more academic work, like the research of some of her female colleagues which also uncovered and analysed women's communities and women's legal position, was set firmly within the traditions of ecclesiastical history or of economic history.

The first women to be recognised as academic historians, with rare exceptions, pursued the constitutional and legal history that then dominated both medieval and modern history. These exceptions were within the newer traditions of economic history: Elizabeth Dixon's study of the craftswomen of Paris in 1895 and Annie Abram on working women in London in 1916.[9] For those who took up the implications of medieval legal and constitutional developments for women, contemporary issues of property law and political participation were part of the agenda. The Married Women's Property Acts of the nineteenth century stimulated historical inquiry into the legal position of women, such as that pursued by Annie Abram; the movement for women's suffrage stimulated research on women's political participation as a part of medieval local and borough politics, as explored by Mary Bateson.[10] The other major framework for women's history was in ecclesiastical history. Mary Bateson and Rose Graham are good examples of those who wrote women's history out of the framework of ecclesiastical and legal history.

Mary Bateson, as we have seen, brought her suffrage politics into ecclesiastical history. Her early work was on nunneries, the Pilgrimage of Grace and the double monasteries. She turned from this work to municipal history, and became a disciple of Maitland.[11] This was where she made her most celebrated contributions to medieval

---

[8]   *Ibid.*, p. ix.

[9]   Dixon, 'Craftswomen in the Livre des Métiers', 209–28; Bateson (ed.), *Borough Customs*; Abram, 'Women traders', 276–85. See Bennett, 'Medievalism and feminism', 314–15 for a contrast between this early medieval women's history and medieval women's history today.

[10] Barbara Hanawalt, 'Golden ages for the history of medieval English women', in Susan Stuard (ed.), *Women in Medieval History and Historiography* (Philadelphia, 1987), pp. 1–24, at pp. 7, 11.

[11] Tout, T. F., 'Mary Bateson', *DNB Supplement*, vol. I, pp. 110–12; F. W. Maitland, 'Mary Bateson', *The Athenaeum*, 8 December 1906; reprinted in Helen M. Cam (ed.), *Selected Historical Essays of F. W. Maitland* (Cambridge, 1957), pp. 277–8.

history.[12] Rose Graham also took up women's history within the framework of ecclesiastical history. Her famous study of the Gilbertine double monastery was part of the historiography of institutional ecclesiastical history; her later work focused on other aspects of monastic history.[13]

Medieval English Nunneries also used the ecclesiastical framework, but the questions that shaped it were posed in terms of economic and social history. The book broke free of former historical traditions in manorial history and medieval religious thought to present a highly readable account of the wealth distribution of convents, their economic activities and division of labour, and the social backgrounds, daily lives and careers of the nuns. While there had been several such studies of monasteries before this book,[14] there was very little on the nunneries, apart from a specialist study of the Gilbertine order by Rose Graham. Power set out her purpose as writing a social history, and not a further study of the monastic ideal and development of the monastic rule and orders.[15]

In taking this approach, Eileen Power also followed closely in the steps of her two main mentors, both idiosyncratic ecclesiastical historians, Alexander Hamilton Thompson and G. G. Coulton. Their influence on her work was set out earlier. Both represented the traditions of monastic history within which she set her work on the nunneries. Thompson's work on the Cistercians and the church at the end of the Middle Ages was solidly institutional, and he also edited the Visitation Records on which she drew extensively for her research. Coulton, despite his long-running conflict with Gasquet, did produce the readable wide-ranging social history of religious life to which she aspired. Neither of these, however, had given any attention to the nunneries.

Power's book provided the first major monograph on English nunneries; as such it was of lasting significance. But at the end of the day Power presented a picture of institutional failure, based on an incomplete and biased reading of her sources. Like Coulton, she was

---

[12]   Mary Bateson, 'The laws of Breteuil', *English Historical Review*, 15 (1900), 73–8, 302–19, 496–523, 754–7; 16 (1901), 92–110, 332–45. She also edited the records of the Borough of Leicester and the Cambridge guild and borough records.

[13]   Rose Graham, *Gilbert of Sempringham*; Veronica Ruffer and A. J. Taylor (eds.), *Medieval Studies Presented to Rose Graham* (Oxford, 1950), foreword.

[14]   Cf. Hamilton Thompson (ed.), *Visitations of Religious Houses*; also see his later *English Monasteries* (Cambridge, 1923).

[15]   Eileen Power, *Medieval English Nunneries c. 1275–1535* (Cambridge, 1922), p. 1.

keen to avoid an over-optimistic reading of the past, but she left a bleak reading of women's achievements in the religious life of medieval England.

Eileen Power emphasised that her book was essentially a history of upper-class women, for it was only these who could bring with them the requisite dower and education – 'the greater part of the female population was unaffected by the existence of the outlet provided by conventual life for women's energies'.[16] The women of no other class except the wealthy were confined to so narrow a sphere that their only outlets were marriage or the convent. She showed that throughout the later Middle Ages convents recruited not just from the well born, but from bourgeois backgrounds; wealth rather than vocation decided applications. Power added a whimsical gloss to evidence of rising numbers of widows taking the veil:

The conventual atmosphere did not always succeed in killing the profaner passions of the soul; and the advent of an opinionated widow, ripe in the experience of all those things which her sisters had never known, with the aplomb of one who had long enjoyed an honoured position as wife and mother and lady of the manor, must at times have caused a flutter among the doves.[17]

When she moved on to investigate the heads of houses, Power found little piety, scholarship or entrepreneurship, but a set of great ladies 'gadding about the countryside with a retinue which better beseemed the worldly rank they had abjured'.[18] She included sections on wicked prioresses and good prioresses, and concluded: 'The typical prioress of the middle ages ... was a well-meaning lady, doing her best to make two ends of an inadequate income meet ... A good ruler of her house? doubtless; but when Chaucer met her the house was ruling itself somewhere at the "shires ende".'[19]

Power's analysis of the social background of the nuns was less careful than it might have been, and showed a predilection to present a story of internal institutional decay caused by the corrupted values of aristocratic and wealthy inmates. Recent research has established that many of the nuns were from parish gentry families of modest means. As the family wealth of the nuns was less than Eileen Power thought, so too may their religious vocation have been greater.[20]

[16] *Ibid.*, pp. 5–6.   [17] *Ibid.*, p. 39.
[18] *Ibid.*, p. 78.   [19] *Ibid.*, pp. 94–5.
[20] Author's correspondence with Professor Marilyn Oliva, Fordham University, New York,

Power gave extended attention, conveyed in a very popular form, to the economics of the convents. She examined property and incomes, financial administration, household accounts and financial difficulties. *Medieval English Nunneries* did not, however, seriously investigate the manorial histories of the convents, their regional situations, the constraints of manorial rule, and the comparative efficiencies of various nunneries as landlords. Agricultural and other economic activities were roundly summed up as inadequate efforts, and she vividly conveyed the amateurish economic outlook of the nuns:

But it must have been a great day for the impoverished nuns of Yorkshire when slim Italian or stout Fleming came riding down the dales under a spring sun to bargain for their wool crop. What a bustling hither and thither there would be, and what a confabulation in the parlour between my lady Prioress and her steward and her chaplain and the stranger sitting opposite to them.[21]

Power pointed out that on the eve of Dissolution the nunneries were on average only half as rich as the men's houses, and the average number of religious persons in them was larger. Their dire financial straits were compared to the men's houses which were also continually in debt. She pointed to the taxation, feudal services, hospitality, bad management, financial incompetence and overcrowding which exacerbated problems. Ultimately, however, this very important part of her book was superficial and unsatisfactory. In her efforts to avoid the detailed manorial investigations of her contemporary economic historians, such as Elizabeth Levett, she also neglected their findings. She said little about the impact of contemporary economic changes; the decline of villein services and rising wages exacerbated problems of small landlords, and these convents formed an important part of this stratum of landed society.[22]

Eileen Power's negative position on the financial state of the women's houses was also overstated by her reliance in this part of her book on the audits of Henry VIII and his ministers; these overlooked many women's houses, and neglected the resources available to the

24 January 1995. Her critique of the historiography of medieval English nuns will be published in her forthcoming book, *The Convent and the Community in Late Medieval England* (Boydell & Brewer). Also see Roberta Gilchrist and Marilyn Oliva, *Religious Women in Medieval East Anglia*, Centre for East Anglian Studies, 1 (1993); and Roberta Gilchrist, *Gender and Material Culture. The Archaeology of Religious Women* (London, 1993).

21   Power, *Medieval English Nunneries*, p. 112.
22   Bertha H. Putnam, 'Medieval English Nunneries', *American Historical Review*, 29 (1924), 538–9.

houses listed in household accounts. Research on a broader range of sources might well have produced a picture of financial resilience rather than ignominious and culpable failure.[23]

Power was better on the social division of labour of monastic households, and the day-to-day provision and accounting of food, clothing and servants. She dealt in some depth with servants, their numbers, their social division of labour and their wages, for which most of her evidence was garnered from account rolls and Dissolution inventories. She was alert to evidence of social conduct in the management of servants by the nuns, and disorder among the servants.[24]

Much of Power's book was taken up with the failures of the nunneries to keep to the Benedictine rule, with their worldliness, and with the extent to which they provided the basis for the bad press the nun received in medieval literature. Small communities of upper-class women maintained high proportions of servants, but contributed little in the way of education, learning or spirituality. She found them bored with monastic routine and communal living, and reacting against both as well as breaking the rules of silence when their communities were enclosed. Scholarship and spirituality provided no solace. The nuns she wrote of produced no saintly women or great mystics; there were no successors to the learned Anglo-Saxon abbesses. These women did not copy and illuminate manuscripts, and no nunnery produced a chronicle. The chronicles were the most notable contribution of the monastic houses to learning from the eleventh to the fourteenth centuries, but the nuns recorded nothing. The nuns' role as educators of the young was as poor as was their own education.

Power found the explanation for the decline of learning among these women from the Anglo-Saxon period to the high Middle Ages in medieval ideas about women among the upper classes.

The whole trend of medieval thought was against learned women and even in Benedictine nunneries, for which a period of study was enjoined by the rule, it was evidently considered altogether outside the scope of women to concern themselves with writing ... While the monks composed chronicles, the nuns embroidered copes; and those who sought the gift of a manuscript from the monasteries, sought only the gift of needlework from the nunneries.[25]

[23] Correspondence with Marilyn Oliva, 24 January 1995.
[24] Power, *Medieval English Nunneries*, pp. 150–7.
[25] *Ibid.*, p. 238.

The nuns' subordination in matters intellectual, spiritual, political
and economic was confirmed in their sexual behaviour. At many
points throughout the book, Power contrasted the ideal of celibacy
with apostacy and immorality. Nuns' lovers and children were the
stuff of unwitting human frailty, not of thought-out reaction and
resistance to conventual rule. She wrote of convents perceived as fair
game for visitors, students and priests, and of the unsettling effect of
secular boarders who brought worldly ways and possessions: 'It is
amusing to follow the reference to scholars of Oxford in the records
of those houses which were in the neighbourhood of the University.
Godstow was the nearest and the students seem to have regarded
it as a happy hunting ground constituted specially for their re-
creation.'[26]

Power's conclusions on the contributions of the nunneries and the
lives of the women in them were not all negative. She did acknowl-
edge that for unmarried women they 'gave scope for abilities which
might otherwise have run to waste, assuring them both self-respect
and the respect of society ... The nunneries still represented an
honorable profession and fulfilled a useful function for gentlewomen
of the middle ages.'[27] She balanced the good and the bad she had
uncovered, summing up thus: 'Yet this may be said for the nunneries
of the age, over and above the allowance for human frailty: not all,
nor even the majority, were tainted with serious sin, though all were
worldly.'[28]

There was little in Eileen Power's book on the constraints on these
women's lives set by the church itself; their little domains were poor,
half-tolerated communities. Members had no prospect of participation in the career structures or great political affairs of the church.
Nor was their contribution to religious thought and vocation seriously considered. Why the convents of the high Middle Ages in
England failed to overcome these constraints or even to challenge
them was not explored by Power. She did not compare their
conditions with those of abbeys and nunneries of the earlier Middle
Ages or of other European countries. Eileen Power did not very
seriously consider religious vocation and leadership; spiritual ideas
and the language of women's role in these lay outside her frame of
reference. Though choosing to write on the nunneries she was always
an utterly secular historian, with no affinity for spirituality. She

---

[26]   *Ibid.*, pp. 395, 413.   [27]   *Ibid.*, p. 260.
[28]   *Ibid.*, p. 473.

lacked the curiosity in the religious ritual and culture of the past which she might have had coming from another faith or from a lapsed Christianity. Her own sceptical assumptions were deep rooted, and appear never to have been questioned. She regarded the Church of England as hypocritical, and there is no evidence that she appreciated the motivation of her paternal grandfather who became a leading Victorian tract writer. She admitted to this lack of religious response and failure to understand that of others when her maternal grandfather died while she was still an undergraduate.[29] On her travels too, it was the spiritual and religious context of Indian civilisation that she found impenetrable. Commenting on a review of her book later, she conceded: 'I ought to have written a chapter of what Americans call sob-stuff about the monastic ideal, for which I am not by any means without admiration.'[30]

Eileen Power herself lived in a women's community at Girton for nearly ten years; this must have suggested parallels to the convents she studied. Yet she did not enquire into friendships among the nuns, and the aspirations of their communities to participate in the broader religious and public life of the church. She referred at various points in her life to her perceptions of her own and others' situations through the prism of her research on the nunneries. The ennui suffered by some of the shipboard crew on her journey from Suez to Ceylon during her Kahn trip she ascribed to the dead routine of a form of monastic rule. The Buddhist monasteries she visited in China were assessed in terms of the discipline or corruption of their heads of houses. Finally, when explaining her decision to leave Cambridge to go to the LSE she compared life in a community in a Cambridge women's college with the constraints of women in medieval nunneries.[31]

Generations of men and women before her had looked back to the nunneries as a source of inspiration for women's education and as a real alternative to marriage. From the sixteenth to the nineteenth centuries there had been proposals for protestant nunneries and women's colleges. By the late seventeenth and eighteenth centuries the ideal of a protestant nunnery was rekindled; it was argued that the education as well as the piety of women had suffered after the Dissolution, and that unmarried women had been left unprovided

---

[29] Power to MLG, April 1910.
[30] Power to Coulton, 27 September 1923, Power Papers.
[31] Power to Coulton, 13 January 1922, Power Papers.

for.[32] Anglican sisterhoods were started in the nineteenth century; and they were perceived in a very different light from Eileen Power's history of the nunneries. Their historian has written that they were among the first women's communities of the nineteenth century to insist on a woman's right to choose celibacy, to live communally and to do meaningful work. These religious communities 'empowered women, validating women's work and values in a world that seemed materialistic, godless and male'.[33] The nunneries also inspired those who called for the first women's colleges. In Girton, Power's own college, the ideals of study and privacy went hand in hand with the corporate identity and community of united women associated with the nunneries.[34]

Eileen Power certainly offered no romantic story of powerful women's communities. The Godstow Abbey of the later Middle Ages was no ideal precedent for Girton College. Power's whimsical comment on daily life and reaction to monastic routine may well derive its note of sympathetic understanding from her own and her friends' experiences in Girton. But she did not make much of the analogy, and certainly the outside world saw her book not in this light, but in the framework of G. G. Coulton's social histories. Power was delighted when the book appeared, and wrote of seeing it in bookshops where 'I have the greatest difficulty in restraining myself from seizing passers by by the elbow & saying "Hi! *I* wrote that!"'[35] She did not have high expectations of it selling many copies, but had thoughts of writing a popular version without footnotes.[36] But for all that, in the eyes of the profession, she was Coulton's creature, and her book a supplement to his more important and larger scale monastic history.

The reviews were generally positive, but the book was clearly not regarded as a great pathbreaking work. She did not initially have the material out of which to make great history, as one reviewer put it.[37] It was 'a judicious survey', 'conscientious', it was 'heroic devotion' to an 'exceptionally wide range of sources'. Some sources had been ommitted, some emphases could have been

---

[32] Bridget Hill, 'A refuge from men: the idea of a Protestant nunnery', *Past and Present*, 117 (1987), 107–30.
[33] Vicinus, *Independent Women*, p. 83.
[34] *Ibid.*, p. 142.
[35] Power to Coulton, 23 December 1922, Power Papers.
[36] Power to Coulton, 23 December 1922, Power Papers.
[37] 'A melancholy chronicle', *New Statesman*, 20 (27 January 1923), 412.

recast, the book was 'full of suggestive touches, capable of development in subsequent works'. It was a big book written with wit and 'a delightful style'.[38] Power's debt to Coulton was clear to some reviewers. He had supervised her, and had published the book in the series he edited. The book was announced as Coulton's in *The New Statesman*, eliciting Power's remark 'a view of the comparative importance of mother and obstetrician which looks like another injustice to women'.[39] One reviewer even erased her existence from the book, assuming it was another of Coulton's anti-catholic outpourings.[40]

Whatever the gaps in *Medieval English Nunneries* and the shadow cast over it by G. G. Coulton's *oeuvre*, it was a major work of scholarship, and the big book of Eileen Power's life. It was enough to establish her, by the time later books appeared, as a leading authority on monastic life.[41] Power had an almost immediate impact on mainstream monastic histories; within a few years, G. G. Coulton included three chapters on gendered aspects of the early church in the first volume of *Five Centuries of Religion*, and Hamilton Thompson devoted several pages to the nunneries in his contribution on the monastic orders in *The Cambridge Medieval History*.[42]

II

Medieval English Nunneries took Eileen Power into a completely new area of research which, with a major monograph behind her, she felt confident enough to pursue. This was the broader history of medieval women. She had predecessors who had written specialist pieces on nuns, women's legal position or women in the crafts, but none of these had branched out to explore women's history more broadly. During the time at Girton when she was writing her nunneries book, Eileen Power was already doing this broader research. When she went to the LSE she described herself as half-

---

[38] Hilda Johnstone, 'Medieval English nunneries', *History*, 8 (1923), 218–19; Revd E. W. Watson, 'Medieval English nunneries', *English Historical Review*, 38 (1923), 435–6; 'English nunneries', *Times Literary Supplement* (23 December 1922), 869.

[39] Power to Coulton, 9 October 1922.

[40] Power to Coulton, 27 September 1923.

[41] 'Medieval People', *Times Literary Supplement* (11 September 1924), 551.

[42] G. G. Coulton, *Five Centuries of Religion*, vol. 1, *St. Bernard, his Predecessors and Successors 1000–1200 AD* (Cambridge, 1923), pp. 138–197; Alexander Hamilton Thompson, 'The monastic orders', in Tanner et al. (eds.), *The Cambridge Medieval History*, vol. v, *Contest of Empire and Papacy* (1926), pp. 658–96, esp. pp. 671–82.

way through a book on medieval women.[43] The book never appeared, but it was planned, and several chapters were written and given as lectures or published separately as articles over the years.

Early plans for the book envisaged six essays: ideas about medieval women, the lady, the bourgeois, the working woman, the nun, and education.[44] A notebook set out subjects and materials she intended to include. One essay on portraits of middle-class women was to include material on the wife of the ménagier de Paris, and on the carpenter's wife, the miller's wife and the 'wyfe of Bathe', all from *The Canterbury Tales*. For another projected essay on the housewife, she had gathered material on servants including their wages, skills and duties, as well as advice and regulations on the supervision of servants. She intended another chapter on medicine which would include material on women as physicians, surgeons and midwives, and medical remedies. There was to be a chapter on prostitution based on sources gathered on medieval France and England. A wide-ranging chapter on marriage was to cover provisions for the marriage of girls and child betrothals, vows of chastity and marriage vows, provisions for widows by will and widows as guardians of children, wife-beating and murder, husbands and wives before the law, and dower, freebench and feudal dues.[45] These topics of women's medieval history, mapped out by Eileen Power and a number of them substantially researched by her in the years between 1911 and the 1930s, have only reappeared as major historical subjects during the 1970s and 1980s.[46]

Why Power never published her book on medieval women is not known, but her reputation spread during the years after the war for a series of major lectures and published essays on the subject. Her lectures became well known not just in academic circles, but in the wider literary world throughout the 1920s. Ray Strachey recalled her excitement at the prospect of a lecture by Eileen Power on 'Many

---

[43] Power to Beveridge, 26 June 1921.

[44] Postan Papers, box 2, shelf 6, CUL.

[45] Postan Papers, box 2, shelf 6, CUL.

[46] A number of these are discussed in Richard Smith, 'Introduction', in Eileen Power, *Medieval People* (London, 1924; new edn London, 1986), pp. xiii–xlvi. Cf. S. M. Stuard (ed.), *Women in Medieval Society* (Philadelphia, 1976); Eleanor Searle, 'Seigneurial control of women's marriage: the antecedents and function of *merchet* in England', *Past and Present*, 82 (1979), 3–43; Barbara Hanawalt, *The Ties That Bind: Peasant Families in Medieval England* (New York and Oxford, 1986); Barbara Hanawalt (ed.), *Women and Work in Pre-Industrial Europe* (Bloomington, 1986); Judith M. Bennett, *Women in the Medieval English Countryside* (Oxford, 1987).

evil women', and her great disappointment when she arrived to discover it was on 'Medieval women'.[47] Power also undertook extensive reviewing on medieval and other historical topics for *The Nation and the Athenaeum*, the *Times Literary Supplement* and the *Spectator*. This lecturing and reviewing in the weeklies helped to establish women's history as a new and popular subject. Eileen Power's object in these lectures was not medieval romanticism, 'that dead middle ages those noodles praise',[48] but a pioneering attempt to uncover the parts played by women at various levels of society, and to reassess some of the mainstream topics of medieval history, such as the cult of the virgin and chivalry from the standpoint of modern debates on women.

The lectures, survey articles and reviews extended Power's scholarly treatment of the nuns to aristocratic ladies, bourgeois housewives and working women. She published short versions of major lectures on 'The cult of the virgin' and 'Medieval ideas about women' between 1917 and 1918.[49] Long after her death some of these pieces were collected and published together in a popular form in *Medieval Women*, edited by M. M. Postan.

The general article on women for which Power became best known was 'The position of women', eventually published after long delays in Crump and Jacob's *The Legacy of the Middle Ages* in 1926.[50] This was the article for which Power later received harsh treatment from feminist historians critical of her failure adequately to set out the extent of women's subordination in medieval society.[51] But Eileen Power disliked this piece herself, written to please the editors who wanted to include an elegant piece on women, but yet gave the subject no mention in their long introduction. They had rejected her article, 'Medieval ideas about women', she thought, 'because it was not sufficiently respectful to (a) women (b) the Church (c) the Proprieties'. And the article they had her write instead 'could be

---

[47] Barbara Strachey to the author, 11 February 1993.

[48] Bishop Blougram's words cited in Eileen Power, 'A plea for the Middle Ages', *Economica*, 5 (1922), 173–80, at 173.

[49] Eileen Power, 'The cult of the virgin in the Middle Ages', *Cambridge Magazine* (28 April, 5 May, 9 June 1917); Eileen Power, 'Medieval ideas about women', *Cambridge Magazine* (2, 9 November 1918).

[50] Eileen Power, 'The position of women', in C. G. Crump and E. F. Jacob (eds.), *The Legacy of the Middle Ages* (Oxford, 1926), pp. 401–35.

[51] Olwen Hufton, 'Women in history: early modern Europe', *Past and Present*, 101 (1983), 125–41; J. M. Bennett, '"History that stands still": women's work in the European past', *Feminist Studies*, 14 (1988), 270.

safely read aloud at the second form by the kindergarten mistress during needlework – one of the gossips about social life which ought to be bought by the yard at a department store'.[52]

'Medieval ideas about women' provided the much more sustained intellectual history that Power preferred. She tied the origins of ideas on women's subordination to monasticism and the ascetic ideal, as well as to the feudal concept of marriage. Most opinion on women was expressed, she argued, by a very small minority, that is by a celibate clerkly order, and by a narrow aristocracy who regarded women as an ornamental asset subordinated to the primary asset, the land. 'The accepted theory about the nature and sphere of women was the work of the classes least familiar with the great mass of womankind.'[53]

Power argued that medieval attitudes to women arose in an age when clerical and aristocratic groups were able to impose their point of view on the rest of society. With the rise of urban society, town law had to take account of women active in trade with the category of 'femes soles', but bourgeois society in the main took over 'official ideas about women and marriage as a dispensation of nature'. The 'cult of the virgin' and the later age of chivalry with its theory of courtly love briefly raised the women of a small aristocratic class onto a pedestal. But they were deposed in the thirteenth and fourteenth centuries, when the urban classes were at the height of their prosperity and influence, by the resurgence of the secular anti-feminism of the bourgeois fabliaux or rhymed stories.[54] Power argued that the misogyny of these ideas and cultural assumptions was, however, eventually to provoke the discontent of women who played an active part in heretical movements such as Catharism and the Order of the Beguines. Literary works by women were rare, but at the end of the fourteenth century Christine de Pisan in her *Book of the City of Ladies* wrote her attack on *The Romance of the Rose*, taking her famous stand against the denigration of women.[55]

Eileen Power believed that the real contributions of bourgeois and working women had to be placed alongside their inferiority as

---

[52]   Power to Coulton, 5 September 1922, Power Papers.
[53]   Eileen Power, 'Medieval ideas about women', in Eileen Power, *Medieval Women*, ed. M. M. Postan (Cambridge, 1975), pp. 9–35, at p. 9.
[54]   *Ibid.*, pp. 10–11.
[55]   *Ibid.*, pp. 31–3; cf. Christine de Pizan, *The Book of the City of the Ladies*, trans. E. J. Richards (London, 1983); Christine de Pisan, *The Treasure of the City of Ladies or the Book of the Three Virtues* (Harmondsworth, 1983).

conveyed in medieval ideas. She wrote a series of papers conveying a much more optimistic stance on the actual work of women in industry and trade, in medicine and housewifery, while she also set against this their ultimate legal subordination to husbands and their exclusion from craft guilds. Her essay on 'The working woman in town and country' uncovered the extensive place of women in all aspects of medieval industry and agriculture. In addition to this it raised the question of why women occupied such a minimal place in medieval craft guilds. In England even in the silk industry, which was almost entirely in the hands of women, there was no trace of a guild of silkwomen. Power tied her explanation for this to the widespread role of English working women in by-employments, whereas men in craft guilds were confined to a single craft.[56]

While the essay on working women was the most general of her specialist studies, and she never did sustained research on the labouring classes, Eileen Power did give some careful thought to women's role in by-employments and domestic industries. She argued that these were followed by the majority of female workers, and were spread all over the countryside as well as in the towns.

They fall into two great classes: those connected with the textile industries and those connected with the production or sale of food and drink. Whereas men as a rule confined themselves to a single craft, it is not uncommon to find women following two or three by-industries of this sort. It is indeed possible that the practice of duplicating crafts and working for a supplementary wage may be one of the reasons which militated against the organisation of women in guilds, even in proper shopkeeping crafts.

As a good example of the practice she identified Rose the Regrater, wife of Avarice in *Piers Plowman* carrying on business as weaver, brewer and huckster or retailer of food and drink.

> My wife was a weaver and woollen cloth made
> She spake to the spinners to spinnen it out
> ... I bought her barley malt, she brew it to sell
> ... Rose the Regrater was her right name
> She hath holden huckstery all her life time.[57]

The problems created for women who followed a multitude of different crafts did not detract, Power argued, from the economic significance of these activities. They were the most important

[56] Eileen Power, 'The working woman', in Power, *Medieval Women*, pp. 62–70.
[57] Eileen Power, 'The working woman in town and country', in Power, *Medieval Women*, chap. 3, p. 62.

contribution of women to the economic life of the nation, apart from home-making. Most of the textile industry and much of the brewing of medieval England was in the hands of women. Their significance was recognised at the time to be sufficiently professional to earn them the titles of spinster, webster and brewster in official documents.[58] Power was keen to argue for the equal contributions of men and women in peasant society, but her evidence was weakest here, and she was looking through tinted glasses in thinking that the social status of women within their households would reflect recognition for their equal contribution in the workplace.[59]

Power's major work on medieval women after her scholarly work on medieval ideas and religious life was devoted to bourgeois women. During the war she spent time at Coggeshall working on the papers of the medieval clothiers, the Paycockes of Coggeshall. Subsequently she worked on the Cely Papers with their wealth of material on the merchants of the Staple. And she read once again the medieval conduct manual, *Le Ménagier de Paris*. At Coulton's suggestion she was later to translate and publish this work as *The Goodman of Paris*.[60] Power wrote a forty-page introduction to *The Goodman of Paris*, annotated it with extensive notes, and gathered from it detailed evidence on the duties of the bourgeois housewife. She complemented this with intimate details of bourgeois family life, and ideas about love and marriage gathered from the Cely Papers and the wills and accounts of the Paycockes.

Power described *The Goodman of Paris* as a manual on deportment as well as a medieval Mrs Beeton. It set out what was expected of a young medieval housewife by her much older husband. 'On the attitude of wife to husband the Ménagier's ideas are much the same as those of the other men of his age. They may be summed up as submission, obedience and constant attention.' But the Ménagier's attitudes were to be distinguished, she argued, from those of aristocratic and ecclesiastical writers. He wanted 'a helpmeet and not a slave ... In spite of the insistence upon obedience which was characteristic of his period, his ideal of marriage is by no means a low or an unequal one.'[61]

---

58 Power, 'The working woman', p. 65.   59 *Ibid.*, p. 75.
60 Power to Coulton, 23 December 1920, Power Papers; Eileen Power (ed.), *The Goodman of Paris*, trans. Eileen Power (London, 1928).
61 Power (ed.), *The Goodman of Paris*, introduction, p. 12.

Power wrote vividly of marital ideals and practices among merchant families and the gentry in a classic lecture, 'English domestic letter writers of the Middle Ages', based on the papers of four families – the Pastons of Norfolk, the Plumptons of Yorkshire, the Stonors of Oxfordshire, all genteel families, and finally the Celys of London, this last a family of large-scale London woollen merchants from the Company of the Staple. She also drew on material from this lecture for her chapter on 'Thomas Betson, a merchant of the Staple in the fifteenth century' in *Medieval People*. This correspondence showed, she argued, that marriage in the fifteenth century was a strictly business affair. Correspondents were always looking out for good matches for themselves or other members of their families, and discrepancies in age mattered little. Power clearly delighted in the somewhat one-sided correspondence between Thomas Betson, a partner to the Stonors, and the thirteen-year-old Katherine Riche to whom he was betrothed. 'He sits down in his office at Calais across the sea & writes her this charming letter to thank her for a present & to scold her for not eating up her dinner & to send his love to his horse!'[62] Poor Katherine, in another letter, was chastised for failing to keep up her side of the correspondence. 'I am wroth with Katherine, because she sendeth me no writing. I have to her divers times and for lack of answer I wax weary; she might get a secretary if she would and if she will not, it shall put me to less labour to answer her letters again.'[63]

Despite the age differences and the business affairs, Power concluded that the letters showed

a remarkable camaraderie between husbands & wives; the wives always look after their husbands' affairs during their absence & are relied upon implicitly in business, in struggles to keep an estate from a rival claimant & in attempts to raise money. The proportion of businesslike hardheaded ladies shown us by the letters is high. Certainly the middle ages would not have understood the Victorian relegation of women to the purely domestic job of running the home.[64]

---

[62] Eileen Power, 'English domestic letter writers of the Middle Ages', unpublished lecture, Postan Papers; cf. Power, *Medieval People*, pp. 127–31.
[63] Eileen Power, 'Thomas Betson', in *Medieval People*, p. 131.
[64] Power, 'English domestic letter writers'.

III

Eileen Power also made a conscious attempt to connect the history of
women to broader social history. In writing these essays and lectures
on women she turned to writing on the history of medieval ordinary
people. The wills of Thomas Paycocke and the letters of Thomas
Betson lent themselves to an integrated treatment of working lives,
social position and domestic relationships. Eileen Power's commitment to women's history turned to a new zeal for social history. The
result was her most famous work, *Medieval People*, first published in
1924.

In 1918, Power was already well advanced in the writing of *Medieval
People*. Methuen had approached her for a textbook on history, and
she offered him 'a little book on medieval ordinary people, which is
nearly done'. She was also asked to be a general historical editor,
and she related that Methuen had written, saying: 'I am looking out
for books on all educational subjects & especially by the younger
scholars, whose is the future. I am not afraid of *women*.' Her comment
on this was 'damn his eyes!'[65]

Medieval People was the culmination of the first phase of Power's
approach to social history. The genesis of *Medieval People* lay in her
feminist and pacifist political commitment, and in the methodology
she developed of history as literature. Eileen Power articulated in
Medieval People the views on historical methodology and on the social
role of history that she set out in her journalism and other publishing
projects in the early 1920s. She became the exponent of a social
history deploying literary devices and a social history written to
spread a message of internationalism.

The book went into ten editions and, since that last tenth edition,
it has been reprinted three times, most recently in 1986 with an
introduction by Richard Smith. Power in her inaugural lecture in
1933 was to observe that social history in the 1920s was held 'in
disrepute as vague and spineless'. But 'properly defined, social
history is the very reverse of this. It is a structural analysis of society,
a line of approach to historical investigation that requires as rigorous
a mental discipline and as scientific a methodology as any of the
longer-established branches of history.'[66]

The book which was published in 1924 was no formal application

[65]   Power to MLG, 25 September 1918.
[66]   Power, *Medieval People*, preface, p. ix.

of theory. In *Medieval People* she presented medieval society as a series of individuals. She wrote:

I believe that social history lends itself particularly to what may be called a personal treatment, and that the past may be made to live again for the general reader more effectively by personifying it than by presenting it in the form of learned treatises on the development of the manor or on medieval trade, essential as these are to the specialist.[67]

Medieval People was in fact a great achievement of history and literary narrative. In the way she wrote of her subjects, Power deliberately collapsed the boundaries between history and fiction. She speculated and wondered about ideas and emotions for which she had no evidence, but which endowed her historical characters with vivid characterisation. She thus moved away from the positivistic constraints on history to include questions if not answers on the person and the self rather than dealing only with the artefacts of the group. She effectively deployed medieval literature as a part of her historical reconstructions of character and of place. At the same time Power sought to represent individuals as ideal types of medieval social structure. Bodo was peasant life on a typical medieval estate; Marco Polo illustrated Venetian trade with the East; Madam Eglentyne was monastic life and the convent; the ménagier's wife was domestic life and medieval ideas about women. Thomas Betson illustrated the wool trade and the merchants of the Staple; and Thomas Paycocke, the cloth industry in East Anglia. Her characters were all actual historical figures, but they were also illustrations of the main outlines of medieval social history.

The presentation of major historical themes as individual personalities was also a way of setting out some of the main types of historical document acceptable as evidence in medieval history at the time: estate books, church records, wills, chronicles, family papers, household manuals and books of deportment. The range of social experience she had explored in her studies of Madame Eglentyne, the prioress, the ménagier's wife, and the two representatives of the cloth trade, Thomas Betson and Thomas Paycocke, was filled out in *Medieval People* from two other social groups, the peasantry, represented by Bodo, and the traders and travellers, represented by Marco Polo. Power did not draw on rich sources in English manorial records for this portrait of Bodo, the peasant, but on her familiarity

[67] *Ibid.*

with French medieval sources and, in this case, a French estate book, that of the abbot of St Germain de Près near Paris. This essay, together with her later wide-ranging comparative history, 'Peasant life and rural conditions', published in the *Cambridge Medieval History* (Cambridge, 1932), were virtually her only publications on the peasantry and the rural economy. In 1918, she had published a short survey essay, 'On the effects of the Black Death on rural organisation in England', and much later in 1933 she published a short archival commentary on agricultural techniques in the Middle Ages, 'On the need for a new edition of Walter of Henley'. But otherwise Power did not pretend to any expertise on the English medieval rural economy. Both her chapter on Bodo and the later classic essay 'Peasant life' were based mainly on French sources.

The daily life of Bodo, the peasant, and his wife Ermentrude was constructed from the estate book, from Charlemagne's capitulary and works on Charlemagne, and various chronicles and works of medieval French and German literature. Ermentrude is described as going up to the big house of the estate of Villaris on the day her chicken-rent is due, with a chicken and five eggs. She stops at the women's workrooms.

Their workrooms were comfortable places, warmed by stoves, and there Ermentrude (who, being a woman, was allowed to go in) found about a dozen servile women spinning and dyeing cloth and sewing garments ... Ermentrude, however, has to hurry away after her gossip, and so must we. She goes back to her own farm and sets to work in the little vineyard; and after an hour or two goes back to get the children's meal and to spend the rest of the day in weaving warm woollen clothes for them. All her friends are either working in the fields on their husbands' farms or else looking after the poultry, or the vegetables, or sewing at home ... Then at last Bodo comes back for his supper, and as soon as the sun goes down they go to bed; for their hand-made candle gives only a flicker of light.[68]

Power filled out their lives with evidence of their beliefs in combinations of old spells and magic along with the newer Christian faith, their festivals and visits to fairs.

It was, however, long-distance trade and travel during the Middle Ages that was most to fascinate her from the time of her Kahn Travelling Fellowship. She had acknowledged as much some time afterwards in a letter to Coulton.[69] Marco Polo took a prominent

[68] *Ibid.*, pp. 27–8.
[69] Power to Coulton, 5 September 1925.

place in *Medieval People*, and presaged the move in Eileen Power's research towards trade, and especially the cloth trade. Her essay on Marco Polo showed her highly evocative sense of place: 'To Venice, therefore, as if drawn by a magnet, came the spoils of the East, and from Venice they went by horse across the Alps by the Brenner and St. Gothard passes to Germany and France.' A few pages later we are taken to China:

Thousands of miles away from Venice, across the lands and seas of Asia, a little south of the Yangtze River and close to the sea stood the city of Kinsai or Hangchow ... Like Venice, Kinsai stood upon lagoons of water and was intersected by innumerable canals ... In its market-places men chaffered for game and peaches, sea-fish, and wine made of rice and spices; and in the lower part of the surrounding houses were shops, where spices and drugs and silk, pearls and every sort of manufactured article were sold. Up and down the streets of Kinsai moved lords and merchants clad in silk, and the most beautiful ladies in the world swayed languidly past in embroidered litters, with jade pins in their black hair and jewelled earrings swinging against their smooth cheeks ... To the men of Kinsai, Venice would have been a little suburb and the Levant a backyard. The whole of the east was their trading field, their wealth and civilization were already old when Venice was a handful of mud huts peopled by fishermen.[70]

Medieval People was Eileen Power's own demonstration of literary synthetic history, as espoused constantly through her reviewing in the *Nation and the Athenaeum* and the *Times Literary Supplement* during the 1920s. Power distinguished between history and research or scholarship. She saw writing history as an act of creative synthesis out of the raw material of historical research. Macaulay was a model, and not the contemporary developments of what she called 'scientific historians', 'busy substituting Clio, a Card Index, for Clio, a Muse'. 'Learned American professors', she declared, 'are too apt to throw a card index in the public's face.' Good research had to be followed by the analysis and selection of facts that went to make good history.[71] Collections such as the *Cambridge Ancient History* needed the guidance of a common mind to lift them above the level of an encyclopedia for historians.[72] Coulton had played a major role in approach and analysis in Power's first book, but she also adopted his views about

---

[70] Power, *Medieval People*, pp. 40, 46–8.
[71] Eileen Power, 'A study of the press', review of *The Newspaper and the Historian* by Lucy Maynard Salmon, *The Nation and the Athenaeum* (29 September 1923), 813; Eileen Power, 'The dark Rosaleen', *The Nation and the Athenaeum* (26 January 1924).
[72] Eileen Power, 'Joint stock history', *The Challenge* (7 September 1923), 476.

the historian's readership. She admired his ability to write history as literature, though avoiding his vituperative denunciation of his opponents, 'at a time when historical research has nearly killed history'.[73]

Power's reviewers caught the point of *Medieval People*, though several were somewhat bemused by the project. The book was thought to be 'more attractive than the average modern novel';[74] it was 'New History for Old'[75] with fine characterisations of figures who could not really be described as 'ordinary'.[76] And it was 'a border book' between history and literature, which had succeeded in satisfying both audiences.[77]

The women's history and the social history Eileen Power wrote during these years were made in the traditions of literature and history in which she had been trained; this was scholarly archival history, but it was not shaped by social or economic theory. In her aspirations to write social history, some of which she had absorbed from G. G. Coulton, she turned away from the constitutional and manorial history that provided the main framework for medievalists at the time. The models she then perceived as available to her lay in the biographical traditions, studies of characters, and commentaries on diarists and letter-writers long practised by popular female historians, few of whom were academics. Indeed it is likely that her older male mentors, Armstrong, Langlois and Coulton, were directing her towards what they perceived to be a literary and aesthetic kind of history most appropriate for a woman to write. But the legacy of the Coulton traditions can also be found in one of his male students who in turn saw himself as indebted to Eileen Power. This was H. S. Bennett, who pursued a social history of life and times, and included work on marriage, love and women's lives.[78]

Eileen Power took these traditions, but with sustained historical research went some way to turn the study of individuals into a new social history of institutions such as the nunneries and of the social

[73] Power, 'The problem of the friars', 753.
[74] 'Medieval people', *The Times Literary Supplement* (11 September 1924), 551.
[75] Sylvia Lynd, 'New history for old: *Medieval People* by Eileen Power', *Time and Tide* (5 December 1924), 1188–9.
[76] 'Round the library table', *Saturday Review* (13 September 1924), 269; 'Life in the Middle Ages', *The New Statesman*, 24 (11 October 1924), 18.
[77] M. M. Postan, 'Medieval people', *The Clare Market Review*, 5, 1 (1924), 27–8.
[78] See Thirsk, 'The history women', pp. 6–9. See also H. S. Bennett, *The Pastons and their England. Studies in an Age of Transition* (Cambridge, 1922); H. S. Bennett, *England from Chaucer to Caxton* (London, 1928); H. S. Bennett, *Life on the English Manor* (Cambridge, 1937).

classes she revealed in her essays on medieval women. The novelty of her approach lay in the diverse social groups she wrote of together with her ability to make their medieval experiences comprehensible to modern audiences. This was not a methodology Power worked out early in her writing and was to pursue consistently thereafter. She had aspired to theoretical approaches from the days of choosing her thesis subject, but she was not then, nor for some years after, in the kind of intellectual environment to encourage very helpful interchange between historians and the new social theorists.

IV

It was not social theory that was important to this stage of Eileen Power's writing, but political commitment. Power's social history was her response to the First World War. Social history was an intervention in internationalist politics. The reason for *Medieval People* lies as much in this part of Eileen Power's life as it does in debates on the methodology of history. Unlike Coulton, who had written pamphlets in the early years of the war calling for conscription, Power followed other members of the suffrage movement into a new pacifist movement. Her own personal experience, like that of most women of her generation, was loss of family members and friends at the front.

One of the major initiatives arising out of the suffrage movement in the post-war years was a women's peace movement. Eileen Power's friends Alice Clark and her sister Hilda were heavily involved throughout the war with the Quaker War Relief Campaign. Alice Clark was working at the time on her *Working Life of Women in the Seventeenth Century*. Other women Power knew were in the Union of Democratic Control and the Women's International League for Peace and Freedom. But Eileen Power chose the League of Nations Union, the largest and most popular of the peace organisations, and one with an internationalist rather than pacifist programme.[79] The League of Nations Union also had close links with the International Federation of University Women, which developed out of the Committee on International Relations of the British Federation of

[79] Johanna Alberti, *Beyond Suffrage. Feminists in War and Peace 1914–1928* (London, 1989), pp. 71–93; Swanwick, *I Have Been Young* (London, 1935); Martin Pugh, *Women and the Women's Movement in Britain, 1914–1959* (London, 1992), pp. 103–70. On the Peace Movement see Martin Ceadel, *Pacifism in Britain 1914–1945: The Defining of a Faith* (Oxford, 1980); Jill Liddington, *The Long Road to Greenham: Feminism and Anti-militarism in Britain since 1820* (London, 1989).

University Women, and out of an initiative taken by the dean of Barnard College, Virginia Gildersleeve. The International Federation pursued campaigns for peace and international understanding, and set up fellowships for study and travel abroad.[80] Eileen Power spoke to the International Federation in early 1932, describing it as 'a special sort of travel agency' for its members, who welcomed fellow scholars from abroad. There was, she said, 'no more powerful means of binding nations together than by the infinite multiplication of these tiny invisible threads of personal contact and mutual understanding'.[81]

By the time the First World War ended Eileen Power was lecturing frequently for the League of Nations Union. Her stand for international rather than national history, along with the historical presentation of the futility of war, was a popular literary theme also explored at the time in H. G. Wells' *An Outline of History* (1920) and the Hammonds' social histories.[82] J. L. and Barbara Hammond, friends of Eileen, wrote enormously successful books on the social history of the nineteenth century, but their message was much more overtly political than was hers. In the middle of the war they published *The Town Labourer*. In the framework of a book about the early nineteenth-century working class, the Hammonds argued that the war was the outcome of unbridled industrialism.[83]

Eileen Power, too, believed in using her position as a historian to attack militarism and nationalism. But she sought to do so through encouraging comparative and social history. She took up her cause when she started teaching at the LSE; she became closely involved in debates on schools history teaching, and she became famous for her schools broadcasts and childrens' history books. Her lucid writing style and her early efforts to write history for a broad literate public now took on a political urgency. She wrote history to change hearts and minds. One of her lectures on the League argued that direct democracy, an intense political life and active citizenship would promote an active peace and 'that power which alone can drive the

---

[80] See Dyhouse, *No Distinction of Sex?*, pp. 141 and 171–6. The British Federation of University Women was founded in 1909 to further opportunities for research and promotion of women in universities.

[81] See *ibid.*, p. 176.

[82] See J. L. Hammond and Barbara Hammond, *The Town Labourer 1760–1832: The New Civilization* (London, 1917).

[83] *Ibid.*, p. 189.

machinery of a League of Nations'.[84] Eileen Power's own practice during these years was as the historian-citizen.

The essays she wrote on international history and history teaching in schools will be analysed in a later chapter on world history. But it is important to emphasise here that her political activism in the post-war years fed into the history she wrote. She linked international peace movements to the teaching of history, arguing that the success of the League of Nations depended on testing an international community with similar historical ideas. She wrote a bibliography for the school history teacher who wished her subject to foster a sense of world citizenship without which a League of Nations would 'be like a machine lacking power to work it'. She counselled avoiding purely national histories by teaching European and world history, and especially by teaching social history which she argued laid more stress than did political history upon the likeness of nations.[85]

Eileen Power's approach to history during these years might be associated with the contemporary debunking of the heroic view of the past and of war which reached its apogee in Sellar and Yeatman's schoolboy send-up, *1066 and All That* (1930).[86] Raphael Samuel has even argued recently in his review of history in the National Curriculum that in these works we can find the liberal and progressive origins of the emphasis in the new history of the 1960s on world history.[87]

Power did not, however, see her work as part of this type of popularisation. Indeed, in a lecture she gave in the 1930s on 'Internationalism and the new history' she compared historical writing over the past and present, and specifically set her approach apart from that of Sellar and Yeatman. She argued that the old historians had written for the governing classes; they were literary men and philosophers, interpreting history with philosophy, but writing it as literature. They were followed by historians who became obsessed with minutiae and historical documents, and these lost their hold on the general public. The growth of popular education and extension of the franchise had opened a new demand for history but, as Power

---

84   Eileen Power, 'The League of Nations', n.d., Postan Papers; this was later revised as 'A plea for the Middle Ages', *Economica*, 5 (1922), 173–80.

85   Eileen Power, *A Bibliography for Teachers of History* (London, 1919), published by the Women's International League for Peace and Freedom.

86   This popular book was analysed recently by Raphael Samuel in 'One in the eye', *Times Educational Supplement* (18 May 1990), 16.

87   Raphael Samuel, 'Grand Narratives', *History Workshop Journal*, 29 (1990), 120–33, at 123.

put it, this was now read in 'queer forms'. Some of this was produced by journalists and some by the clever 'superior' young men who turned the wrong end of the telescope onto the great figures of the past so that they appeared ridiculous compared with ourselves. Such were Sellar and Yeatman, the writers for *Punch* and students in Evelyn Waugh's Oxford. Alongside these were historical novelists who wrote history and called it fiction. In recent years 'scientific historians' saw that their small monographs had little appeal. But none of these elite byways, satire, historical novels, or scientific history met the new broadly based demand for historical writing. The revulsion to the traumas of the First World War, and the hopes for a new internationalism, found new, politically articulate exponents among the recently enfranchised women and working men. History, in Eileen Power's view, mattered to this new citizenship as providing a framework for routes to new political and social orders. That history, in Power's view, had to include those formerly excluded from the franchise, and it had to provide the background on which to build international co-operation. It was thus that she explained the rise of a new kind of history of interest to ordinary people – social and economic history and world history.[88]

Eileen Power's immediate object in the post-war years and the early 1920s was focused on getting the message into schools. She started the New World History Series with Bernard Manning, wrote the first volume herself in 1920 and recruited several of her friends including M. G. Jones, Alice Gardner and Lucy Hanson to write later volumes. With her sister Rhoda she started a series of children's history books. The most well known of these was their first, *Boys and Girls of History*, published by Cambridge in 1926. With the old friend she had met on her Kahn Fellowship, Sir Edward Dennison Ross, she edited *The Broadway Travellers* in 1926, with G. G. Coulton *The Broadway Medieval Library*, and with her good friend at Girton Elizabeth Drew, she followed this with *The Broadway Diaries, Memoirs and Letters*.[89] For a wide reading public, she contributed her series on

---

[88] 'How history can foster international goodwill', newspaper report on a lecture by Eileen Power on 'Internationalism and the new history', n.d., Postan Papers.

[89] *The New World History Series*, ed. Eileen Power and B. L. Manning, 4 vols. (London, 1920). Book 1, Eileen Power, *From the Beginning to 1485* (London, 1920); Eileen Power and Sir Edward D. Ross (eds.), *The Broadway Travellers*, 26 vols. (London, 1926–38); Eileen Power and G. G. Coulton (eds.), *The Broadway Medieval Library*, 10 vols. (London, 1928–31); Eileen Power and Elizabeth Drew (eds.), *The Broadway Diaries, Memoirs and Letters*, 7 vols. (London, 1929–31).

foreign craftsmen, 'Alien immigrants and English arts and crafts', and her essay 'The opening of the land routes to Cathay'.[90]

All of these spread the message of social and comparative history, and presented themes of medieval and early modern history in a personalised approach deploying literary anecdote and verse. Eileen Power also found new frontiers in schools in which to use her literary knowledge, and her interests in history and literature. With A. W. Reed she edited six volumes of *English Life in English Literature* between 1928 and 1930, and in 1929 edited *Poems from the Irish*. She was also soon to discover the use of a new medium, radio, for reaching yet wider audiences, and especially children.

Eileen Power's views on, as well as her successful practice in, the writing of social history in her early works were thus deeply bound up with her political ideas. If feminism and methodology formed part of the framework for *Medieval People*, so too did internationalism and education. *Medieval People* also reflected Power's internationalist politics in the years during and following the First World War. It was clear that this was a book about the social rather rather than the military side of history.[91] The subjects tackled in the book, drawn as they were from several European countries and China, and emphasising the place of long-distance trade and travel, revealed an internationalism in her approach to social history that was to distinguish her from Coulton and later from Trevelyan. The book started with the simple Carolingian peasant, and with the newest of all the branches of history, economic history. And with these she made her famous proclamation, one that was put in a way which perhaps only a female historian would phrase it:

We still praise famous men, for he would be a poor historian who could spare one of the great figures who have shed glory or romance upon the page of history; but we praise them with due recognition of the fact that not only great individuals, but people as a whole, unnamed and undistinguished masses of people, now sleeping in unknown graves, have also been concerned in the story. Our fathers that begat us have come to their own at last. As Acton put it, 'The great historian now takes his meals in the kitchen.' This book is chiefly concerned with the kitchens of History.[92]

---

[90]   Eileen Power, 'Alien immigrants and English arts and crafts', *Home-reading Magazine* (October 1922–May 1923); Eileen Power, 'The opening of the land routes to Cathay', in Newton (ed.), *Travel and Travellers of the Middle Ages*, pp. 142–58.

[91]   'Life in the Middle Ages', *The New Statesman*, 24 (11 October 1924), 18.

[92]   Power, *Medieval People*, p. 19.

CHAPTER 6

The LSE, economic history and the social sciences
1921–1940

Eileen Power moved to London and the LSE on her return from her Kahn Travelling Fellowship in September 1921. The LSE was a very different institution from Cambridge, and with it went a whole new way of approaching economic history. Power's closest association there in her early years was with R. H. Tawney, and their complementary ideas of economic history informed the evolving structure of teaching the subject at the LSE. These were the years during which Power's sociological and comparative approach was developed and matured, and her message spread through her teaching. They were also the years in which economic history was institutionalised through the creation of a society and a journal, and Eileen Power took a leading part in both these ventures.

I

Eileen Power finally decided to go to the LSE while she was in Peking. The prospect, however, was daunting – after eight years teaching in a Cambridge women's college, she was to move to the metropolis to teach in a new university with a mixed student body and a progressive social scientific stance. All of this was to take place within three weeks of her return home from her world tour. Despite the anxieties she expressed when she first received the offer, there was never much doubt that she would accept the post. It would provide an outlet for the new directions she sought in writing history, as well as the opportunity to live in London. Eileen's more intimate letters to Margery Garrett had for some years conveyed her feelings of being confined if not imprisoned in Cambridge. Once she had accepted the job she also felt vindicated in her feelings about Cambridge's treatment of female students and academics. The vote in Cambridge against giving women university degrees and making

6.1   Eileen Power at the London School of Economics

them full members of the university continued to make her very angry, and she wrote about it to Bertrand Russell shortly after she started at the LSE. 'Cambridge really has cut our throats now: it would have been much better to get nothing than to get the titular degree ... our position in the university exactly where it was. I've never felt so bitter in my life.'[1]

The first priority was finding somewhere to live. Though Eileen preferred to live alone, she expected to 'go into digs' for a term, then to find someone to share a flat with. 'I'd rather live alone, but don't think I can afford it.'[2] She went back initially to the Ebury Street flat she had shared with Karin Costelloe.

[1]   Power to Bertrand Russell, 20 October 1921, Bertrand Russell Papers, McMaster University, Hamilton, Canada.
[2]   Power to MLG, 21 July 1921.

Eileen's transition from world traveller to LSE lecturer was bridged in other ways by the Russell household, with which she stayed in close touch during her early months back in England. No longer in awe of the Bertrand Russell of her Court Place student days, she was now a close friend of 'Bertie' and Dora. They asked her, with Russell's brother, Frank, to witness their marriage shortly before the birth of their baby. Dora described the scene at a registry office in Battersea, 'myself now rather large in a black cloak'. Eileen and Frank Russell had arrived first, and 'Frank alleged that the Registrar was on the point of marrying them, when we came in the nick of time'.[3]

Eileen followed Bertrand Russell's lectures and journalism on China, seeking out and sending him American newspaper cuttings,[4] and took a sisterly concern in the birth of the Russell baby. She wrote to Russell in November, 'I am delighted to hear that Snooks is already adorning a less restricted sphere ... I will remember that his name is John Conrad, but I shall never, never think of him as anything but Snooks!'[5] Letters characteristic of this stage of their friendship ranged from babies and prams to Einstein and China.[6]

When Eileen went to the LSE she saw herself as joining a more cosmopolitan environment with more opportunities for women than Cambridge had offered. A later vote in 1923 for women's degrees in Cambridge did succeed, but women were not made full members of the university until 1948. The LSE, by contrast, had been co-educational from the time it opened in 1895, and the University of London had opened its degrees to women in 1878, long before Oxford and Cambridge had done so.[7]

At the LSE there was already a strong women's presence, not just among the students but among the staff. The LSE developed the social sciences, which University College had failed to do, and the presence of women in a new subject at a new institution was unmistakable. The first students included five women and four men brought from the University Extension Movement by Graham Wallas. The first LSE research studentships in 1896 went to three

3   Russell, *The Tamarisk Tree*, p. 149.
4   Power to Bertrand Russell, 24 and 25 October 1921, Russell Papers.
5   Power to Bertrand Russell, 17 November 1921; also see letter of 22 February 1922, enquiring about John Conrad's visit to the doctor, Russell Papers.
6   Power to Russell, 21 November 1921, Russell Papers.
7   Harte and North, *The World of University College London*; N. B. Harte, *The Admission of Women to University College London: A Centenary Lecture* (London, 1979), pp. 6, 21.

women and one man, and between 1897 and 1932, ten of the twenty-
seven research studentships went to women. Four women including
Eileen Power and Alice Clark shared in the ten Shaw research
studentships awarded between 1904 and 1915, and there were
thirteen female winners of the Hutchinson silver medal for research
out of thirty-two awards between 1900 and 1932.[8] Of the total of two
hundred on the regular teaching staff between 1895 and 1932, forty-
three were women, proportions at least comparable to those on
university teaching staffs today.[9] The estimates for the numbers of
female tutors and lecturers in London compared favourably with
estimates for the rest of the country; they were between 13 and 20 per
cent, depending on the categories for including women on the
university staff. There was effectively no change in the proportions of
women teaching in British universities between the 1920s and the
1970s. Similarly, the proportions of women in senior posts did not
improve at all over the period up to the 1970s.[10]

The presence of women at the LSE was certainly noticeable, in
contrast to their impact at Cambridge. It was all too much for some
men. Esmé Wingfield Stratford was the author of a book entitled *The
History of English Patriotism*, a man of conservative political views and
quaint ideas on women. After King's College, Cambridge where he
did his first degree, he went on to the LSE which impressed him as
'not so much of a school at all, as a collection of earnest fanatics,
principally women. Principally at any rate as far as tone and
influence are concerned for the male students played a comparatively
humble part ... It was not the male students who really counted in
the L.S.E. The dynamic impetus was imparted by the ladies.'
Stratford thought the real core of the School was in the body of 'lady
students': 'I am not sure they would have liked to be called by this
name ... they were emphatically and consciously women, and
women with the most enormous W's ... Woman with a big W, had
something more earnest to think about. She had the Cause with a
big C, or possibly two or three Causes.'[11]

By the 1930s the feminist presence subsided, and a number of
women who came to the LSE to study then did not see themselves as

8   *LSE Register*, pp. 219–29.
9   *Ibid.*, p. xv; information from staff office, registry, University of Warwick and personnel
    office, LSE.
10 Dyhouse, *No Distinction of Sex?*, p. 138.
11 E. Wingfield Stratford, *Before the Lamps Went Out. Autobiographical Reminiscences* (London,
    1945), p. 192. I owe this reference to Negley Harte.

distinctive. They were studying, if not in equal proportions with men, then in the relatively good proportions for the day of at least one woman to four men. Many, therefore, no longer saw the need for a feminist perspective on their lives and careers.[12]

For Eileen Power, just coming from Cambridge (and now with a rather differerent attitude from that she had held on her first encounter with the LSE, as a candidate for the Shaw fellowship), the LSE was refreshingly open, with easy access to a range of exciting personalities on the staff and a mixed student body of different ages, experience and nationality. Sociability and personal relationships with staff were important. There were no departments and the atmosphere was 'one of appealing amateurishness when practically no-one was teaching the subject in which he or she had taken a first degree, and few paraded their expertise'.[13] An unhierarchical, anti-snobbery atmosphere prevailed. H. L. Beales, a social historian at the LSE from the 1930s onwards, recalled an institution in the 1920s that was 'informal, associative and free'. It was a 'friendly place where there was no kind of barrier between the good and the great and the humble lecturers like myself. But after the Second World War it was "never quite the same", as it became "more stereotyped, more departmentalised." '[14]

The staff consisted of a whole series of highly individual characters. Eveline (Richardson) Burns' recollections of her teachers there catches the atmosphere. There were the economists A. L. Bowley and H. S. Foxwell, 'rather wraith-like figures with drooping mustaches'. Eileen Power exchanged clerihews with Bowley in the common room: from Eileen there was:

> Holy, Holy, Holy
> Arthur Lionel Bowley
> Decomposing Slowly

to which Bowley responded:

[12] Conversation with Dr Jean Floud, who was a student at the LSE 1933–6, and later taught there, 1947–61.
[13] Recollection of Jack Fisher, cited in David Ormrod, 'R. H. Tawney and the origins of capitalism', *History Workshop*, 18 (1984), 138–59, at 142.
[14] T. C. Barker, 'Interview with H. L. A. Beales', video recording, 1976, University of Kent archives. Hugh Lancelot Beales (1889–1988) was lecturer in economic history at the LSE 1926–31, then reader 1931–56. He wrote *The Industrial Revolution* (1929) and *Early English Socialists* (1932). He was editorial advisor to Penguin and Pelican Books until 1945; *Who Was Who* (London, 1990).

Eileen Power
Blooms like a Flower
Things will come to a pretty pass
When she withers like grass.[15]

Burns remembered the other great LSE economist Edwin Cannan as a 'frugal man'. 'When I had to substitute for him he would send me a package containing a complete lecture typed out word for word on the backs of paper shopping bags or of private correspondence, all tied together by one of his wife's staylaces.'[16] Then there was Lilian Knowles, always noticeable for her flamboyant hats. She was an 'ardent imperialist who was always reminding the Indian students how fortunate they were to be part of the British Empire. She was known as Britannia, for she had the same ample figure and always lectured holding her pointer like a trident.'[17] She 'combined outspoken anti-sacerdotalism and anti-snobbery with violent Toryism'.[18] Knowles was a Conservative, but was also one of the few female academics of her generation with a child. Motherhood did not, however, affect her views on social policy. When Beveridge introduced a scheme of family allowances for the LSE staff she opposed it, arguing it was a premium on irresponsibility, for it would make a colleague with five children immensely better off than she, with only one.[19]

Eveline Burns also remembered that when she married Arthur Burns, Hugh Dalton[20] and Knowles were very kind, and were concerned lest I ' "start having babies right away", and gave me detailed advice about contraception and where to purchase supplies – this at a time when birth control was almost a taboo subject. I well remember the frisson that went through the class when Dalton in a lecture on population casually remarked "of course we all know that it is possible to control births by the the use of contraceptives." '[21]

Eileen's colleagues at the LSE during the 1920s also included a

---

[15] Recollection of Lady Cynthia Postan; Bowley's answering clerihew was quoted in the *Clare Market Review* (April 1931), 8.

[16] Eveline M. Burns, 'My LSE: 1916–1926', *LSE Magazine*, 66 (November 1983), 8–9. Eveline Burns was assistant then assistant lecturer in economics 1921–8.

[17] Burns, 'My LSE', 8.

[18] Harris, *William Beveridge*, pp. 264–5.

[19] W. H. Beveridge, *The London School of Economics and its Problems 1919–1937* (London, 1960), p. 49.

[20] Dalton at the time was reader in economics at the LSE, and pursued a moderate socialist economics.

[21] Burns, 'My LSE', 9.

new generation of scholars. Harold Laski came from Harvard in the
year she joined the School. Laski was at this time a liberal internationalist, but he later turned to Marxism.[22] Edwin Cannan was succeeded
(though briefly) in 1927 by Allyn Young from Harvard.[23] The other
economists were a politically diverse group including Theodore
Gregory, Hugh Dalton, Lionel Robbins and F. A. Hayek. Sociology
was taught by L. T. Hobhouse and Morris Ginsberg. Anthropology
was taught by Bronislaw Malinowski and Raymond Firth.[24]

   Sir William Beveridge was the director; he had come to the LSE
only a few years before, and he was to remain there as director until
1937, for most of Eileen Power's career. During these years he built
the LSE up to the major centre for the social sciences in Britain; its
premises were tripled in size, and its annual budget grew sevenfold.[25]
Beveridge also carried on some idiosyncratic research on the history
of prices. This combined the search for social laws with inductivism,
using five female research assistants to gather enormous quantities of
price data ranging from medieval to modern times. He never
connected the project in any way with the the work of the economic
historians at the School, and he never finished it.[26] The work was
fundamentally flawed by Beveridge's single-minded quest for the
mechanism of the trade cycle in factors affecting the price of wheat;
and he thought the secret of these lay in astronomy and meteorology.

[22] See Isaac Kramnick and Barry Sheerman, *Harold Laski. A Life on the Left* (Harmondsworth, 1993), pp.153–291.
[23] Allyn A. Young was professor of political economy at the LSE from 1927 to 1929, when he died suddenly. He was previously professor of economics at Harvard, and was a member of the Economics Consultative Committee of the League of Nations from 1928. He wrote *Outlines of Economics* (1907 and later editions) and *Economic Problems New and Old* (1927), as well as a famous article, 'Increasing returns and economic progress', *Economic Journal*, 38 (1928).
[24] Harris, *William Beveridge*, p. 271. Theo Gregory started to teach economics at the LSE in 1913, and became a professor in 1926. Lionel Robbins (1898–1984) was assistant lecturer, then lecturer and professor of economics at the LSE 1925–61. F. A. Hayek (1899–1991) was professor of economics at the LSE 1931–50. L. T. Hobhouse (1864–1929), a philosopher, was lecturer then professor of sociology at the LSE 1904–29. Morris Ginsberg became an assistant in sociology in 1921, a reader in 1924 and a professor in 1930. Bronislaw Malinowski, the leading anthropologist of his generation, was educated in Cracow, then came to the LSE in 1910. He became professor in 1927. Raymond Firth was an occasional lecturer in anthropology at the LSE 1924–32, then lecturer until 1935. He became a reader in 1935 and professor in 1944. See *LSE Register*, pp. 217–66; *Who was Who, Who's Who*.
[25] Harris, *William Beveridge*, p. 261.
[26] Beveridge, after leaving the project for a number of years, did attempt to pick it up again, and wrote to Power, making a few overtures of some form of collaboration with M. M. Postan, then a lecturer in economic history at the LSE. Beveridge to Power, 7 April 1932, William Beveridge Papers, BLPES.

He was not interested in linking his price data with specific structural and institutional factors, and many of his academic contemporaries were suspicious of his efforts.[27]

Beveridge's secretary and the school administrator was Jessy Mair, and she was the thorn in otherwise harmonious memories many held of the LSE. She was married to a cousin of Beveridge, and came to the School first as business secretary in 1919, then as academic secretary in 1921. She rapidly asserted herself, and the directorship was soon effectively a partnership. She eventually married Beveridge after her husband's death in 1942, but carried on a long platonic affair with him before this.[28] She was regarded by many on the staff as a meddler and was much disliked. One of Eileen's contemporaries on the staff was Harold Laski, the controversial radical. His wife, Frida, described Mrs Mair as 'a dragon who bullied the staff and hated Harold'. Her approach put a stop to conversation in the hallways, and there was no rapprochement over 'breaking the bread' at lunch.[29] Mrs Mair took an early dislike to Eileen, and tried at various points to block promotions and salary increases for her.

With its personalities, the other big difference the LSE offered from Cambridge was a political vitality, and close involvement with the issues of the day. Eileen's friend Mary Stocks was an undergraduate there just before the First World War, and was inspired by a teaching staff that was itself making social and political history.

There was the Irish Question – and we had Irish students ... Norman Angel's 'Great Illusion' had been published – he came to talk to us about it. The women's suffrage agitation was in an acute phase and for some weeks two policemen were posted at the gardens of Clements Inn from which Christabel Pankhurst was on the run – and they never caught her.[30]

Indeed, what the LSE offered was political diversity combined with a progressive social and educational stance. Some members of the School fitted its associations with socialism and Fabianism, but equally important to its make-up was a radical Milnerite con-

27 Harris, *William Beveridge*, pp. 285–6.
28 For a careful assessment of the relationship between Beveridge and Mair, see Ralph Dahrendorf, *A History of the London School of Economics and Political Science 1895–1995* (Oxford, 1995).
29 Kramnick and Sheerman, *Harold Laski*, p. 322.
30 Cited in Janet Beveridge, *An Epic of Clare Market: Birth and Early Days of the London School of Economics* (London, 1960), pp. 80–1.

servatism and opposition to free trade.[31] Both political strands
favoured an extension of state intervention. Beatrice Webb in 1895
set out her view of the politics of the LSE as academic excellence
within a collectivist framework.[32]

When Eileen Power arrived, new political issues were on the
agenda, and the LSE staff was no less involved. The political frisson
of Eileen's time in India was revived again at the School when the
Dyer incident became the subject of a notorious libel case, *O'Dwyer v
Nair*, in 1924.[33] This went over once again the whole debate on the
Dyer episode, or the Amritsar Massacre, in which General Dyer had
ordered troops to fire on a crowd, killing 379 people. This had
dominated politics during Eileen's visit to India in the autumn of
1920. One of the members of the jury on the libel case was Harold
Laski, who intervened with a number of embarrassing questions to
General Dyer, and entered the sole dissenting voice on what was
eventually agreed as a majority verdict in favour of the plaintiff. The
incident established Laski's commitment to Indian independence.[34]
Re-entry into academic life, by going to the LSE, was not a break for
Eileen from that feeling of active participation in world politics she
had experienced on her world tour.

Eileen had her own early experience of political conflict when she
was invited during her first term at the LSE to dine with the Webbs.
The dinner was not a success, and Eileen wrote to Bertrand Russell
afterwards: 'I don't think I ever shall be [asked] again for we nearly
came to blows over the relative merits of China and Japan!'[35]

II

Economic history, from the early years of the School, played a
unifying role, providing a discipline with the ammunition for prac-

[31] Harris, *William Beveridge*, pp. 264–5; and José Harris, 'The Webbs, the COS and the Ratan
     Tata Foundation: social policy from the perspective of 1912', in M. A. Bulmer, J. Lewis
     and D. Piachaud (eds.), *The Goals of Social Policy* (London, 1989), pp. 27–63.
[32] Beatrice Webb, *The Diaries of Beatrice Webb*, ed. Norman and Jean MacKenzie, 4 vols.
     (London 1982–5), vol. II, p. 85.
[33] Sir Michael O'Dwyer had been the civilian lieutenant-governor of the Punjab when the
     massacre happened. Sir Sankaran Nair, an eminent Indian jurist, had written a book,
     Gandhi and Anarchy, published in 1922, accusing O'Dwyer of terrorism in the events.
     O'Dwyer then sued Nair for libel.
[34] Kramnick and Sheerman, *Harold Laski*, pp. 220–2.
[35] Power to Bertrand Russell, December 1921, Russell Papers; Webb, *Diaries*, vol. II, 16
     February 1922, p. 396.

6.2   R. H. Tawney at work on WEA affairs, early 1930s

tical policy by tariff reformers on the one hand, and by the ethical R. H. Tawney and the socialist Webbs on the other. Eileen Power entered into the spirit of this, working with Tawney to build the ethical foundations of social history, with Laski to deploy medieval political ideas in current politics, and developing her lecture series to build on her internationalist and pacifist sentiments, which found fertile ground at the LSE.

Power's closest early association at the LSE was with R. H. Tawney. It was with him that she organised her teaching, and together they produced *Tudor Economic Documents*[36] in 1924, one of the most long-lived texts of undergraduate history teaching. When Power joined Tawney at the LSE he was already well known for his

[36]   R. H. Tawney and Eileen Power, *Tudor Economic Documents*, 3 vols. (London, 1924). Tawney later wrote in his obituary of Power that she was responsible herself for finding a number of new documents which went into the collection. See Tawney, 'Eileen Power', *Economic History Review*, 10 (1940), 91–4.

first book, *The Agrarian Problem in the Sixteenth Century*, published in 1912, and was developing his work on religion and capitalism, the first results of which appeared in *The Acquisitive Society* in 1921. Tawney had a class background and variety of experience of great appeal to Eileen. He was born in India, the son of a Sanskrit scholar, and educated at Rugby and Balliol College, Oxford. After Balliol, he had taught at Glasgow and led the first WEA tutorial classes. This was followed by work for the Oxford University Tutorial Classes Committee, directing the Ratan Tata Foundation at the LSE, and finally being severely wounded at the Somme. After piecing together new WEA work with a fellowship at Balliol in 1918, he was appointed to a lectureship at the LSE in 1919.[37]

Tawney had the donnish background she understood, but his WEA leadership was an inspiration to her own views on history and citizenship, and her work for schools. Tawney was not so much older, being in his early forties when Eileen came to the LSE at the age of thirty-two, and he had been in an economic history post there for only a relatively brief time. They were, therefore, able to build together the courses that were effectively to create the new fields of economic and social history both at the LSE and elsewhere.

They taught joint courses and corresponded about course changes and developments, and Power was eager to step in to do Tawney's teaching during the time he was ill in the year after she arrived.[38] Eileen Power worked with Tawney on a day-to-day basis, and lived virtually next door to him. There is little in the way of correspondence or other papers to throw light upon the personal relationship between Eileen Power and Tawney. Recollections convey something of the closeness of their friendship. Beales remembered Tawney's affection for Eileen as one which it 'would be hard to overestimate'.[39] Barbara Wootton noticed that Tawney's feelings for Eileen were special, for 'with the spectacular exception of Eileen Power he did not warm to intellectual women'.[40] Others were more

---

[37] J. M. Winter, 'Introduction' in Winter (ed.), *History and Society*, pp. 1–36; Ross Terrill, *R. H. Tawney and his Times* (London, 1974), pp. 21–47.

[38] Power to Beveridge, 24 September 1922, Power personal file, LSE.

[39] Cited in Terrill, *R. H. Tawney and his Times*, p. 66.

[40] Cited in *ibid.*, p. 82. Barbara Wootton (née Adam) was educated at Girton, then was director of studies in economics there 1920–2. She worked for the TUC and the Labour Party research department 1922–6. She was director of studies for tutorial classes in the University of London 1927–44, then became reader in social studies in 1944. See *Girton College Register*.

direct, and said that he loved her. In 1930, before he went to China, Tawney wrote to Laski at length, setting out why the vacant chair in economic history should go to Power.[41] Eileen Power's death was the one that devastated him more than any other.[42]

The great partnership of the 1920s was that of Tawney and Power. This was a partnership between two very different approaches to economic history. While he provided inspiration, Tawney was not at all the same kind of historian as Eileen Power. He was a Christian and a socialist prophet.[43] Her earlier background was the anti-Catholic stance of G. G. Coulton which, though she thought it went to ideological excess, nevertheless appealed to her own secular preferences. Power never aspired to write history in the same way or with the same kind of conviction as Tawney. While Power believed that history was a way of explaining the present, Tawney took this much further to explore fundamental truths. He chose a personal engagement with the processes of history, and explored 'the interplay of ideas and material forms in history'.[44] Jack Fisher, who succeeded Tawney at the LSE, set out the kind of position Tawney held during the 1920s:

> The most widely read historians were Tawney and the Hammonds ... [but] neither claimed to be economic historians. They were very similar: the Hammonds were classical scholars and what they tried to explain was why an upper class with a classical education could allow the things that they thought happened during the Industrial Revolution to actually happen. Now Tawney above all else was a Christian and what interested him was why an upper class which claimed to be Christian could have allowed history to take the way it did.[45]

Power, by contrast, had no religious convictions, and moved her history from the time she came to the LSE from the study of religious communities towards a much more materialist economic history. Her internationalism prompted an interest in merchants and trade, and her lecture series from her first years at the LSE developed these

---

41   Tawney to Laski, letter in possession of the late Lance Beales, cited in Terrill, *R. H. Tawney and his Times*, p. 67. Discussion of the chair, frozen since 1926, and an earlier candidate, W. R. Rees, are in the Beveridge Papers: Beveridge to Sidney Webb, 25 May 1926; J. Mair to Beveridge, n.d. [1926], Beveridge Papers.

42   Recollection of Lance Beales, cited in Terrill, *R. H. Tawney and his Times*, p. 107; Tawney to J. U. Nef, 22 August 1940, cited in *ibid.*

43   Ormrod, 'R. H. Tawney', 140.

44   Cited in *ibid.*, on p. 141.

45   Cited in *ibid.*, on p. 140.

interests. From the later 1920s, furthermore, she was concentrating on the medieval cloth trade.

The Christian socialist framework of Tawney's thought informed his books *The Agrarian Problem, The Acquisitive Society* and *Religion and the Rise of Capitalism*. Tawney's study of religion and capitalism analysed the break with the traditional social ethics of the medieval church.[46] He found in Puritanism a new moral dynamic for early modern English society, but the legacy of Calvinism was contradictory, both applauding economic virtues and condemning economic licence. Tawney's analysis of Puritanism revealed a marked preference for the 'soldier-saints and the prophets rather than the merchants and businessmen'.[47]

When Eileen Power came to the LSE she was about to publish her book *Medieval English Nunneries*. This established her as an authority on English monasticism; she was not, however, a historian of religious ideas, but a social historian of religion. Her prior work in the history of ideas, as in 'Medieval ideas about women' and 'The cult of the virgin', was set in a feminist and social historical framework. With her agnosticism and much more materialist approach she was a very different historian of religious life from Tawney.

Alongside Tawney's writing on the role played by religious ideas in the rise of capitalism, however, must be placed his economic history lectures at the LSE. These were developed in parallel with Eileen Power's lectures, and a comparison of the topics and lines of analysis offered by both reveals many overlapping themes. While Tawney's books may have dwelt on soldier-saints, his lectures were about the commercial origins of capitalism – trade, finance and mercantile activity. He gave a series of lectures covering the period up to the Restoration, including topics on exploration and geographical discoveries, international finance, the revolution in prices, and commerce and commercial companies. He particularly emphasised the expansion of international trade and the rise of the absolutist state.[48] Tawney's emphasis on the commercial side of capitalism in these lectures runs parallel to similar themes explored by Power in her lectures on the medieval economy. Tawney has been credited with providing a Christian socialist critique of the history of capitalism, along with avoiding a nostalgia for the Middle Ages as a rural

---

[46] Winter (ed.), *History and Society*, p. 19.
[47] Ormrod, 'R. H. Tawney', 146.
[48] This summary of Tawney's lecturing follows up points made by Ormrod, *ibid.*, 147–8.

utopia. Eileen Power, working alongside him, was providing the new
medieval history that gave equally little credence to such nostalgia.
Her lectures at the LSE at the same time portrayed medieval society
in motion, with an emphasis similar to Tawney's on international
connections, trade, merchants and manufacturers, and travellers.

These two figures, the saintly man and the secular, elegant
woman, created the new face of economic history at the LSE. Two
more contrasting personalities would be difficult to find. Their lives
were intertwined in many ways, but they lived completely differently.
Within months of arriving at the LSE, Eileen Power found the house
where she spent most of the rest of her life. This was a half-house at
20 Mecklenburgh Square, which she shared with her old friend from
Girton, M. G. Beard. Beard had left her fellowship at Girton, and
was now head of Crofton Grange School; she would use the house at
weekends. The house was only two doors down from Tawney's.
Eileen wrote to Coulton of her pleasure when she found the place:
'My idea of life is to have enormous quantities of friends, but to live
alone. And I do not know whether Girton or the study of medieval
nunneries did more to convince me that I was not born to live in a
community.'[49]

The social gatherings at these two virtually adjacent flats in
Mecklenburgh Square often included the same people and some of
the same discussions. But they were in every other way completely
different. Of Tawney's flat, Ross Terrill has written: 'There was no
Bloomsbury smartness about the gatherings in Mecklenburgh
Square. Nor did they brim with ideological zeal ... Rather, the talk
was of history, economics, and how to change England without
wrecking it.' In the 1930s the domestic chaos in Mecklenburgh
Square was noticeable amidst the highpoints of the conversation:

Tawney wore his sergeant's jacket. His pipe he would empty into the cuff of
his tweed trousers. Bits of half-eaten food sat among piles of books ... But
Tawney's imperious bearing was not shaken. The young, such as Postan,
Gaitskell and Durbin, were undeterred: 'We were prepared to sit and listen,
amused by the wit and aptness of his language and enraptured by the image
of the man himself, to us the greatest living Englishman.'[50]

A few doors down, at number 20, Eileen's Mecklenburgh Square flat
was filled with beautiful things, some of them from the packing case

[49] Power to Coulton, 30 January 1922.
[50] M. M. Postan, 'Hugh Gaitskell', cited in Terrill, *R. H. Tawney and his Times*, p. 79.

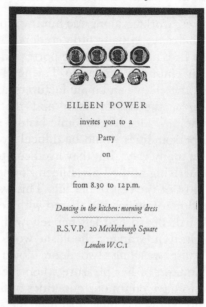

EILEEN POWER

invites you to a

Party

on

from 8.30 to 12 p.m.

Dancing in the kitchen: morning dress

R.S.V.P. *20 Mecklenburgh Square*

London W.C.1

6.3   Invitation to 'Dancing in the kitchen'

she had sent home from China, and presided over by her highly
competent daily housekeeper, Mrs Saville. Mrs Saville did all the
cooking, and arranged the dinner parties that graced this rather
different gathering place. Eileen wore her Chinese dresses, or
fashionable outfits bought in Paris. (It was said that every time she
got an article published she would go to Croydon, and take a flight
on Imperial Airways to Paris, buy herself a new dress, then return.[51])
She arranged frequent and memorable 'kitchen dances' in the basement of the Mecklenburgh Square house: her guests included
Humbert Wolfe, Tawney, Laski, Charles Webster, Michael
Clapham, and from later in the 1920s, Michael Moissey (known as
Munia) Postan.[52]

Eileen particularly delighted in taking friends for dancing at her
club, the Gargoyle in Soho, a nightclub frequented by writers and

---

[51]   Recollections of Sir Michael and Elizabeth Clapham, 21 July 1993.
[52]   Interview with Sir Michael Clapham, 21 July 1993. Humbert Wolfe (1886–1940) was a
major civil servant and poet. He wrote and edited over forty books and was a well-known
reviewer for the weeklies; *Twentieth Century DNB*. Charles Webster was the professor of
international history at the LSE from 1932, and Michael Clapham was Professor John
Clapham's son. He was at this time apprenticed as a printer to Cambridge University
Press. He later became a company director.

intellectuals. Jazz and dance bands dominated an L-shaped room; it was the place to go to run into friends and acquaintances, and definitely a sought-after place to take visitors and friends who were not members. This only continued, however, until when in 1933 she tried to bring in Paul Robeson, and he was refused entry because he was black. She went home and wrote a letter of resignation, and never returned to the place again.[53]

III

These were the two leading personalities who shaped the economic history teaching at the LSE during the 1920s. With Tawney and Eileen Power, and later M. M. Postan, medieval and Tudor and seventeenth-century history easily dominated not just economic history teaching, but teaching in the social sciences generally at the LSE. Students flocked to their lectures, and remembered them in later years. Eileen Power's lectures always filled large lecture halls. Students from all subjects at the LSE attended; hers and Laski's were known as the lectures to attend. Indeed, Eileen Power saw her teaching in medieval history as making a unique contribution to the social sciences. She regarded her lectures in the same light as radio broadcasts, and perfected clarity and presentation.[54] She always wrote them out in point form, but with a fairly full text. Her argument was always built up layer on layer, and her points were set out with a rich texture of literary anecdote, verse and allusion. She deployed narrative as her own literary device, holding her audience to her argument as if she was telling a story. She was not a charismatic lecturer in the sense of one who speaks spontaneously, and easily deploys rhetorical flourish. Laski's lectures, for instance, were always memorable for starting with phrases such as 'Well, I just saw the PM yesterday'; Webster's were full of gossip; Lionel Robbins' were exciting, delivered from a few notes on a card as if he was having a conversation with himself.[55] Eileen Power was different. She made an immense impression on everyone, and was remem-

[53] Interview with Sir Michael Clapham, 12 July 1993.
[54] See her views on lecturing in 'Too many lectures spoil the student', *The Clare Market Review*, 12, 2 (Lent term, 1932), 7–8, 7–8; The late Dorothy Marshall wrote an extended and laudatory description of Eileen Power's lectures in her diary. Diary extracts sent to author.
[55] Interview with Nadine Marshall (née Hamburg), student at the LSE 1933–6. After graduating she translated the work of Alfons Dopsch with M. G. Beard at Power's suggestion. She was married to T. H. Marshall.

bered as absolutely exceptional. She had a cool demeanour and a distinction that impressed all who heard her. She was methodical; though she wrote out her lectures virtually in full, she knew the stages of her argument so well that few realised she had a written text. Her students remembered vivid lectures lucidly delivered by a beautifully dressed and brilliant woman.[56] Dorothy Marshall described the effect on her at the time as a young student:

she would flash one charming smile round the room, take you all into her confidence & then start lecturing in her low trilling voice. She seldom joked or played to the gallery more than most lecturers but when she did ... it swayed you to mirth or indignation just as she wished ... I think it was her voice & that smile that demanded and entreated at the same time.[57]

Power had a very good rapport with students. Some of the undergraduates were in awe of her mainly due to her reputation, but those in her seminars were attracted by an open, eager face and a supportive seminar leader, adept at interacting and bringing people together. Her graduate students were a very mixed group of part-time older students, some of whom had come from unconventional educational backgrounds or had done unexpectedly badly in their examinations and others who were the bright sparks of their years. She put a lot of time into making up the deficiencies in their backgrounds, getting them all to work together and finding opportunities for them afterwards.[58]

When Eileen Power first arrived at the LSE, the economic history courses were shared between Lilian Knowles' industrial revolution and empire courses and Tawney's sixteenth- and seventeenth-century economic history and history of social and economic thought courses, with some medieval lectures and the medieval economic history seminar presided over by Hubert Hall. Power first slotted into pre-existing courses on the history of the modern world, and contributed to the general series on medieval economic history, but within a year she was giving new core lecture series on the economic

[56] Recollections of Nancy Raphael, 5 April 1995.
[57] Dorothy Marshall, diaries, 1922. Dorothy Marshall (1900–94) was educated at Girton under Eileen Power, then did research at the LSE under Lilian Knowles. She taught afterwards at Bedford College, Durham, and then at Cardiff, where she stayed as lecturer then reader 1936–67. Her books included *The English Poor in the Eighteenth Century: A Study in Social and Administrative History* (1926); *The Rise of George Canning* (1938); and *English People in the Eighteenth Century* (1956).
[58] Interview with Elizabeth Crittall, 27 November 1991. Cf. Eileen Power's notebook on her research students in London 1922–6, which shows the wide range of backgrounds, ages and first degree results of her students: Power–Postan papers.

history of western Europe in the Middle Ages, and a special series, 'Everyday life in the Middle Ages', based on what she was writing for *Medieval People*. By 1923 she was running a seminar on the economic and social history of Tudor England with Tawney, and her own seminar on medieval trade. Both seminars were flanked by their own lecture courses, with hers on medieval economic history and Tawney's on the Tudor period.

By the autumn of 1926 Lilian Knowles had died; H. L. Beales was hired to cover some of her courses, and he was soon joined in this by Vera Anstey.[59] Power took over Knowles' course on the industrial revolution, 'The growth of English industry'. In addition she split her old lecture course on the history of the modern world into one on the West and one on the East, and covered the lectures on both. Another new lecturer, Valentine Judges, joined Power in running the modern European history course, and he later went on to lecture in her place in several of the core European and world history courses. Eileen Power's research student and assistant, M. M. Postan, now joined her in the seminar on medieval trade, and mounted his own lecture course on the trade of northern Europe in the later Middle Ages. Tawney continued with his lecture and seminar courses on the sixteenth and seventeenth centuries, and Hubert Hall kept up his seminars on medieval famine and agrarian history. T. H. Marshall, who had started lecturing in political history, turned increasingly to history of economic thought and economic history.[60]

Two other economic historians, Lance Beales and Valentine Judges, later taught nineteenth- and twentieth-century labour history and courses on the Industrial Revolution respectively; they were joined in the 1930s by F. J. (Jack) Fisher. Beales and Fisher soon built up a large and enthusiastic following among the students.[61] Power clearly worked closely with Judges. He was young, and struggling to support a family when he came to the LSE. He published a few articles in the *Economic History Review*, but nothing in the subject afterwards. Power not only taught several courses with

---

[59]　Vera Anstey (1889–1976) was assistant lecturer, lecturer then reader in commerce at the LSE 1921–54. She was dean of the faculty of economics 1950–4. Her main books were *The Trade of the Indian Ocean* (1929), and *The Economic Development of India* (1929; new edns 1936 and 1952).

[60]　See *Prospectus of the London School of Economics and Political Science*, volumes for session 1921–30, London School of Economics; T. H. Marshall was an assistant lecturer in economic history at the LSE 1925–6, then a reader in commerce, then sociology.

[61]　Recollection of H. J. Habakkuk from when he knew them in 1940, 12 November 1995.

him, but put his name forward for proposed Rockefeller Foundation
grants, and for secretary of the editorial committee of the *Economic
History Review*. He witnessed her will, and she named his baby
daughter, Eve, as its main beneficiary in the form of an educational
insurance policy.

Eileen Power's teaching interests were developed within the framework of the mainstream courses she taught in medieval economic
history from the early 1920s through the 1930s, but her lecture series
dwelt upon medieval trade and European history. She also developed the world history courses to include one course specifically on
the East, which she taught many times during her years at the LSE.
The medieval economic history seminar she started in 1923–4 as a
seminar in medieval trade was shared in the later 1920s with M. M.
Postan, and became for a time the seminar in medieval trade and
industry. During the 1930s it became a general seminar in medieval
economic history. She shared the Tudor economic and social history
seminar with Tawney throughout the 1920s, and they resumed
teaching it together once more during the later 1930s.[62]

The detailed lecture notes, notes on reading and syllabuses allow
us to reconstruct the content and main purpose of her lecture
courses. Eileen Power's early lecture series include sets on medieval
women, but somewhat surprisingly she does not appear to have given
these at the LSE. They may have been written for Summer Sessions
she did at Girton, and were certainly adapted for the lecture course
she did in 1930 at Barnard College, New York. The early lecture
series at the LSE and outside it instead show a broad coverage of
economic and social history topics, including women's history. A
number of lectures written later during the early 1930s for the Girton
Summer Session in 1933 related to themes out of *Medieval People*,
covering a range of other individuals, including medieval missionaries to the East, student life, and the lives of various merchants and
clothiers. These were intended to be collected together for a new
book, to be called 'More medieval people'.[63]

---

[62] See *Calendar of the London School of Economics and Political Science*, volumes for the sessions
      1921/2 to 1939/40.
[63] Her new characters included Etienne Boileau, a thirteenth-century merchant of Paris;
      Hermann Budde, a Hanse merchant; William Budrier, a Parisian goldsmith exiled in
      Karakorum in 1254; Thomas Lord Berkely and his wife; Usama Iln Mungidh, an Arab
      gentleman of the twelfth century; and Ibn Battuta, the great Arab medieval traveller. See
      M. G. Jones, 'Memories of Eileen Power', Postan Papers, box 2, notes for *Medieval People*,
      shelf 3.

By far the predominant preoccupations that emerge from Power's teaching files were trade and the comparative history of the East and the West. The series she gave at the LSE on trade between East and West was a strikingly wide-ranging investigation into Norse, Arab, Ottoman and Venetian trade routes, accounts of travellers' journeys to China, Ceylon and India, and the opening of trade routes to the Far East. There were her classic lectures on Marco Polo and Ibn Battuta, and the early versions of her famous set piece on the silk routes to China. She read and recommended to her students the major German, Austrian, French, Belgian and British authorities.[64]

Eileen Power's medieval world was open, expansionist and commercial. Her lectures on the economic history of Tudor England followed very similar topics to Tawney's with a substantial bias towards commercial and financial topics – capital in industry, international money markets, foreign trade, monopolies, trading companies and guilds, and taxation and finance.[65] The keynote of Power's teaching during the 1920s was internationalism and comparative history. This was to mature during the 1930s, when she also applied the social sciences. After she became professor of economic history in 1931, she devised and introduced a new course. This was economic history since 1815 (including England and the Great Powers), which she organised and taught for the Bachelor of Commerce degree in 1936–7. This was a two-year course comparing Britain, France, Germany and America. It was to replace the one originally taught by Lilian Knowles, and which in its new format was an attempt to combine economics and history, and to apply Sombart's model of the capitalist system. The course drew on teaching from Postan, Beales, Tawney and Durbin as well as Power.[66] Alongside the teaching, Power initiated research projects and seminars to develop links between history and the social sciences.

---

[64] These included Kovalewsky, Schmoller, Meitzen, Pirenne, Sée, Levasseur, Maitland and Vinogradoff. By 1926 she had added to these Kötzschke and Dopsch, as well as several major French studies, by Espinas, Bourquelot, and Huvelin. *Calendar of the London School of Economics*, 1922/3 and 1926/7; lectures by Eileen Power in Postan Papers.

[65] Postan Papers, case 69, lecture boxes.

[66] 'Proposed rearrangement of the Great Powers course', Power to Tawney, 6 May 1936, R. H. Tawney Papers, 11/1, BLPES; Eileen Power, 'Introductory lecture, Great Powers course', Postan Papers. For general syllabus and preliminary reading see *Prospectus of the London School of Economics*, (London, 1936/7–1939/40).

IV

Eileen Power was an inveterate organiser of discussion groups and projects. She brought together men and women across disciplines, and saw such groups as an important way of setting new research agendas. Discussion with a broad mixture of colleagues was also her own way of learning. In this way she was never an individualist, working on her own for her own self-advancement. The groups, projects and research seminars shook things up at the LSE and outside; they were a more co-operative way of learning, and they contributed to a stimulating research atmosphere, involving younger colleagues, students and researchers.

She turned her medieval history seminar for a time during the later 1920s and early 1930s into a research project focusing on the use of the customs accounts to reconstruct English trade in the fifteenth century. The seminar and research project included students and visiting foreign historians, as well as other academics from outside the LSE. At least half those regularly attending were women. Publication of the volume on fifteenth-century trade was partly financed with contributions from the Rockefeller Foundation. Power submitted other grant proposals to the Rockefeller Foundation in 1930 and 1931. These resulted in two major projects. The first was for a five-volume economic history of London to include contributions by Power, Tawney, Judges and Beales, with the co-option of Miss E. Jeffries Davis and of Dorothy George. Dorothy George was a former Girton and LSE student who had worked for MI5 during the First World War, then gone on to write major works on the economic and social history of eighteenth-century England.[67] The second was for a register of London business archives and a depository for business archives.[68] Power was the moving spirit behind the founding in 1934 of the Council for the Preservation of Business Archives, now the Business Archives Council.[69] The Rockefeller history of London

---

[67] Rockefeller Foundation Papers, 1931, LSE archives, BLPES. E. Jeffries Davis published some bibliographical works on history and topography, and edited the journal *History*. Mary Dorothy George (née Gordon) (1878–1971) studied at Girton until 1899, then held a series of research fellowships. She married the painter Eric George in 1913, and was employed from 1930 in compiling the British Museum Catalogue of Political and Personal Satires. *Who was Who* (1971); *Girton College Register* (1896).

[68] Rockefeller Foundation Papers, 1932, LSE archives, BLPES.

[69] *Ibid.*

project soon took on a full-time researcher, Mr F. J. Fisher, who later taught for the economic history degrees.[70]

Along with these more formal projects and seminars Eileen Power also initiated informal groups and discussion, especially across history and the social sciences at the LSE. The fact that she worked in this way is important for understanding her research and her broader conception of the role of economic history at the LSE. The more open structures of the LSE may have contributed; so too might the early dependence of the LSE on grants from the Rockefeller Foundation, and the availability of more of these grants for research projects. Discussion groups and workshops have also been the common practice in more recent years in marginal, new and interdisciplinary subjects or in radical approaches, such as in socialist and feminist history or in Marxist economics in the 1970s, and in cultural studies and literary theory in the 1980s and 1990s. Eileen Power certainly saw herself as on the frontiers of her discipline. Crossing boundaries led to new approaches. Leading but also learning from young colleagues and students was her way forward. Economic history was changing rapidly, away from its earlier focus on policy; medieval history was moving beyond its prior constitutional and administrative frameworks. She made a vital contribution to these developments, not only through her writing, but through the debates she initiated and in which she participated.

There is also another possible explanation for this research style. Was this a woman's way of working to a greater extent than a man's? We can point to factors such as making connections, the sociability of discussion, co-operative approaches, the nurturing of a discipline and the younger people joining it, and the confidence to look beyond the cultivation of a narrow expertise in order to challenge the traditional hierarchies and parameters. Certainly all these factors were important to Eileen Power's research activities. Was she, however, representative of her sex in working in this way, or merely following the characteristics of her own personality as well as the special contingencies of her institution and her discipline at the time?

---

[70] See *Review of the Activities and Development of the LSE during the Period 1923–37* (prepared for Rockefeller Foundation, February 1938, LSE archives, BLPES. F. J. Fisher (1908–88) became known for a number of seminal articles on overseas trade and London's economic significance during the sixteenth and seventeenth centuries. He became professor of economic history at the LSE after T. S. Ashton. See University of Kent videos 'F. J. Fisher', 1975; *Prospectus of the London School of Economics*, 1935/6–1942/3; 'Obituary', *Economic History Review*, 40 (1988), 343–5.

We know too little about research methodologies and ways of
working to test such propositions. Eileen Power was unusual among
women in attaining high levels of academic leadership. Whatever the
key factors that animated her research, what we see is a woman who
was a leader, a doer and a catalyst in research as well as a scholar
and a writer.

As far back as her early days at the LSE as a Shaw research
student, Eileen Power had taken part in the first of many clubs to
bring together various academic disciplines. The Query Club was a
student group with a mixed membership of about a dozen third
years and postgraduate students. These included Hugh Dalton,
Mary Stocks, William Piercy and Theo (Gugenheim) Gregory, and
they had met in Hugh Dalton's room in the Temple, to discuss
political, philosophic and aesthetic subjects.[71]

Anthropology was one of her major interests; she saw it as the
social science with the closest connections with history. From 1929
Eileen Power co-operated with Bronislaw Malinowski for projects in
history and anthropology. Together with A. V. Judges, in economic
history, she drew up a series of topics where history and anthropology might both gain from more interaction. These included
studies of family and marriage customs, political organisation,
territorial and ethnic groups, religion and magic, and voluntary
associations. This co-operation broadened out to larger group
discussions on history and the social sciences. She drew parallels
between the comparative method pursued by anthropologists –
variations in social systems at different points of space – and that
followed by historians who correlated variations at different points of
time.[72] In addition to general methodology, she talked with and
wrote to Malinowski about anthropological approaches to her own
research on medieval miracles and medieval women.[73]

---

[71] Stocks, *My Commonplace Book*, p. 92. Mary Stocks (1891–1975) was one of Eileen's close
female friends; she was an undergraduate at the LSE while Eileen was Shaw research
student. She later taught economics at the LSE and at King's College for Women until
1919. She married John Stocks, a philosophy tutor at St John's College, Oxford, then after
1924 professor of philosophy at Manchester. After years as an external lecturer, JP and
administrator she became principal of Westfield College, London 1939–51. William Piercy
was an assistant lecturer then lecturer at the LSE from 1913, where he taught public
administration, modern history then commerce. See *LSE Register*, pp. 217–66; *Who was
Who*.
[72] A. V. Judges to Malinowski, 30 January 1929, Bronislaw Malinowski Papers, BLPES
archives.
[73] Power to Malinowski, 24 April 1931, 14 January 1937, Malinowski Papers.

She continued throughout the 1930s to take part in and to lead groups of historians and social scientists in discussions of theory and methodology. Postan recalled groups organised by her from about 1926 including historians and other social scientists. Two of these merged into one which met between 1928 and 1934, 'erroneously called the sociological history group'. It included Power, Postan, D. W. Brogan, Gaitskell, J. A. Hawgood, W. G. S. Adams and K. B. Smellie at different times.[74] At another point Postan recalled a group started by Power in 1932 to discuss the sociological and historical implications of economic problems.[75] She later took part in the Institute of Sociology conferences on 'The social sciences: their relations in theory and in teaching'. Postan gave a paper, 'History and the social sciences', at the first of these in 1935 at Bedford College, and both also attended the next one at Westfield College in 1936.[76]

The discussion groups, seminars and projects generated methodological debate. Power lectured on Marxism and history and on medieval history and the social sciences during the 1930s. The major influence on the social sciences during the later 1920s and the 1930s was Marxism. The most prominent Marxist then at the LSE was Eileen's close friend Harold Laski. A number of the economists she was close to – Dalton, Gaitskell and Durbin – were socialists, of more or less moderate persuasion. Tawney's socialism was ethical not Marxist, and Postan, now lapsed from his radical socialist youth, was widely conversant with Marx's writings, but no longer a Marxist. Eileen Power who saw herself as a socialist faced the problem of just how far she would take Marxist positions and methodologies in the writing of history. In a lecture on the Marxian interpretation of history she praised the insights Marx had brought to historical writing. She was attracted by the emphasis Marxism brought to the historical process and its rejection of the individualist theory of

[74]   Postan to Webster, 10 October 1940. D. W. Brogan was assistant lecturer then lecturer in political science at the LSE from 1930. K. B. Smellie was an assistant lecturer in public administration at the LSE from 1921. J. A. Hawgood was an assistant lecturer in history at University College 1929–31, and after this a reader then professor of American history at Birmingham University. W. G. S. Adams was professor of political theory in Oxford 1912–33, but also an occasional lecturer in economics at the LSE. *LSE Register*, pp. 217–66; *Who was Who*.

[75]   M. M. Postan, 'Hugh Gaitskell: political and intellectual progress', in M. M. Postan (ed.), *Fact and Relevance* (Cambridge, 1971), pp. 169–82, at p. 171.

[76]   The paper to the Bedford conference is reprinted as in Postan (ed.), *Fact and Relevance*, pp. 15–21. Conference programme, Westfield College, 1936. Power–Postan Papers.

history, and she liked its analytical approach and its search for change through contradictions in the old order. But it was the new emphasis Marxism brought to social history that especially impressed her. It created the history of a people and not just of governments. It was a new structural analysis of society's history quite unlike the surface descriptions or scene-setting, such as was found in Macaulay. It not only created a new social history, but gave a special emphasis to economic history, displacing the former position of political history.

Yet Power never became a Marxist; the formulations and practices of her colleagues were after all too restrictive. She disliked their tendency to overlook the individual. She thought they made a too direct translation of history into the terms of economics, and she found their formulation of the relations between culture and economic conditions crude. Her real objection was to Marxism's claim to powers of prediction. In the end she saw Marxism as bringing a rejuvenation of history, but preferred for herself a more flexible approach to methodology which would allow the place of the individual and the personal, and the use of other theories of motivation.[77]

In 1931 Eileen Power was promoted to the chair of economic history at the LSE, and it was to the social sciences that she turned for the subject of her inaugural lecture, 'On medieval history as a social study', not delivered and published until 1933. This addressed the problems of the social sciences at the LSE, and their relationship to history, especially medieval history. Tawney had published his inaugural, 'On the study of economic history', the year before, and emphasised economic history's place in the historical disciplines. Power's inaugural, by contrast, was overtly methodological. She blamed the historians' snobbery for the gap between history and sociology. Sociologists, as a result, ignored the process of change, for historians never wrote in a way they could use. And historians produced the 'vague and spineless' social history that served as their substitute for sociology. She hoped for a social history that would be 'a structural analysis of society', and 'a line of approach to historical investigation which requires as rigorous a mental discipline and as scientific a methodology as any of the longer-established branches of history'.[78]

She saw little hope, however, for any integration with economics.

[77]   Eileen Power, lecture on the Marxian interpretion of history, Postan Papers.
[78]   See R. H. Tawney, 'The study of economic history'; and J. M. Winter, 'Introduction',

It was perfectly true that economic historians often mistook the nature of some of their problems through an inadequate knowledge of economic theory. But economics as a deductive science had gone too far; obsessed with formalism, it had become too much like medieval scholasticism to comment on the 'dusty realm of reality'. Elsewhere she denounced the turn taken by economics at the School; under Robbins and Hayek it had turned to neo-Austrian marginalism and *laissez-faire* market models.[79]

Despite the deficiencies of social science, however, Power held firmly to the belief that the historians should be seeking to answer some of the questions raised by sociologists and economists; ultimately observation and comparison should be integrated with more deductive methods. She believed that Weber's ideal types and Sombart's economic systems and economic epochs had contributed valuable abstractions, and delineated the distinctive features of various economic orders.

Power thought that medieval history had a very special contribution to make to sociology since it provided the best territory for the comparative method.[80] The study of medieval history also illuminated analysis of present problems. There were parallels between the methods of economic control in the bureaucracies of Soviet Russia and those of medieval Europe. Knowledge of medieval history moreover helped in understanding current problems in the development of Asia. 'Why did not the great medieval trading societies of the Arabs, the Indians and the Chinese produce industrial capitalism as a stage following commercial capitalism, as was the case in the West?'[81]

Power's interest in non-economic motivations in economic systems and in the different path followed by the East set her apart from the evolutionary theories and Marxist and other stage theories then prevalent. As a medievalist looking to anthropology and sociology, she was saved from some of the cruder results of nationalist versus

both in Winter (ed.), *History and Society*; Power, 'On medieval history', 14. This was also published in *Economica*, 12 (1934), 13–29.

[79] Power, 'On medieval history', *Economica*, 12 (1934), 16; Power to Webster, 5 April 1932, C. K. Webster Papers, BLPES. Robbins and Hayek were professors of economics at the time. They stood for the neoclassical conceptions of economic policy in opposition to John Maynard Keynes, and drew on the Austrian school of economics which introduced theories of 'marginalist economics' and subjective theories of value. Power did not, however, discount the value of all economics. She described Allyn Young as 'one of the wisest men who ever taught in this School': 'On medieval history', 16.

[80] *Ibid.*, 23.   [81] *Ibid.*, 48.

Marxist historical writing during the 1930s. Her comparative method grew out of what she learned in her early discussion groups, out of her political statements on the role of history, from before and during the early 1920s and out of her meeting with the social sciences. The mature expression of this, her inaugural lecture, was her major methodological contribution to medieval and economic history.

v

Teaching and research at the LSE under Power, Tawney and their younger colleagues had created a new and prominent profile for economic history. Power and Tawney now took their initiatives in the discipline outside the School to form a society and a journal. Initiatives to start something were already afoot in other quarters from the early 1920s. Ashley, Pirenne, Posthumus and Febvre discussed this at the International Historical Congress in Brussels in 1923, but nothing came of it. In Britain, economic history still fell between two stools – in Cambridge the economists, following Marshall's ascendancy, claimed it; elsewhere it was a branch of history.[82] The *Economic History Review* was the idea of Ephraim Lipson, the reader in economic history at Oxford, and an independent figure trained in the Cunningham tradition. He was an outsider in Oxford, a Cambridge man and not a fellow of any college. He had no claim except his work. It was because of his initiative that the *Review* was established as a historical not an economics journal.

Lipson was an admirer of Tawney, and recruited him and with him Eileen Power to the cause of a journal for the subject. The Economic History Society was launched in a joint meeting with the Anglo-American Historical Conference in London on 14 July 1926, the meeting at which Tawney made his statement on the future of economic history. Before the society was formed there was already an economic history section of the Anglo-American Conference. This was chaired by W. J. Ashley, with Eileen Power as secretary. Power now moved on from her position in the economic history section of the Anglo-American Conference to the key positon of secretary of the new Economic History Society.[83]

[82] Kadish, *Historians, Economists and Economic History*, pp. 223–45.
[83] This paragraph is summarised from T. C. Barker, 'The beginnings of the Economic History Society', *Economic History Review*, 30 (1977), 1–19, esp. at 7–13.

The first membership list of the society in 1927 included 500 members; 100 of these were women. Eileen Power was the centre of the society, and clearly at the helm from its start. For the society in its early years was a small band, largely London based and relying on friendship networks. This was partly due to Lipson's relative isolation in Oxford, and the little interest shown there in the initiative. There was also little interest in Cambridge. J. H. Clapham, the professor of economic history at Cambridge, kept his distance from the society and the *Review* until the 1930s. He attended the inaugural meeting, but expressed a note of scepticism.[84] Clapham was asked to be president in 1928, but wrote begging to be let off on the grounds of work and involvement in other societies, so he was elected vice-president instead.[85] He did not become actively involved in the society until 1940, some time after his retirement from the Cambridge chair in the late 1930s.[86]

In spite of his distance from the society, Clapham was close to Eileen Power. She was a friend of the family from the time she taught in Girton. Mrs Clapham had been entrusted with assembling the final parts of her *Nunneries* book for the publisher after Eileen had set off on her Kahn journeys, and they shared a common pleasure in the French language and literature. She stayed frequently at the Clapham home in Storeys End on trips back to Cambridge, and was friendly with Clapham's daughters and his son, Michael. Michael Clapham met his fiancée frequently at the Power kitchen dances and other social gatherings at Mecklenburgh Square. Mrs Clapham and her daughters loved talking about the fashions with Eileen until she was summoned away by Clapham with, 'Now Eileen, enough Ladies Page, it's time to talk economic history.'[87]

The end result of institutional if not personal distance from Cambridge was a society closely tied to the LSE. With this went close links with the schools and university extension classes of its founders. Women were important in these networks, and they also entered and took up positions in the society. Tawney insisted on keeping the

---

[84] Cited in Barker, *ibid.*, 15.
[85] Minutes of the meetings of the Economic History Society, 4 January 1925 and 19 May 1928, Economic History Society Papers, Nuffield College, Oxford.
[86] There were, however, clearly other reasons for his limited involvement. He was a central figure in Cambridge, indeed a rival with Keynes for the provostship of King's, and had heavy claims on his time from the college, and from his commitment to writing the *Economic History of Modern Britain*. Interview with H. J. Habakkuk, 12 November 1994.
[87] Interview with Miss Barbara Clapham, 21 July 1993.

society close to these roots. Due to his influence the conferences were always held at simple venues which people could afford and where they could easily talk to each other.[88] Most of the early conferences were held at the Institute of Historical Research, and it was only after the war that they started to travel around the provincial universities.[89]

Power orchestrated the society, working tirelessly herself and drawing on her own women's networks to get the society off the ground and keep it going. She recruited Gwladys Jones and badgered her into taking on the treasurership. She used her aunt Ivy as the secretary for society business,[90] and her own home as the office. She paid a number of the bills herself, and used her social connections to raise funds. She built up a team of friends and colleagues in Britain and the US. These included a number of women, several of whom had been colleagues or students at the LSE, including Mabel Buer, Vera Anstey, Dorothy Marshall and Ivy Pinchbeck. Others were fellow medievalists outside the LSE such as A. E. Levett, Bertha Putnam, Nellie Neilson and Helen Cam.

The major female figures in the society and the *Review* in the early years besides Eileen Power were Elizabeth Levett and Julia de Lacy Mann. They were very different to Power. Both were trained in Oxford; Levett was Vinogradoff's disciple, and Mann was trained by her and by Lipson. Mann started her research at the LSE on the cotton industry, under Lilian Knowles, but soon returned to Oxford to succeed Levett at St Hilda's College. Levett went to King's College, then Westfield in London. Neither was close intellectually to the group at the LSE nor personally to Eileen Power. Levett was put on the committee of the *Economic History Review* in 1926, and attended meetings of the council of the society from that time until her death in 1932. She chaired several of the council meetings, took an active part in discussions, and helped Power with the society business.[91] Mann was appointed editorial assistant on the *Review*, alongside Lipson and Tawney as editors, and was made a member of the council from July 1928.[92] When Lipson stepped down from his

[88]   Terrill, *R.H. Tawney and his Times*, p. 67.
[89]   Economic History Society Papers.
[90]   She was eventually paid £50 per year for two days a week – minutes, Economic History Society, 15 May 1929.
[91]   Minutes, Economic History Society, 1926–32; annual reports, 1931–2.
[92]   Minutes, 14 July 1926, and 5 July 1928.

editorship in 1934, an editorial committee was formed, with M. M. Postan as editor, and including Julia Mann, along with Eileen Power, J. H. Clapham, G. N. Clark, R. H. Tawney, and A. V. Judges as secretary.

A small band of women did a substantial amount of the work to shape the society. In addition to this, a schools committee was one of the first activities of the society, and several female teachers served on this committee, including V. A. Hyett, A. E. Pinnick and J. Hyslop. While the involvement of schools in the activities of the society was seen later as one of its worthy, but not terribly interesting, activities,[93] during these early days the schools and university extension classes were seen as the key to changing ideas about history. The crusade to take the subject out to the schools and adult education frontiers gave the society momentum through the 1920s. Membership rose to 768 by 1928, but remained steady from that time.

The society and the *Review* attracted the main economic historians in Britain and abroad, as well as the schools and WEA audiences. Here Eileen Power's own internationalism and Tawney's connections came into play. The early society included her close correspondents H. L. Gray of Bryn Mawr and N. S. B. Gras, who became professor of business history at Harvard. There was also E. F. Gay of Harvard, one of the first vice-presidents, and Bertha Putnam from Mount Holyoke. E. A. Kosminsky in Moscow, Pirenne in Belgium, and Henri Sée and Marc Bloch in France also played an important part as foreign correspondents. Eileen Power herself never published any mainstream articles in the *Review*, but acting as secretary of the society and a member of the editorial committee of the *Review*, she may have felt that this was not the place to put her own work. She did, however, publish a substantial number of reviews. Postan, by contrast, published several major articles, a number of short survey articles, and did by far the most reviewing for the journal.

The society hit hard times during the 1930s. Individual membership fell, though library subscriptions continued to grow; subscriptions were in arrears and costs of the *Review* drove the society into difficult financial straits. Power was still in command as secretary, and rescued the society by seeking donations from her friends. Among these were Laurence Cadbury, Jonathan Cape and Donald Brace.[94] She edited the first wartime number of the *Review* herself

---

[93]   Barker, 'The beginnings', 14–15.
[94]   Barker, 'Interview with M. M. Postan', video recording, University of Kent archives.

after Postan went off to the Ministry of Economic Warfare. She wrote to friends reminding them of unpaid subscriptions, and a week before she died badgered Beales for a revision on free trade for the *Review*. 'I simply can't carry on the review without some collaboration from economic historians . . . I know it's not as interesting as planning Pelicans – but if scholarship is at all worth keeping up in wartime I do feel you owe us a small contribution . . . I keep getting letters from the USA urging me to keep the Review going.'[95]

[95]   Power to Beales, 1 August 1940, Postan Papers. See also Power to E. F. Gay, 11 January 1940, E. F. Gay Papers, Huntingdon Library, San Marino, California.

CHAPTER 7

Love, marriage and careers

In the years between 1929 and 1940 Eileen Power built up the teaching and research relationships that made her reputation as a comparative economic historian. Through her research groups and teaching she became a leading exponent of the connections between history and the social sciences. This was the time when she took a major part in exciting new ventures which gave economic history a more systematic framework – her internationalist aims took shape with the social sciences, and she developed a genuinely comparative approach. Her own career took off: she was fêted in America, elected to the chair of economic history at the LSE and given honorary degrees. She considered, then decided against, putting her name forward as Clapham's successor in Cambridge. These were also the years of major changes in her personal life. There was another trip to China, where she became engaged to Reginald Johnston. When this was broken off she became closely involved with her former research assistant, then colleague, Munia Postan, finally marrying him in 1937 shortly before he became professor of economic history at Cambridge.

I

Eileen Power's second trip to China, in 1929, held out the promise of another turning point in her life. In the end, however, it could not have the same kind of effect upon her as the first one. She was now an established figure, not a young unknown woman on her first travels, eagerly absorbing all impressions and experiences that came her way. She already knew several of the other travellers she met. She travelled for a time with Arnold Toynbee, and met a number of her colleagues at an international conference in Japan. She was still, however, susceptible to her long-held images of China, in spite of recent political turmoil, and she fell again under the spell of Reginald Johnston.

Eileen started to make plans as early as 1926 for a major expedition. She planned this time to travel through Central Asia and on to Peking. She hoped to leave in March with a few others, led by a Syrian traveller, and to retrace some of the great medieval trade routes, including part of the silk road. That year she had published an article, 'The opening of the land routes to Cathay', in A. P. Newton's *Travel and Travellers of the Middle Ages*, and in this had discussed and mapped out all the major trade routes, as well as the itineraries of the great medieval travellers. She wanted to go from the Persian Gulf via Bokhara and Samarkand along Alexander the Great's march, through Turkestan and the Lesser Gobi to Peking.[1] At the time she wrote this she thought the only obstacle was raising the money, but in fact there was then a civil war in Sunkiang, or Chinese Turkestan, and the journey as planned would have been impossible. Eileen was forced therefore to abandon the expedition, but did not give up hope, and instead planned again for a rather different trip to Mongolia in 1929.

In the meantime there were invitations from Barnard College, Columbia for her to spend the year 1929/30 or part of it teaching there.[2] By March 1929 it was clear that conditions in Mongolia were still too unstable to make another Central Asian journey feasible. She therefore decided on a journey to China via the Trans-Siberian Railway in August, followed by four months in the Far East. She accepted teaching at Barnard for January to March 1930.[3] Eileen's project while she was in the East was to take up the topic of her short article on travellers and her abortive journey of 1926, and to do the research for a book about European travellers to China at the time of the Mongol Empire.[4] Her trip conveniently coincided with a significant London University presence in China and Japan, for she met Charles Webster and Arnold Toynbee at the Institute of Pacific Relations Conference in Kyoto, and Tawney was in China later in 1930.

Before going on to Kyoto Eileen spent time in Peking, and went to

[1]   Power to Postan, 13 July 1926, Power–Postan Papers.
[2]   Virgina Gildersleeve to Eileen Power, 23 November 1928, Virginia Gildersleeve Papers, Wollman Library, Barnard College, Columbia University, New York.
[3]   Power to Gildersleeve, 6 December 1928, 24 February 1929, 4 March 1929; Gildersleeve to Power, 6 March 1929; Power to Beveridge, 12 March 1929, Power personal file, LSE.
[4]   Power to Beveridge, 12 March 1929, Power personal file, LSE.

7.1   Reginald Johnston in the sable coat given to him by the last emperor of China
in the Forbidden City, Peking, 1922

the Western Hills, where she rekindled her enchantment of ten years before with Reginald Johnston, the scholar of her 'Haunted Valley'. Friendship and fascination blossomed into love, and their time together ended in a marriage engagement. Eileen left no record of her time in Weihaiwei, but Johnston wrote to his friend Sir James Stewart Lockhart about her visit in October, and again later at Christmas. He did not reveal a great deal apart from an obvious delight in having her in his house: 'I have a ... charming person ... staying with me at present, namely Miss(!!!) Eileen Power ... I met her when she visited Peking 7 years ago & again when I was in London 3 years ago ... She is spending a fortnight with me – Mrs. Walkinshaw being the only chaperone.'[5]

Another of Eileen's old acquaintances, the novelist Stella Benson,[6] spent a month there in the summer. Her diary recorded aspects of Johnston's character, and suggested that something of a shadow was cast over her own visit after, by comparisons with Eileen's. Johnston did not tell Stella Benson of the engagement, but she clearly worked out the feelings he had for Eileen. She wrote of his 'personal resentment of my "non-magnetism" as contrasted with his loved Eileen', and referred to Eileen at several other points in relation to Johnston.[7] Stella Benson's descriptions of Johnston were bound up with her own introspection, but she provided some insight into the reputation and personality of this 'tutor to the last emperor of China'. Johnston was then a decade and a half older than Eileen, a large-built white-haired man secure in his reputation as scholarly orientalist. He was a poseur, who liked to play to the image of the scholar, and clearly enjoyed being considered an eccentric by the rest of the expatriate community. He was also susceptible to attractive women. Benson found him 'much simpler and more accessible to public opinion than I remembered – somehow, since he is so much cleverer than anyone else in China, a nest of legend seems to have

[5] Johnston to Sir James Stewart Lockhart, 14 October 1929 and 2 February 1930, Lockhart Papers. I owe copies of these letters to Shiona Airlie and Robert Bickers. See Shiona Airlie's biography of Sir James Stewart Lockhart, *Thistle and Bamboo* (Oxford, 1989).

[6] Stella Benson (1892–1933) lived in Hong Kong 1921–33. She wrote *I Pose* (1915), *Tobit Transplanted* (1931) and *Mundos* (published posthumously, 1935). *Twentieth Century DNB*. See R. Ellis Roberts, *Portrait of Stella Benson* (London, 1939).

[7] Stella Benson, diary, 22 July 1930, 4, 9, 10 July 1930, Stella Benson Papers. I owe this reference and the following references from Stella Benson's diary to Robert Bickers. Benson's disappointment over the reception of her host during this visit is also related in Roberts, *Portrait of Stella Benson*, p. 243.

formed itself around him, and it is surprising to find him at the core of that ... a flesh and blood person'.[8]

Stella Benson was a very self-absorbed person, and her view of Johnston's character clearly reflected her own anxieties. Still, there was probably a good deal of truth to aspects of her depiction, for some of these were corroborated later by others after his return to England. She wrote that he was 'the most conspicuously consistent creature ... no wonder he is a confirmed celibate ... no wonder he became tutor to a dummy emperor – no wonder he enjoys being saluted by police & soldiers'. She thought that he held 'colonial' attitudes to women, 'absorbed from his Chinese circumstances', 'that women should not only be seen and not heard – but should not even be allowed, silently, to respect themselves and hold opinions and come to conclusions'. These attitudes, she thought, stemmed from his position in China.

I believe if he had lived a normal life amongst his own equals, he would have been a delightful person, but the world has presented itself to him purely as a territory to be governed – he has never met people of his own stature, either intellectual or official – he has always been able to feel unique, and to withdraw himself from all challenges to his uniqueness.[9]

If Benson's impressions and recollections of conversations are at all accurate, Johnston was an extraordinary person for Eileen Power, at the age of forty still a beautiful and much sought-after woman, to decide to marry. She was clearly fascinated by Johnston's 'Chinese' erudition, and he was one of those 'older men' she had always been attracted to. He left China in the autumn of 1930, and prepared to set up a career in London, and to marry Eileen.

Eileen went on to Japan after Peking and found friends and colleagues gathered for the Third Meeting of the Institute of Pacific Relations in Kyoto. After the meeting Eileen travelled with Arnold Toynbee through Manchuria and northern China. Toynbee was a member of Eileen's social and academic circles. He was the same age as she, and had by this time been married for sixteen years to Rosalind Murray, the daughter of Gilbert Murray. He was a close friend of Tawney; Toynbee had followed in Tawney's footsteps to Rugby, then Balliol, and they saw each other for a time in the summers in Oxford when Tawney came back to teach WEA classes. Toynbee by 1929 was at the Royal Institute of International Affairs

[8] Benson, diary, 5 July 1930.
[9] Benson, Diary, 22 July 1930.

in Chatham House at the University of London. He also knew the Hammonds as 'virtual members of his inner family circle'.[10]

At the end of their trip Eileen told Toynbee in secret of her engagement. The announcement had a devastating effect on Toynbee, who had been powerfully attracted to her himself during the trip. Eileen was beautiful and elegant, and was also deeply interested in his project of a universal history. Toynbee's biographer, McNeill, has described how Toynbee, after a sleepless night, burst into Eileen's room, begged her not to marry the man and declared his own love for her.[11] Eileen, shocked and embarrassed, asked him to leave. They parted soon afterwards, and Toynbee wrote her a confused letter about the event after his return to England.

After my first reaction to the news of your engagement it is still a bit on my mind that I shall be one of a rather small number of people whom you will have told about it before making your final decision, for the way your picture fitted into my frame obviously threw out my judgement, besides going through my guard ... "The unreal world" [of foreigners in China] *is* to the point ... (That is easily tested when you come home.) Not so that other thing that was on my mind a propos of myself. This strange and unexpected thing that has happened to you in the unreal world not only may vanish, but certainly will vanish, as soon as you leave the unreal world behind – and thank God for that, for it is a bad thing which leads nowhere. This, while true for me, has, I am sure, *no* application to you, and it was just an irrational and most devastating association of ideas in my mind, at first thoughts, when taken by surprise.

Toynbee had hoped to influence Eileen's decision, if not in favour of himself, then at least against Johnston, but realised when he declared himself what a mistake he had made.

So perhaps I might have spared myself a night of wondering what to do and the experience of being shown the door by an angry lady who thought I was going to forget – or had forgotten – my manners – though I hadn't and wasn't, but was only desperately embarrassed and tongue tied.[12]

Toynbee was churned up by what he had done, and his long letter went over his horror at finding himself like other men at the mercy of

---

[10]   Arnold J. Toynbee, *Acquaintances* (Oxford, 1967), pp. 86–94.
[11]   McNeill, mistakenly, however, thought the man was Postan – see W. H. McNeill, *Arnold J. Toynbee: A Life* (New York and Oxford, 1989), p. 141; cf. Toynbee's record of his trip in A. J. Toynbee, *A Journey to China: Or, Things Which Are Seen* (London, 1931).
[12]   Toynbee to Power, n.d., c. January 1930, in A. J. Toynbee Papers, Bodleian Library, Oxford; cited in McNeill, *Arnold Toynbee*, p. 142.

his elemental passions. Eileen wrote back to him briefly some weeks later from Barnard College:

I meant, my dear Arnold, to say nothing about that unlucky episode; but a passage in your letter (which I have just re-read) causes me to take up my pen again. I really can't have you thinking that I tried to eject you lest you should "forget your manners." ... You gave me a sudden and violent shock, for which I was totally unprepared, and what really animated me was a frantic and quite irrational desire to stop you from putting into words what I didn't want to hear ... It was silly of me, for the damage had been done ... And that's the last I shall speak of it. I am glad that you came out of it at once, for I should hate to have anything spoil our being friends, and I did so much enjoy wandering about with you.[13]

McNeill has argued that Toynbee's encounter with Eileen Power marked a watershed in his life. In poetry that Toynbee wrote immediately after the event he invoked for the first time the help of an unknown God in conquering his sexual passions. He also wrote to his wife of the encounter, and she wrote back twice confirming her love for him despite his lapse.[14]

After this momentous journey Eileen went on in January 1930 to a term's teaching at Barnard College in New York, one of the 'seven sisters', those pioneer women's colleges founded in America in the same spirit as the Oxford, Cambridge and London women's colleges. Her visit was arranged by the dean of Barnard, Virginia Gildersleeve, already known to Eileen through her work for the Federation of University Women and the links she was seeking to foster with the British Federation of University Women. Power taught two medieval history courses there with four or five hours of teaching a week, and was offered $3,500 for this, along with a teaching assistant and a guest suite in the residences, Hewitt Hall.[15] She also did another course of lectures for Vassar College, another of the seven sisters, and some teaching for the New School for Social Research.[16] As if this hectic schedule was not enough, there were invitations from all who heard she was in the US. She visited and gave guest lectures at most of the other seven sister colleges, Bryn Mawr, Radcliffe

[13] Power to Toynbee, 23 February 1930, Toynbee Papers. See McNeill, *Arnold Toynbee*, pp. 141–2.

[14] Rosalind Toynbee to Arnold Toynbee, 11, 14 December 1929, Toynbee Papers; cited in McNeill, *Arnold Toynbee*, p. 145.

[15] Gildersleeve to Power, 23 November 1928; Gildersleeve to Lucile A. Huber, 22 January 1930, Gildersleeve Papers.

[16] Power to Gildersleeve, 27 April 1929; Henry N. MacCracken to Gildersleeve, 11 April 1929.

College, Mount Holyoke, Sweetbriar and Wellesley, and also spoke at Cornell. She addressed both the Federation of University Women and the Medieval Academy of America: 'The last was great fun, because all the medievalists were there & I met everyone whose work I had ever known; we had a most convivial & not at all prohibitionist dinner together & made after dinner speeches at each other till the wee small hours.'[17]

Eileen Power was so popular at Barnard that her return to England was soon followed by an offer of a professorship of history at Barnard which she turned down with not a little regret, pleading the hold of her work at the LSE and her friends in London.[18] There were still other reasons for turning down a job offer in the US, for by the autumn of 1930, Johnston had returned to England, where he was appointed professor at the School of Oriental Studies. His appointment was controversial, and his subsequent career there until 1937 an unsuccessful one.[19]

Eileen now told her friends of her engagement, and Johnston bought her a ring. She wrote to Margery Garrett to say, 'My toreador's ring is *greatly* admired here.'[20] Some time later when he started to get settled, he bought a house in Kew. Eileen was horrified, however, when she visited, to find a hodgepodge of tasteless fittings and decorations with mixtures of modern furnishings and priceless Chinese curtains and artefacts given him by the emperor.[21]

The house was a harbinger of what was to come, for the course of the engagement did not go smoothly. Eileen had expected to marry in January, but Johnston, now aged fifty-six and a bachelor all his life, was undecided, and procrastinated. The day in the house at Kew had followed a wretched evening with Margery Garrett, who was in the midst of marital breakdown with her second husband, Dominick Spring Rice, and an unhappy affair with Dick Mitchison.

I felt a pig afterwards that I talked so much about myself when your affairs are so much more distressing. I feel as if I had been knocked down & someone was counting me out. But doubtless I shall get up again & it is unreasonable to expect to be happy all one's life.[22]

[17] Power to Gildersleeve, 6 August 1930.
[18] Power to Gildersleeve, 28 November 1930; cf. Gildersleeve to Power, 13 November 1930.
[19] Bickers, ' "Coolie work" '.
[20] Power to MLG, 25 December 1930.
[21] Power to MLG, 7 January 1931.
[22] Power to MLG, 7 January 1931. Naomi Mitchison, in her autobiography, *You May Well Ask*, alluded to the affair between Margery and her husband, Dick Mitchison, without

Eileen's own misgivings were matched by a series of postponements of the wedding date by Johnston, and by the summer of 1931 it appeared that marriage was off. Johnston offered his own version of the end of the affair when he resumed contact with Stella Benson in the summer. 'I finally decided not to because I had a strong feeling that for Eileen's sake it was very much better that we should not be married.'[23] Breaking off the engagement did not end their friendship; Johnston visited her while she was on holiday in Marlow, and a few days later she came to see him off in Southampton as he set off back to China to attend another Institute of Pacific Relations conference as a British delegate. He wrote of getting to know the London that Eileen loved, and meeting a host of her literary and journalistic friends.[24] In his view he had managed to keep the relationship he wanted, and to avoid the marriage he clearly did not want.

Decisions were not, however, quite so final. On Johnston's return from China, they were again talking of marriage. After yet another postponement by Johnston in February 1932, Eileen finally brought the long and unsatisfactory engagement to an end. She wrote frankly to Charles Webster, newly appointed professor of international history at the LSE, of what had happened:

I think Ref is uncertain of his plans; & in any case it became quite clear to me in the course of these two months that he no longer wanted to marry. So that it seemed best to me to end it, for I found adjournment sine die rather nerve racking. He was very much in love with me in Weihai, but I suppose it was stupid of me to think it would last; & we shall no doubt do better as friends.[25]

She did indeed keep up her friendship with Johnston. Over the years he gave her a number of his 'imperial treasure' pieces, and when he died suddenly in 1938 he left her a small legacy. Eileen Power, in her turn, was clearly shocked at his death, and wrote warmly about him afterwards.[26]

naming them, but wrote at several points of the very close friendship between the two couples. See pp. 68, 70–1, 79–80, 183.
[23] Johnston to Benson, 12 August 1931, Benson Papers.
[24] Johnston to Benson, 12 August 1931, Benson Papers.
[25] Power to C. K. Webster, 5 April 1931, Webster Papers, BLPES.
[26] Power to Mrs Joel, 10 March, 25 and 31 May 1938, Sir James Stewart Lockhart Papers, National Library, Edinburgh.

II

Disappointment in love did not set Eileen Power back for long. Her career was blossoming, research and teaching at the LSE were intense and exciting, and friendships were close and fulfilling. She was appointed to the chair of economic history at the LSE in 1931. She was a real pioneer, for she was only forty-two, and was only the second woman to become a professor at the LSE and in her subject generally. Lilian Knowles was the first, and though she taught full time at the LSE from 1904, she was only appointed to a chair in 1921, at the age of fifty-one, and died five years later.[27] There were no other female professors in the subject, unless A. E. Levett is included. Levett was a reader in economic history at the University of London, but was given a chair in history in 1929. This was to remain the situation until 1953, when Eleanora Carus-Wilson was promoted to a personal chair at the School. Even she remained alone, though over twenty years had elapsed since Eileen Power was elected to the chair. Since Carus-Wilson's time there have been no women in named chairs in the field of economic and social history, despite the massive expansion of economic and social history departments in Britain in the 1960s and 1970s.[28] Only through personal promotion and appointments to new or more broadly defined history chairs have a few women attained the highest academic levels during recent years.

It is hard to overestimate the academic status Eileen Power had achieved at such a young age. The chair enhanced her already well-established international reputation in a new and innovative field of study, and her own cosmopolitan connections across literary London raised the profile of her discipline. There were many other major female historians in the field, and a substantial female constituency of students and followers, but none of these ever achieved her academic recognition.[29]

We know little of how Eileen Power felt in the rarefied atmosphere of the female professoriate. She now ranked well above most of her female friends and colleagues. She was just as close to her oldest

---

27 *LSE Register*, Appendix A; Wallas, 'Lilian Knowles'.
28 Joan Thirsk recalled the years (and the dispiriting experience) when she sat as the only woman elected to the Council of the Economic History Society, 'and it was at a time when countless new chairs of economic history were being created, not one of which went to a woman', letter to the author, 2 March 1990. There are still no women in these chairs, though recently a few women have achieved personal promotions to professorships.
29 Berg, 'The first women economic historians', 308–11.

female friends, Margery Spring Rice and Gwladys Jones, but inevitably saw less of them as work became busier and personal life more entangled. She was conscious of her special position, and sought out female students and the disadvantaged, and she drew on wide contacts with many female graduates and researchers when seeking candidates for posts as research secretaries and assistants, and lectureships. However conscious she was of the support the women in her own life had given her from the time of her earliest education, it is also true that reaching the top must have isolated her. As Jo Manton Gittings put it, 'she was the queen'; despite her own efforts to be herself, her position, to those who did not know her, made her less approachable than she would have liked.[30]

What did this position mean in relation to the men she worked with? She herself did not perceive any problem. As we have seen, she led research initiatives and worked closely with graduates. She deferred to Tawney as chairman, but did most of the organising of the teaching in the department herself, sending him proposals for approval. She was dean of the faculty of economics from 1931 to 1935; her first and only female predecessor in this post was Lilian Knowles, from 1920 to 1924. What stands out, however, is how little access promotion gave her to the power that might have gone with a chair at a major university. She was not put on any professorial appointment committees in her own or any other institution. She was not put on the government inquiries and commissions that her younger male colleagues were called to, and she was not called to any significant war work during the Second World War.[31] Becoming a professor had not given her access to the male club of power and political influence.

Behind the façade of egalitarianism at the LSE lurked practices and personalities that had discriminated against her from her early days at the LSE. First, both she and Lilian Knowles were paid less than their male contemporaries. When Power was first hired there were long negotiations over her salary, some of which she never knew about. The appointments committee had originally decided on a readership for Power; the current salary for readerships was £800.

---

30 Conversation with Jo Gittings, September 1992. For Jo Gittings' work, see Jo Manton, *Elizabeth Garrett Anderson* (London, 1965); Robert Gittings and Jo Manton, *Dorothy Wordsworth* (Oxford, 1985); Robert Gittings and Jo Manton, *Claire Clairmont and the Shelleys 1798–1879* (Oxford, 1992).

31 Occasionally these commissions did include a woman, for example, Lilian Knowles served as the only woman on the Royal Commission on Income Taxes 1919–1920; Mary Stocks was a member of the Royal Commission on Lotteries and Betting in 1932. *LSE Register.*

But when she was actually offered the post, it was a lectureship at £500. She was not promoted to a readership until 1924, and then with a rise of only £100. Knowles discovered this when she was asked for a reference for Power's readership in 1924: 'I thought Miss Power was a Reader long ago. When I was on the appointments committee it was agreed to put her through as *Reader in History* with Kings to avoid clashing with Dr. Hall who is Reader in Medieval Economic History and Tawney.'[32]

Power asked for a salary rise again in 1927, and this was finally granted, bringing her salary to £750, still short of what it should have been. This rise was also in spite of the protestations of Mrs Mair, who claimed that Power did not deserve one because 'medieval history as a subject was merely "descriptive and limited", and because E.P.'s interest in administration was definitely nonexistent'.[33] Power's case was only a repetition of the treatment meted out to Lilian Knowles in previous years. She was paid less than male colleagues Cannan, Bowley, Foxwell and Sargent,[34] though she had started her job at the same level of £300 per year. She had protested vigorously to the administration about this on a number of occasions.[35] The discrimination experienced by Lilian Knowles and Eileen Power was felt to a much greater extent by many other female academics. The salaries for lecturers and readers were lower in many provincial universities; indeed, the general average in the country for lecturers, both men and women in 1923–4, was £444, and for readers or assistant professors it was £582. For example, Margaret Murray, a professor at University College London, started as a junior lecturer in 1898 at £40 a year, and when she retired in 1933 as an assistant professor, her salary was £450.[36]

Being appointed to her chair was no straightforward matter for Eileen Power either. She was not an automatic choice. Knowles' chair had, in fact, been suspended since 1926, for at that time it was

---

[32] Knowles to Beveridge, 12 February 1924, Power personal file.

[33] Mair to Beveridge, 26 July 1927, Beveridge Papers, Supplement, 1/12, BLPES.

[34] Edwin Cannan was lecturer then professor of economics at the LSE 1895–1926; A. L. Bowley was lecturer then reader and professor in statistics 1895–1936, though he was only in a full-time post at the LSE from 1919–36. H. S. Foxwell was professor of banking and currency 1895–1922, but he lectured at the same time at University College, London 1881–1927. See *LSE Register*, pp. 217–66; *Twentieth Century DNB*.

[35] Knowles to Miss Mactaggart, 12 October 1911, Lilian Knowles personal file, LSE.

[36] Dyhouse, *No Distinction of Sex?*, pp. 149–51. Dyhouse paints a sad picture, not just of wage discrimination, but of obstacles put in the way of female academics in terms of working conditions and career advancement: see pp. 147–67.

thought that no suitable applicants had come forward. Power had been in a readership since 1924, but even Tawney was a only a part-time reader with the added responsibility of head of the history department. In 1931 the faculty was reorganised; Tawney was appointed to a new research chair in economic history, and the chair in economic history was filled by promoting Power. One readership was left in place, and Beales was promoted to this. There was also a lecturer, A. V. Judges, and an assistant lecturer, F. J. Fisher.[37]

III

Soon after Eileen Power's appointment to a chair came another new professor to the LSE. This was Charles Webster (1886–1961), who became one of her closest male friends, her confidant and a firm supporter in her internationalist projects. Webster was appointed in 1932 to the Stevenson chair of international history, a new post developed after the first Sir Daniel Stevenson chair of international history shared at Chatham House between the LSE and The Royal Institute of International Affairs in 1926–7, but afterwards held at the Royal Institute of International Affairs. Webster was a big, bluff Yorkshireman. He had studied diplomatic history in Cambridge, and worked in the main on the Congress of Vienna and the foreign policy of Castlereagh. He had held chairs at Liverpool and Aberystwyth, and had served as part of the British delegation to the Paris peace conference after the First World War.[38] Power had spent time with the Websters during the Institute of Pacific Relations conference in Kyoto, and she was Charles Webster's closest contact at the LSE during the negotiations over the Stevenson chair. She telegraphed the results of the appointments committee to him, then wrote: 'I hope you will accept & it will be too lovely to have you here.'[39] By March, Webster had accepted the job.[40]

Eileen Power now planned a new course of lectures on the modern

[37] Mair to Beveridge, n.d., 1926; Beveridge to Webb, 25 May 1926; university readership in economic history, 1931; Beveridge Papers; Alexander Carr-Saunders, *Review of the Activities and Development of the London School of Economics and Political Science During the Period 1923–1937* (prepared for the Rockefeller Foundation, February 1938).

[38] Christopher Parker, *The English Historical Tradition since 1850* (Edinburgh, 1990), pp. 110–11; 'Webster, Sir Charles Kingsley (1886–1961)', *Who Was Who, 1961–1970*; J. A. S. Greville, 'C. K. Webster, 1886–1961', *LSE*, 51 (June 1976), 4–5.

[39] Power to Webster, 3 February 1932, Webster Papers.

[40] Beveridge to Webster, 16 March 1932, Beveridge Papers, 6/1 (55).

East, to be taught by Webster, Tawney and herself, and engaged Webster in her project to set up an international committee to revise school textbooks to provide greater emphasis on international friendship. She took on the National Committee of Intellectual Co-operation and the National Committee of Historical Sciences, but needed them to appoint the committee she wanted, to include herself, Webster, a few history teachers, and a few more historians, with G. P. Gooch as president. 'I think most of the work will be done in the basement of 20 Mecklenburgh Square!'[41] Alongside the urgency she expressed for more internationalism in history was her growing alarm over Japanese incursions in Manchuria and Shanghai.[42]

Eileen's friendship with Webster became the subject of yet more recrimination from the pen of Mrs Mair. Clearly no love was lost between them. Mrs Mair's diary entries in 1940, one of these after Eileen Power's death, recorded her dislike, and her accusations of a flirtation with Webster.[43] 'How mean a thing it is of any woman to use another woman's husband.'[44] The entries tell us more about Jessy Mair than they do about Eileen Power.

There is no doubt that Eileen's friendship with Webster was close, but her letters to him always enquired closely after his wife, or included warm wishes to her. Nora Webster had a delicate constitution, and Webster was well known to be devoted to her. Webster himself was so sure in the status of his friendship that he liked to tell people he had 'two wives', Nora and Eileen Power.[45] She wrote to Webster with great frankness of the end of her engagement to Reginald Johnston, and reported to him an otherwise confidential visit to Oxford to investigate job prospects for Postan. She also made Webster a member of a new club she had recently concocted with her sisters, the 'Honorary Powers'. 'People who are only friends of *one* sister are ineligible. It is a most select society, and those who do not disqualify themselves under Rule 2c usually disqualify themselves under Rule 2d.'

The Honorary Powers
Watchword. Principalities and Powers
Rules

1. This Society shall be called the Honorary Powers.

---

[41] Power to Webster, 5 April 1932, Webster Papers.
[42] Power to Webster, 3 February and 5 April 1932, Webster Papers.
[43] Jessy Mair's diary, 4 May 1940, 8 October 1940. I owe these references to José Harris.
[44] Mair, diary, 8 October 1940.
[45] Reported by Sir Isaiah Berlin.

2. Members must be possessed of the following qualifications.
   a. The members must be personally known to at least two of the Power sisters.
   b. The members must be of the male sex, nature having amply provided the Power family with females.
   c. The members must at no time have proposed to any of the Power sisters, such proposal constituting an implied slight upon the Honorary surname.
   d. The members must be able to recognise the Power idea of a joke at sight.
3. The Society shall consist of a President, the Vice Presidents & any number of ordinary members.
4. The President of the Society shall be one of the Power sisters, each sister serving in rotation for a period of two years, beginning with the eldest.
5. The late Vice Presidents must be known to & elected by the unanimous vote of all three of the Power sisters & shall serve for a period of five years & be eligible for reelection.
6. Candidates for membership of the Society must be duly proposed & seconded by two of the Power sisters & can be elected by the vote of those two. The third sister has, however the right to blackball any candidate.
7. Members can be deposed by the unanimous vote of the three Power sisters for conduct unbecoming to a Power. As the views of the Power sisters on conduct are exceedingly diverse such deposition is unlikely, but a breach of rule 2(c) shall be regarded as coming within the definition.

The current president was Eileen Power, the vice presidents Sir Matthew Nathan and Sir Victor Sassoon.[46] Members were C. K. Webster, M. M. Postan, and the publisher Curtice Hitchcock (of the Century Co., New York).[47] Later members were thought to be Sir Denison Ross, Donald Brace, another publisher (of Harcourt, Brace & Co.) and Humbert Wolfe.

Several of these friends were mentioned in a set of verse written by Beryl for a birthday celebration for Eileen after she returned from the US. This 'Ode to EEP on reaching the age of 40' set out advice from her sisters and her friends Gwladys Jones, Sir Denison Ross, Sir Matthew Nathan, Sir William Vincent and Humbert Wolfe:

---

[46] Sir Victor Sassoon (1881–1961) was the governing director of E. D. Sassoon Banking Company Ltd. He was a member of the legislative assembly of India 1922–3 and 1926–29, and later in 1929 a member of the Royal Commission for Investigating Labour Conditions in India, the same commission that Rhoda Power served on. See *Who was Who*.

[47] Power to Webster, 5 April 1932, Webster Papers.

I'd heard that Eileen Power
Shewed signs of being sour
Because she'd reached the age of 40.
She ne'er did need a dower
But in her maiden tower
Did fiercely scowl and glower,
Most dismal grown, as well as haughty
But sudden came an offer
(at which she was no scoffer)
To overbrim her coffer
By rapid nipping off to U.S.A ...
Her wisdom ripely garnered
She did disperse at Barnard.
Then hopping on a liner
She hied her thence to China
Where hearts did flame and rage
Since NO-ONE KNEW HER AGE!...

Yet she returned to London ...
She now was – FORTY-ONE!
So, forty-one and single
She exits from this jingle.

This is a gallant story
Of non-connubial glory.
The legend has no hero,
Because this female Nero
Watched all men's hearts a-burning
Without a qualm or yearning,
Grew younger every year,
And never shed a tear.
Although by menfolk harried
She never did get married.
Her charms, they ne'er grew lesser
SHE DIED A FAIR PROFESSOR![48]

IV

The rules of the Honorary Powers were particularly odd in relation to the person who was to have the greatest influence over Eileen during the 1930s, if not before. This was Michael Moissey Postan, otherwise known as Munia Postan. Postan was born in Bessarabia, Russia, probably in 1899, though no one was sure of his birth date,

[48]   Power–Postan Papers.

and he either did not know it himself, or changed it to suit his circumstances. Postan came to the LSE in 1921 or 1922, one of Eileen's early students. He had landed in England in 1920 after periods at the universities of St Petersburg, Odessa and Kiev and, some months before coming to England, had failed to gain entry to the universities of Vienna and Cernowitz. He had studied sociology, methodology, law and economics, and was reputed to have spent some time as an assistant to Sombart in Vienna. He was a small, red-haired man, some ten years younger than Eileen, though the age gap may well have been rather less than this.[49] He was gifted with languages and possessed of a formidable intellect and charismatic presence. It is quite possible that he also had a political background in the Zionist socialist movement in early revolutionary Russia.

Postan had come to England because though at this time he was a socialist, he was opposed to the Bolsheviks. He seems to have worked as a journalist and organiser for Jewish organisations in England during the time he was studying at the LSE and for some years afterwards.[50] This part of Postan's past was not made part of his personal biography once he was in England, though he did he not try actively to conceal it, for his name appeared in the *Jewish Yearbook* until 1945–6.[51] Postan did the B.Sc. (Econ.) (economic history) degree at the LSE, and studied there with Eileen Power and Tawney while scraping together a living on sporadic journalism. Eveline Burns remembered 'Mounia' Postan as an undergraduate. He was 'one of my first advisees, who terrified me for he was so much older,

---

[49] Postan, honorary degree of doctor of science in social science, laureation address, University of Edinburgh, 14 August, 1978; M. W. Flinn and Peter Mathias, 'Obituary: Professor Sir Michael Moissey Postan, 1899–1981', *Economic History Review*, 35 (1982), iv-vi; Edward Miller, 'Michael Moissey Postan 1899–1981', *Proceedings of the British Academy*, 69 (1983), 543–57. Even Eileen Power seems to have had a different idea of Postan's birthdate. See Power to Postan, 29 January 1932, Power–Postan Papers. There was also some disagreement over Postan's educational background as related in these obituary notices.

[50] It seems that Postan was a member of the secretariat of the Jewish Autonomy Movement in the Ukraine. This was a branch of the Zionist Socialists, and advocated setting up a Jewish parliament in an independent Ukraine. During his early years in England Postan may have been employed by the Jewish Democratic Agency and the Jewish Demographic Organisation. Some details of this background have been recollected by Sir Isaiah Berlin and Professor Chimen Abramsky. Letter from Chimen Ambramsky to the author, 29 September 1994.

[51] Postan is also recorded in the 'Who's Who' entries of the *Jewish Yearbook* between 1927 and 1932 as working for the Council of the Jewish Health Organisation of Great Britain. One full entry with his title, his educational background and address is recorded in 1945–6, but not thereafter. This political and religious background is not mentioned in Postan's obituary notices in the *Economic History Review* and the *Proceedings of the British Academy*.

.

7.2   Postan with postgraduate students in anthropology, 1926. Left to right: Camilla Wedgwood, Hortense Powdermaker, Munia (Michael) Postan, Miss Shirtcliffe

better educated and sophisticated than I was at the age of 21'.[52] He gained a second in 1924, experiencing difficulties with the English examination system common to those encountered by many mature students. Eileen wrote to him while she was staying in Girton. She commiserated over his difficulties in working with the time constraints of the examination system, and without his typewriter. She assured him, however, that testimonials and a doctorate or published piece of work would make good the lack of a first, and he would eventually be able to find an academic post. She also at this time fixed him up with funding from the LSE to employ him as her research assistant.[53] He did an MA in the following year, with a thesis on 'Credit in medieval trade'.[54]

Postan became closely involved from this time with Eileen Power's research plans. He worked for her while he was writing his MA thesis, collecting material on the cloth trade and miscellaneous bibliographical material used in her reviewing.[55] She wrote to him in July, telling him that she would read his thesis during the summer,

[52]   Burns, 'My LSE'.
[53]   Power to Postan, 26 July 1924; Power personal file.
[54]   Power to Postan, 26 September 1926, Power–Postan Papers.
[55]   Postan to Power, 26 April 1926; 4 May 1926, Power–Postan Papers.

and telling him of her research on the wool trade. She asked him to read her work, asking advice especially on finance. She also told him of the launch of the Economic History Society and the *Economic History Review*, and asked him to submit an article to the second number on the financing of trade.[56] She was effusive in most of her correspondence with him in her gratitude for his research assistance.

Postan took up Power's interests in the social sciences, and from the later 1920s they formed a close intellectual partnership. Postan also took part in many of her initiatives to bring the social sciences and history closer together. Power's lectures during the 1930s on modern economic history included several on Marx and Sombart in which she made reference to Postan. In the mid-1930s when she revised the course on the economic history of the Great Powers, substantial lecture slots were given to Postan. The student bibliography he drew up for his part of the course consisted, in characteristic uncompromising style, almost exclusively of a whole series of German and Russian works, with virtually none translated into English. Postan's references in lectures and research notes extended to a large range of German and Russian economists, social scientists and methodologists, and sometimes medieval historians. The simplicities of Power's course outlines were exchanged in Postan's sections for intricate discussions of contemporary economic debate, along with commentaries on a number of Marxian propositions on industrial concentration, on the tendency of rates of profit to fall, and of the immiseration of the working classes.[57] His ideal of analytical history was very different from hers. She too, it must be said, however, was conversant with many of the German authorities used by Postan; these formed part of the bibliographies used by most economic historians at the time, but unlike him she did not expect her undergraduates to grapple with this material themselves.[58]

Postan and Eileen Power clearly worked closely together in their teaching through the 1930s; both were pursuing aspects of the study of the medieval wool trade at the time. But their approaches, reading

---

[56] Power to Postan, 22 July 1926, Power–Postan Papers; See M. M. Postan, 'Credit in medieval trade', *Economic History Review*, 1 (1928), 234–61.

[57] Power, 'The economic history of the Great Powers, introduction; revised syllabus', Power to Tawney, 6 May [1936], Tawney Papers, 11/1, BLPES.

[58] They feature in Power's bibliographies, as they did in those of Knowles, Tawney and Clapham. There is a good discussion of Tawney and the historical school in Winter (ed.), *History and Society*, introduction. Knowles and Clapham both spent time in Germany after their degrees, and Knowles in particular saw herself as an apostle of the historical school.

and writing were different. Postan's methodological position was stated in his essay, 'History and the social sciences' which he presented to the Institute of Sociology conference in 1935, and later in his inaugural lecture, 'The historical method in social science' at Cambridge in 1938. Postan's approach in both these papers was a highly theoretical discussion of particular and general laws. He made reference to comparative history, but his key preoccupation was to push historical enquiry beyond its current empiricism towards the generalisation characteristic of the social sciences. The difficulty was that social scientific enquiries then available, notably in economics and sociology, were both sadly lacking in their sensitivity to social processes, assuming rather than investigating behaviour. In 1935, Postan contrasted the macrocosmic subject of the general sociologist to the microscopic subjects of the antiquarian. The subject of the scientific historian, by contrast, was 'microcosmic', that is 'a recognition of the need for making his investigations relevant to the wider issues of social science and a yet further recognition of the special difficulties and peculiar shortcomings of social investigation'.[59]

By 1938 he offered a more wide-ranging analysis of the differences in the methods of economics, sociology and history, but was more critical of the claims of social science. The contingency of the social facts should make the social scientist question 'whether it is worth his while to set up in business at all'. By this time he accepted that economic and social historians should go on studying individual situations, but that they should 'ask questions and look for answers capable of revealing the action of social causes'.[60]

Eileen Power differed from Postan not only in her conscious methodology but also in the focus and methods of her research. She was never the system builder and historical economist that he was. His contributions in research notes and letters to her focused on financial matters and on price and other quantitative data. Postan's closest friends through the 1930s were economists, Hugh Gaitskell and Evan Durbin. Power concentrated on processes, mercantile networks and descriptive analysis of manorial economies. She had developed her own distinctive method of comparative history;

[59] M. M. Postan, 'History and the social sciences', in *The Social Sciences: Their Relations in Theory and Teaching*, Bedford College (London, 1936), repr. in Postan, *Fact and Relevance*, pp. 15–22, esp. pp. 20–1.
[60] M. M. Postan, 'The historical method in social science', inaugural lecture (Cambridge, 1939), repr. in Postan, *Fact and Relevance*, pp. 22–34, at pp. 32–3.

Postan's influence added a gloss of mid-European methodology and social science system, but she never really internalised these. Instead, she built on her comparative beliefs and approaches, though possibly turning her earlier interests in medieval merchants and clothiers, in tune with some of his interests, to a more economic study of the wool trade and the pastoral economy.

Postan through the 1930s was no doubt her closest collaborator, and she was always aware of the inequality of their positions. Her chair in 1931 led her to redouble her efforts to find a more senior appointment for Postan. From early in 1932 she was investigating the prospects of the readership in economic history in Oxford for him. Lipson had stepped down, and the post was now open. She went to Oxford to sound out G. N. Clark, the professor of economic history, and a number of other historians, but clearly met with little enthusiasm for her suggestion of Postan. Afterwards she wrote to both Postan and Webster of her reactions:

I should have thought the extreme remoteness of the Oxford mind was carrying the contrast rather too far ... at one moment I am reminded of Frederick II's experiment of shutting twelve new born infants up with dumb nurses to see what language they would evolve in their segregations; I feel sure that when he returned they were all talking with Oxford accents! At another moment I am reminded of the Irish fairy people, the Sidhe; they walk upon the hills & they cast no shadows & their eyelids do not blink. It is not that they are unaware of the outer world, but by some odd optical elusion they are aware of it as a part of Oxford – like Carfax – no, not quite so central as that – like Boar's Hill. They are slightly warmer about the British Empire, but that, of course, is because it was invented by Lionel Curtis.[61] It is marvellous to be able to live like flies in amber (or are they more like prawns in aspic?), but God alone knows why you want to do it.[62]

The readership went to Reginald Lennard, a fellow of Wadham and friend of Tawney. Lennard had even at this stage written not much more than Postan, and did not write a great deal afterwards, though he stayed in the readership for the next twenty years. He was also one of Eileen's admirers, and never forgave Postan for his success with her.[63]

---

[61] Lionel Curtis (1872–1955) led 'Milner's Kindergarten' in setting out proposals for a Union of South Africa, took part in the Montagu–Chelmsford reforms in India, and assisted in negotiations for the Irish treaty and constitution. He was known later for his gospel of Commonwealth unity. *Twentieth Century DNB.*

[62] Power to Postan, 26 February 1932, Power–Postan Papers; cf. Power to Webster, 5 April 1932, Webster Papers.

[63] R. V. Lennard (1885–1967) wrote 'The alleged exhaustion of the soil in medieval England',

Eileen was also planning bigger things for Postan. By this time the
relationship may have moved on from academic partnership and
friendship to romantic involvement. She was nearing the end of a
long-drawn-out and frustrating engagement to Reginald Johnston.
Postan joined her for a holiday in the Lake District, at the house in
Patterdale owned by the Llewellyn Davis family. Together they were
making plans for the *Cambridge Economic History of Europe*. Eileen wrote
beforehand about the holiday, and set out her views on the *Cambridge
History*. She stated that she had had the idea of the work some years
before, and regretted that the first medieval volume would be
published under the aegis of Cambridge rather than the LSE. She
was especially candid then about their working relationship, and the
letter bears quoting fairly fully:

I do, I confess, feel rather worried about you. You would be a much better
editor than I, and you are continually having to give me advice & help in
work for which I get the credit. I don't really know quite what to do about
it. I can't *help* asking for the best advice I can get over things, & I have an
extremely high opinion of you – & not nearly such a high opinion of myself
as I had 10 years ago (this is partly inferiority complex, but partly because
I'm beginning to know something about my subject). I suppose I could plan
this without consulting you at all, but it would be so silly. It is just the
unfortunate fact that I am 12 years older that puts me in Chairs and on the
editorial page of these things ... after all it is part of my job to keep your
interests in view, apart altogether from the fact that affection would cause
me to do so in any case).
    Actually I don't think even from your point of view that it will be a bad
thing for Cambridge to do this book. Clapham's chair will be vacant in
about 7 years time. You can't get a chair in London or Oxford, because you
are blocked by myself & Clark; but I have for some time had my eye on
Cambridge for you. It is a snag that you are not a Cambridge man; but as
far as I can see there aren't going to be any Cambridge men available, for
Clapham has failed to train up any successor of the right calibre. I think if
you get your big book out, get a Readership in London, *and* if I can play
Clapham carefully, you ought to stand a good chance. I shall never say this
to anyone but you, because it would be most unsafe, but I have had it for
some time in my mind. It depends entirely on how big a reputation you can
amass in the next 7 years, & on how we manage Clapham.

She contrived to get Clapham together with Postan, by inviting the

Economic Journal, 32 (1922), 12–27; 'Rural Northamptonshire under the commonwealth', in
Vinogradoff (ed.), *Oxford Studies in Sociolegal History* (Oxford, 1916), and edited *Englishmen at
Rest and Play 1558–1714* (Oxford, 1931). Information on hostility between Lennard and
Postan reported to the author by the late Charles Wendon, February 1989.

Claphams to Patterdale while he was there, and advised Postan on how to handle him: 'He is a very suggestible man (despite his rock-like obstinacy) provided that ideas are presented to him in such a form that he thinks they are his own ... you will have to be deference & brilliance combined!'[64] Clapham would not have had any say in who filled his chair after he retired; by convention professors did not take part in choosing their successors. Presumably, Eileen thought that if Clapham favoured Postan, his views would become known by others who might have more direct influence on the choice of an incumbent.

In an even more revealing letter, undated, but most probably written in the autumn of the year following, Power discussed the extent to which she relied on Postan to read her work and provide suggestions for topics and writers for the *Cambridge Economic History of Europe*. The letter also indicates how close their relationship was by this time.

In case I am too late to ring you up, are you going to be very busy on Monday? Because (a) Economica wants my inaugural "as soon as convenient" (b) the Cbridge Econ. Hist. is announced in the Times L.S. Could you possibly help me with these on Monday before our seminar? I shan't be with you till 6:30 or 7:00 on Sunday, so we shan't have much time that evening. I want to understand what you think I shld do abt the inaugural, with the proviso that I simply can't rewrite it completely & we must be content with the minimum of revision in order to make it join up better: I enclose my copy of it. Also I want to block out a very rough scheme of chapters for the 3 vols. of the CEH w. wh I'm concerned & discuss authors with you. I will come armed with some ideas as to general topics & want you to help me with additions & dovetailing – as I shall have to see Clapham before Xmas. I wish you were doing it, not I. You'd do it much better – & I make such demands on your time & thought. But this at least *shall* happen – we'll treat ourselves to a month in Europe when I get the first cheque.

Don't get tired, my lamb – I thought you were rather piano last night ... Anyhow I'll see you at the Hon Powers. If you want to be nice to Aunt Ivy bring her *not* a box of chocolates, but some violets or other flowers (& not a lot).[65]

In December 1937 Eileen Power married Postan, a shock to many because of the difference in their ages, their positions and their

---

[64] Power to Postan, 29 January n.d., Power–Postan Papers. Internal referencing to the planning of the *Cambridge Economic History* indicates this was 1932. In fact, Clapham retired from the Cambridge chair in 1937 at the age of sixty-four.

[65] I am grateful to John Hatcher for a copy of this letter. The letter is undated, but internal references reveal that it was written in the autumn of 1933.

physical appearance. Eileen visited her friends Nadine and Tom Marshall shortly before she married. She went to dinner there with Dennis Robertson, and both stayed a long time. When eventually Robertson left, she told the Marshalls she had decided to marry Postan. They like many others were very surprised, for as Nadine Marshall recalled, 'She was very British, and he very Russian'.[66] Thus was the long affair of over six years concluded.

Postan's persistence had paid off in the end, and friends who had assumed that Eileen would never marry him were duly astonished. She told the Claphams, but not their daughters, who however guessed at the marriage on the day, after their mother, Margaret Clapham, dropped little hints. They then toasted 'Harriet Vane and Lord Peter Wimsey'.[67] Eileen's housekeeper, Mrs Saville, on hearing of the marriage, said, 'I don't like to think of Miss Eileen being walked over at her age, but these foreigners are rather good at it.' Eileen's friend Gwladys Jones was shattered by the marriage, for they had not only always taken their holidays together, but the marriage broke the unique and close bond she perceived between them.[68] Whatever their views on the suitability of the marriage, however, Eileen's friends could also see her great happiness. Sir Raymond Firth was a witness at their wedding, and recalled Power saying to him that she was very happy, and her only regret was that she would not be able to give Postan children.[69]

The partnership between Eileen Power and M. M. Postan was one of the great historical associations. There are many stories of the marriages or love affairs between historians, and in all cases the woman took the subordinate role. These women either did the research for or did some or much of the writing in their husbands' *oeuvres*. Among Power's own predecessors and contemporaries there were J. R. and Alice Stopford Green, J. L. and Barbara Hammond, G. D. H. and Margaret Cole. The wives, lovers and daughters who assisted major historians in various ways with writing, research, indexes and editorial tasks were commonplace – among them Margaret Clapham, Toynbee's second wife Veronica, Lucie Varga, lover of Lucien Febvre, Paule Braudel, Florence Halévy, Janet Trevelyan and Jane Wells. Their contributions were only rarely

---

[66]   Interview with Nadine Marshall, 12 February 1993.
[67]   Recollection of Miss Barbara Clapham, 21 July 1993.
[68]   Recollection of Miss Barbara Clapham, 21 July 1993.
[69]   Conversation with Sir Raymond Firth, June 1988.

acknowledged, for they acted as unofficial, unpaid researchers. They receive but small mention from the biographers of their husbands and fathers, for their contributions have been considered as little more than an extension of their household and family duties.

David Cannadine provides an exemplary case of such biography. He recounts the attributes of Janet Penrose Ward, Trevelyan's wife: she translated Julicher's *Commentary on the New Testament*, a volume of 635 pages, from German into English before her marriage, wrote *A Short History of the Italian People* (1920) and a biography of her mother, the writer Mrs Humphrey Ward. According to Cannadine, 'Janet Penrose Ward was thus an ideal Trevelyan wife: well connected, independent-minded, public-spirited, and more than averagely intelligent'.[70] She barely rates another mention throughout the book.

Eileen Power's partnership with Postan was clearly a working relationship with a difference. In this case she was the senior partner, ten (or as she thought, twelve) years his senior, his teacher, supervisor and employer, and established as a writer and lecturer with an international reputation before she even met him. His exotic background and his middle European theoretical training, however, placed him in a special position as Power's research assistant from the time he embarked on his MA thesis. He had acquired all his background in medieval history from her, but as an assistant was able to contribute insight into gathering and interpreting quantitative data as well as economic analysis in areas such as finance. He also had a broad knowledge of contemporary economics and sociology, in German and Russian as well as in English, to add to Power's own reading of continental and English medieval historiography, as well as her English and French literary and historical background. In this way they complemented each other.

In the early years of Postan's assistantship he did library work for Power, sending her short summaries of books and reporting references. He soon moved onto a major research project with her on material on woollen merchants she had found at the Public Records Office. From this time, their collaboration was close as they both gathered material on the woollen industry, and they ran a joint research seminar, and sometimes taught together on joint courses. They worked, however, in parallel. Power gathered her own research material, and wrote this up herself; Postan did likewise. The drafts of

---

[70] David Cannadine, *G. M. Trevelyan. A Life in History* (London, 1992), p. 10.

her papers and the notes for her lectures were not marked by Postan. This is exactly as one would expect. They were both extraordinarily busy academics, with no time for a close monitoring of each other's work. They did, of course, discuss their work, and Eileen acknowledged the particular assistance Postan provided in her understanding of credit in the woollen industry, by noting this in her first article on the subject.[71] He in turn, in his first published article for the *Economic History Review*, acknowledged what she had written on the wool trade based on the Cely accounts, and also thanked her for material she had given him on Edward III's transactions with wool merchants.[72]

It was Eileen Power who cultivated Postan's career, and did her best to open doors for him, from the time she arranged the funding for his first assistantship right through his lectureships at the LSE and University College, London to the chair in economic history at Cambridge. She proposed him for the lectureship at the LSE, and asked him to join her in running her internationally known medieval economic history seminar. She groomed him for the Cambridge chair, going to lengths verging on the improper, but kept her strategy and their relationship quiet. Postan went to a university lectureship in Cambridge and a fellowship at Peterhouse in 1934. The Cambridge chair came up in January 1938, shortly after their marriage, and Eileen herself was encouraged to put her name forward.

She wrote while on her honeymoon to her friend Helen Cam, telling her the reasons why she would not stand for the chair; she seemed to accept that she was the obvious candidate, and there was no mention of Postan standing.[73]

I feel frightfully torn about it. On balance Munia is anxious for me to come, both for personal reasons & because he doesn't think we shld get in each other's way to any appreciable extent, or find the situation awkward once people were used to us. For personal reasons I, too, should like to come, for I should see more both of him & of MGJ. But for nearly all other reasons I shouldn't. I shall drop a sabbatical year. And I do find the L.S.E. a much more stimulating place to work in & London a more congenial place to live

[71]   Power, 'The English wool trade in the reign of Edward III', *Cambridge Historical Journal*, 2 (1926), 17–35, at 17.
[72]   See Postan, 'Credit in medieval trade', 240, 245.
[73]   Her letter says she had done nothing all holiday except answer a million letters, while Postan had written two chapters of his book on manorial profits. The book never appeared. Postan did, however, publish an article on the issue in the *Economic History Review*, 'The rise of a money economy', 14 (1944–5), 123–34, and the work he was doing then was probably the first stages of his turning towards the study of medieval agriculture, where his reputation as a medievalist was to be made.

in than Cambridge. I like people to be all different kinds – I like dining with H.G. Wells one night, & a friend from the Foreign Office another, and a publisher a third & a professor a fourth; and I like seeing all the people who pass through London & putting some of them up in my prophet's chamber. I know all these sound small things, but they *are* one's life, & I'm not sure how I should settle down in the much more formal society of Cambridge. However, you may be quite sure that I shall consider it very carefully. It would be an honour to hold Clapham's chair (tho' not more of an honour than to hold Mrs. Knowles') and I know that it *would* be a good thing from the point of view of the position of women for one of us to get it.[74]

She did not allow her name to go forward, and was delighted to hear from Cam at the beginning of February of the success of her designs. The chair had gone to Postan. 'I am perfectly delighted – I never thought the Committee would have the sense. I *do* feel rewarded for choosing London. The P-P household is now commodiously furnished with two chairs!'[75]

By the early spring Power was writing up her material on the wool trade into the Ford lectures and chapters for a book, and both were planning new joint ventures. One of these was to be a source book on the economic history of England 1377 to 1485, a combination of articles and documents, most of it written by Power and Postan, along with a few other contributors.[76] Clapham soon heard of it, and wrote reminding Eileen of other commitments.

I'm sorry I didn't tell you that I had heard of the P-P project. I think it very relevant. I didn't expect it very soon (pardon me!) because besides manors and wool there are chapters for the *Cambridge Economic History* which have I think a prior claim.[77]

Postan wrote shortly after Power's death of their working partnership. He told Webster that they had collaborated in a way few people realised. Each wrote independently, but by the time one or the other sat down to write, 'the other was so familiar with what was going to be written that he (or she) could easily have done the writing'. 'This was possible not only because we collected our evidence together, mostly working on the same mss. (we began doing that in 1925), and always discussed it, but because we were evolving towards the same views at the same time.'[78]

[74] Power to Cam, 6 January 1938, Helen Cam Papers, Girton College archives.
[75] Power to Cam, 6 February 1938, Cam Papers.
[76] File on source book, Postan Papers.
[77] Clapham to Power, 21 May 1938, Power–Postan Papers.
[78] Postan to Webster, 10 October 1940, Webster Papers.

The collaboration was a fruitful one for both throughout most of Eileen Power's career at the LSE. Postan was always clear that it was Tawney and not he who shaped the development of Power's historical interests towards the large-scale comparative economic history she pursued through the later 1920s and 1930s.

She very much admired his philosophical habit, and was much influenced by it. Of course she would not and could not imitate him, but her *penchant* for social analysis and evolution away from 'manners & customs' was induced by Tawney's example. It was already there in 1921, when I began to work with her.

And he attributed to Pirenne and Bloch the transformation in her work from *Medieval English Nunneries* to the Ford lectures, for in these cases she had found historians whom she both admired and could consciously try to imitate.

Postan saw Power's urge to write 'analytical' history as responsible for her article in the *Cambridge Medieval History*, and for a number of other projects she wished to pursue 'analytically'. In her search for theory that might help to shape such history, she started the socio-logical discussion groups to which they both belonged between 1926 and 1934. Postan saw the reshaping of the Great Powers history course at the LSE, Power's inaugural, his own inaugural and his own articles on method as direct products of their common evolution in these groups. He saw her Ford lectures as an indirect product, and 'the most important and the most successful'.[79]

Postan's perception of the common project of a historical partner-ship changed in emphasis in the later years of his life. He came to claim at a time when his reputation was not only secure, but as high as it could ever be, that he had played a much greater part in the research and writing of some of her articles than the letter to Webster conveyed. When he edited *Medieval Women* in 1975, he pointed out in the preface that the third chapter, 'The working woman in town and country', was based on his researches, and 'embodied numerous passages written by me'.[80] In 1980 he wrote that he had written her article 'Peasant life and rural conditions' together with her.[81] There is, however, nothing in the papers to corroborate this. Power's own notes and an extensive text of the

[79] Postan to Webster, 10 October 1940, Webster Papers.
[80] Power, *Medieval Women*, preface by Postan, p. 7.
[81] Postan to Peter Linehan, 1980.

lecture on the 'Working woman' are all written in her own hand; her piece in the *Cambridge Medieval History* was similar in its general reading and scope to those written at the same time by Laski and Clapham for the same collection, and the evidence in both was drawn from the French medieval sources she knew so well.

Whatever roles Power and Postan played in each others' scholarship and careers, they were both brilliant figures in their own individual ways. Eileen Power gathered many honours through the 1930s, and she was fêted by great professors and ordinary university porters alike. The letters poured in after her inaugural lecture, describing the pleasure of hearing and seeing 'a historian in her prime'.[82] She was the first woman to give the Ford lectures in Oxford, and was praised by the head porter of the Oxford examination schools for the record audiences she attracted.[83] She was awarded an honorary LL D at Manchester in 1933, another at Mount Holyoke in 1937, and was elected a corresponding fellow of the Medieval Academy of America in 1936. She wrote to Beveridge after this election, with her offhand humour:

There are not many of them and they are drawn from all over Europe ... though I put it all down to an uproarious Annual Dinner of the Fellows, at which I was a guest in Cambridge (Mass) five years ago; I always knew I could drink any American (weakened by years of prohibition) under the table and make an after dinner speech on top of it, but little did I know how much this feat would impress the medievalists of America.[84]

[82] Dorothy George to Power, 18 January 1933, Power–Postan Papers.
[83] G. H. White to Power, 7 March 1939, Power–Postan papers.
[84] Power to Beveridge, 13 April 1936, Beveridge Papers, supplement 2/1, BLPES.

CHAPTER 8

Eileen Power's medieval history

Eileen Power's career and the honour she was accorded during her lifetime were based on the contribution she made to medieval and economic history. What was this contribution, and what more did she have planned when her life was cut short? Eileen Power's work on medieval social history was not just a history of ordinary people, as against that of political elites and armies, states and empires. This kind of social history was pursued by many of the early social and economic historians working on various periods – Tawney, the Hammonds, Marc Bloch and many others, and she was certainly a part of this tradition. But more than this, Power's was an internationalist history. Her work ranged across countries. She was particularly fascinated by immigrant craftsmen, by travellers, merchants and scholars. From early in her career she aimed to write comparative and world history. The stages by which she came to do this took her out of the Coulton style of social history, and back to a reassessment of the legal-constitutional and Germanic traditions. She then brought this foundation together with the insight she gained from social theory, especially the comparative method, to develop a new kind of comparative economic and social history. Finally, she started and shaped some of the major international collaborative histories of the time. The driving force behind this contribution was her commitment to an internationalist political and economic programme.

I

Eileen Power is perhaps best remembered now for breaking free of the traditions of constitutional and legal history to move out to write the kind of accessible and human economic and social history associated with *Medieval People*. But she did not abandon those traditions; instead, she drew on their political ideas to develop a new comparative history.

A clue to her ties to these traditions can be found in her lecture, 'The League of Nations', which became the essay, 'A plea for the Middle Ages', published in *Economica* in 1922. The essay looked back to medieval political institutions as a source of ideas for federal structures to underpin the League of Nations. She wrote: 'While in theory the principles of unity and peace governed medieval politics, in practice pope fought with emperor, nation with nation, and city factions raised their clamour to the skies ... but ... the Middle Ages, though they failed in practice, did solve in theory the problem of what sort of political institutions are necessary for men living in society.' She pointed out that the new school of political thought was in the process of discarding the ideal of the sovereign state in favour of a theory of multiple sovereignty, 'a theory with medieval roots'.[1] These roots lay in medieval corporatism and community. She argued that the Holy Roman Empire functioned alongside small local and functional associations within which men lived and worked. A theory of sovereignty that gave recognition to smaller entities and local initiatives would give greater scope for social service and a greater sense of man's duty to the community.

Power argued that the advances of modern transport and communications had created the opportunity to resuscitate these political ideals.

In the Middle Ages the world could be regarded as one, because it actually was a small place ... Sharp and clear lay the little world of Europe, round the Mediterranean Sea, still what it had been for the Romans, the centre of the earth. Today the extreme rapidity of transport and communication, the railway, the telephone, wireless telegraphy, the steamboat and the aeroplane, have made the world small again.[2]

Power regarded current trends in political thought as close to the principles of the medieval world. Internationalists attacked the state from without as being too small; the sovereignty of the state should be limited by its relation to the larger whole. The state was also being challenged from within by various groups, seeking home rule, devolution and regionalism: 'And when these ideas have transformed our political philosophy, it will be almost identical with the philosophy of the despised Middle Ages.'[3]

[1]   Power, 'A plea for the Middle Ages', 174.
[2]   *Ibid.*, 179.   [3] *Ibid.*, 180.

Despite professing a different approach to medieval history, Eileen Power's internationalism drove her back to a reassessment of the legal-constitutional school. The social history she evolved during the 1920s and 1930s drew to an important, neglected extent on these foundations. The cosmopolitan and comparative social history to which she aspired in her early writing was also reinforced during her years at the LSE by close contact with social and economic theory.

Among Eileen Power's sources for 'A plea for the Middle Ages' were Gierke, Maitland and Laski in his early pluralist phase.[4] She looked again, in the light of the current politics of pluralism, at a debate in the late nineteenth century among German and English historians of the Middle Ages. The issue then was the extent to which medieval political institutions had their origins in the early medieval Germanic corporations and communities, or in a continuity with ancient Roman institutions. Frederic Seebohm's *The English Village Community*, published in 1883, opened up a debate with 'Germanic' views and myths of a free peasant society and communal ownership of land in England during the Anglo-Saxon period. Seebohm used medieval court rolls to show that the manorial system, serfdom and private ownership of land were introduced to England by the Romans.[5]

Seebohm's challenge was taken up and subjected to a new critique by Sir Paul Vinogradoff and by Frederic Maitland. Vinogradoff's study of English legal records and manorial documents, *Villeinage in England*, first published in English in 1892, argued for the more recent development of serfdom during the twelfth century. Maitland followed with his study of a Cambridgeshire manor, which demonstrated the resilience of serfdom into the early fifteenth century, and the economic interdependence of medieval villages.[6] The nine-

---

4   See Otto von Gierke, *Community in Historical Perspective. Translation of Selections from Das deutsche Genossenschaftsrecht 1868*, ed. Antony Black (Cambridge, 1992); F. W. Maitland, *Domesday Book and Beyond* (1897; London, 1960); Harold Laski, *Studies in the Problem of Sovereignty* (New Haven, 1917); *Authority in the Modern State* (New Haven, 1919) and *The Foundations of Sovereignty and Other Essays* (New York, 1921). On Laski's pluralism, see Kramnick and Sheerman, *Harold Laski*, pp. 101–4.

5   Razi, 'The historiography', 8.

6   F. W. Maitland, 'The history of a Cambridgeshire manor', *English Historical Review*, 35 (1894), 417–39; Frederick Pollock and F. W. Maitland, *The History of English Law* (Cambridge, 1895). Cf. Razi, 'The historiography', 13; and Richard M. Smith, '"Modernization" and the corporate medieval village community in England: some sceptical reflections', in Alan R. H. Baker and Derek Gregory (eds.), *Explorations in Historical Geography* (Cambridge, 1994), pp. 140–70, esp. pp. 153–4; J. W. Burrow, '"The village community" and the uses of history in late nineteenth-century England', in Neil

teenth-century debates on the origins of manorialism and of natural law in England took on new meaning in a post-war world. Eileen Power, and Laski too in his essay on medieval political thought for the *Cambridge Medieval History*, took an old debate into the 1920s by giving it a radical twist, and relating it to the problems of the League of Nations. Laski set out the connections between the medieval doctrine of natural law and the new international law.[7] Power drew for her sources not just on the debate on the English manor, but on German historiography.

II

Maitland's position and that of many medievalists of the time was heavily influenced by the debate among German historians over the origins and impact of the village community.[8] Their most important influence was Otto Gierke's *Das deutsche Genossenschaftsrecht*. Part of this was translated by Maitland in 1900, though Gierke's books had been published long before, in 1868, 1873 and 1881, at the time of German unification. Gierke's work was published in the context of the land problem in the Germany of his day. This was perceived in terms of the persistence of the breakup of old agrarian communities. Gierke traced the long continuity of medieval ideals of community and fellowship. He argued they were succeeded by the rise of state power, a tendency towards a dissolution of all intermediate communities, and the development of the notion of the state as the exclusive community. He argued that the medieval idea of the empire was shattered by the modern idea of the state. Modern philosophical doctrine had accepted the Aristotelian definition of the state and of its exclusive character.[9]

Gierke set out his concept of 'Genossenschaft', or fellowship and corporate group personality, in the first volume of his great work. He stressed the central role of associations in social life, and their moral independence from the state, and he conveyed a warm sympathy for voluntary associations. Gierke's pluralistic liberalism,

McKendrick (ed.), *Historical Perspectives. Studies in English Thought and Society in Honour of J. H. Plumb* (London, 1974), pp. 255–84, esp. pp. 275–84.

[7]   H. J. Laski, 'Political theory in the later Middle Ages', *Cambridge Medieval History*, vol. VIII, chap. 20 (Cambridge, 1936), pp. 620–45.

[8]   R. Kötzschke, 'Manorial system', *Encyclopaedia of the Social Sciences* (1933), vol. IX/X (New York, 1948), pp. 97–102, at p. 98.

[9]   Gierke, *Community*, introduction by Black, pp. xiv–xx.

however, changed after German unification, and the later volumes
of his work focused on the supreme fellowship of the German
nation state, or the Second Empire.[10] The early Gierke, however,
influenced a generation of English pluralists, including Maitland,
Figgis and Cole.

Through his main English exponent, Maitland, Gierke's work on
the early guilds and rural communities was particularly influential.[11]
Maitland sided with Gierke against the Roman foundations of rural
organisation and, in particular, of English manorialism. He took up
Gierke's investigation of different associations, both rural and urban,
and of their linkages to a greater whole in the Holy Roman Empire.
On this basis Maitland stressed the variety of forms of seigniorial
power, and the different origins and forms this took in different parts
of England. He went outwards to discuss land ownership by individuals, communities and corporations.[12] The role of the free
communities was taken further by the Russians Vinogradoff and
Kovalevsky, who carried their own perceptions of the problems of
contemporary agrarian reform in Russia into their analysis of
medieval society.[13]

The debate on the free peasant community, inspired initially by
land issues in Germany, the debate over the 'mir' (or rural
commune) in Russia, and Liberal land policy in England, acquired
new dimensions by association with fresh ideas on the state and
internationalism in the years following the First World War. The
breakdown of old empires, the emergence of new national identities
and regional autonomies, and the internationalist project of a
League of Nations to act as a higher sovereign power all seemed to
have parallels in the end of the Roman Empire and the rise of the
medieval world. Eileen Power's early paper pointed out the parallels
between medieval ideas of association and the new anti-nationalist
political thought. Her research from this time on merchants and
traders was also clearly affected by Gierke's ideas on the associations
and fellowships of the early guild communities.

Most of Power's reading in German historiography was similar to

---

[10] *Ibid.*   [11] *Ibid.*, pp. 58, 70, 98, 107, 114.

[12] Maitland, *Domesday Book and Beyond*, pp. 396–7 and chap. 6, 'The village community'. See
      the introduction by Edward Miller.

[13] Powicke, *Modern Historians*, pp. 9–19; E. Levett, 'Sir Paul Vinogradoff', *Economic Journal*, 36
      (1926), 310–17; Cantor gives biographical details of Vinogradoff and Maitland, and
      recounts stories of their meeting. See Cantor, *Inventing the Middle Ages*, pp. 48–66; W. J.
      Ashley, 'The history of English serfdom', *Economic Review*, 3 (April 1893), 153–73.

that of other medieval and economic historians of her day.[14] She drew primarily on Gierke, who had been reinterpreted for the British by Maitland. Her other sources, however, included the Germans Meitzen, Kötzschke and Bücher, the Russians Kovalevsky and Vinogradoff, and the Austrian Dopsch. These nineteenth-century historians stood out at the time for their large-scale regional and comparative histories; the origins of the Annales school and of English economic history alike owed much to their foundations.[15]

III

Eileen Power took what she needed from legal-constitutional history and German historicism, and put them into the modern framework of the comparative method. Her 'Peasant life and rural conditions', published finally in 1932 in the *Cambridge Medieval History* after long delays, was the practice of comparative history she advocated in her inaugural lecture. She argued that the legal historians had treated the peasant mainly in relation to his lord; instead of this, peasant societies and their religious and cultural lives needed to be compared across Europe.[16]

Her paper was a great comparative survey of the different geographical conditions of feudalism. She ranged over the wide plains and arable cultivation of the large manors and serfdom across northern and central Europe to the hilly country and pasture farming associated with weak manorialism interspersed through these regions. These were contrasted in turn with the smallholdings, individual cultivation and free peasantry of the vine- and olive-growing districts.[17] She followed the frontier of medieval societies, writing of the Germans as the great colonisers of the Middle Ages. They expanded over the Slav lands in the same manner as did the

---

[14] For the influence of German historiography on Tawney and Unwin, see Winter (ed.), *History and Society*, introduction, pp. 7–11; Cf. J. H. Clapham, 'Commerce and industry in the Middle Ages', *Cambridge Medieval History*, vol. vi (1929), pp. 473–503. For a sophisticated discussion of the influence on Marc Bloch of German historiography see S. R. Epstein, 'Marc Bloch: the identity of a historian', *Journal of Medieval History*, 19 (1993), 273–83, esp. 278–9.

[15] N. S. B. Gras, 'The rise and development of economic history', *Economic History Review*, 1 (1927), 12–34 draws attention to these regional histories. Also see J. A. Schumpeter, *History of Economic Analysis* (1954; Boston, 1981), p. 311. Also see A. W. Coats, 'The historicist reaction in English political economy 1870–90', *Economica*, 21 (1954), 143–53.

[16] Eileen Power, 'Peasant life and rural conditions (*c.* 1100–1500)', in *Cambridge Medieval History*, vol. vii (1932), pp. 716–40, at p. 740.

[17] *Ibid.*, pp. 717–19.

Americans from the Atlantic to the Pacific, and the Slav took on the
role of the native American, or 'Red Indian'.[18] She compared the
process of the decline of serfdom across west and east. And she
compared transhumance in parts of Scotland, Wales and England
with its role in Spain, southern France, south-eastern Italy and the
Roman Campagna, and northern Greece. She lucidly presented
current medieval scholarship on the contours of the manorial system
across Europe, and characteristically drew on her own range of
literary and cultural sources to discuss peasant superstition, manners
and morals. She concluded her essay:

> These inarticulate and despised masses had two achievements to their
> credit which are worthy to be set beside the greatest works of art and
> literature and government produced by the Middle Ages. They fed and
> colonised Europe; and slowly, painfully, laboriously they raised themselves
> from serfdom to freedom, laying hands as they did so upon a good
> proportion of that land which they loved with such a passionate and
> tenacious devotion.[19]

Power's comparative piece had come into the *Cambridge Medieval
History* by a circuitous route. The *Medieval History*, first mooted in
1904, had started out with the same principles of 'universal history'
as those espoused by Acton for the *Cambridge Modern History*. But few
foreign historians were considered as first choices for contributions.
Furthermore, in 1916, seven German and Austro-Hungarian historians, several of them highly eminent scholars, were dropped from the
list of contributors as enemy aliens.[20]

In 1918 J. R. Tanner had been appointed as a new editor, and the
enterprise was cranked up once more; the third volume was published in 1921, and the fourth and fifth prepared. Power had
originally been engaged under the first editors to write for the
seventh volume, and was reminded of this by Tanner in 1922. She
wrote back: 'I had got into the habit of regarding Volume III as
something remote as the day of judgment, but I am glad to hear that
the Cambridge Medieval History is going along so quickly.'[21] She
took the opportunity to change the topic allotted to her from

---

[18] *Ibid.*, p. 725.   [19] *Ibid.*, p. 750, pp. 740–6.
[20] P. A. Linehan, 'The making of the *Cambridge Medieval History*', *Speculum*, 57, 3 (1982), 463–
      94. For discussion of the original editors, Previté-Orton and Z. N. Brooke, see Powicke,
      Modern Historians, pp. 127–41.
[21] Power to Tanner, 10 July 1922, J. R. Tanner Papers, St John's College archives,
      Cambridge.

'England: Edward III and Richard II' to 'Rural conditions and the peasantry'.[22] She discussed the scope of her paper which was at that time intended to cover the whole period between 1000 and 1500, and to give comparative treatment over the whole of Europe.[23] When the chapter was finally published ten years later it did not depart very far from these original plans.

Power had been recruited before the war,[24] but now found herself among a new group of replacement historians recruited from a missing generation, and avoiding German contributors. Some of these were women, whose names were put forward by T. F. Tout, not 'from any prejudice but because since the War the male researcher has almost ceased so far as I am concerned'. In the event, eleven of the hundred and forty-three chapters of the post-war volumes were written by women, as compared to two of the forty-three prewar chapters, and only three of the two hundred and eighty-three in the *Cambridge Modern History*.[25] Tanner's editorial preferences were also insular: 'His natural instinct was to turn to men he knew, British historians ... to replace one set of old men, some of them aliens to boot, with another set of old men, all of them British.'[26] Among these essays by 'old men', however, were major essays by Clapham and Pirenne[27] which drew on a common range of secondary works, indicating the significant place of the German historical school, and the part played by the constitutional and legal historians in the making of this broadly based comparative economic history.

M. M. Postan later claimed that he had written the paper with Eileen Power. He recalled that he and Power met the editors, Previté-Orton and Brooke, both before and after the chapter was delivered:[28] 'In discussing our chapter with Previté both Eileen and I were taken aback by his view that the chapter was "not sufficiently historical", i.e. not arranged in a strictly chronological order. He was by instinct and training opposed to historical writing focussed on

---

22 Power to Tanner, 13, 25 July 1922, Tanner Papers.
23 Power to Tanner, 21 August 1922, Tanner Papers.
24 Power to Tanner, 10 July 1922, Tanner Papers.
25 Linehan, 'The making', 485.
26 *Ibid.*, 486.
27 Clapham, 'Commerce and industry'; Henri Pirenne, 'Northern towns and their commerce', *Cambridge Medieval History*, vol. VII (1929) pp. 332–60.
28 J. R. Tanner, the senior editor for vols. IV–VII, died in 1931, just before the proofs of vol. VII were completed. See Powicke, *Modern Historians*, p. 132.

problems.'[29] Clapham always referred to him as 'dear little Previté-Orton', and held a higher opinion of him than did Postan.[30] But there is no other evidence of Postan's involvement in the writing of the chapter.

It was to Pirenne and to Marc Bloch that Postan himself earlier ascribed the greatest influences on Eileen Power's work. He thought their books and Bloch's conversation played an important part in the transformation from *Medieval Nunneries* to the Ford lectures. Power certainly took detailed notes on the work of both.[31] Tawney, Postan thought, had provided the example which turned her from 'manners and customs' to social analysis.[32] In a lecture delivered in 1930 Power wrote critically of typologies which both Bücher and Sombart had imposed on the medieval period, drawing on recent medieval and archaeological research to demonstrate that transitions between systems were more continuous than they allowed. In Pirenne she found a social analysis of entrepreneurial and capitalist values in the early stages of the history of capitalism.[33] She was inspired by Pirenne's studies of commerce and industry and their impact on medieval urban and social developments. She took up his theses on the impact of the seventh- and eighth-century Arab conquests, and out of this pursued her own research on Arab commerce. Pirenne's *Mohammed and Charlemagne* (1935), first published as an article in 1922, was a major influence on the course of her historical research, as it was on that of other major intellectuals then and later.[34] When the English translation of the book appeared in 1939, she subjected it to the sustained critique of the seventeen years of medieval scholarship it had inspired.[35] His anticipation of her interest in traders and

[29] Postan to Peter Linehan, 10 November 1980, Power–Postan Papers.

[30] See Postan to Linehan, 10 November 1980; see Power–Clapham correspondence on the *Cambridge Economic History of Europe*, Clapham to Power, 10 October 1938, Power–Postan Papers.

[31] Postan Papers, case 69, box 2, box 5.

[32] Postan to Webster, Webster Papers, 10 October 1940.

[33] Power, 'Problems in the history of the social and economic development of the Middle Ages', October 1930, Postan Papers. On Henri Pirenne (1862–1935) see Bryce Lyon, *Henri Pirenne. A Biographical and Intellectual Study* (Ghent, 1974), pp. 417–18, 429. See also Powicke, *Modern Historians*, pp. 96–108.

[34] Both the Marxist economist Paul Sweezy and the economic historian David Landes, educated in economics and in history at Harvard, claimed that *Mohammed and Charlemagne* was the key influential book of their intellectual formation. See M. Berg, 'Introduction', in M. Berg, *Political Economy in the Twentieth Century* (London, 1991), p. 17; interview with David Landes, May 1992.

[35] Eileen Power, 'A problem of transition: review of Henri Pirenne, *Mohammed and Charlemagne* (1939)', *Economic History Review*, 10 (1940), 60–2.

travellers, and of her aspirations to world history, made Pirenne Eileen Power's first mentor after Coulton's early influence.

From the Germanic tradition, it was the Austrian medievalist Alfons Dopsch from whom Power gained most. She made notes on his work, lectured on him, and eventually arranged for an English translation of his most well-known work by her friends M. G. Beard and Nadine Marshall, wife of T. H. Marshall. Dopsch had considerably modified the view that the Germanic invasions of the fifth century brought about a great breach in the continuity of social and economic development between the ancient and medieval world. Dopsch and Pirenne both attacked the old German catastrophic divide between the Mediterranean and the medieval world.[36] Marc Bloch too was influenced by Dopsch. Though he wrote a critical review of Dopsch's work, he intended to contribute to his Festschrift, and only withdrew his contribution after the Austrian Anschluss.[37]

From comparative history, Eileen Power moved on to commercial and industrial history. The whole enterprise of Power and Postan's medieval economic history seminar through the late 1920s and the early 1930s was part of her pursuit of the international side of economic history. The result was her work on the wool trade, and the collaborative volume, *Studies in English Trade in the Fifteenth Century*, ranged over many aspects of England's trade with Europe. The volume included her own and other studies of the wool trade, Postan's paper on the Hanseatic League and specialist studies on the overseas and distributive trades.[38] The book and the seminar behind

---

[36] Alfons Dopsch, *The Economic and Social Foundations of European Civilization* (condensed by Erna Patzelt from *Wirtschaftsliche und soziale Grundlagen der europäischen Kulturentwicklung aus der Zeit von Caesar bis auf Karl den Grossen*), trans. M. G. Beard and Nadine Marshall (London, 1937); Power, 'A problem of transition'; Henri Sée, 'Review of Alfons Dopsch, *Naturalwirtschaft und Geldwirtschaft in der Weltgeschichte* (Vienna, 1930)', *Economic History Review*, 4 (1933), 359–60.

[37] See Fink, *Marc Bloch*, p. 198; Epstein, 'Marc Bloch', 278. Bloch withdrew from the Festschrift because he did not wish to be associated with other contributors who might be supporters of the National Socialist regime.

[38] Eileen Power and M. M. Postan (eds), *Studies in English Trade in the Fifteenth Century* (London, 1933). The book contained chapters by Howard Gray from Bryn Mawr, Power and Postan, Eleanora Carus-Wilson, Sylvia Thrupp and Winifred Haward, and a further contribution on the Hanseatic trade by Doris Leech. Those who attended Power's seminar left major books on medieval economic history, many of these on aspects of trade. The members of the seminar included R. A. L. Smith, who died young; Elizabeth Crittall (*Victoria County History, Wiltshire*); Eleanora Carus-Wilson (ed.), *Medieval Merchant Venturers: Collected Studies* (1954); Alwyn Ruddock, *The Port Books or Local Customs Accounts of Southampton* (1937) and *Italian Merchants and Shipping in Southampton 1270–1600* (1951); Sylvia Thrupp, *The Merchant Class of Medieval London 1300–1500* (1948); Marjorie Chibnall, *Select Documents of the English Lands of the Abbey of Bec* (1971); Edward Miller, *The Abbey and Bishopric of Ely* (1951);

it created a centre at the LSE for the study of aspects of medieval trade and commerce that lasted well into the 1950s. It was an introduction to the enterprise she would turn to next, the *Cambridge Economic History of Europe*. Another contribution to Power's thinking in the 1930s lay in the contemporary work and new historical enterprises being started by Marc Bloch.

IV

Power's comparative history with its international framework had a parallel in the work in France of Marc Bloch and Lucien Febvre. The *Annales*, initially conceived by Bloch and Febvre in 1921 as an international journal on the model of the *Vierteljahrschrift für Sozial und Wirtschaftsgeschichte*, was later created in 1928 as a 'national journal with an international spirit'. It was to provide a forum for problem-oriented history, history based on attention to present-day concerns and large questions.[39] Bloch came to Britain in 1934, where he delivered three lectures on comparative history at the LSE,[40] and sought as collaborators on the *Annales* Tawney, Power and Postan. He went on to Cambridge where he saw Coulton and Clapham, and where he was invited to contribute to the *Cambridge Economic History of Europe*. Though Bloch did not get very far in identifying authors, reviewers and subscribers for the *Annales*,[41] he recognised Power and Tawney in particular as pursuing goals similar to his own. Tawney published an extended and laudatory review of Bloch's *Les caractères originaux de l'histoire rurale française* (1931) in the *Economic History Review* in 1933, and Bloch wrote to Tawney in 1936 about references and archives on the *ancien régime*. Bloch published a bibliography on the economic history of France in the *Review* in 1938,[42] and he lectured

---

Menna Prestwich, *Cranfield: Politics and Profits under the Early Stuarts* (1966); Philippe Wolff, *Commerces et marchands de Toulouse vers 1450–1850* (Paris, 1954); Florence MacClure and Dorothea Oschinsky. I am grateful to Marjorie Chibnall and Elizabeth Crittall for details about the seminar. Elizabeth Crittall photographed the seminar group, but unfortunately the photograph was too dark to include in this book.

[39] Fink, *Marc Bloch*, pp. 132–4.

[40] The lectures were later published as *Seigneurie française et manoir anglais* (Paris, 1960), with a preface by Georges Duby. See Epstein, 'Marc Bloch,' 275.

[41] Fink, *Marc Bloch*, p. 179.

[42] R. H. Tawney, 'Review of Marc Bloch', *Economic History Review*, 4, 2 (1933), 230–3; Bloch to Tawney, 20 May 1936, Tawney Papers; Marc Bloch and Paul Leuilliot, 'Books and articles on the economic history of France', *Economic History Review*, 9 (1938), 104–7.

once again in Cambridge in 1938, on 'Some economic and psychological aspects of feudalism'.[43]

In his methodological piece, 'A contribution towards a comparative history of European societies', published later in *Land and Work in Medieval Europe*, Bloch acknowledged his debt in his idea of comparative history to articles by Pirenne and Henri Sée, but not to the German historians who had clearly played such a large part in Clapham, Tawney, and Power and Postan's intellectual formation.[44] He had, however, studied with Sering, Eberstadt and Bücher in Berlin and Leipzig, and at Leipzig had absorbed the idea of the region as an appropriate unit of interdisciplinary analysis.[45]

The early manifestos of the Annales school were internationalist, espousing similar aims in the writing of social and economic history to those expressed by Power in her own combination of pacificism and social history. There was also, however, a strong nationalist background to the Annales school. Bloch and Febvre had sought to drive out the German kind of history that had reigned supreme at the Sorbonne and the *Revue historique* since 1876.[46] It was perhaps Bloch's French patriotism that led him to present the manifesto and methodological piece first published in 1928 with so little reference to his own intellectual formation. But some German sources were there, despite Nazism and the insecurity Bloch felt as a Jew, by the time 'The rise of dependent cultivation and seigniorial institutions' was published in *The Cambridge Economic History of Europe* in 1941. Dopsch, in particular, was prominently cited in several places. Bloch failed to acknowlege the earlier German comparison across Europe, but introduced his own sources of comparison in Morocco, Hungary, Wales, Mexico, Chile and the Celtic countries.[47] Bloch's early writing in the *Annales* preached his comparative method, often at the expense of English historiography, which he frequently denounced for parochialism and for overindulgence in political and legal history. He dismissed English local history: 'Every local monograph is, in this way, a monument to the dead.' Yet he was delighted with

[43] Fink, *Marc Bloch*, p. 194.
[44] M. Bloch, 'A contribution towards a comparative history of European societies', in M. Bloch, *Land and Work in Medieval Europe: Selected Papers by Marc Bloch*, trans. J. E. Anderson (New York, 1969), pp. 44–81, esp. pp. 44, 76.
[45] Epstein, 'Marc Bloch', 279; Max Sering, Rudolf Eberstadt and Karl Bücher.
[46] See Georges Huppert, 'The Annales school before the Annales', *Review*, 1 (1978), 215–19.
[47] Marc Bloch, 'The rise of dependent cultivation and seigneurial institutions', *The Cambridge Economic History of Europe*, vol. 1 (Cambridge, 1941), pp. 224–77, 587.

the challenges that Elizabeth Levett's work on the Winchester manor posed to previously accepted interpretations of manorialism, and he welcomed the comparative project of Power and Postan, though neither had created a school to turn back traditional history.[48]

In spite of Bloch and Febvre's protestations over the novelty of their comparative method, the basis for this was simultaneously being laid in England by Power and her colleagues. As we have seen, the framework provided by the LSE took her into other fields, especially anthropology and sociology. The foundations of English economic history in the German school already pointed to comparative methods. Finally, the first great comparative initiative in economic history, *The Cambridge Economic History of Europe*, was first discussed by Clapham and Power in 1932.

v

The *Cambridge Economic History* was conceived initially by Clapham and Power. Postan was also already involved, as Power had made clear in her letter to him about the planning of the volume. Postan later claimed that his part in the enterprise had been equal to hers:

The first blue-prints of the series was almost entirely Clapham's. He drew Eileen into the project and she accepted it on the understanding that she would share her part with me. We did not want this arrangement to be officially divulged for purely personal reasons, but the personal reasons were no longer valid after I had moved to Cambridge and married E.E.P. Though the plans for volume I were almost entirely Clapham's the contributors had to be chosen by E.E.P. and me, as Clapham was not in touch with medievalists in the field.[49]

In fact, Clapham showed rather more knowledge of the medievalists than Postan allowed him. Clapham's memories from much earlier, in his obituary of Power in *Economica*, attributed the idea of the edition to Power.[50] Power, in her letter to Postan discussing plans for the edition in 1932, confirms this. She wrote frankly to him then about his part in her work and about his prospects, but she said in

[48] See his reviews of Postan in *Annales d'histoire economique et sociale*, 6 (1934), 202, and one he wrote later on Elizabeth Levett, 'Sur les terres d'une grande abbaye anglaise', *Mélanges d'Histoire Sociale*, 1 (1942), 108. Also see *Annales d'histoire economique et sociale*, 6 (1934), 510; and 10 (1938), 150; see J. A. Raftis, 'Marc Bloch's comparative method and the rural history of medieval England', *Medieval Studies*, 24 (1962), 349–68.
[49] Postan to Linehan, 10 November 1980, Power–Postan Papers.
[50] J. H. Clapham, 'Eileen Power, 1889–1940', *Economica*, 7, 27 (1940), 359.

the letter that the idea of the volumes was hers.[51] The first draft of
the plans for the three volumes was, furthermore, set out in her
hand.[52]

When the first volume came out in 1941 Power was credited by
Clapham with planning the first volume as a complete whole. Postan
was thanked for helping Power in the planning of the volume. Marc
Bloch was also thanked for putting at the command of Power and
Clapham his 'knowledge of European scholarship and scholars'.[53]
Clapham and Power corresponded closely over the contributions
from early in 1933, when the format, scope, title and plans for the
contents of the first three volumes were decided on.[54] The first
volume, as Clapham set out in his preface, was to lay the foundations
of medieval economic life, and in many places what was almost the
complete superstructure too. It was to 'cover the earth, the crops, the
peasant's toil; how villages and fields were occupied and laid out;
how and with what cattle and implements they were tilled; what the
society was that they maintained'. The great movements affecting all
of Europe – settlement and colonisation, agricultural techniques, and
the rise of the manor – were to be described in four great general
and comparative chapters. The country sections of one large compo-
site chapter on medieval agrarian society in its prime were ranged
according to region back to the early Middle Ages and forwards, in
the case of Russia, to the serfdom of the nineteenth century. The
volume was European, spatial, comparative, and problem oriented.

Despite the internationalism of the project, however, Clapham
revealed nationalist prejudices on a whole range of possible contributors. He did not want an American volume in the series at all, and
only conceded that America 'must come in somehow' when they
came to the volume on the nineteenth century.[55] He agreed to ask an
Italian or a Belgian to write on Mediterranean trade out of
'courtesy', but preferred to ask Byrne, an American settled in
England, or even better Runciman, as he was 'local'. 'We want
English folk ... I am ... against remote aliens when a denizen may
suffice.' 'Cambridge ought to do what it can.'[56] His Cambridge
preferences were checked fairly sharply by Power, who wrote back:

[51] Power to Postan, 29 January 1932, Power–Postan Papers, cf. this vol., chap. 7, n61.
[52] Correspondence between Power and Clapham, Power–Postan Papers.
[53] Clapham, preface to *Cambridge Economic History*, vol. 1 (Cambridge, 1941), pp. v, viii.
[54] Clapham to Power, 7 February 1933, 13, 24 September 1933.
[55] Clapham to Power, 1 October 1934.
[56] Clapham to Power, 7 March 1936.

'Do whatever you like about Runciman. The only thing I had against him was that Baynes [Norman H. Baynes] does not think well of him, and in general I think people dealing with economic history ought to know something about economic problems.'[57] Clapham also felt 'safer with an American than with a German who might always give us generalisations which were really German not European – as the best of 'em often do'.[58] By 1938 he was not so keen on American generalisations either, and denounced a particular American as

too repulsive for words ... a man who says he has dealt with 'social history and the history of institutions' – and incidentally has explained the rise of towns on Pirenne lines – and has 'never really dealt with economic history' is an obvious charlatan. We never asked him for 'the lectionability of trade' etc. No doubt like a good specialised American he thinks that is 'economic' and the things of wider interest 'social?'[59]

From 1936 Power and Clapham were having problems finding a suitable Italian to do both Mediterranean agrarian history for the first volume and the Italian cloth industry for the second. In fact there were a number of Italian medieval economic historians, but the editors clearly did not know whom to ask. A language barrier, limited access to Italian publications and the small number of international conferences that might have brought such historians to their attention were all factors. Power, after persuading Clapham to allow Eleanora Carus-Wilson to do the English woollen industry, tried to press her into a comparative piece on the English and Italian industries.[60] She had given up on this by 1938, reporting that 'both de Sagher and Miss Carus-Wilson, with deplorable lack of enterprise, refused to tackle it', and she proposed to do it herself in order to keep the account of the cloth industry a single whole.[61]

By 1938, Clapham had also given up on the Italians – 'the wops are no gentlemen' – and Power wrote to Marc Bloch for suggestions for a French historian and to Previté-Orton for other suggestions.[62] Fascism was now part of the agenda. Bloch wrote back suggesting Bognetti in Genoa: 'A competent worker, he is, moreover, certainly not loathe to collaborate with "non-fascist" scholars ... But you will

57 Power to Clapham, 11 March 1936.
58 Clapham to Power, 21 April 1936.
59 Clapham to Power, 21 May 1938.
60 Power to Clapham, 11 March 1936; Henri E. de Sagher.
61 Power to Clapham, 11 March 1936, 13 October 1938.
62 Clapham to Power, 21 May 1938; Power to Clapham, 24 May 1938.

perhaps – and not without reason – despair getting any Italian to work for you.'[63] He then suggested several French historians. Previté-Orton also pinned the difficulties on the fascist regime in Italy. 'I conjecture the causes are political. They are afraid of making a false step and losing their jobs.'[64] Clapham rejected Bloch's suggestion of Bognetti, but took up Previté-Orton's suggestion of a Dane, Johan Plesner: 'Scandinavians are honest folk.'[65] Power at this point agreed with Clapham's prejudices: 'There is nothing rotten in the state of Denmark – how different from the "wops". Here is a friendly acceptance from Plesner, who even proposes to fly instantly to the Regno in order to do our chapter properly.'[66] And they also took up another Previté-Orton suggestion of a Finn, Gunnar Mickwitz.[67]

Power started to translate Bloch's piece then, busy with teaching, turned it over to Clapham.[68] She translated Ganshof, and expected to translate some of the French pieces in the second and third volumes. Clapham, by now retired and with more time available, completed the Bloch translation, and took on most of the German pieces, in order to speed things up.[69] Dopsch did not live up to his former high standing in Power's estimation. She rewrote his piece, which she described as 'an extremely bad article'. Clapham had earlier denounced the piece for 'bias towards a rather flabby "continuity" and a quite unnecessary polemic against the (extinct) view that early European agriculture was thoroughly communistic'.[70] He was also critical of Bloch for 'degeneration into a kind of manorialism'.[71]

Clapham had hopes in January 1939 that the volume would be out by the autumn of that year. Most of the pieces were in by then, apart from the Scandinavian section, the piece on Italy by Mickwitz, and part of the general piece on medieval agrarian society by Nabholz.[72] When the volume finally went to press nearly two years later, it was

63 Marc Bloch to Power, 25 May 1938, G. P. Bagnetti.
64 Previté-Orton to Power, 26 May 1938.
65 Clapham to Power, 1 June 1938.
66 Power to Clapham, 15 June 1938.
67 Clapham to Power, 10 October 1938.
68 Power to Clapham, 19 January 1938.
69 Power to Clapham, 19 January 1938, 3 August 1938, 11 January 1939; Clapham to Power, 11 August 1938, 25 April 1939.
70 Power to Clapham, 28 April 1939; Clapham to Power, 10 October 1938.
71 Clapham to Power, 29 October 1938.
72 Clapham to Power, 7 January 1939, Hans Nabholz.

marked by the ravages of war and death Clapham opened his preface with a report of the death of Eileen Power, the loss of the editor 'upon whom, as a medievalist, the main responsibility for the first three volumes rested'. The great exercise in international co-operation had been struck by the onset of war. Koebner, author of the first chapter on the settlement and colonisation of Europe, had been forced to transfer from Breslau to Jerusalem, and to delay his work by learning to lecture in Hebrew. An Italian scholar had succumbed to fascist dictates in Italy, been replaced by a Dane who then died, and finally by a Finn, Mickwitz, who finished, then wrote ' "from somewhere in Finland" in November 1939 that he hoped to get back to economic history but that "it was a small thing compared with the independence of his country". We have not heard from him since.' The Spanish contributor had to give up because he was a refugee in Santander and his notes were in Seville. 'There has been no later news of him either.' 'Of Professor Rutkowski all that we know with certainty is that he cannot be at his University of Poznan; we believe that Professor Ganshof, an officer of the reserve, is alive in Belgium.'[73]

Writing to Eileen Power in 1938 with advice on French scholars who might do the section on Italy, Bloch had commented:

I am extremely anxious about the European situation ... The great crisis seems to be at our doors: a long play of bluff and blackmail which ends in the blackmailed ones becoming so desperate as to take the pistol in hands. What will the blackmailers decide? What *can* they decide?[74]

By the end of 1940 when the first edition of the *Cambridge Economic History* went to press, Clapham wrote: 'We believe ... that Professor Marc Bloch, after serving with the armies, is safe in America.' Bloch had by this time moved to Clermont-Ferrand, teaching at the University of Strasbourg, which had been evacuated there, but his applications for emigration to the United States were in limbo.[75] At the issue of the next edition a year later, Clapham reported that Marc Bloch was safe in France, not in America, that Mickwitz had died in the first Finnish war, and that no one knew what had happened to Peter Struve and Georg Ostrogorsky, Russian exiles in Belgrade. Bloch, his attempts to move to America with his family

[73] Clapham, preface to Eileen Power and J. H. Clapham (eds.), *Cambridge Economic History*, vol. I (Cambridge, 1941), pp. v, viii; F. L. Ganshof, Richard Koebner, Jan Rutkowski.
[74] Bloch to Power, 25 May 1938, Power–Postan Papers.
[75] Fink, *Marc Bloch*, pp. 246–50.

frustrated, was by then teaching in Montpellier.[76] By 1943 he was in the Resistance, but still kept in touch with the editors through clandestine routes. His last letter with enquiries and suggestions for the next volume was sent a few months before he died at the hands of the Gestapo in 1944.[77]

The first volume was hailed by Tawney as a great international enterprise which had succeeded despite the war. 'At a time when to speak of the unity of Europe seems a cruel jest, the present work, to which scholars of some 13 different nationalities have made their contributions, is a welcome reminder of the reality of spiritual bonds, which preceded the war and which will survive it.'[78]

The second volume of the *Cambridge Economic History* did not come out until 1952; it too was the victim of wartime ravages on contributors. Power's death meant not only loss of an editor, but of a key contributor of one of the two general chapters, that on the trade of the Mediterranean south. With Bloch the volumes had lost a key guide to continental contributors. Then A. E. Sayous died soon after submitting a first draft of a chapter on commercial technique. Only one foreign contributor, M. H. van Werveke, had been able to send his contribution before Hitler occupied western Europe, but his chapter had been moved to the third volume.

Postan and E. E. Rich, the new editors, tried in spite of these losses of contributors to keep to the schema over the first three volumes originally devised by Power and Clapham. The volumes displayed, rather than concealed, the conflicts of opinion among contributors; they were a testimony to Postan's defence, in the preface to volume II, of the vitality of a frontier subject.

Economic history is a new and a growing study. The facts and theories with which economic historians operate are even more provisional than the facts in the older and more stabilized branches of historical study. The authorized and established versions of economic history are therefore very few and will, let us hope, remain very few for many years to come. In their absence the study of economic history has done very well, for the striking advances in recent years have been greatly stimulated by the clash of opposing views. Is it too much to hope that the differences exhibited in the

---

[76] *Ibid.*, p. 270.
[77] M. M. Postan, 'Marc Bloch: an obituary note', *Economic History Review*, 14 (1944), 161–2; Fink, *Marc Bloch*, p. 303n.
[78] Tawney, draft of 'Review of the Cambridge Economic History of Europe ... Vol. I', Tawney Papers.

present volume will make their contribution to the stress and conflict of new discovery?[79]

VI

Power's co-operative ventures through the late 1920s and the 1930s in the medieval history seminar, in the *Studies in English Trade in the Fifteenth Century*, and in the *Cambridge Economic History of Europe* were complemented by her own work on the medieval wool trade. This had been her main research interest since her work on the Celys and the Paycockes of Coggeshall before she went to the LSE. What she did during the course of the early 1920s was to shift her interest outwards from individual merchants and their families to the whole economic structure of the woollen industry. In this she was no doubt influenced by the work she was doing with Tawney for the three-volume *Tudor Economic Documents*, published in 1924. She was also influenced later by the work brought back by her research assistant, Postan, sent out to gather data on wool prices, and later in 1926–7, by his dissertation on the finance of the wool trade. Power was collecting data on wool prices from at least 1925.[80] From 1926, there is evidence that her work on the subject, from this point, became joint work with Postan. She corresponded with Howard Gray at Bryn Mawr and with Hubert Hall over merchants' accounts, wool prices and customs returns.[81] She collected voluminous material through the later 1920s on customs accounts, and material on individual clothiers and merchants. During the 1930s she embarked on more major research into sheep farming and sheep breeds, consulting agricultural colleges and institutes of horticulture and animal genetics. On finance she drew on Postan's notes on credit in the Mediterranean trade, and credit in the wool trade.[82]

In the spring of 1938 she was ensconced with her new husband at a farm near Glastonbury, setting her 'medieval sheep farms in the right surroundings', and trying to write her Ford lectures on the wool trade. She found herself 'overcome with the mass of material which I seem to have accumulated, & at present I really do not know how to

---

[79] Postan, preface to *Cambridge Economic History of Europe*, vol. ii (Cambridge, 1952), p. ix.
[80] Letters from Allan Evans, August 1925, Power Papers.
[81] Postan to Power, 26 April 1926; Power to Postan, 21 August 1926, Power–Postan Papers. Letters from H. L. Gray to Power, 1926–8, Power–Postan Papers.
[82] Postan Papers, shelf 1, shelf 5, letters and papers 1934 and 1938, case 69, box 2. Cf. Power, 'The English wool trade', 32.

start on it'.[83] Despite taking some time to write then, she had a particularly heavy teaching term the following autumn. Then, just before term started, the Munich crisis broke. The lectures were still unfinished the following January, a week before she was to give them. 'I am nearly dead over the still unwritten Ford lectures wh. start next Friday.'[84] Directly she had started the lectures, however, she was thinking once again of the *Cambridge Economic History*, and wrote to Clapham of her plans to devote her time to it from the end of February.[85]

The Ford lectures on the wool trade in English medieval history were the first to be given by a woman. Tawney had given the lectures three years before. The lectures ranged widely over the organisation of the wool trade, and its social implications for later structures of British society. They also delved into the techniques of sheep farming and the mercantile connections of large and small producers. Her core lectures focused on taxation and the Staple system, culminating in the Company of the Staple of Calais in the late fourteenth century. Power argued that monopoly price-setting by the Staple secured low domestic and high foreign prices for English wool, and had as its by-product the rise of the English cloth industry.[86] With this, however, went a reduction in the English export of wool, which Power followed through the customs accounts gathered during her earlier work for *Studies in English Trade*.

Power deployed her material on the institutions of the wool trade in order to test the great thesis of Henri Pirenne in *The Social History of Capitalism* that capitalism developed in a series of waves between periods dominated by adventurers or *haute bourgeoisie* and others of respectable prosperity.[87] She speculated freely on the connections between the social institutions of the wool trade in the medieval period and the rise of the English middle class. She reduced the significance of the 'haute bourgeoisie', the speculative financiers of the fourteenth century. Their power was the short-lived product of a specific historical context – wartime finance. The struggle between crown, parliament and merchants in the fourteenth century resulted in the Staple system, which effectively destroyed the conditions

[83] Power to Tawney, 23 March 1938, Tawney Papers.
[84] Clapham to Power, 8 October 1938, Power–Postan Papers; Power to Webster, January 1939, Webster Papers.
[85] Power to Clapham, 11 January 1939, Power–Postan Papers.
[86] Eileen Power, *The Wool Trade in English Medieval History* (Oxford, 1941), p. 101.
[87] *Ibid.*, p. 108.

under which the great financiers operated. The boom and bust of the earlier *haute bourgeoisie* was followed in the fifteenth century by a levelling out, 'a more widespread, but more modest prosperity'.[88]

The Ford lectures set out Power's perspectives on the economic and social framework of the English industrial and mercantile community. They focused on the connections between trade, industry and the land, but her story was above all one of the international basis of medieval society. The wool trade provided the key to unlock the international themes she relished. It broke down images of the self-sufficing natural economy; it was founded in a pastoral world which featured migration and in some cases transhumance; its pastoral economies were freer, less manorial; its international fairs and merchant associations went with cosmopolitan cities established along trade routes.[89]

The lectures were published virtually as Power had delivered them. Postan wrote in his preface to the posthumously published lectures that the book to follow the lectures had been planned by Power for her sabbatical leave in 1940. Wartime conditions prevented him bringing them out with footnotes, appendices and additional chapters. He wrote then that he hoped to do so in future: 'The material has all been collected and digested, and so much of the work was interwoven with my own researches and done in my company, that, given time, I could have tried to piece together something not far removed from the book she herself intended to write.'[90]

Postan published the lectures as lectures, though taking advice from Gwladys Jones on syntax.[91] In fact, however, Power was well advanced with the book by the time she died. She left four chapters typed and heavily footnoted: the wool trade in the Hundred Rolls of 1274-5; the great producers; the evolution of sheep farming; and monasteries and wool contracts. She also left a typescript version of the lectures, complete with their footnotes. For some reason Postan included only one of the four separate chapters, that on sheep farming appearing in the published lectures. Neither the version of the Ford lectures with notes, nor anything containing the separate chapters, was published; and the fuller version Postan hoped one day to do never emerged.[92]

---

[88]   *Ibid.*, p. 123.   [89]   *Ibid.*, pp. 1–19.
[90]   *Ibid.*, p. vi.
[91]   Jones to Postan, n.d., 1940, Postan Papers.
[92]   See Postan Papers for these other versions.

During 1939 Power not only presented her Ford lectures, she also wrote a new series of lectures centred on agrarian organisation and trade, and focused particularly on Marc Bloch and Henri Pirenne. With the coming of war, her sabbatical was given up, and her lectures were presented between the LSE and Cambridge, for part of the LSE was evacuated to Cambridge that year. Postan meanwhile went to the Ministry of Economic Warfare, and so went back to London. The new lectures were devised on a grand format, and covered topics such as 'the decline of the Roman Empire', 'the rise of the great estate', 'crown finance and financiers', 'English trade in the Middle Ages' and 'the Hanseatic League and the Northern Trade'. The lectures ranged across Europe, they were all on large-scale themes of economic history, and none of them were on women or on the themes of social-cultural history upon which she had lectured so frequently in the 1920s and earlier 1930s.

As well as writing these lecture series, Eileen Power planned a volume with Postan, and continued her work with Clapham on the *Cambridge Economic History*. She edited the first wartime issue of the *Economic History Review*, and dealt with the problems of paper shortages.[93] She ran the medieval economic history seminar with its twenty-odd participants on her own.[94] It was a busy year.

[93]   The volume was the 'source book'; see this vol., chap. 8 nn73, 74. See Power to Beales, 1 August 1940; Power–Postan Papers; Power to Beveridge, n.d., Beveridge Papers.
[94]   See membership list 1938–9, Power–Postan Papers.

CHAPTER 9

World history and the end of the world

Eileen Power's internationalism went far beyond academic history. The First World War had affected her deeply, and from that time she believed in using her position as a historian to counteract militarism and nationalism with social history. She pursued these aims in her teaching at the LSE and her writing in medieval economic history through the 1920s and 1930s. She also took an active part in trying to change the content and methods of schools history teaching, she spread her message in her journalism and schools history broadcasts, and she conceived the idea of writing her own history of the world for use in schools. She wrote this book, 'An introduction to world history', though it was never published, against the background of H. G. Wells' *Outline of History* and A. J. Toynbee's *A Study of History*. Then in 1938, faced with choices to be made after the Munich crisis, she became active in anti-appeasement circles, and gave one of her finest lectures, 'The eve of the Dark Ages: a tract for the times'.

I

Eileen Power's activism over history teaching in schools during the interwar years presented an early mirror image of recent debates in Britain over the history curriculum for schools. The introduction of a National Curriculum for schools in 1990 opened up major fissures between protagonists of a 'national' history with a grand narrative structure and supporters of a 'new' history which valued multiculturalism and project-centred methods. This debate on the content and methods of history has centred on attempts to restore British history to a central place in the school curriculum, and new political concerns over the nation and its 'identity'.[1]

---

[1]   Anna Davin, 'Introduction to history, the nation and the schools', *History Workshop Journal*, 29 (1990), 92–4; Samuel, 'Grand Narratives'.

During the years after the First World War there was a very similar debate over history teaching in schools. Historians of liberal-left persuasions turned their energies to the role of history teaching in the making of a new kind of citizen. Debate over changing the content of history towards more international and social history went with proposals for less ministry control over the school curriculum, and the introduction of more project- and child-centred education as a progressive ideal.[2]

Eileen Power's contributions to these debates emphasised the place of teaching world history in the training of future citizens. In a paper entitled 'The teaching of history and world peace' she drew comparisons between the First World War and the Thirty Years War. She reported an examination question on the Thirty Years War where students showed 'great familiarity with the clauses of the Treaty of Westphalia, but only one spoke of the misery of the people upon whose soil that war was fought'. The writers of this examination

were living in a world bled white in an even more devastating war; its horrors must have reached every home; yet so strong was the hold of traditional history upon them that they did not think of turning back to the Seventeenth Century with some of the experience which *this* war has given them of what war means, or of asking what results the Thirty Years War had upon the people of Europe, who are today in the grip of starvation and of typhus.[3]

In a later essay, 'The approach to political and economic problems in schools', Power argued for the history lesson as a medium of political and economic education; as such it should be world history and social and economic history. History, she argued, 'is one of the most powerful cements known in welding the solidarity of any social group'. 'If we can enlarge the sense of group solidarity and use history to show the child that humanity in general has a common story, and that everyone is a member of two countries, his own and the world, we shall be educating him for world citizenship.'[4]

Power continued her campaign to change schools history teaching through the 1930s. She was put on an international committee to revise school textbooks in history towards more international themes,

2   Samuel, 'Grand Narratives', 123.
3   Eileen Power, 'On the teaching of history and world peace', in F. S. Marvin (ed.), *The Evolution of World Peace* (Oxford, 1921), pp. 179–91.
4   Eileen Power, 'The approach to political and economic problems in schools', Postan Papers, 3–4.

and set out to prepare a bibliography of textbooks on world history.[5]
She started broadcasting for schools on the new BBC schools
programmes during the 1920s and continued this, and she embarked
on an ambitious new textbook for children, an 'Introduction to
world history', which was left in her papers, nearly complete, in
typescript but never published.

II

The starting point for Eileen Power's broadcasts, journalism and
book on world history is to be found in her anger with the nationalist
histories written during the First World War and with her disappointment over the Eurocentric focus of the major global histories
begun just after it. A turning away from the nationalist perspectives
of the German historical school, and from the imperial tariff-reform
policies lying behind early economic history, was followed initially
among some historians by a jingoistic condemnation of Germany
and her political and intellectual traditions. A set of Oxford historians – Ernest Barker, H. W. C. Davis, C. R. L. Fletcher, A. Hassall,
L. G. Whickham Legge and F. Morgan – published *Why We Are at
War: Great Britain's Case* (1914). Davis followed this up with *The Political
Thought of Heinrich von Treitschke*, his attack on German idealism and
the German doctrine of the state. On the home front, those identified
with the spread of German Idealist views on the state were seen as
traitors to their own national tradition. Hobhouse identified Bosanquet as a 'pedlar of an alien philosophy'. Bosanquet replied that the
war was not the product of the Idealist conception of the state; on
the contrary, it was the result of a failure to live up to that
conception.[6]

Eileen Power developed her idea for writing a world history in the
context of the two most influential global histories produced during
these years – H. G. Wells' *Outline of History*, published in 1920 and
Arnold Toynbee's *A Study of History*, the first six volumes of which
were published between 1932 and 1939. Power was deeply impressed
by Wells' *Outline of History*. It was a book that 'never loses perspective
... was never provincial'. Though its judgements were often per-
verse, and the details sometimes incorrect, Wells 'never loses sight of

[5] Power to Webster, 3 February 1932; Rhoda Power to Webster, 21 September 1940, Webster Papers.
[6] Parker, *The English Historical Tradition*, p. 108, L. T. Hobhouse and Bernard Bosanquet.

the unities of time and space'. In the *Outline of History*, East and West developed together, and 'civilization as a whole grows before the readers' mind: it *is* the story of mankind'.[7]

Wells had first come to Eileen's attention during her student days, when he was notorious for his sexual peccadilloes (rather than for the racism, elitism and crypto-fascism for which his novels have since been condemned).[8] Eileen's early encounters with Wells were distant views of a notorious progressive.[9] But she later moved in his social circles, and she endorsed him as a Labour candidate for London University in 1921. In 1938 he featured as part of that interesting life in London that stopped her from taking up the Cambridge chair in economic history, 'dining with H. G. Wells one night, a friend from the Foreign Office the next, a publisher another'.[10]

Wells attributed the origins of his *Outline of History* to his discovery of perpetually recurring differences of opinion among members of the League of Nations Union due to their different views of history. He wanted, naively enough even at the time, to provide a general history to which all members could subscribe.[11] The *Outline of History* would also provide a route to salvation through education: 'The war was an educational breakdown ... and in education lay whatever hope there was for mankind.'[12] His *Outline of History* was not based on any background of study in history, nor on any direct experience of travel by Wells himself. The book was written out of *The Encyclopaedia Britannica*, Winwood Reade's *The Martyrdom of Man*, Holt's *World History* and Cruch's *Botanical Memoirs*. He assembled a team of his more serious academic friends and experts as consultants and editors, and paid them 100 guineas apiece for their advice.

Wells was reputed to have written most of the book in a year, publishing it in instalments first, then in a summary version as *A Short History of the World*. But the team of helpers played a large part; indeed, sections of the book were written in his absence, notably by his wife, Jane Wells. She worked long and hard as his unpaid

---

7   Eileen Power, 'The story of half mankind', draft review of Hendrik van Loon, *The Story of Mankind*, Postan Papers.

8   Michael Corran, *The Invisible Man: The Life and Liberties of H. G. Wells* (London, 1992); John Carey, *The Intellectuals and the Masses* (London, 1992).

9   Eileen Power, diary, 1911.

10 Power to Cam, January 1938, Cam Papers.

11 See H. G. Wells, *History is One* (London, 1919); H. G. Wells, *Experiment in Autobiography* (London, 1934).

12 Norman and Jeanne MacKenzie, *The Time Traveller. The Life of H. G. Wells* (London, 1973), p. 317.

9.1   H. G. Wells with Professor Eileen Power at a theatrical première in the
late 1930s

research assistant, distilling passages from his main sources.[13] Within
two years he had sold two million copies in America and England,
and by 1934 it was 'translated into most literary languages except
Italian'.[14] Wells certainly exploited his assistants and collaborators,
but the arguments and structures of the book were his own. As
Toynbee later put it, the book 'detected trends, cycles and movements in world history. Wells saw history as confirming his predictions and hopes for the future.'[15]

Wells described this world history in a way that had great appeal
for Power, for she used similar phrases in her schools proposals. He
saw his effort as

a new sort of history that will twist the minds of its readers round towards a
new set of values ... No one has ever attempted to teach our children the
history of man as Man ... that they are all engaged in a common work, that

[13]   Corran, *The Invisible Man*, p. 153.
[14]   Wells, *Experiment*, p. 179; MacKenzie and MacKenzie, *The Time Traveller*, p. 323.
[15]   Corran, *The Invisible Man*, p. 155.

they have sprung from common origins, and are all contributing some special service to the general end.[16]

The big message of the *Outline of History* was that war was a general disaster, and that there could be no peace but a common peace, no prosperity but a general prosperity, and neither without common historical ideas.[17] The book was journalistic, and contained a number of radical *aperçus*, none of them very systematically connected, but several points fitted with Power's own thinking.

Wells was fascinated by nomadic civilisations, especially the Mongolians. He argued that there were two great systems of development interacting in the story of human society. There were the great primordial civilisations on the one hand; these had created systems of subjugation and obedience. On the other hand there were the nomadic and wanderer peoples, the Nordic Aryans, the Hun-Mongol peoples and the Semites of the Arabian deserts. These 'hardier, bolder, free spirited peoples of the steppes and desert' created a 'nomadization' of civilisation. He praised the Mongolian conquests for diffusing and broadening men's ideas and stimulating imaginations: 'For a time all Asia and Western Europe enjoyed an open intercourse; all the roads were temporarily open and representatives of every nation appeared at the court of Karakorum.'[18]

Power was also attracted by Wells' analysis of the rise of the state. 'Those vast vague phantoms, the "Powers" crept insensibly into European political thought', and were dominant by the later eighteenth and nineteenth centuries. He argued that Europe had given itself up to the worship of a state mythology.[19]

Wells' world history was ultimately a progressive history. It adopted the metaphors of Social Darwinism, charting the rhythms of the historical process as if they were the rise and fall of species in biological evolution. Political ideas, social systems and ruling classes took form, prospered and died just as did biological species. He argued that the human drive to adaptation and survival would find new constructive elements in the emergence of a world consciousness.[20]

Another global history with a message was conceived shortly after

16   Cited in MacKenzie and MacKenzie, *The Time Traveller*, p. 321.
17   Wells, *Outline of History*, introduction.
18   *Ibid.*, pp. 362–3.   19   *Ibid.*, p. 424.
20   *Ibid.*, p. 590; MacKenzie and MacKenzie, *The Time Traveller*, p. 323; Corran, *The Invisible Man*, p. 155.

Wells' *Outline of History*. This was Arnold Toynbee's *Study of History*.
Toynbee's background was also in the liberal-left intelligentsia, but
he produced a philosophy of history with a great deal more
pretension than Wells' downbeat one-world political document. The
background of his work was also the war and, in the first three
volumes at least, the idealism of the League. But Toynbee had much
more to go on than Wells' journalism, the *Encyclopaedia Britannica* and
one year of writing. He was a classical scholar, a member of the
intellectual elite, and he was well travelled, especially in the Far
East. From 1924 he was responsible for the *Surveys of International
Affairs* for the Royal Institute of International Affairs. When Wells
published his book, Toynbee had just read Oswald Spengler's *Der
Untergang des Abendlandes* (1918), which predicted the decline of Western civilisation after the historical pattern of the decline of earlier
civilisations. It was then that Toynbee wrote an early outline of his
Study of History.[21]

Eileen Power had known the Murrays, including Toynbee's wife,
for some time, and had no doubt encountered Toynbee at the LSE.
She visited the Toynbees for a week at Castle Howard in the summer
of 1927, where she reported: 'He always works in the long gallery,
which is a splendid library, so I did too & I became quite accustomed
to strutting along under Gainsboroughs & Reynoldses as though the
place belonged to me, instead of trailing meekly in the rear of a
guide.'[22] She certainly came to know him rather better than she
wished during their ill-fated travels in China after the Institute of
Pacific Relations conference in 1929. Toynbee had by this time been
gathering material for some years for his *Study of History*, but had not
yet started to write it. While they travelled together through
Manchuria and northern China, they discussed his ideas about the
clash of civilisations in the Far East. After Toynbee's return to
England and the end of his infatuation with Power, he settled down
to write his *Study of History*.[23]

Toynbee saw his work as addressing the resemblance between
classical and modern European history, and the perennial encounter
of 'east' and 'west'. He surveyed the past for plausible equivalents to
the Roman Empire, and for equivalents to the combination of
Christianity and barbarian invasions that had led to its fall, and

[21] McNeill, *Arnold Toynbee*, pp. 98–101, 111, 122.
[22] Power to MLG, 21 September 1927, Power–Postan Papers.
[23] McNeill, *Arnold Toynbee*, p. 146.

discovered no fewer than twenty-one civilisations whose rise and decline could be charted.

Toynbee also believed, as Wells did, in a progressive current underlying the reciprocal motions of civilisations rising and declining. He thought that the process led to higher forms of life and culture, and that for this ascent the existence of leading men and leading societies was essential.[24] For Toynbee too, war was the constant destructive force, the occasion of the breakdown of civilisations. He argued that persistent flaws in human nature meant that sooner or later the growth of every recorded civilisation had been checked by the unleashed brutality of war. The repair of war's ravages permitted a dominant minority to achieve peace by establishing a universal state; this 'creative minority' was the repository of a healing pattern for new beginnings. Toynbee looked to a new religion of the universal state.[25]

Toynbee's idealism and political elitism were more polished and more scholarly than were Wells', but his message was not so very different. What it lacked of Wells' racy journalism it made up for in pretension. When the first six volumes were published in 1934, his message still had some credibility, and he had not yet made the monumental political misjudgements he was to make in the later 1930s. According to McNeill, 'the power and sweep of Toynbee's portrait of the past impressed his English contemporaries profoundly'. There were rave reviews by his father-in-law Gilbert Murray, by Leonard Woolf and J. L. Hammond. He found only one shadow of an academic attack, from E. L. Woodward, who questioned Toynbee's selection of facts.[26] But in fact, McNeill did not look too far for hostile reviews. Postan was dismissive in the *Sociological Review*, and much later, when all the volumes were published, the eighteenth-century historian Richard Pares attacked the books in the *English Historical Review*.[27]

Personal reactions were also more circumspect. Clapham was very funny about it. He reported back to Power:

I read 3 vols. of Toynbee on holiday. Queer book. Great in patches. But far too long. He has a pontifical way of telling stories of himself – how once

---

[24] See M. M. Postan, 'A study of history. A review of Professor Toynbee's book', *The Sociological Review*, 28 (1936), repr. in Postan, *Fact and Relevance*, pp.144–54, at p. 145.
[25] McNeill, *Arnold Toynbee*, p. 141.   [26] *Ibid.*, p. 162.
[27] Postan, 'A study of history'; Richard Pares, 'A study of history by Arnold J. Toynbee', *English Historical Review*, 71 (1956), 256–72.

(bless him!) he motored thro' the West Riding into Lancashire (he will call it
the Black Country) and what his 'reactions' were. When he wants to drive
home to us Westerns that Chinese and Negroes dislike our smell, he can't
just say that but tells 1 1/2 pp. of anecdote to establish it ... And I can't
picture *his* picture of his typical reader. This bloke can read stiff Greek and
stiff German at sight. But he has to be told Plato's parable of the cave
almost verbatim. I could talk a lot more but spare you.[28]

III

Eileen Power's own 'Introduction to world history'[29] was started
during the mid-1930s; parts of it drew on radio talks she had given
during this time. The book was virtually complete at the time of her
death, but was never published. It avoided Toynbee's ostentatious
display, and was merely offered as her contribution to her long-
standing involvement in educational initiatives and committees to
promote the study of world history in schools. There are few clues to
the book's provenance, but after her death, her sister Rhoda alluded
briefly to it. She described it as 'her part of a text book on World
History which we were going to write together', and as 'almost
complete'. She wrote that she would finish it, as it was for children of
twelve.[30] The book, however, was a substantial twenty-eight chapters, each of approximately five thousand words, the bulk of it
centred on the Middle Ages and the early modern period, and its
intended audience was much more likely to have been fifteen- and
sixteen-year-olds.

Eileen Power's idea of writing a book on world history arose
directly out of her involvement with her sister Rhoda in schools
history broadcasts. Out of their collaborative book for children, *Boys
and Girls of History*, and its sequels, evolved a unique partnership for
conveying history through the medium of radio.[31] Shortly after a

[28]   Clapham to Power, 18 September 1934, Postan Papers.
[29]   Eileen Power, 'Introduction to world history', Power–Postan Papers; incomplete version in
       Postan Papers.
[30]   Rhoda Power to Webster, 21 September 1940, Webster Papers.
[31]   E. E. Power and Rhoda Power, *Boys and Girls of History* (Cambridge, 1926); E. E. Power
       and Rhoda Power, *Cities and their Stories* (London, 1927); E. E. Power and Rhoda Power,
       Twenty Centuries of Travel (London, 1926); E. E. Power and Rhoda Power, *More Boys and Girls
       of History* (Cambridge, 1928). See also some of Rhoda Power's own productions: *Union Jack
       Saints. Legends Collected and Rewritten by Rhoda Power* (London, 1920); *The Age of Discovery from
       Marco Polo to Henry Hudson* (London, 1927); *How it Happened. Myths and Folk Tales; Stories from
       Everywhere* (London, 1931); *Richard the Lionheart and the Third Crusade*, ed. Eileen Power
       (London, 1931); *Great People of the Past* (Cambridge, 1932); *The Kingsway Histories for Juniors*

9.2   Eileen Power broadcasting

pioneering survey of schools in 1927, schools broadcasting was developed in new directions under Mary Somerville. One of the great success stories in these initiatives was Rhoda Power's dramatised history lessons.[32] These were a departure from the more formal radio lecture suited only to adults and older children. Eileen Power frequently wrote the historical background for these lessons, and Rhoda then conveyed them. Several of the best remembered were on familiar Eileen Power territory – the wool trade dramatised through the day-to-day lives of a fifteenth-century woollen merchant and his three sons; or life in a medieval village through the story of a serf, Simon the Tod, who runs away from a nearby manor.[33]

(London, 1937). There were more volumes in the 1940s and 1950s related to Rhoda Power's BBC broadcasts.

[32]   Asa Briggs, *The History of Broadcasting in the UK*, vol. II, *The Golden Age of the Wireless* (London, 1965), p. 195; See BBC *Memorandum of Information: School Broadcasting*, June 1932; Rhoda Power, 'Dramatization in the teaching of history', Paper to the NUWT, 30 April 1932, BBC written archives.

[33]   Richard Palmer, *School Broadcasting in Britain* (London, 1947), p. 84.

9.3 Rhoda Power at the BBC

Eileen and Rhoda started a series on world history from 1932 onwards.[34] Eileen played a major part herself in a series of world history programmes she devised during the mid-1930s for children aged thirteen and older. From 1934 through 1936 she was broadcasting major series of twelve programmes a term for which she was paid eight guineas a programme.[35] She found the programmes difficult to write, and she frequently missed her deadlines. But she was clearly a popular broadcaster; one BBC official commented on a programme she did in 1938: 'Good as ever, even if she does sound like a headmistress on Prize Day.'[36]

By March 1936 Eileen was discussing her plans for a world history textbook with Oxford University Press, but early plans for the book were hatched a few months before during an acrimonious exchange with the BBC. During 1936 Eileen was in dispute with the BBC over

[34] *BBC Broadcasts to Schools*, vols. XVI, XXII–XXIV, 1932–5, BBC written archives.
[35] *BBC Broadcasts to Schools*, vols. XXV–XXVII, 1934–6; Eileen Power, talks, file 3, 1936–40, BBC written archives.
[36] Comment of N. G. Luker, 16 December 1938, Eileen Power, talks, file 3, 1936–40; Power to Edith MacQueen, several letters in 1935–6, Eileen Power, talks, file 3, BBC written archives.

differences in the conception and content of the programmes and the accompanying pamphlets. At issue was the use of dramatic interludes, with Eileen this time on the side of the lecture format. Mary Somerville suggested to Eileen that she devise her world history courses for younger audiences and use more dramatic interludes rather than the straight lecture formula she had followed for her older audiences, but Eileen objected that there was a lack of textbooks to back up the interludes, and that the subject was being taken less seriously by the BBC. She was clearly regarded as a prima donna by Mary Somerville, who scribbled on one of Eileen's letters: 'Is EP the only person who can treat the world in the round?' But Eileen Power fought her corner with the BBC, writing in visible anger in late January:

It seems an essential purpose of history teaching in schools to explain his wider as well as his narrower environment to the child, who is a future citizen of the world as well as of Britain. It is doubly essential today, when the front page of every newspaper is full of America, China, Japan and India. But such an explanation can only be given at an age when it can be understood *as an explanation* ... it is impossible to do this in the form of desultory stories and dramatic interludes for small children.

She dismissed the suggestion that world history should be taught in relation to the history of Great Britain: 'It seems to me highly undesirable to intensify the egocentric tendency of most history teaching by treating the history of the world as a mere background to that of Britain. It is a negation of all that we have tried to do for the last five years.' She refused to collaborate on any course in British history, and declared her absolute commitment to getting world history into schools as a subject for older children. One of her means of doing so was 'by devoting what little spare time I have to preparing a textbook on the subject'.[37]

Relations with Mary Somerville and the BBC went from bad to worse a few months later when the BBC published a picture, 'Bolivar and his generals discussing the campaign of the Andes' in the pamphlet to go with her term's lecture series. She wrote Mary Somerville the most angry letter that survives in the entire collection of her correspondence: 'It is, as you know, entirely against my principles to concentrate attention on wars in the world history

[37] Power to Mary Somerville, 27 January 1936; cf. Mary Somerville to Power, 13 January 1936; and Power to Mary Somerville, 2 January 1936. All letters are in Eileen Power, talks, file 3, 1936–40, BBC written archives.

course ... it is obvious that a fancy picture of generals whom I am not going to mention, in a war on which I am not going to dwell, is a most unsuitable choice.' She pointed out that she had chosen a picture of the 'Great Christ of the Andes', but her instructions had been ignored, and her reference to the picture deleted from the proofs.

I most strongly object to being treated this way by the BBC, especially in view of the great deal of time & trouble I always give to the preparation of the pamphlet. *I* am responsible for what goes out to the schools for use with my talks, and I consider it a gross impertinence to ignore my instructions.[38]

This outburst was followed by another protest a few months later over a programme on China. An editor cut out a criticism of the missionaries: 'We rather felt the missionary societies might object, and it is not really essential.' Power was not prepared to allow this to slide:

I note that you have cut my phrase about the quarrels of the missionaries in the 18th Century. As you know it was this which resulted in the shutting of China to the West, and I strongly deprecate these attempts of the BBC to tamper with the presentation of history in order to save the susceptibilities of a class of its listeners.[39]

Power had, by this time, clearly lost her battle with the BBC for a serious course on world history. In July she and Rhoda were cut off from the schools broadcasting programmes for a time, though at whose instigation was not clear.[40] In the autumn a new series on world history by Mary Beggs, a lecturer at Goldsmith's College, was introduced. This followed exactly the format sought by Mary Somerville, of a series of stories for younger children with dramatic interludes.[41] The following year Rhoda was asked to take on the narration of the world history and the British history series, and in July that year was given a new contract for thirty broadcasts on British history for a fee of £225.[42] Eileen did individual broadcasts from time to time after this, but no further series.

---

[38]   Power to Mary Somerville, 29 March 1936, Eileen Power, talks, file 3, BBC written archives.
[39]   PP to Power, 10 June 1936; Power to Edith MacQueen, 11 June 1936, Eileen Power, talks, file 3, BBC written archives.
[40]   MWS to Power, 2 July 1936, Eileen Power, talks, file 3, BBC written archives.
[41]   *BBC Broadcasts to Schools*, pamphlets, vol. XXVII, 1936.
[42]   Edith MacQueen to Rhoda Power, 23 March 1937, 20 July 1937, Rhoda Power, talks, file 1, BBC written archives.

Eileen, therefore, turned her efforts instead to her textbook, 'Introduction to world history'.[43] She followed the moral precepts of her famous contemporaries Wells and Toynbee in denouncing war and the rise of the absolutist state, and in seeking principles of unity among nations. But she had no predictions to make over the rise and fall of civilisations, nor did she offer any panaceas in universal states. The key difference in terms of scope from the world histories of Wells and Toynbee, as well as from others written at the time, was the emphasis Power gave to the Arabs and the Chinese. Toynbee and Wells professed to write about the world, but Toynbee knew about the Greeks, and Wells about Europe. Power brought the medieval and early modern Arab and Chinese civilisations to the forefront of her story, and dwelt on periods of religious toleration and foreign trade.

She compared great principles of international co-operation in the Holy Roman Empire, in the Islamic Empire from the sixth to the twelfth centuries, in the Mongol Empire of the thirteenth and fourteenth centuries, and in China under the T'ang dynasty from the seventh to the tenth centuries and later in the early Manchu dynasty in China during the seventeenth century. She followed a rough chronological format in the book, but pursued similar themes across periods and empires.

She saw in the Arab conquests the creation of a great unity across the world from the Atlantic Ocean to the centre of Asia. Through this vast area pilgrims, merchants and men of learning passed freely. Power admired the scholarship and religious toleration of this civilisation, and even more she admired its significance as a great trading civilisation – merchants were much respected in Muslim society. She retold the stories of the great caravan routes from East to West – the caravan route from China across Central Asia to Samarkand and Bokhara, where it was joined by caravan routes from India, then south of the Caspian Sea into Persia. This was both the silk route from China to the Roman Empire and the route by which Buddhism went from India to China. The land and sea routes that bound together the West and the Far East all through the ancient and medieval periods were forged by the Arab merchants.

The major result of the crusades in Power's view was the increase in contacts between Christian, Byzantine and Arab civilisations

[43]   Power, 'Introduction to world history'.

around the Mediterranean. There was greater trade, and a mingling of these civilisations in the three doors between Europe and the East – the Latin kingdom of Jerusalem, Sicily and Spain.[44] The significance of the timing of Power's analysis should not be missed. She wrote these words on religious and cultural toleration, and on the interconnected role of Arab and Jewish merchants in forging cross-cultural links, in the years of the growth of anti-Semitism and trade barriers before the Second World War.

Her eye was also turned to China. China under the T'ang emperors had contributed to the great trading connections by conquering westward until the two great empires of China and Persia came face to face. The next two hundred years were known for religious toleration, travellers and trade, the beginning of printing and paper money.[45] Power, like Wells, also admired the Mongolian Empire. She condemned its destruction of Muslim civilisation in Central Asia, but in the wake of these conquests, she argued, the Mongols created a peaceful, well-ordered realm, divided into four Khanates run from Peking, Samarkand, Persia and Russia. The Mongol Empire brought peace for trade, and right across Asia the roads were open to traders with their goods, to missionaries with their gods, artists carrying Chinese designs to be woven into Persian carpets, or those carrying the Persian art of enamelling to China.[46] Power pronounced the breakup of the Mongol Empire on the one side and the Holy Roman Empire on the other to be responsible for the rise of the Ottoman Turks, whose conquests brought not new connections but an unbridgeable divide between East and West. The siege of Constantinople in the fifteenth century ended the Byzantine Empire, the former bridge between the ancient and the medieval worlds. 'Now the great city had fallen and the sound of its fall was the sound of a closing door.' The roads between East and West closed, and the Ming dynasty which arose in China looked to the old China and shut her doors to the world outside.

The Japanese model of civilisation, however, never attracted her. She had disliked the Japan she saw on her Kahn Travelling Fellowship, describing its civilisation as one borrowed from China, India and Europe, 'a people who had adopted the Western idea of civilization as material progress while clinging to the Eastern idea of

[44] *Ibid.*, part ii, chap. 2.   [45] *Ibid.*, part i, chap. 5.   [46] *Ibid.*, part ii, chap. 5.

religion in the shape of a blind patriotism'.[47] She had read the news of Japanese incursions in Manchuria which culminated in the Japanese seizing control in September 1931, and had disagreed with Webster on their intentions.

What do you think of the Japanese now? Did I tell you my theory that it was they who stole the Lindbergh baby in order to get themselves off the front page? ... the Mitsui & another big Japanese bank are going to advance a vast loan without interest to the new Manchurian Govt. Could there be clearer proof that the Japanese intend to stick to the place ... There could be no more cynical flouting of the League Committee. Meanwhile I observe that even the Japanese have ceased to pretend that the forces they are fighting are mere bandits.[48]

It was in this spirit that she wrote of the failures of the shogunates in Japan. She depicted the split in Japanese civilisation between the art and poetry of the Ashikaga shogunate (1334–1573) and its war-mongering administration. And later the great Tokugawa shogunate (1603–1867) shut itself off from other peoples, living its own life like a hermit in a cell.[49]

Passing from medieval Europe and the Arab and Mongolian Empires into the Europe of the sixteenth to eighteenth centuries was for Power a transition from unity, peace and trade to nationalism, war and religious conflict. It had taken Germany over a century to recover from the Thirty Years War. Louis XIV, after the War of the Spanish Succession, had left his country in a miserable state of poverty. The Dutch Republic, the great symbol of political liberty, had only emerged after two exhausting struggles against Spain then France, struggles which drained away her lifeblood, so that she soon lost the status of a great power. England was the only winner, because she had kept war off her own territory and emerged with the colonial possessions she wanted. Power depicted the eighteenth-century architects of nation states and benevolent despotism as international brigands responsible for the enormous international crime of the destruction of Poland:

It is only now, after four centuries in a world of great states ending in a terrible world war that we are beginning to feel that ' "patriotism" is not enough' and that Europe lost something of great value when it turned away from the ideal of these ancient and medieval thinkers ... we shall have to

[47] Power, *Kahn Report*, p. 56; Eileen Power, 'Japan the enigma', *The Athenaeum* (24 November 1923), 319–20.
[48] Power to Webster, 5 April 1932, Webster Papers.
[49] Power, 'Introduction to world history', part II, chaps. 7 and 11.

take up their task again and find some new means of expressing an international unity, to which we must be as loyal as we are to our own country.[50]

Eileen Power took her 'Introduction to world history' up to the end of the eighteenth century. It was complete in typescript apart from a few chapters she intended to write out of revised versions of some of her radio talks. She was still writing the book in 1938, but there is little reference to it after that. Did other work and wartime pressures cause her to set it aside? Or was its message of internationalism and peace no longer something she could believe in after the German occupation of Poland?

IV

The 'Introduction to world history' was certainly as much about the Europe of the later 1930s as it was about the Arab and Chinese cultures Eileen Power sought to introduce to British schoolchildren. The nationalism, trade barriers and political aggrandisement of the later 1930s threatened to cast Europe once again into the state of war created by the eighteenth-century nation builders. Their partition of Poland then was to be replayed over a century later at the outbreak of the Second World War.

In 1939 Eileen Power attended the League of Nations Assembly in Geneva, and wrote movingly of the speech of the Polish delegate, 'the pathos of the occasion ... enhanced ... by the appearance ... of the aged Paderewski, who sat in the auditorium, chin on stick, like an image cut in ivory, listening to the voice of a Poland once more partitioned'.[51] She was at this time still defending the League, hoping that its existence and condemnations of aggression backed up with even minimal sanctions was better than mere dreams of federal union.[52] But by now she was no pacifist. She had always been deeply critical of fascism, and was part of a prominent anti-appeasement circle in the later 1930s.[53] Much of the Labour Party, except for some members of the Labour left, opposed appeasement on the grounds that it condoned fascism. Her friends Hugh Gaitskell and

---

[50] *Ibid.*, part III, chap. 2.
[51] Eileen Power, 'Geneva impressions', *The Spectator* (22 December 1939), 892.
[52] *Ibid.*, 893.
[53] Eileen Power, 'A guildsman on fascism', *The Nation and the Athenaeum* (8 September 1922), 719; Postan, 'Hugh Gaitskell: political and intellectual progress', in Postan, *Fact and Relevance*, p. 179.

Hugh Dalton stood for resistance to Germany, though another friend from this group, Evan Durbin, reluctantly followed other Labour Party supporters of peace. Eileen Power was immediately appalled by the Munich agreement, as she made clear a few days afterwards in a letter to Clapham. In this she stood out against many in her literary and political circles, for the *New Statesman* took sides with *The Times* in supporting the series of conciliatory British actions in the weeks leading up to the crisis.

When Chamberlain returned from Munich at the end of September 1938, the response of several of her contemporary internationalists was to support him in his policy of appeasement. Clapham replied to her in the following week with his reasons for supporting Chamberlain:

> I find myself behind Halifax. Samuel, whose speech in the Lords I thought as noble a thing as the debate produced – Jimmy Maxton and, today, McGovern. Halifax also has an old school tie and I always respected Maxton ... So my personal allegiances are happier than yours ...
>
> From village after village in France people ran out to stop an English car driven by a woman I know and tell her to take their thanks to Chamberlain – Jimmy Maxton's common people.[54]

Toynbee's immediate reaction was to write that 'the [Germans'] mischief making power will turn out to have been much clipped', and 'the principle of self-determination of nations has now at last been applied equally for the benefit of the nations that happened to be on the losing side in 1919–21'.[55] A few weeks later, Toynbee had changed his tone and predicted that the principle of national self-determination in Europe was 'bound to produce a Mitteleuropa under German hegemony'.[56] Trevelyan, the other great liberal historian of the day, found himself 'wholly on Chamberlain's side', and 'could not understand how any pacifist or peace lover can be anything else'.[57]

Eileen Power rejected these views, and she found plenty of supporters among other friends. Wells, whom she saw on occasion during 1938, denounced Chamberlain's capitulation to Hitler's blackmail.[58] A Labour Party socialist group which included Power,

---

[54] The Earl of Halifax was foreign secretary at the time of Munich; Marcus Samuel was MP (Nat. C) for Wandsworth 1934–42; Jimmy Maxton was Labour MP for Glasgow; John McGovern was MP (ILP) for the Shettleston division of Glasgow 1930–47, then Labour MP 1947–59. Clapham to Power, 7 October 1938.
[55] McNeill, *Arnold Toynbee*, p. 173.   [56] Cited in *ibid.*, p. 174.
[57] Cannadine, *Trevelyan*, pp. 133–4.
[58] MacKenzie and MacKenzie, *The Time Traveller*, pp. 410, 419–40.

Postan and Tawney, as well as Durbin, Gaitskell, Barbara Wootton, Leonard Woolf and others had met in 1934–5 and decided on an active campaign against fascism.[59] Eileen Power had long been a critic of anti-Semitism. Her correspondence with J. H. Clapham over the *Cambridge Economic History of Europe*, and the efforts of both herself and Clapham over finding jobs and publishers for some refugee historians and researchers reveal their attitudes.[60] But the world she lived in, the liberal left, literary London and the academic establishment, was uncomfortable with Jews, considered them as outsiders, and used racial jokes and slurs with little thought. Eileen Power's friend Harold Laski experienced the full brunt of socialist anti-Semitism, especially from another of her friends, Hugh Dalton.[61] Laski attended her kitchen dances; Sir Matthew Nathan, Sir Victor Sassoon and Humbert Wolfe[62] were Honorary Powers. Moreover, M. M. Postan was her closest collaborator, friend then husband. But it is not known to what extent Postan's Jewishness affected her attitudes, or indeed even what she knew about his background.

Eileen Power and Postan took a leading part in campaigning against appeasement, and in 1938 Power applied her knowledge of medieval history to the task of denouncing Chamberlain. That autumn she had set aside both her 'Introduction to world history' and much of her work on the *Cambridge Economic History of Europe*, for she was locked into a very heavy teaching term at the LSE, taking over courses left by colleagues on sabbatical.[63] But with the Munich crisis in the autumn, she dropped her teaching preparation to prepare a lecture to the Cambridge History Club which she gave at the end of November or early December 1938. She wrote to Helen Cam on 21 November: 'At present I am in despair for I *can't* make

---

[59] Elizabeth Durbin, *New Jerusalems. The Labour Party and the Economics of Democratic Socialism* (London, 1985), p. 189.

[60] Clapham was chairman of the Society for the Protection of Science and Learning during this time, and was very active in helping Jewish refugee scholars. Eileen Power tried to find a publisher for A. D. Hessell's book, 'The rise of the House of Commons and the wool trade 1215–1343'. He had been unable to publish in German because he was a 'non-Aryan'. She also sought out a research secretary post for a female refugee. Postan Papers, case 69.

[61] See Kramnick and Sheerman, *Harold Laski*, pp. 206–8, 353–7; Tony Kushner, *The Persistence of Prejudice. Antisemitism in British Society during the Second World War* (Manchester, 1989), pp. 85–92.

[62] Humbert Wolfe was referred to as 'Humbert the Jew' in the doggerel Beryl Power concocted for Eileen Power's fortieth birthday, 'Ode to EEP on reaching the age of 40', Power–Postan Papers.

[63] Clapham to Power, 7 October 1938; Power to Clapham, 11 January 1939.

the paper 'come'.[64] But during the preceding months she had gathered together an enormous range of material to illustrate and support a remarkable rhetorical intervention into the whole debate on Munich. This was her lecture 'The eve of the Dark Ages: a tract for the times'. 'Munich' was pencilled over the title.[65]

She began with the observation that the Renaissance preoccupation with the age of Greece and Rome had been due to an inner feeling of recognition, of a sense that the world's great age begins anew. She compared this to her own feelings now of being drawn as a historian to the centuries that saw the fall of Rome and entry into the dark tunnel of barbarism. She contrasted what they stood for: Rome stood for a civilisation, trade and ideas, peace and security, law and government. The barbarians stood for race, tribes loyal to a leader, personal relations (as distinct from citizenship), and war. Roman civilisation, she added, was about intellectual achievement, and contributing to the legacy of Greece; learning in the barbarian world was in its infancy. The parallels with appeasement were clear throughout the lecture. She argued that the Roman army had been barbarised, and the legions in turn barbarised the emperor. 'For them he is no longer the majestic embodiment of law, he is their leader, their Führer, and they raise him on their shields.'[66]

In her conclusion Power asked why the Romans had been so blind to what was happening: 'The big country houses go on having their luncheon and tennis parties, the little professors in the universities go on giving their lectures and writing their books; games are increasingly popular and the theatres are always full.'

She answered that the process of disintegration was a slow one ... it is only because we can look back from the vantage point of the future that we can see the inexorable pattern that events are forming, so that 'we long to cry to these dead people down the corridors of the ages, warning them to make a stand before it is too late'.

They suffered from the fatal myopia of contemporaries. It was the affairs of the moment that occupied them ... At what point did barbarism within become a wasting disease? ... Was it the withdrawal from Dacea in 270 –

---

[64] Power to Cam, 12 November 1938, Cam Papers.
[65] The unpublished lecture as well as drafts of it, and research notes compiled for it, are in the Power–Postan Papers. Further research notes towards the lecture are in the Postan Papers. A shortened version of the lecture, entitled 'The precursors', was later included by Postan in the tenth edition of *Medieval People* in 1963.
[66] Eileen Power, 'The eve of the Dark Ages', lecture to the Cambridge History Club, 12. The phrase is repeated in 'The precursors', *Medieval People*, p. 5.

give the Germans *Lebensraum* in the East of Europe, fling them the last-won recruit to Romania and they will be satiated and leave the West alone? Was it the settlement of the Goths as foederati within the Empire in 382 ... Was this policy of appeasement the fatal error?

They were deluded, she argued, by the error of imagining that Rome was a condition of nature. 'They took it for granted that civilisation could not die. But it died.'[67] The Romans were blinded, Power went on, by the perfection of their material culture. 'The roads grew better as their statesmanship grew worse, and central heating triumphed as civilisation fell.'

Power concluded her great parable with some words on the role of the historian:

But however strongly you may believe that civilization is in the end immortal and must rise again, you cannot gainsay the immense significance of the fact that in the West it was dead for five hundred years ... Of course there were lights in the Dark Ages – there are stars in the night – but 'never glad confident daylight again'. If historians were less obsessed with an outworn fetish of progress, less convinced that all is always for the best, they might be of greater help to their generation. The men of the Dark Ages had no such illusion; they knew what they had lost and the memory of Rome haunted their wistful minds like the dream of a golden age.

Characteristically, she also reminded her readers of China. The Romans 'could not see across the mountains & deserts of Asia in the then unknown East, the only other great secular civilization, the Han Empire of China, going down (it too) during those same disastrous centuries, before the attack of barbarians from the North.'[68]

When Postan put together the tenth edition of *Medieval People* in 1963, he included a version of the essay under the title 'The precursors'. For this he replaced the first two pages and the last (which were topical comments – 'I am sure that she never intended these passages to be perpetuated in her *Medieval People*') with a reconstruction of what he referred to as pages from her first draft.[69] Yet it is evident to any reader that the whole essay, and not just its introduction and conclusion, resounds with parallels with the Europe of the 1930s.

Power, in this lecture, equated Rome with internationalism, and not with imperial power and military dictatorship. In so doing she

[67] Power, 'The precursors', pp. 14–15.
[68] Power, 'The eve of the Dark Ages', conclusion.
[69] Power, *Medieval People* (10th edn, 1963), p. xi.

stepped aside from the imagery the Nazis themselves had adopted as leaders of a new world empire with all its attendant Roman iconography, holding back the Asiatic barbarism of Stalin's communism. Toynbee had echoed such images in his disillusioned forecast of the imminence of a new world empire. He thought there would be a competition between Russians and Germans for the role of twentieth-century Romans: 'Personally, I am inclined to think that the Germans rather than the Russians will play the Roman part.'[70] But for Power, the 'Romans' were those who had been unable to see that barbarism was a denial of civilisation, and had sat by complacently while the barbarians encroached and civilisation perished.

v

The war broke up the new life with Postan into which Eileen Power had so recently settled. In the year before the Munich crisis, they had married, Postan had gained the chair in Cambridge she had planned for him, and they had moved to the new modernist house in Cambridge at 2 Sylvester Road that they had had built for their new life together. They kept the house in Mecklenburgh Square, for Eileen carried on with her teaching and her medieval economic history seminar at the LSE. With the war, however, Postan was called to the post of Assistant Secretary at the Ministry of Economic Warfare, and he returned to London. A part of the LSE was evacuated to Cambridge, and Eileen went with it. She divided her time between London and Cambridge, and in Cambridge carried on her medieval history seminar and took on Postan's work in editing the *Economic History Review*. One of the young members of her seminar, Elizabeth Crittall, assisted her with the editing, then became one of her evacuees along with another student from the LSE. Her house in Cambridge became a gathering place for her students and for economic historians. The dinner parties and dances once held in Mecklenburgh Square were now replaced in Cambridge by Sunday afternoon 'at homes' for economic historians and large gatherings of other friends, colleagues and visitors from Cambridge and London.

Through the summer of 1940, Eileen travelled back and forth to London, and took pleasure in working in her garden at Sylvester

---

[70] Toynbee to Quincy Wright, 1936, cited in McNeill, *Arnold Toynbee*, p. 173.

Road, along with Elizabeth Crittall. Postan had been away on his ill-fated 'mission to Moscow' with Stafford Cripps since the end of May. Cripps had been sent as ambassador to Moscow; Postan, as head of the East European section of the Ministry of Economic Warfare, was to accompany him. They had waited for credentials and Soviet agreements in Sofia, and Postan had been refused a visa. Cripps flew to Moscow, and Postan set out to return home via Italy, but was diverted after Italy entered the war. He eventually returned via the Cape in the last week of July.[71]

During that week Eileen had a busy day going to London for a General Purposes Committee, back to Cambridge, then down to London again on the midnight train so as to meet him at Euston the next morning. While he was away she herself had worked at the Ministry of Economic Warfare, but her work there fell through after a few days because the woman she was replacing had returned. She looked forward, however, to other war work as soon as she had completed the new issue of the *Economic History Review*.[72] Some days later she was gardening again in Sylvester Road, and was forced to stop after a sharp pain in her back.[73] She returned to London that week and wrote to May Wallas from Mecklenburgh Square on 7 August about her friend Florence Halévy. 'I have thought about her such a lot. I am told that communication with unoccupied France is almost impossible except by telegram ... The trouble is that I too feel very doubtful about the wisdom of sending communications from England to a Frenchwoman. The anti British feeling is bound to grow & I should hate to embarrass her in any way ... What a world.'[74] The next day she went shopping in Bourne and Hollingworth's and collapsed. Eileen Power died of a heart attack in the ambulance on the way to the Middlesex Hospital.[75] She was fifty-one.

The will that Eileen Power had drawn up the previous December was a characteristic document of her friendships and the things she cared for. Her husband was her executor, and her witnesses were Val

---

[71] See Gabriel Gorodetsky, *Stafford Cripps' Mission to Moscow 1940–42* (Cambridge, 1984), pp. 41, 68–9. For more on Postan's wartime work see Keith Hancock, *Country and Calling* (London, 1954) and W. N. Medlicott, *The Economic Blockade* (London, 1952).
[72] Power to Beales, 1 August 1940, Power–Postan papers.
[73] Interview with Elizabeth Crittall.
[74] Power to May Wallas, 7 August 1940.
[75] The death certificate gave as cause of death heart tumour or myxomatous. General Register Office, death certificate, 13 August 1940.

Judges and Hugh Gaitskell. There was not a lot of money. She left a life insurance policy valued at £3,300 for the education of A. V. Judges' small daughter, Eve. Her personal property came to £2,080 in capital and £1,231 in other assets. She left her capital to her closest sister, Rhoda, and the rest of her property and most of her personal possessions to Postan, with a series of provisos: that he should secure publication of her friend Sir Matthew Nathan's book, that he should keep up payments on the educational insurance policy she had taken out for Eve Judges, and that he complete repayment of the loan made to her by her sister Rhoda. She remembered her special friends, M. G. Jones, Margery Spring Rice and Elizabeth Downs, and left them particular pieces of Chinese jewellery. In the case of M. G. Jones there was a picture by Vulliamy, a number of books and the armchair she had been given by the Girton staff when she left Cambridge. But Margery Spring Rice was left the salutary gift of her copy of *Ecclesiasticus*. Her sisters both received Chinese jewellery, coats, pictures and scrolls. She also remembered her housekeeper, Mrs Saville, and a god-daughter, Antonia Clapham and a godson, John Cowell. She wanted her books, together with Postan's on his death, to be left to the LSE for the founding of a history seminar room, to be known as the M. M. Postan and Eileen Power Library.[76]

---

[76] Register of Wills, Somerset House, 9 December 1940. Postan eventually secured the publication of Sir Matthew Nathan's book, *The Annals of West Coker* (Cambridge, 1957). *Ecclesiasticus* or *The Wisdom of Jesus the Son of Sirach commonly called Ecclesiasticus* (Oxford, 1932) was collated and edited by Arnold Danvers Power, a cousin of Eileen Power. It contained 'wise sayings, dark sentences, parables and certain ancient godly stories', and may have been given as a parting joke to Power's best friend. The LSE could not accommodate the books Eileen Power bequeathed to it. They were later sold through book dealers.

CHAPTER 10

Clio, a muse

The last fifty years have witnessed great changes in the management of Clio's temple. Her inspired prophets and bards have passed away and been succeeded by the priests of an established church; the vulgar have been excluded from the Court of the Gentiles: doctrine has been defined; heretics have been excommunicated; and the tombs of the aforesaid prophets have been duly blackened by the new hierarchy. While these changes were in process the statue of the Muse was seen to wink an eye. Was it in approval, or in derision?[1]

G. M. Trevelyan was drawn to address the muse because he saw history in its eighteenth- and nineteenth-century meaning as an art, not a science. It was a form of literature, like poetry, that required the imagination. Great historians were dedicated to the art of narrative, and wrote history as literature. He disliked the 'Germanising hierarchy' which attempted to train historians as scientists. The heroic historical narrative he admired was written by Gibbon, Carlyle and Macaulay.

It was believed that few women practised the art of narrative in this higher literary form; instead, they used the lower literary form of the novel. The Germanising influences, however, had brought greater credibility to the archival research methods that women interested in history had long pursued. Simultaneously, however, the Germanising hierarchies professionalised the innovations and practices of the historical fields in which women had made their contributions. Others have discussed the extent to which women carved out their own historical subjects in biographies, foreign social histories, historical novels, and social

[1]   G. M. Trevelyan, 'Clio, a muse', in G. M. Trevelyan, *Clio, a Muse and other Essays Literary and Pedestrian* (London, 1918), pp. 1–55, at p. 1.

histories.[2] History was a young discipline, much less prestigious than jurisprudence and moral philosophy.

Female historians practised their craft, not just as scholarly gentle-women, but in the interstices of subjects relatively new to the university. In Ireland, for example, history as an academic discipline only started in the first decade of the twentieth century, and women held three of the first six chairs established in the subject.[3]

Female historians appeared to be particularly prominent before the Second World War in medieval history and in economic and social history. Eileen Power in 1940 stood at the pinnacle of a new kind of history, economic and social history, which precisely because it was so new included more women than other more established historical disciplines.[4] She was also a medievalist, an area of history already attractive to many female scholars. The accommodation of women within medieval history, however, went with much more limited professional recognition. In America, for instance, though women were part of the Medieval Academy from its beginning, that part was a very small one. Of the thirty-three fellows elected in 1926, only one, Nellie Neilson from Mount Holyoke, was a woman.[5] Another American, Frances Davenport, pioneered the statistical analysis of medieval court rolls at the beginning of the twentieth century, but her work had little impact precisely because, as Zvi Razi has argued, her work was ahead of its time.[6] Since she did not occupy a central position in the academic hierarchy, her innovation was marginalised.

What impact did Eileen Power make on her contemporary historians? Trevelyan's *English Social History*, published in the US and Canada in 1942, and in Britain in 1944, was one response. He dedicated it to the memory of Eileen Power, economic and social historian. Trevelyan wrote most of the book before the war. In the introduction to the book he made the well-known statement: 'Social history might be defined negatively as the history of a people with the politics left out.' He went on to argue that many history books

---

2 See Thirsk, 'The history women'; Smith, 'The contribution of women'; Melman, 'Gender, history and memory'.

3 Mary O'Dowd, 'Women's history and Irish history', unpublished paper presented to the Warwick Regional Seminar on Gender, History and Historiography, 28 February 1994.

4 See Berg, 'The first women economic historians'.

5 Bennett, 'Medievalism and feminism', 312. Nellie Neilson (1873–1947) was a student of Maitland and Vinogradoff, and taught at Bryn Mawr and Mount Holyoke, and wrote extensively on medieval agrarian history and English common law.

6 Razi, 'The historiography', 18.

had consisted of political annals with little reference to their social environment, and that a reversal of this might have its uses. To this, significantly, he added:

During my own lifetime a third very flourishing sort of history has come into existence, the economic, which greatly assists the serious study of social history. For the social scene grows out of economic conditions, to much the same extent that political events in their turn grow out of social conditions. Without social history, economic history is barren and political history is unintelligible.[7]

Trevelyan saw social history as not just a link between economic and political history; it had its own positive value and peculiar concern – its scope 'the daily life of the inhabitants of the land in past ages'.

The book that Trevelyan dedicated to Eileen Power's memory was a 'sensational success'.[8] It sold 100,000 copies within a year of its publication, and by the early 1950s had sold half a million. Power and Trevelyan had known each other, though not well, for Trevelyan was well over a decade older than Power, and had been Regius professor at Cambridge since 1927. Her death at the point where she had achieved a major position as a historian, but still appeared to be so young, cut off in the middle of creating so much more, was a great tragedy to her contemporaries. This was Trevelyan's tribute. She was there among the good and the great, but still the representative of the younger historians, the standard bearer of new directions in the economic and social history she had helped to create.

Yet it is clear that Trevelyan had not fully understood those new directions. He appears to have seen his own social history as a continuation of what Power had presented in her *Medieval People*. In that early work Power had tried to personalise social history, and so to bring it alive in the form of individual characters who yet represented whole social classes or groups within medieval society. Likewise, in *English Social History*, Trevelyan had tried to 'tell the story as life is presented on the stage, that is to say by a series of scenes divided by intervals of time'.[9] His method was to present successive scenes of English life, the first of which was the lifetime of Chaucer.

Trevelyan's social history was, as Cannadine has argued, literary and poetic, an act of imagination as much as of research. He was a

7   G. M. Trevelyan, *English Social History* (London, 1944), p. vii.
8   Cannadine, *Trevelyan*, pp. 174, 23.
9   Trevelyan, *English Social History*, p. xi.

literary craftsman, 'possessed' by the idea of writing, and his prodigious learning was always lightly borne.[10] These ideals were in some measure shared by Power, who also valued fine writing and despised the 'cardbox' historians who felt the necessity of informing the reader of every morsel of archival research. But in every other way Trevelyan's history stepped back to a social history she had long left behind. It encompassed the ideals she had once admired in G. G. Coulton's work, but its denial of 'scientific history' and the professionalisation of history showed that Trevelyan was blind to the role of theory in historical explanation.

Power's idea of social history from the time she came to the LSE developed away from simply revealing the lives of ordinary people towards offering a historical analysis of social structures. Her close contact with the social sciences at the LSE stimulated her to think in conceptual terms. But she applied economic and social models as a historian, not for their own sakes, but as keys to a better understanding of social change. Thus she had turned to the analysis of the underlying trends of medieval agrarian society and to comparative commercial and industrial development. This work took social history onto an altogether different plane, and bound it into the new discipline of economic history.

There were two other ways in which Power's idea of social history was quite different from that presented in the book Trevelyan dedicated to her. First, she could never have written a book with the limited national focus of *English Social History*. Trevelyan started with Chaucer's England because for the first time England began 'to emerge as a distinct nation'. 'In Chaucer's time the English people first clearly appear as a racial and cultural unit.'[11] The book was the kind of elegiac, parochial and national account she had tried so hard to displace from the historical outlook of both popular and schools audiences. Her own *Medieval People* was a European history; her last work was a world history. Her own identification with Marc Bloch made it all the more ironic that Trevelyan's text, dedicated to her, should be castigated by another French historian, François Crouzet, as 'un pamphlet de propagande nationaliste et xenophobe', with a tone of 'complaisance et d'autosatisfaction'.[12]

The second way in which Eileen Power's idea of social history was

10 Cannadine, *Trevelyan*, pp. 183–96.
11 Trevelyan, *English Social History*, pp. l, xii.
12 Cited in Cannadine, *Trevelyan*, p. 222.

different was in its very sense of the professional creation of her discipline. Power worked in archives, and had a reputation for finding primary sources and using these in new ways. She was chosen by the British Academy to give a special lecture on the significance of Walter of Henley's papers. She also started major new archive collections, such as the London business records collection and initiatives such as the project on the history of London, and sought Rockefeller grants to fund these. Eileen Power developed research projects, set up her research seminar to pursue these, and had a clear idea of developing her subject, if not in a directed school, then through a range of research students who would take her subject in various directions. Although her fame today lies in the individual legacy she left to the study of women's history, the main school of research students she left at the LSE developed a specialism there on aspects of medieval trade. Finally, she had a sharp sense of the gulf between those she would identify as writing economic history, and having some idea of economics, and those who pursued the subject in an amateur way. She had disapproved of Clapham's choice of Runciman for the Italian chapter of the *Cambridge Economic History of Europe* because he had no idea of economic problems.[13] Likewise, she had preferred Carus-Wilson because she had a close, archivally based knowledge of the woollen industry.

Eileen Power's professionalism and her hopes of turning history outwards from its focus on English political history towards comparative economic and social history did leave a mark, if only for a short time. Her own research students pursued their work on medieval trade and commercial history, and published articles and volumes during the following two decades. Some of the other students and colleagues she had influenced wrote the big books of social history and women's history which were not overtaken until the 1970s and 1980s – Alice Clark, Dorothy George, Ivy Pinchbeck, Dorothy Marshall and H. S. Bennett among them. Neither the subjects nor, in most cases, the authors of these histories, however, achieved the recognition to enable their own careers and Eileen Power's legacy to flourish. Many of these historians were women. Several did become dons in women's colleges, or lecturers, sometimes eventually promoted to readers, in other universities. But only Eleanora Carus-Wilson became a professor; the few others who achieved prominence

---

[13]   Power to Clapham, 6 March 1936, Power–Postan Papers.

did so by leaving for America – Sylvia Thrupp and Power's Girton friend and colleague Helen Cam. In this way Power's legacy was confined and marginalised, and she herself dropped out of the historical canon.

Another historian, Marc Bloch, only a few years older than Eileen Power and engaged in similar historical initiatives, also died during the war. Natalie Davis has compared aspects of their lives and work. But we can also compare their reputations in terms of the making of historical memory – the creation of a 'founding father' figure on the one hand, and the forgetting of the feminine presence on the other.[14] There is no need here to make claims for similar degrees of brilliance, innovation and contribution, but our knowledge today of what Marc Bloch did achieve rests on the way his fame was enhanced after his death through the active creation of historical memory. In the case of Eileen Power, who had considerable fame, if not the same kind of creativity as Marc Bloch, during her lifetime, the process was reversed. She was forgotten, and with this so were the particular directions she sought for economic and social history.

Marc Bloch died during the war, a martyr of the Resistance. Many eulogies were published after the discovery of his death; his unpublished work was published in the *Annales d'histoire économique et sociale*, in the *Revue de Synthèse* and in books.[15] An intellectual biography by Charles-Edmond Perrin was published in 1948. Bloch's reputation was associated with the new institutional base in economic and social history and the social sciences, the Sixième Section of the Ecole des Hautes Etudes en Sciences Sociales, founded in 1947. The tenth anniversary of Bloch's death was marked with memorial articles in the *Annales* and in the press, and the new head of the *Annales* and of the Sixième Section, Fernand Braudel, was deeply committed to keeping Marc Bloch's memory alive. Collections of his articles were brought out in the 1960s, and his reputation remained central as the Annales school gained in popularity and international fame.[16] There was a sense in which the memory of Marc Bloch took the place of a founding myth for the *Annales*.[17]

How was Bloch's contemporary, Eileen Power, a parallel founder

[14] Davis, 'History's two bodies', 23–5; see also her 'Women and the world of the "Annales"', *History Workshop* 33 (1992), 121–38, which discusses the female scholars associated with Bloch, Febvre and Braudel.
[15] Fink, *Marc Bloch*, p. 326.
[16] *Ibid.*, pp. 329, 335, 338–40.   [17] Epstein, 'Marc Bloch', 282.

of the discipline of economic and social history, remembered in her country? The institutional responses were limited, and Eileen Power was remembered for her personal qualities and for being a woman to a much greater degree than she was for her scholarship or her vision of economic and social history. An institutional tribute to Power's contributions to history was immediately launched by Tawney and Webster in the form of a memorial fund. This was to celebrate her interest in foreign countries and belief in the value of travel, and was to provide a fellowship for studying economic and social history abroad. Within a month of Power's death Tawney had drawn up a list of suggestions for a committee to include the director, Alexander Carr-Saunders, Webster and himself at the LSE, Mary Stocks at Westfield College, Clapham, M. G. Jones and Coulton in Cambridge, Powicke and G. N. Clark in Oxford, T. S. Ashton at Manchester, Bertha Putnam in the US, a French historian, to be identified, possibly Marc Bloch himself (still at this time alive, and not yet active in the Resistance), Jonathan Cape, one of the Cadburys, and a Chinese historian. There had been some suggestion of Sir John Neale at University College, and of H. G. Wells, but Tawney decided against these.[18] By January 1941 the committee had been set up at a meeting in Cambridge with Carr-Saunders as chairman, M. G. Jones and Betty Behrens as joint secretary, and Lawrence Cadbury as treasurer.[19] The memorial fund was announced in the press in August 1941, with plans to raise capital of £10,000.[20] It still exists today as the Eileen Power Memorial Studentship.[21]

Tawney also hoped that a volume of Power's writings would be produced, to include as an introduction Webster's article about her from the *Economic Journal*.[22] Postan pressed on with an early publication of the Ford lectures with only slight revisions. He also had plans for a later edition with full footnotes and appendices to include the technical material upon which her conclusions rested.[23] Neither the first nor the last of these projects was pursued.

The memories of Eileen Power conveyed in obituaries and other accounts in the years immediately following her death mourned the

[18] Tawney to Webster, 7 September 1940.   [19] Tawney to Webster, 10 January 1941.
[20] *The Times*, 15 July 1941.
[21] See the particulars of the Eileen Power Memorial Studentship in the *Economic History Review*, 48 (1995). The preference for candidates studying a foreign country has, however, disappeared from the particulars.
[22] Tawney to Webster, 10 January 1941, Webster Papers.
[23] Clapham to Webster, 29 September 1940.

personality, but failed to convey her particular historical contributions. All who knew her wanted to convey the shock and tragedy of her early death. The common theme in the balance sheet drawn up for Eileen Power was an emphasis on her pioneering role as a female historian. She appeared to some to be a unique and extraordinary case of mainstream academic achievement in her field. Notices about her life included that she was the first woman to hold the Kahn Travelling Fellowship, that she was the first female Ford lecturer, and that she was one of the first female professors of economic history.

The notices did not, however, draw out the contribution she made to scholarship and the formative part she took in the creation, institutionalisation and popularisation of economic and social history. Certainly, all the notices about her life listed her publications, but few of these, at such close remove, were able to assess the differences made by her work to the directions taken by medieval and economic history. Clapham, in his obituary notice, and Marjorie Chibnall, in a more recent interview, pointed to some key contributions. Clapham praised her leadership in the *Cambridge Economic History*, and her innovation in avoiding rigid chronological treatment, drawing on a few contributors, and asking each to take a big theme and to treat it comparatively. As we have seen, however, she had found few scholars with the nerve to do this. Marjorie Chibnall credited Power with taking medieval history beyond its previously limited constitutional and political framework. She brought in a much broader archival base, and sought to relate agrarian structures to local and international trade.[24] Yet such serious notice as there was of her work neither subjected it to any sustained critique nor assessed the kind of contribution made by her new social and comparative history. Soon after Power's death the types of history she stood for were no longer central. Women's history as an academic subject taught within the universities, and incorporated within broader historical surveys, was her creation, but it fell out of academic history after the Second World War, and only re-emerged in the 1970s. The broad comparative economic and social history informed by sociological and anthropological concepts she sought to foster with projects such as the *Cambridge Economic History of Europe* lost impetus in Britain, and economic approaches took priority. This is

[24] Clapham, 'Eileen Power', 359; interview with Marjorie Chibnall, 15 March 1990.

despite the fact that Postan carried on with subsequent volumes of the *Cambridge Economic History*, and they have been continued since by Peter Mathias to cover historical periods up to the 1960s. Power brought together economic and social history, and she was an evangelist for what she did, somewhat in the manner of Marc Bloch. Yet his followers were able to carry the movement forward; hers were not. The achievement of social history was attributed to Tawney alone; the combined field with its international dimensions was split asunder. What she had written, taught and organised thus became a lost byway, and eventually a list of disconnected antiquarian pieces of social history.

The impression left by accounts of Eileen Power was above all else of a personality and of a woman who had been loved by those who knew her. It was the fascination and inspiration provided by a beautiful but utterly scholarly woman that really stood out in the accounts left by men and women. Eileen Power was not a bluestocking: her physical appearance and feminine charisma turned learning into elegance, even beauty. Most were fascinated by her beauty and her clothes, as well as the interests she chose to list in *Who's Who*: travelling and dancing. Clapham wrote: 'Her rooms were full of beautiful things, mostly Chinese. And – this is important – her dress was appropriate to her rooms, although not mostly Chinese.' He remembered commenting to her at some learned gathering: 'Eileen, you look like Semiramis.' She had replied: 'I thought I looked like a professor of economic history.'[25] Her former mentor, Coulton, had managed to add a characteristic comment on religion to his epithet and had written: 'Her costume and the serene composure of manner came up to Henry James' standard: "A woman who feels herself to be perfectly well dressed has a sensation of inward peace such as religion can never bestow." '[26] Webster described her impact on other scholars in terms of her physical presence:

I was once invited to dine with her at Harvard with a number of scholars who admired her work. She came late into the room in a New York frock that suited her perfectly, with long ear-rings of exactly the right shape and colour, looking about fifteen years younger than her years, her eyes sparkling with enjoyment of a 'party' in her honour. There was an audible

[25] Clapham, 'Eileen Power', 355–9.
[26] G. G. Coulton, 'Memories of Eileen Power', *Cambridge Review*, 52 (1940), 28–9.

gasp of surprise when it was realised that this enchanting creature was the learned lady whom they had come to meet.[27]

Eileen Power became the 'learned lady', dressed up in the character-istics of romantic memory, now in death receiving the 'praise of ladies dead and lovely knights' spurned by her contemporary medieval historian Nellie Neilson. She was admired for her feminine gifts, friendship, personal charm, wit, vivacity and beauty,[28] and she evoked the special affection expressed so movingly by Tawney:

One sees her after a heavy day's work, scampering off light-heartedly to one of her parties, coming home at midnight to sit up till 2 a.m. writing next day's lectures, and then, when, on seeing her light, one looked in to insist that she really must go to bed, asking sweetly whether she couldn't do one's next week's work for one.[29]

The women who remembered her used a similar language of appreciation and even of love for an embodiment of beauty, love-liness and youthfulness.[30] This glamour, along with her political integrity, made Eileen Power an attractive role model to a genera-tion of female students and academics. These features attracted many women into the discipline she played such a vital part in transforming.

By contrast, Power's intellectual originality was passed over or even slighted. Her work was remembered for her writing style,[31] as well as other 'female' traits, lucidity, intellectual modesty, industry, methodical work.[32] Some critical assessment of her methods ques-tioned her use of theory. Clapham and Webster both commented on the absence of economic theory from Power's work. Webster referred to her lack of training in economic science; Clapham wrote of his personal impressions to Webster: 'She was no economist in the strict

27 Webster, 'Eileen Power', 572.
28 Obituary, *The Manchester Guardian*, 12 August 1940; obituaries, J. H. Clapham, *The Times*, 13 August 40, and others in *The Times*, 15 August 1940; 19 August 1940; R. H. Tawney, *Eileen Power*, address delivered at Golders Green Crematorium, 12 August 1940 (London, 1940); J. M. Keynes to Webster, 29 October, 5 November 1940; Tawney to Webster, 10 January 1941, Webster Papers. Other more recent recollections by Maurice Beresford, H. J. Habakkuk and Asa Briggs referred to a 'Renaissance face', elegance and a brilliant style.
29 Tawney, *Eileen Power*.
30 Jones, 'Memories of Eileen Power', 4, 10; Jones to Cam, n.d. [10 August 1940], Cam Papers; Nellie Neilson to Tawney, 21 October 1940, Tawney Papers.
31 Jones, 'Memories of Eileen Power', 5; Dorothy Marshall, diaries; Webster, 'Eileen Power', 564.
32 Webster, 'Eileen Power', 564; R. M. Haig Brown to M. G. Jones, 23 September 1940, Power–Postan Papers; Tawney, 'Eileen Power'.

sense, but had a splendid range of knowledge in economic and social history ... She knew the economic historians of nearer Europe far better than I do and was highly esteemed by them – technically I mean: of course they were all her slaves personally.' He pointed out again that Power would most certainly have been offered the Cambridge chair if she had stood for it. 'I repeat it to show that, economist or not, her mastery of the subject was acknowledged.'[33] Clapham, finally, wrote in his article about her: 'She would have hated to spend her life with attention concentrated on one aspect of human activity, and could never have brought herself to neglect men and women for generalisations about them, bankers for their liquidity preferences or horse dealers for J. A. Hobson's doctrine of their bargains.' She had 'scores of books of poetry to one "Principles of Economics".'[34]

The point about the use of economics in economic history was not, however, taken further to compare her work with that of other contemporary economic and medieval economic historians. Nor was it made clear whether 'economics' was the application and testing of contemporary economic theories, whether it was the collection and presentation of quantitative data on various aspects of the economy, or whether it was the description and analysis, drawing on a variety of techniques and theories, of the functioning of the medieval economy. In later years the lack of economics was simply equated with lack of analysis – completely overlooking Power's attempt to draw anthropological and sociological concepts into economic history.[35]

The characterisations of Eileen Power in the years following her death clearly sought to go beyond the dry dust of scholarly contributions and intellectual legacies. This was a historian who had had a major personal impact on those around her. The words they used drew out the personal, with all the feminine attributes they most admired – friendship, beauty, wit, personal charm, hard work and clarity of writing. The accolade she had been given when presented with her honorary degree at Manchester was that 'she combined the graces of the butterfly with the sober industry of the bee', and

---

[33]   Clapham to Webster, 29 September 1940, Webster Papers.
[34]   Clapham, 'Eileen Power', 358; Webster, 'Eileen Power', 568. Yet Clapham himself made little explicit use of economic theory. Postan indeed objected to Webster's words on her lack of economics, pointing out that 'she knew much more of the technical stuff than she ever revealed'. Postan to Webster, n.d., Webster Papers.
[35]   See Coleman, *History and the Economic Past*.

Tawney repeated this to encapsulate what she represented to him.[36] None of her friends, colleagues and students meant these as a denigration of her place as a scholar and intellectual. But they had the effect of closing off her originality.

There is, perhaps, a sense in which Eileen Power herself conspired in the creation of this myth of the female scholar. She wanted, in her own being, to express the aesthetics she admired. In the years that followed, however, she was left with the feminine attributes, now belittled, and much less of the scholarly recognition. In Clio, the muse of history, Power had sought both inspiration and scholarly achievement as a historian. In memories of Power the female historian, it was the inspiration, not the writing of history, that was recalled.

What Eileen Power had done was now completely overshadowed in Cambridge by the new prominence of her husband, M. M. Postan. His knowledge of philosophy and the social sciences, and his dialogue with economics, carried the field forward in new directions.[37] These did not develop the start Power and her students had made on the study of the commercial and mercantile aspects of medieval history; rather, they centred on agrarian and demographic change. Postan's new departures brought a fresh outlook on the medieval agrarian economy, overturning the older concerns of the manorial-constitutional school. What he wrote was not quite the new turning it appeared to be, for he built on what he had learned from R. H. Tawney's *The Agrarian Problem in the Sixteenth Century*,[38] and from the work he had done with Eileen Power on the cloth trade and pastoral agriculture. But the impact of his few, seminal articles was none the less profound. The shift in the framework of medieval economic history that Postan led also fitted much more easily into a more general shift in the questions asked by economic historians. These moved from the interwar concerns over the origins of capitalism to the post-war emphasis on the sources of economic growth.[39]

Like that of Marc Bloch, Postan's reputation was carefully culti-

[36] Cited in Tawney, 'Eileen Power'.
[37] 'Sir Michael Moissey Postan, 1899–1981', *Economic History Review*, 30 (1982), iv–vi.
[38] This point was made by Zvi Razi, 'Rural society and the economy', unpublished paper presented to the Economic History Society Conference, Edinburgh, 1995.
[39] Cannadine, 'The past and the present' points out this interest among post-war historians in economic growth, but does not adequately explain the concerns of the interwar economic historians. There were intellectual as well as institutional reasons for the prominent place occupied then by medieval economic historians in the historical disciplines generally.

vated. He had a long life, and dominated his field for much of it. His
brilliance was not in doubt, but he also fostered his own reputation
in a cult of story-telling about himself which others delighted in
repeating, and embellishing with their own stories long after his
death, and even to this day.[40] He set himself 'in the frame' by
creating a mythology of himself, which is now handed down through
the generations.

What Eileen Power aspired to in her inaugural lecture, and in the
comparative and international history she was pursuing in her later
years, was to integrate economic history on a large scale with
sociological questions and concepts to achieve an economic and
social history. The possibility of such an integrated economic and
social history only re-emerged at the end of the 1960s and in the
1970s in dialogue with Marxism.[41] That possibility was in turn cut off
by the rise in econometric economic history on the one hand, and on
the other by the rise of a new social history 'from below', which
turned away from economic issues. Two of Power's approaches set
her apart from these developments, and raise questions about an
alternative route which she might have taken had she lived longer.
These were, first, her own independent socialist stance and critical
attitude towards Marxism, and second, her long campaign for and
practice of an institutional, comparative economic and social history.
With her death and a combination of factors following the war the
subject of economic history changed. It narrowed its concerns to
those of economics, with long-run trends of economic growth,
economic development and demographic trends to the fore, and the
anthropological and sociological questions she had raised were
pushed aside, and left to the new, separate field of social history. The
discipline lost the political and social commitment that had marked it
during the interwar years, and it became increasingly professionalised. With all of these factors went a sharp decline in the involvement of female historians, and especially of those occupying
mainstream academic positions.

The reasons for the decline of women in the field after the Second
World War are social, institutional and intellectual. First, there was a
more general decline in the numbers of female academics in the

---

[40]   I owe this point to Natalie Davis, who noticed the Postan stories that form a common
currency among economic historians.
[41]   See Richard Smith, 'Introduction', in Power, *Medieval People* (10th edn, London, 1986),
p. xvi.

post-war era. Women had a much higher chance, due to changing demographic factors, of marriage and children; spinsterhood and careers were no longer regarded as equal, if not better, alternatives. It was still difficult to combine marriage and careers, and those who did so were relatively few. They were not given the support they needed by male or single female colleagues, or by married women outside the workplace.[42] Institutional constraints grew; hierarchies rigidified; newer fields such as economic and social history, sociology and anthropology became professionalised and departmentalised. Women who had previously found a niche in more flexible structures were now marginalised. But these problems, common to women in academic life, were not enough in themselves to account for the dramatic fall in women's participation in economic and social history.[43] The reasons were intellectual as much as they were institutional. The priority given after the war to economic growth and capital formation forced underground former mainstream subjects in social history, labour history and women's history. Women and many men with broader historical interests left the field, and turned their attention to the founding of a separate social history.

I have emphasised that Eileen Power took a professional attitude to the history she wrote, an attitude that set her apart from Trevelyan. She respected economic history that was based in close archival research and demonstrated a knowledge of economic issues and concepts. Most of Power's own generation of medievalists sought such professionalism through the study of institutions and politics as against what they perceived as a past legacy of 'romantic antiquarianism'.[44] Power sought her professionalism in developing the new discipline of economic history. She nevertheless saw this economic history as an analytical history, integrated into the social sciences and responding to theoretical questions. She deployed enormous energy in developing and organising her discipline, using the research seminar and collaborative research projects on major archives such as the customs accounts, in creating a society and a journal, in fostering international scholarly co-operation and in using the lecture podium and the media to demonstrate to a wide audience what economic history was about. But, in the years following her death, the professionalisation she believed in turned

[42] Dyhouse, *No Distinction of Sex?*, pp. 161–7.
[43] For more discussion of this see Berg, 'The first women economic historians'.
[44] Scott, 'American women historians', p. 181.

into academic hierarchies, narrow specialisation and the 'card-box' histories she had long before denounced. This new form of pro-fessionalisation offered little encouragement to a broadly based participation in historical writing and in particular to the female historians who had once constituted an important part of Power's research community.

Eileen Power was cosmopolitan and internationalist, and at the forefront of progressive intellectuals. She was also a medievalist, an exacting and careful scholar, and a writer of high literary merit and aesthetic sensibility. Some of these qualities were, perhaps, products of the older perception of history as an art, an extension of classical training and literary sensibility. But in Power's, and indeed in Tawney's hands too, they could both claim the respect of colleagues who still valued these qualities, and the attention of a broader readership who could now study the new history of the lower and middling orders, and through this understand some of the new social science concepts of the time. As a woman writing the new history in an immediately approachable way she shaped her subject and made it a central part of the contemporary national culture.

From the 1970s a new generation of feminist historians rediscovered Eileen Power, above all, ironically, through the essay she had most disliked, 'The position of women' from Crump and Jacobs' *The Legacy of the Middle Ages*, and she once again appeared in historical footnotes. A collection of her lectures, *Medieval Women*, edited by Postan, and published at the instigation of his second wife, Lady Cynthia Postan, was issued in 1975. Eileen Power has come to be regarded, perversely enough, as an easy target for critics, representing the 'romantic' view of the Middle Ages.[45] More positively, she has been remembered as the historian of nunneries and medieval housewives, continuing the tradition going back to the nineteenth century of women writing social history and private lives.[46] For Natalie Zemon Davis, who rediscovered Power in a remarkable comparison with Bloch, what distinguished Power was her aim to write about the one group that Bloch never considered: the women of different social estates.[47] Power was praised by Cantor, unlike most of the historians who appear in his recent quirkish *Inventing the Middle Ages*, but praised among the 'dissenters, the eccentrics, the nonconformists' for her

[45] See Bennett, ' "History that stands still" '.
[46] Smith, 'The contribution of women', 709–32.
[47] Davis, 'History's two bodies', 22.

feminist history.[48] He described *Medieval English Nunneries* as 'the most underrated major work in medieval history'. The new feminist consciousness, he argued, had not penetrated medieval studies until the 1970s, but Power had made a definitive response to the question of women's condition in 1922: 'Little attention was paid for half a century to what she was saying.'[49]

Would Eileen Power have liked a position as an icon of feminist or women's history? Perhaps she might, for it is better to be remembered for some of the things one has written and fought for than for none of them. In her own lifetime she was certainly recognised as the major historian of medieval women, and she devoted her guest lecture series at Bryn Mawr, Aberystwyth and at Girton during the 1930s to social history and women's history. She by no means abandoned the subject. As feminist history and women's history comes of age and seeks the move from 'margins' and 'frontiers' to 'core' and 'established' will it not seek its own founding myths and female saints? Will Eileen Power fill that role, providing the potent mixture of struggle against adversity, achievement, sympathetic political views, and historical denigration by a predominantly male professional hierarchy? But before yielding to this temptation, it should be recalled that Power wrote most of her women's history in the earlier parts of her life, and women did not feature so much in her later work. Her later work ensures that she deserves a larger place in the history of her discipline.

From the early 1920s until her death Eileen Power saw herself as an economic historian, and she pursued this subject through a comparative approach in studies of the peasantry, trade and the woollen industry. When she wrote about women, it was within this framework. She saw the importance of an institutional basis for the discipline of economic history in a journal, in university courses, in school history teaching and in publishing. Tawney knew how she saw herself: 'Economic history, however, was not only her profession, but her dominant interest, and her allegiance to it did not waver ... she threw herself into its advancement with unflagging zeal.'[50]

The economic history that Eileen Power fostered at the LSE, and through the *Economic History Review* and the *Cambridge Economic History of Europe*, was closely tied to current issues and concerns. She brought

[48] Cantor, *Inventing the Middle Ages*, p. 376.
[49] *Ibid.*, pp. 387–8.
[50] Tawney, 'Eileen Power', 92.

the present into the past, and shaped economic history at the LSE within a broad and politically relevant mould that was both her own and a part of the tradition of the LSE. When she wrote of the coming of war in 1938, she wrote 'The eve of the Dark Ages: a tract for the times', and spoke of the position of the historian: 'The ears of the historian are full of echoes, but since his own existence is the thing most real to him, some sound more clearly than others, because his ear is attuned to the ring of a clarion or the toll of the passing bell.' Women were integral to this conception of the discipline; they were there in large numbers in the field before the war, and Power occupied a prominent position in the predominantly male professional hierarchy. She had an enormous appeal to her female as well as male readership, and in turn she fostered women's participation in the field both through her own example and the individual encouragement and teaching she gave to women, and finally through the combination of social and economic history she wrote.

Perhaps as another female economic historian, I might speculate on the huge gap between the great project of a comparative and an integrated economic and social history of Eileen Power's day, and the narrow quantitative economic history that now dominates our field. One woman standing up for this integrated history, had she lived and remained in the prominent intellectual position she held, might not have made a difference to this, but a number of women in such positions could certainly have done so. More than inspiration was needed from Clio, the Muse; her own writing and teaching were vital. Eileen Power wrote in *Medieval People*: 'This book is about the kitchens of history.' If only, perhaps, there had been more dancing in the kitchen.

Pekin

If wishes were rickshas, beggars would ride
I wish I were a mandarin
And lived in yellow-roofed Pekin.
I'd have a courtyard with a tree
Through which the moon should shine on me,
And there below the rustling leaves
I'd have a house with curly eaves.
I'd have a spacious cushioned k'ong
Where I might dream the whole night long,
And hear the curtain at my door
Swish to and fro across the floor.
I'd have some goldfish in a bowl,
And on my wall a painted scroll
Of hills and waterfalls should hang
Made in the lovely age of T'ang.
Kwan Yin in painted ivory
On stand of carven ebony
Should clasp her child upon her knee,
And dimly lacquered o'er with gold
Brought from some temple shrine of old
Buddha, the lord who knew no guile,
Should smile his immemorial smile.
A pig-tailed boy should bring to me
Thin cups of amber-coloured tea
And fragrant rose-leaf-scented wine;
And when my friends came in to dine
With clicking chop sticks they should stoop
O'er jellied eggs and bird's-nest soup,
Sharkfins and duck and lichees sweet,
Peanuts and melon seeds should eat.
I'd have a robe of blue and gold
All sewn with dragons fold on fold,
And buttons set with many a gem
And broidered waves about the hem.

Time and Tide, 2 January 1925, 15.

I'd wear a chain from neck to knee
Of jade and lapis lazuli,
With amber beads an inch apart
Brought from a far Malaccan mart.
And in a case of old brocade
With silken knots and tassels made
Should hang my fan of ivory
Adorned with poems two and three
By Hanlin scholars writ for me.
And I would have a lady rare
With moth-dark brows and cloudy hair
And all the day she should be fair.
Oh, I would have a lady bright,
More beautiful than pale starlight,
And she should love me all the night.
Sometimes beside me she should lie
When high the moon stood in the sky
And sing me love songs of Li Po
Set to a tune of long ago.
And sometimes she should dance for me,
Slim as a waving bamboo tree
And light as foam above the sea.
So day should follow happy day
And life should slowly drift away,
And when I reached mature old age
I'd keep a cricket in a cage,
And gamble on him half the night
With four old men by candle light.
And when next morn from sleep I woke,
I'd sit beside my door and smoke,
And smile and watch the blue-clad folk.
And when at last I came to die
Adown the road with gong and cry
Banner and text and canopy,
My funeral should stretch for miles
With green robed beggar men in files,
And weeping mourners all in white
And scarlet coffin huge and bright.
With paper rickshas, paper arbours,
And paper boats for heavenly harbours,
With paper money scattered free
And paper secretaries three,
Opium and rice and tea and wines,
And rows of paper concubines,
All the delights that man can boast

To please my disembodied ghost.
But oh! I should be far away,
My spirit should forever stray
High in a lonely western hill,
Where day and night are very still,
And there where winds and white clouds play
I should be one with night and day.

But I am not a mandarin,
I do not live in old Pekin.
No blue coats flutter in the breeze
Here are no whispering ginko trees,
No green and blue and yellow tiles
That shimmer in the sun for miles.
No paper-latticed windows dim
Are lit by candles pale within,
No dogs and dragons guard the eaves,
No courtyards sleep beneath green leaves
Behind the walls of shady lanes.
Here dust is on the window panes
And dust upon the stunted planes.
Here in a smoke-encircled town
The sad faced folk go up and down,
And houses rise so gaunt and high
They blot the sun and hide the sky.
Here is no time for lovely leisure
Wherein the heart may store its treasure
Of fair things seen and bright truths known
And knowledge unto wisdom grown.
Here even love must furtive be
In darkened rooms snatched hastily.

I wish I were a mandarin
And lived in yellow-roofed Pekin.

Select bibliography

WORKS BY EILEEN POWER

PUBLISHED BOOKS

A Bibliography for Teachers of History (London, 1919)
The Paycockes of Coggeshall (London, 1920)
Report to the Trustees September 1920–September 1921, Alfred Kahn Travelling Fellowship, University of London (London, 1921)
Medieval English Nunneries c. *1275 to 1535* (Cambridge, 1922)
Medieval People (London, 1924)
The Industrial Revolution 1750–1850. A Select Bibliography (London, 1924)
The Wool Trade in English Medieval History (published posthumously, Oxford, 1941)
Medieval Women, ed. M. M. Postan (Cambridge, 1975)
with R. H. Tawney, *Tudor Economic Documents*, 3 vols. (London, 1924)
with M. M. Postan (eds.), *Studies in English Trade in the Fifteenth Century* (London, 1933)
with J. H. Clapham (eds.), *The Cambridge Economic History of Europe*, VOL. I (Cambridge, 1941)

EDITIONS, TRANSLATIONS AND CHILDREN'S BOOKS

P. Boissonade, *Life and Work in Medieval Europe. Fifth to Fifteenth Centuries*, trans. and introduction (London, 1927)
The Goodman of Paris, ed. and trans. (London, 1928)
Joannes Herolt, *Miracles of the Blessed Virgin Mary*, ed. and introduction (London, 1928)
The New World History Series, ed. with Bernard Manning, 4 vols. (London, 1920). First book by Eileen Power (London, 1920)
Europe Throughout the Ages, ed. with N. H. Baynes (London, 1929)
The Broadway Travellers, ed. with Sir Edward Dennison Ross, 26 vols. (London, 1926–38)
The Broadway Medieval Library, ed. with G. G. Coulton, 10 vols. (London, 1928–31)

The Broadway Diaries, Memoirs and Letters, ed. with Elizabeth Drew, 7 vols. (London, 1929–31)
Poems from the Irish selected by Eileen Power (London, 1927)
with Rhoda Power, *Boys and Girls of History* (Cambridge, 1926)
  Twenty Centuries of Travel (London, 1926)
  Cities and their Stories (London, 1927)
  More Boys and Girls of History (Cambridge, 1928)
Rhoda Power, *Richard the Lionheart and the Third Crusade,* ed. (London, 1931)

SELECTED PUBLISHED ARTICLES

'The cult of the virgin in the Middle Ages', *Cambridge Magazine* (28 April, 5 May, 9 June 1917); republished in *Medieval Women,* ed. Postan
'Medieval ideas about women', *Cambridge Magazine* (2, 9 November 1918); republished in *Medieval Women,* ed. Postan
'The effects of the Black Death on rural organisation in England', *History,* 3 (1918), 109–16
'On the teaching of history and world peace', in Marvin (ed.), *The Evolution of World Peace,* pp. 179–91
'A plea for the Middle Ages', *Economica,* 5 (1922), 173–80
'Pierre Du Bois and the domination of France', in F. J. C. Hearnshaw (ed.), *The Social and Political Ideas of Some Great Medieval Thinkers* (London, 1923), pp. 139–66
'The English wool trade in the reign of Edward III', *Cambridge Historical Journal,* 2 (1926), 17–35
'The position of women', in C. G. Crump and E. F. Jacob (eds.), *The Legacy of the Middle Ages* (Oxford, 1926), pp. 401–35
'The opening of the land routes to Cathay', in Newton (ed.), *Travel and Travellers of the Middle Ages,* pp. 142–58
'Peasant life and rural conditions (*c.* 1100 to *c.* 1500)', in Tanner et al. (eds.), *The Cambridge Medieval History,* vol. VII (1932), pp. 716–50
'On the need for a new edition of Walter of Henley', *Transactions of the Royal Historical Society,* 7 (1933), 101–16
'The wool trade in the fifteenth century', in Power and Postan (eds.), *Studies in English Trade in the Fifteenth Century*
'On medieval history as a social study', inaugural lecture, LSE, 1933, republished in *Economica,* 12 (1934), 13–29
'A problem of transition: review of Henri Pirenne, *Mohammed and Charlemagne* (1939)', *Economic History Review,* 10, 1 (1940), 60–2

UNPUBLISHED WORKS

'Introduction to world history', in papers of Eileen Power held by Lady Cynthia Postan, hereafter called Power–Postan Papers. Incomplete

version in Eileen Power's papers in the Postan Collection, Cambridge University Library (CUL), hereafter called Postan Papers
Unpublished lectures, Postan Papers
Unpublished lectures, Power–Postan Papers
'Mahatma Gandhi's boycott: another view', Power–Postan Papers
'Survey of evidence available for a historical enquiry into the family', Postan Papers
'The approach to political and economic problems in schools', Postan Papers
'The eve of the Dark Ages', lecture to Cambridge History Club, 1938, Power–Postan Papers
'The League of Nations', n.d., Postan Papers
Plans for a history of women, Postan Papers
'The economic history of the Great Powers, introduction; revised syllabus', R. H. Tawney Papers, British Library of Political and Economic Science (hereafter BLPES)
'Diaries – tour du monde 1920–21', Power–Postan Papers

JOURNALISM: SELECTED ITEMS

'Women of Cambridge', *The Old Cambridge*, 14 February 1920
'A guildsman on fascism', *The Nation and the Athenaeum*, 8 September 1922, 719
'Japan the enigma', *The Athenaeum*, 24 November 1923, 319–20
'Alien immigrants and the English arts and crafts', *Home-reading Magazine*, October 1922–May 1923
'The story of half mankind, review of Hendrik van Loon, *The Story of Mankind*, *The Challenge*, 20 September 1922, 17–18
'Joint stock history', *The Challenge*, 7 September 1923, 476
'Bismarck's universal robots', *The Nation and the Athenaeum*, 17 November 1923, 279
'Light and flashlight on the Irish Question', *The Nation and the Athenaeum*, 20 December 1924
'Early Ireland', *The Nation and the Athenaeum*, 16 May 1925
'The problem of the friars', *The Nation and the Athenaeum*, 18 January 1928, 753–7
'Too many lectures spoil the student', *Clare Market Review*, 12, 2 (Lent term, 1932), 7–8
'The achievement of medieval art', *The Listener*, 4 January 1933, 18–20
'Wool gathering in the Cotswolds', *The Highway*, October 1933, 7–9
'Geneva impressions', *The Spectator*, 22 December 1939, 892

COLLECTIONS OF PERSONAL PAPERS

Stella Benson Papers, CUL, Add. 8367
William Henry Beveridge Papers, BLPES

Helen Cam Papers, Girton College, Cambridge
G. D. H. Cole Papers, Nuffield College, Oxford
G. G. Coulton Papers, St John's College, Cambridge
Margaret Llewellan Davies Papers, Girton College, Cambridge
E. F. Gay Papers, Huntingdon Library, San Marino, California
Virginia Gildersleeve Papers, Barnard College, Columbia University, New
    York
J. L. and Barbara Hammond Papers, Bodleian Library, Oxford
Lilian Knowles Papers, BLPES
Lilian Knowles personal file, LSE
Sir James Stewart Lockhart Papers, National Library, Edinburgh
Bronislaw Malinowski Papers, BLPES
Dorothy Marshall diaries (in the possession of the family of the late Dorothy
    Marshall)
John U. Nef Jr Papers, University of Chicago Library, Chicago
Minute books of the education committee, Newnham College, Cambridge
Economic History Society Papers, Nuffield College, Oxford
Postan Papers, Cambridge University Library
Power Papers, Girton College, Cambridge
Eileen Power personal file, LSE
Eileen Power and Rhoda Power Papers, BBC written archives, Caversham
Power–Postan Papers (in the possession of Lady Cynthia Postan)
Rockefeller Foundation Papers, LSE archives, BLPES
Russell Papers, McMaster University, Hamilton, Canada
Charlotte Shaw Papers, BLPES
J. R. Tanner Papers, St John's College, Cambridge
R. H. Tawney Papers, BLPES
A. J. Toynbee Papers, Bodleian Library, Oxford
C. K. Webster Papers, BLPES

INTERVIEWS AND RECOLLECTIONS

Barker, T. C., 'Interview with H. L. A. Beales', video recording, University
    of Kent archives
Barker, T. C., 'Interview with Miss J. de L. Mann', video recording,
    University of Kent archives
Barker, T. C., 'Interview with M. M. Postan', video recording, University
    of Kent archives
Lord Briggs, recollections, March 1995
Marjorie Chibnall, interview, 15 March 1990
Clapham family recollections, 21 July 1993
Sir Michael Clapham, interview, 21 July 1993
Clark family recollections, 12 June 1990
Elizabeth Crittall, interview, 27 November 1991
Sir Raymond Firth, conversation, June 1988

Jean Floud, conversation, 23 July 1993
Sir John Habakkuk, recollections, February 1989; October 1994
Christopher Hill, recollections, February 1989
Dorothy Marshall, interview, 20 December 1991
Nadine Marshall, interview, 16 February 1993
Lady Cynthia Postan, interviews, June 1988, 4 November 1991
Martin Robertson, interview, 17 February 1993

PRIMARY SOURCES

Abram, Annie 'Women traders in medieval London', *Economic Journal*, 26 (1916), 276–85
Anstey, V. *The Economic Development of India* (London, 1929; new edns 1936, 1952)
Armstrong, Edward 'Italy in the time of Dante', in Tanner et al. (eds.) *The Cambridge Medieval History*, vol. VII (1932), pp. 1–48
'The Papacy and Naples in the fifteenth century', in Tanner et al. (eds.) *The Cambridge Medieval History*, vol. VIII (1936), pp. 158–201
Ashley, W. J. 'The history of English serfdom', *Economic Review*, 3 (April 1893), 153–73
Atkinson, Mabel 'The economic foundations of the women's movement', Fabian Women's Group Series, *Fabian Tracts*, 175 (1914); repr. in Alexander (ed.) *Women's Fabian Tracts*, pp. 256–82
Bateson, Mary 'The laws of Breteuil', *English Historical Review*, 15 (1900), 73–8, 302–19, 496–523, 754–75; 16 (1901), 92–110, 332–45
Bateson, Mary (ed.) *Borough Customs*, Selden Society 18 and 21 (London, 1904, 1906), vol. I, pp. 222–30; vol. II, pp. c-cxv, 102–29
Bennett, H. S. *Life on the English Manor* (Cambridge, 1937)
Beveridge, Janet *An Epic of Clare Market: Birth and Early Days of the London School of Economics* (London, 1960)
Beveridge, W. H. *Prices and Wages in England from the Twelfth to the Nineteenth Century* (London, 1939)
The London School of Economics and its Problems 1919–1937 (London, 1960)
Bloch, Marc *The Historian's Craft* (1914), trans. from the French (Manchester, 1954)
French Rural History: An Essay on its Basic Characteristics (1931), trans. from the French (Berkeley and Los Angeles, 1970)
'Pour mieux comprendre d'Europe d'Aujord'hui', *Annales d'histoire économique et sociale*, 10 (1938), 1942–3, 62
Feudal Society (1939), trans. from the French (London, 1961)
'The rise of dependent cultivation and seigneurial institutions', in Clapham et al. (eds.) *The Cambridge Economic History of Europe*, vol. I (1941), pp. 224–77

'A contribution towards a comparative history of European societies', in Bloch, Marc *Land and Work in Medieval Europe: Selected Papers by Marc Bloch*, trans. J. E. Anderson (New York, 1969), pp. 45–81

Bloch, Marc and Leuilliot, P. 'Books and articles on the economic history of France', *Economic History Review*, 9 (1938), 104–7

Braun, Lily *Die Frauenfrage, ihr geschichtliche Entwicklung und wirtschaftliche Seite* (Leipzig, 1901)

Briggs, Asa *The History of Broadcasting in the UK*, vol. II, *The Golden Age of the Wireless* (London, 1965)

Brittain, Vera *Testament of Youth* (1933; London, 1978)
Testament of Friendship: The Story of Winifred Holtby (London, 1940)

Bücher, Karl *Die Frauenfrage im Mittelalter* (Tübingen, 1910)

Buer, Mabel *Health, Wealth and Population in the Early Days of the Industrial Revolution* (London, 1926)

Burns, Eveline 'My LSE: 1916–1926', *LSE Magazine*, 66 (November 1983), 8–9

Cam, Helen M. *The Hundred and the Hundred Rolls. An Outline of Local Government in Medieval England* (London, 1930)

Campion, Sarah (pseud.) *Father. A Portrait of G. G. Coulton at Home* (London, 1948)

Clapham, J. H. *An Economic History of Modern Britain*, 3 vols. (Cambridge, 1926–38)
'Commerce and industry in the Middle Ages', in Tanner et al. (eds.) *The Cambridge Medieval History*, vol. VI (1929), pp. 473–503

Clapham, J. H. Power, E. E., Postan, M. M., Habakkuk, H. J., Coleman, D. C., Mathias, Peter and Pollard, Sidney (eds.) *The Cambridge Economic History of Europe*, 8 vols. (Cambridge, 1941–89)

Clark, Alice *The Working Life of Women in the Seventeenth Century* (London, 1919; new edns London, 1982, 1992)

Cole, G. D. H. *The World of Labour* (London, 1913)
A Short History of the British Working-class Movement (London, 1948)

Cole, Margaret *Growing up into Revolution* (London, 1949)

Collier, Frances *The Family Economy of the Working Classes in the Cotton Industry 1784–1833* (1921; new edn Manchester, 1965)

Coulton, G. G. *Fourscore Years: An Autobiography* (Cambridge, 1943)
Five Centuries of Religion, 4 vols. (Cambridge, 1923–50)
The Medieval Village (Cambridge, 1925)

Coulton, G. G. (ed.) *Cambridge Studies in Medieval Life and Thought*, 18 vols. (Cambridge, 1920–50)

Court, W. H. B. *Scarcity and Choice in History* (London and New York, 1970)

Cunningham, William *The Growth of English Industry and Commerce in Modern Times* (6th edn, Cambridge, 1907)

Dexter, E. *Colonial Women of Affairs: Women in Business and Professions in America before 1776* (Boston, 1924)

Dickinson, Goldsworthy Lowes *Letters from John Chinaman and Other Essays* (London, 1901)

Albert Kahn Travelling Fellowships. Report to the Trustees, October 1913 (London, 1913)

An Essay on the Civilizations of India, China and Japan (London, 1914)

Dixon, E. 'Craftswomen in the Livre des Métiers', *Economic Journal*, 5 (1895), 209–28

Dopsch, Alfons *The Economic and Social Foundations of European Civilization* (condensed by E. Patzelt), trans. M. G. Beard and Nadine Marshall (London, 1937)

Eckenstein, Lina *Women under Monasticism: Chapters on Saint-lore and Convent Life between AD 500 and AD 1500* (Cambridge, 1896)

Fabian Women's Group 'Summary of six papers and discussion upon the disabilities of women as workers ' (private circulation, 1909), *Fabian Tracts*, 140–84; repr. in Alexander (ed.) *Fabian Women's Tracts*, pp. 105–28

'Summary of eight papers and discussion upon the disabilities of mothers as workers' (private circulation, 1910), *Fabian Tracts*, 140–84

Fawcett, Millicent Garrett *What I Remember* (London, 1924)

Gasquet, Cardinal F. A. *The Eve of the Reformation* (London, 1900)

English Monastic Life (London, 1904)

George, Dorothy *London Life in the Eighteenth Century* (London, 1925)

England in Transition (London, 1931)

Gierke, Otto von *Community in Historical Perspective. Translation of Selections from Das deutsche Genossenschaftsrecht 1868*, ed. Antony Black (Cambridge, 1992)

Girton College Register 1869–1946 (Cambridge, 1948)

Gnauck-Kühne, Elizabeth *Warum organisieren wir die Arbeiterinnen?* (Leipzig, 1905)

Graham, Rose S. *Gilbert of Sempringham and the Gilbertines* (London, 1901)

Gras, N. S. B. 'The rise and development of economic history', *Economic History Review*, 1 (January 1927), 12–34

Grier, Lynda *The Life of Winifred Mercier* (Oxford, 1937)

Hamilton, Mary Agnes *Remembering My Good Friends* (London, 1944)

Hamilton Thompson, A. (ed.) *Visitations of Religious Houses in the Diocese of Lincoln*, Lincoln Record Society Publications, vol. VII (Lincoln, 1914)

English Monasteries (Cambridge, 1923)

Hammond, J. L. and Hammond, Barbara *The Town Labourer 1760–1832: The New Civilization* (London, 1917)

The Skilled Labourer 1760–1832 (London, 1919)

The Rise of Modern Industry (London, 1925)

Hodgkins, Winifred Howard *Two Lives* (Leeds, 1983)

Hutchins, B. L. 'The working life of women', Fabian Women's Group Series, *Fabian Tracts*, 157 (1911); repr. in Alexander (ed.) *Women's Fabian Tracts*, pp. 164–78

Women in Modern Industry (London, 1915)

Johnston, Sir Reginald F. *Twilight in the Forbidden City* (London, 1934)
Confucianism and Modern China. The Lewis Fry Memorial Lectures 1933–1934 (London, 1934)

Jones, E. E. C. *As I Remember. An Autobiographical Ramble* (London, 1922)

'Knowles, Lilian Charlotte Anne', *Who Was Who*, vol. II (1916–1928), p. 595

Knowles, L. C. A. *The Industrial and Commercial Revolutions in Great Britain during the Nineteenth Century* (London, 1921)

Kötzschke, Rudolf 'Manorial system', *Encyclopedia of the Social Sciences* (New York, 1933), vol. IX/X (New York, 1948), pp. 97–102

Kovalevsky, Maxime *Die ökonomische Entwicklung Europas bis zum Beginn der kapitalistischen Wirtschaftsform* (Berlin, 1901)
Allgemeine Wirtschaftsgeschichte des Mittelalters (Jena, 1924)

Laski, H. J. 'Political theory in the later Middle Ages', in Tanner et al. (eds.) *The Cambridge Medieval History*, vol. VIII (1936), pp. 620–45
A Grammar of Politics (London, 1925)

Langlois, C. V. and Seignobos, Charles *Introduction aux études historiques* (Paris, 1898)

Lehmann, Rosamund *Dusty Answer* (London, 1927; Harmondsworth, 1936)

Levett, A. E. 'The consumer in history', in Sir Percy Redfern (ed.) *Self and Society: First Twelve Essays on Social and Economic Problems from the hitherto Neglected Point of View of the Consumer* (London, 1930), pp. 1–38
Studies in Manorial History, ed. H. M. Cam, M. Coate and L. S. Sutherland (Oxford, 1938)
'The Black Death on the estates of the See of Winchester', in Vinogradoff (ed.) *Oxford Studies in Social and Legal History*, vol. V (1916)

Lewis, J. and Chaytor, M. 'Introduction', in Clark *The Working Life of Women* (1982 edn)

London School of Economics (LSE) *Calendar for the Session* (London, 1921–41)
LSE Register 1895–1932, ed. Mildred Bulkley and Amy Harrison, intro. by W. H. Beveridge (London, 1934)

Lyell, Laetitia *A Medieval Post-bag* (London, 1934)

Maitland, F. W. *Domesday Book and Beyond* (1897; new edn, with an introduction by Edward Miller London, 1960)
Township and Borough (Cambridge, 1898)
'The history of a Cambridgeshire manor', *English Historical Review*, 35 (1894), 417–39

Marshall, Dorothy *The English Poor in the Eighteenth Century. A Study in Social and Administrative History* (London, 1926)

Marvin, F. S. (ed.) *The Evolution of World Peace* (Oxford, 1921)

Meitzen, August *Siedlung und Agrarwesen der Westgermanen und Ostgermanen, der Kelten, Römer, Finnen und Slawen*, 3 vols. (Berlin, 1895)

Mitchison, Naomi *Small Talk: Memories of an Edwardian Childhood* (London, 1973)
All Change Here. Girlhood and Marriage (London, 1975)
You May Well Ask. A Memoir, 1920–1940 (London, 1979)

Newnham College Register (Cambridge, 1979)

Newton, A. P. (ed.) *Travel and Travellers of the Middle Ages* (London, 1926)

Oxford Directory (Oxford, 1904; 1907; 1910)

Palmer, Richard *School Broadcasting in Britain* (London, 1947)

Phillpotts, Bertha *Kindred and Clan* (London, 1913)

Pinchbeck, I. *Women and the Industrial Revolution 1750–1850* (London, 1930)

Pirenne, Jean Henri *Medieval Cities: Their Origins and the Revival of Trade* (1925; New York, 1956)

'Northern towns and their commerce', in Tanner et al. (eds.) *The Cambridge Medieval History*, vol. VII (1929), pp. 332–60

Mohammed and Charlemagne (1937), trans. B. Miall (London, 1939)

Pisan, Christine de *The Treasure of the City of the Ladies or the Book of the Three Virtues* (Harmondsworth, 1983)

[Pizan, Christine de] *The Book of the City of the Ladies*, trans. E. J. Richards (London, 1983)

Pollock, Frederick and Maitland, F. W. *The History of English Law* (Cambridge, 1895)

Postan, M. M. 'Credit in medieval trade', *Economic History Review*, 1 (1928), 234–61

'The economic and political relations of England and the Hanse from 1400 to 1475', in Power and Postan (eds.) *Studies in English Trade in the Fifteenth Century*

'Medieval capitalism', *Economic History Review*, 4 (1933), 212–27

'Recent trends in the accumulation of capital', *Economic History Review*, 6 (1935), 1–29

'History and the social sciences', in *The Social Sciences: Their Relations in Theory and Teaching*, Bedford College (London, 1936)

'The chronology of labour services', *Transactions of the Royal Historical Society*, 20 (1937), 169–93

'The historical method in the social sciences', inaugural lecture (Cambridge, 1939); repr. in Postan *Fact and Relevance*, pp. 22–34

'The rise of a money economy', *Economic History Review*, 14 (1944–5), 123–34

Preface to Clapham et al. (eds.) *The Cambridge Economic History of Europe*, vol. VII (1952), p. ix

Fact and Relevance (Cambridge, 1971)

Honorary degree of Doctor of Science in Social Science, laureation address, University of Edinburgh, 14 August 1978

Power, Rhoda *Under Cossack and Bolshevik* (London, 1919)

Russell, A. 'Appendix on social democracy and the woman question in Germany', in Russell, B. *German Social Democracy* (London, 1896), 175–95

Russell, Bertrand *The Autobiography of Bertrand Russell, 1914–1944*, vol. II (London, 1968)

Russell, Dora *The Tamarisk Tree: My Quest for Liberty and Love* (London, 1975)

Schreiner, Olive *Woman and Labour* (English edn, London, 1911)

Sombart, Werner *Der Moderne Kapitalismus* (4th edn, Munich and Leipzig, 1916)
Spruill, J. *Women's Life and Work in the Southern Colonies* (Chapel Hill, 1938)
Stephen, Barbara *Girton College, 1869–1932* (Cambridge, 1933)
Stocks, Mary Danvers *My Commonplace Book* (London, 1970)
Strachey, Rachel Conn *The Cause: A Short History of the Women's Movement in Great Britain* (London, 1928)
Stratford, E. Wingfield *Before the Lamps Went Out. Autobiographical Reminiscences* (London, 1945)
Strong, L. A. G. *English Domestic Life during the Last 200 Years* (London, 1942)
Swanwick, Helen M. *I Have Been Young* (London, 1935)
Tanner, J. R., Previté-Orton, C. W. and Brooke, Z. N. (eds.) *The Cambridge Medieval History*, 7 vols. (Cambridge, 1911–32)
Tawney, R. H. *The Agrarian Problem in the Sixteenth Century* (London, 1912)
The Establishment of Minimum Rates in the Tailoring Industry under the Trade Boards Act of 1909 (London, 1915)
Religion and the Rise of Capitalism: A Historical Study, Holland memorial lectures (1922; London, 1926)
Land and Labour in China (London, 1932)
'Postan, Eileen Edna le Poer (1889–1940)' in Wickham Legge, L. G. (ed.) *Dictionary of National Biography 1931–1940* (London, 1949), pp. 718–19
Beatrice Webb 1858–1943 (London, 1945)
'China 1930–1931', in Tawney, R. H. *The Attack and Other Papers* (London, 1953), 35–51
Toynbee, A. J. *A Journey to China: Or, Things Which Are Seen* (London, 1931)
A Study of History, vols. I–VI abridged by D. C. Somervell (London, 1946)
Acquaintances (Oxford, 1967)
Trevelyan, G. M. 'Clio, a muse', in Trevelyan, G. M. *Clio, A Muse and Other Essays Literary and Pedestrian* (London, 1918), pp. 1–55
English Social History (London, 1944)
Tuke, M. J. *A History of Bedford College for Women 1849–1937* (London, 1939)
Unwin, George *The Guilds and Companies of London* (London, 1908)
Samuel Oldknow and the Arkwrights (Manchester, 1924)
Studies in Economic History, ed. R. H. Tawney, with an introductory memoir by R. H. Tawney (London, 1927)
Vinogradoff, P. (ed.) *Oxford Studies in Social and Legal History*, 9 vols. (Oxford, 1909–27)
Wadsworth, A. P. and Mann, J. de L. *The Cotton Trade and Industrial Lancashire 1600–1780* (Manchester, 1931)
Webb, M. Beatrice, *The Diaries of Beatrice Webb*, ed. Norman and Jeanne MacKenzie, 4 vols. (London, 1982–5)
Webb, Sidney and Webb, Beatrice *The Webbs in Asia. The 1911–1912 Travel Diary*, ed. George Feaver (London, 1992)
Wells, H. G. *History is One* (London, 1919)
Experiment in Autobiography (London, 1934)
An Outline of History (London, 1920)

Woolf, Virginia *A Room of One's Own* (London, 1928)
  Three Guineas (1938; London, 1991)
  The Diary of Virginia Woolf, ed. Anne Oliver Bell (1977; Harmondsworth, 1979)
Wootton, Barbara *In a World I Never Made* (London, 1967)

SECONDARY WORKS

Agulhon, Maurice *The French Republic 1879–1992* (Oxford, 1993)
Airlie, Shiona *Thistle and Bamboo* (Oxford, 1989)
Alberti, J. *Beyond Suffrage. Feminists in War and Peace, 1914–1928* (London, 1989)
Alexander, Sally *Becoming a Woman and Other Essays in Nineteenth and Twentieth Century Feminist History* (London, 1944)
Alexander, Sally (ed.) *Women's Fabian Tracts* (London, 1988)
Annan, N. G. 'The intellectual aristocracy', in Plumb, J. H. (ed.) *Studies in Social History: A Tribute to G. M. Trevelyan* (London, 1955), pp. 243–87
Barker, T. C. 'The beginnings of the Economic History Society', *Economic History Review*, 30 (1977), 1–19
Baron, Lily 'Girton in the First World War', *Girton Review* (Easter term, Cambridge, 1965)
Bennett, J. M. *Women in the Medieval English Countryside* (Oxford, 1987)
  ' "History that stands still": women's work in the European past', *Feminist Studies*, 14 (1988)
  'Medievalism and feminism', *Speculum*, 68 (1993), 308–31
Berg, Maxine *The Age of Manufactures: Industry, Innovation and Work in Britain 1700–1820* (1st edn, London, 1985)
  Introduction to Berg, Maxine (ed.) *Political Economy in the Twentieth Century* (London, 1991), pp. 1–25
  'The first women economic historians', *Economic History Review*, 45 (1992), 308–29
  'Eileen Power and women's history', *Gender and History*, 6 (1994), 265–74
  'A woman in history: Eileen Power', in O'Dowd and Wichert (eds.) *Chattel, Servant or Citizen*, pp. 12–21
Bickers, Robert 'Changing British attitudes to China and the Chinese, 1928–1931' (University of London, Ph.D. thesis, 1992)
  ' "Coolie work": Sir Reginald Johnston at the School of Oriental Studies, 1931–1937', *Journal of the Royal Asiatic Society*, 5 (1995)
Bonney, M. 'The English medieval wool and cloth trade: new approaches for the local historian', *The Local Historian* (February 1992), 18–40
Boos, Florence S. (ed.) *History and Community: Essays in Victorian Medievalism* (New York, 1992)
Brown, J. M. *Gandhi's Rise to Power. Indian Politics 1915–1922* (Cambridge, 1992)
  Modern India: The Origins of an Asian Democracy (Oxford, 1985)

Burrow, J. W. ' "The village community" and the uses of history in late nineteenth-century England', in McKendrick, Neil (ed.) *Historical Perspectives. Studies in English Thought and Society in Honour of J. H. Plumb* (London, 1974), pp. 255–84

Caine, Barbara 'Beatrice Webb and the "woman question" ', *History Workshop*, 14 (1982), 23–43

Victorian Feminists (Oxford, 1992)

Caine, Sydney *The History of the Foundation of the LSE* (London, 1963)

Cam, H. M. (ed.) *Selected Historical Essays of F. W. Maitland* (Cambridge, 1957)

Campbell, R. H. 'Scottish economic and social history: past developments and future prospects', *Scottish Economic and Social History*, 10 (1990), 5–20

Campbell, Stuart L. *The Second Empire Revisited. A Study in French Historiography* (New Brunswick, NJ, 1978)

Cannadine, David 'The past and the present in the English industrial revolution, 1880–1980', *Past and Present*, 103 (1984), 149–58

G. M. Trevelyan. A Life in History (London, 1992)

Cantor, N. F. *Inventing the Middle Ages* (Cambridge, 1991)

Carey, John *The Intellectuals and the Masses* (London, 1992)

Ceadel, Martin *Pacifism in Britain 1914–1945: The Defining of a Faith* (Oxford, 1980)

Christianson, G. 'G. G. Coulton: the medievalist as controversialist', *Catholic Historical Review*, 57 (1971), 421–41

Clark, G. Kitson 'A hundred years of the teaching of history at Cambridge, 1873–1973', *The Historical Journal*, 16 (1973), 353–553

Clarke, Peter *Liberals and Social Democrats* (Cambridge, 1978)

Coats, A. W. 'The historicist reaction in English political economy 1870–1890', *Economica*, 21 (1954), 143–53

Coleman, D. C. *History and the Economic Past* (Oxford, 1987)

Collini, Stefan *Public Moralists: Political Thought and Intellectual Life in Britain 1850–1930* (London, 1991)

Corran, M. *The Invisible Man: The Life and Liberties of H. G. Wells* (London, 1992)

Cunningham, Valentine *British Writers of the Thirties* (Oxford, 1989)

Dahrendorf, Ralf *A History of the London School of Economics and Political Science 1895–1995* (Oxford, 1995)

Davidoff, Leonore *The Best Circles* (London, 1973)

Davin, Anna 'Introduction to history, the nation and the schools', *History Workshop Journal*, 29 (1990), 92–4

Davis, N. Z. 'History's two bodies', *American Historical Review*, 93 (1988), 1–30

'Women's history in transition: the European case', *Feminist Studies*, 3 (1976), 83–103

'Women and the world of the "Annales" ', *History Workshop*, 33 (1992), 121–38

Dewey, Clive *Anglo-Indian Attitudes. The Mind of the Indian Civil Service* (London, 1993)

Durbin, Elizabeth *New Jerusalems. The Labour Party and the Economics of Democratic Socialism* (London, 1985)

Dyhouse, Carol *Feminism and the Family in England 1880–1939* (Oxford, 1989) *No Distinction of Sex? Women in British Universities, 1870–1939* (London, 1995)

Epstein, S. R. 'Marc Bloch: the identity of a historian', *Journal of Medieval History*, 19 (1993), 273–83

Faderman, Lilian *Surpassing the Love of Men: Romantic Friendship and Love between Women from the Renaissance to the Present* (New York, 1981)

Fink, Carole *Marc Bloch. A Life in History* (Cambridge, 1989)

First, Ruth and Scott, A. *Oliver Schreiner* (London, 1980)

Floud, Roderick, 'Words not numbers: John Harold Clapham', *History Today*, 39 (April 1989), 42–7

Forster, E. M. *Goldsworthy Lowes Dickinson* (London, 1934)

Freeden, Michael *Liberalism Divided. A Study in British Political Thought 1914–1939* (Oxford, 1986)

The New Liberalism. An Ideology of Social Reform (Oxford, 1978)

'George, Mary Dorothy', *Who Was Who*, vol. VII (1980), p. 293

Gilchrist, Roberta and Oliva, Marilyn 'Religious women in medieval East Anglia', *Studies in East Anglian History*, 1 (Centre for East Anglian Studies, Norwich, 1993)

Goldin, Claudia 'The economic status of women in the early Republic: quantitative evidence', *Journal of Interdisciplinary History*, 16 (1986), 375–404

Gorham, D. 'Have we really rounded seraglio point? Vera Brittain and inter-war feminism', in Smith, H. L. (ed.) *British Feminism in the Twentieth Century* (Aldershot, 1990), pp. 84–103

Gorodetsky, Gabriel *Stafford Cripps' Mission to Moscow 1940–1942* (Cambridge, 1984)

Halsey, A. H. 'Provincials and professionals: the British post-war sociologists', *LSE Quarterly*, 1 (March 1987), 43–74

Hanawalt, Barbara 'Golden ages for the history of medieval English women', in Susan Stuard (ed.) *Women in Medieval History and Historiography* (Philadelphia, 1987), 1–24

The Ties that Bind: Peasant Families in Medieval England (New York and Oxford, 1986)

Hanawalt, Barbara (ed.) *Women and Work in Pre-industrial Europe* (Bloomington, 1986)

Hancock, Keith *Country and Calling* (London, 1954)

Harris, José *William Beveridge: A Biography* (Oxford, 1977)

'Political thought and the welfare state 1870–1940: an intellectual framework for British social policy', *Past and Present*, 135 (May 1992), 116–41

Private Lives, Public Virtues (Oxford, 1993)

'The Webbs, the COS and the Ratan Tata Foundation: social policy from the perspective of 1912', in Bulmer, M., Lewis, J. and Piachaud, D. (eds.) *The Goals of Social Policy* (London, 1989), pp. 27–63

Harrison, B. 'Women in a men's house. The women MPs 1919–1945', *Historical Journal*, 29 (1986), 623–54

Prudent Revolutionaries: Portraits of British Feminists between the Wars (Oxford, 1987)

Harte, N. B. 'Trends in publications of the economic and social history of Great Britain and Ireland, 1925–1974', *Economic History Review*, 30 (1977), 20–41

The Admission of Women to University College London: A Centenary Lecture (London, 1979)

Harte, N. B. (ed.) *The Study of Economic History* (London, 1971)

Harte, N. B. and North, J. *The World of University College London, 1828–1978* (London, 1978)

Hastings, M. and Kimball, E. G. 'Two distinguished medievalists – Nellie Neilson and Bertha Putnam', *Journal of British Studies*, 18 (1979), 142–59

Hayeck, F. A. 'The London School of Economics 1895–1945', *Economica*, 13 (1946), 1–31

Hill, A. O. and Hill, B. H. 'Marc Bloch and comparative history', *American Historical Review*, 85 (October 1980), 828–57

Hill, Bridget 'A refuge from men: the idea of a Protestant nunnery', *Past and Present*, 117 (1987), 107–30

The Republican Virago. The Life and Times of Catharine Macaulay, Historian (Oxford, 1992)

'Women's history: a study in change, continuity or standing still?', *Women's History Review*, 2 (1993), 5–22

Howarth, Janet and Curthoys, Mark 'The political economy of women's higher education in late nineteenth and early twentieth century Britain', *Historical Research*, 60 (1987), 208–31

Howell, Martha, Wemple, Suzanne and Kaiser, Denise 'A documented presence: medieval women in Germanic historiography', in Susan Stuard (ed.) *Women in Medieval History and Historiography* (Philadelphia, 1987)

Hufton, Olwen 'Women in history: early modern Europe', *Past and Present*, 101 (1983), 125–41

Hughes, H. Stuart *Consciousness and Society. The Reorientation of European Social Thought 1890–1930* (New York, 1958)

Huppert, Georges 'The Annales school before the Annales', *Review*, 1, c/4 (1978), 215–19

Jann, Rosemary 'From amateur to professional': the case of the Oxbridge historians', *Journal of British Studies*, 22 (1983), 122–47

Kadish, Alon *The Oxford Economists in the Late Nineteenth Century* (Oxford, 1982)

Historians, Economists and Economic History (London, 1989)

Kennard, Jean E. *Vera Brittain & Winifred Holtby: A Working Partnership* (Hanover and London, 1989)

Kenyon, J. P. *The History Men* (London, 1983)

Kowaleski, M. and Bennett, J. M. 'Crafts, guilds, and women in the Middle Ages: 50 years after Marian K. Dale', *Signs: Journal of Women in Culture and Society*, 14 (1989), 474–501

Kramnick, Isaac and Sheerman, Barry *Harold Laski. A Life on the Left* (Harmondsworth, 1993)

Kushner, Tony *The Persistence of Prejudice. Antisemitism in British Society during the Second World War* (Manchester, 1989)

Levine, Philippa 'Love, friendship and feminism in later 19th-century England', *Women's Studies International Forum*, 13 (1990), 63–78

Lewis, Jane *The Politics of Motherhood* (Montreal, 1980)

Liddington, Jill *The Long Road to Greenham: Feminism and Anti-militarism in Britain since 1820* (London, 1989)

Linehan, P. A. 'The making of the *Cambridge Medieval History*', *Speculum*, 57, 3 (1982), 463–94

Lyon, Bryce *Henri Pirenne. A Biographical and Intellectual Study* (Ghent, 1974)

The Middle Ages in Recent Historical Thought. Selected Topics (Washington, 1959)

Mack, Phyllis *Visionary Women: Ecstatic Prophecy in Seventeenth-Century England* (Berkeley, 1992)

MacKenzie, Norman and MacKenzie, Jeanne *The Time Traveller. The Life of H. G. Wells* (London, 1973)

MacKerras, Colin *Western Images of China* (Oxford, 1991)

Mayeur, Jean-Marie and Rébérioux, Madeleine *The Third Republic from its Origins to the Great War 1871–1914* (Cambridge, 1984)

Matthew, David *Lord Acton and his Times* (London, 1968)

McNeill, William H. *Arnold J. Toynbee: A Life* (New York and Oxford, 1989)

Medlicott, W. N. *The Economic Blockade* (London, 1952)

Melman, Billie 'Gender, history and memory: the invention of women's past in the nineteenth and early twentieth centuries', *History and Memory*, 5 (1993), 5–41

O'Dowd, Mary 'Irish historiography and women historians in Ireland', unpublished paper presented to the Warwick Regional Seminar on Gender, History and Historiography, 28 February 1994

O'Dowd, Mary and Wichert, Sabine (eds.) *Chattel, Servant or Citizen. Women's Status in Church and State*, Irish Historical Studies, xix (Belfast, 1995)

Ohlander, Ann-Sofie 'Ellen Fries – female historian and historian of women's history', *Gender and History*, 4 (1992), 240–7

Ormrod, David 'R. H. Tawney and the origins of capitalism', *History Workshop*, 18 (1984), 138–59

Parker, Christopher *The English Historical Tradition since 1850* (Edinburgh, 1990)

Pimlott, Ben *Frustrate Their Knavish Tricks: Writings on Biography, History and Politics* (London, 1994)

Postan, M. M. 'Political and intellectual progress', in Rogers, W. T. (ed.) *Hugh Gaitskell 1906–1963* (London, 1964), pp. 49–66

Powicke, F. M. *Modern Historians and the Study of History* (London, 1955)
Prévost, M., D'Amat, R. and Tribout de Movembert, H. *Dictionnaire de biographie française*, vol. XVII (Paris, 1989)
Pugh, Martin *Women and the Women's Movement in Britain 1914–1959* (London, 1992)
Pugh, Patricia *Educate, Agitate, Organise: 100 Years of Fabian Socialism* (London, 1984)
Raftis, J. A. 'Marc Bloch's comparative method and the rural history of medieval England', *Medieval Studies*, 24 (1962), 349–68
Raverat, Gwen *Period Piece. A Cambridge Childhood* (London, 1952)
Raymond, Janice *A Passion for Friends: Towards a Philosophy of Female Affection* (London, 1986)
Razi, Zvi 'The historiography of manorial court rolls before World War II', in Razi, Zvi and Smith, R. M. (eds.), *Medieval and Small Town Society* (forthcoming Oxford, 1996)
  'Rural society and the economy', unpublished paper presented to the Economic History Society Conference, Edinburgh, 1995
Ringer, Fritz *Fields of Knowledge. French Academic Culture in Comparative Perspective 1890–1920* (Cambridge, 1992)
Roberts, J. A. G. *China through Western Eyes. The Nineteenth Century* (London, 1991)
Roberts, R. Ellis *Portrait of Stella Benson* (London, 1939)
Robinson, J. *Wayward Women. A Guide to Women Travellers* (Oxford, 1991)
Ruffer, Veronica and Taylor, A. J. (eds.) *Medieval Studies Presented to Rose Graham* (Oxford, 1950)
Said, Edward *Orientalism: Western Conceptions of the Orient* (1978; Harmondsworth, 1991)
Samuel, Raphael 'Grand narratives', *History Workshop*, 29 (1990), 120–33
Schumpeter, Joseph *History of Economic Analysis* (1954; Boston, 1981)
Scott, J. W. 'American women historians 1884–1984', in Scott, J. W. *Gender and the Politics of History* (New York, 1988), pp. 178–231
Searle, Eleanor 'Seigneurial control of women's marriage: the antecedents and function of *merchet* in England', *Past and Present*, 82 (1979), 3–43
Simmons, Clare A. *Reversing the Conquest. History and Nineteenth-century British Literature* (New Brunswick, 1990)
Skidelsky, Robert *John Maynard Keynes*, vol. I, *Hopes Betrayed* (London, 1983)
Smith, B. G. 'The contribution of women to modern historiography in Great Britain, France and the United States, 1750–1940', *American Historical Review*, 89 (1984), 709–32
Smith, R. J. *The Gothic Bequest: Medieval Institutions in British Thought, 1688–1863* (Cambridge, 1987)
Smith, R. M., introduction to Power, Eileen, *Medieval People* (10th edn, 1986), pp. xiii–xlvi
  ' "Modernization" and the corporate medieval village community in England: some sceptical reflections', in Baker, A. R. H. and Gregory,

Derek (eds.) *Explorations in Historical Geography* (Cambridge, 1994), pp. 140–70

Smith-Rosenberg, Caroll 'The female world of love and ritual: relations between women in nineteenth century America', *Signs*, 1 (1975), 1–29

Sondheimer, Janet *History of the British Federation of University Women 1909–1957* (London, 1957)

Steedman, Carolyn *Childhood, Culture and Class in Britain: Margaret McMillan, 1860–1931* (London, 1990)

Stock, Phyllis H. 'Students vs. the university in pre-world war Paris', *French Historical Studies*, 7 (1971–2), 93–110

Strachey, Barbara *Remarkable Relations. The Story of the Pearsall Smith Family* (London, 1980)

Stuard, S. M. (ed.) *Women in Medieval Society* (Philadelphia, 1976)

'A new dimension? North American scholars contribute their perspective', in Rosenthal, Bernard and Szarmach, Paul (eds.) *Medievalism in American Culture* (Binghampton, NY, 1984), pp. 67–84

Terrill, Ross *R. H. Tawney and his Times* (London, 1974)

Thirsk, Joan 'Foreword', in Prior, Mary (ed.) *Women in English Society 1500–1800* (London, 1985), pp. 1–21

'The history women', in O'Dowd and Wichert (eds.) *Chattel, Servant or Citizen*, pp. 1–11

Thom, Deborah 'The bundle of sticks: women, trade unionists and collective organization before 1918', in John, Angela (ed.) *Unequal Opportunities* (Oxford, 1986)

Todd, Janet *Women's Friendships in Literature* (New York, 1980)

Trevor-Roper, H. R. 'The twilight of the monks', in Trevor-Roper, H. R. *Historical Essays* (New York, 1975)

Tullberg, Rita McWilliams *Women at Cambridge* (London, 1975)

Vicinus, Martha 'Distance and desire: English boarding-school friendships', *Signs*, 9 (1984), 600–22

Independent Women: Work and Community for Single Women 1850–1920 (London, 1985)

Wall, Richard and Winter, Jay (eds.) *The Upheaval of War. Family, Work and Welfare in Europe, 1914–1918* (Cambridge, 1988)

Weber, Eugen *The Nationalist Revival in France 1905–1914* (Berkeley, 1968)

'Webster, Sir Charles Kingsley (1886–1961)', *Who Was Who, 1961–1970* (London, 1970), p. 1181

Winter, J. M., introduction to Winter, J. M. (ed.) *History and Society: Essays by R. H. Tawney* (London, 1978), pp. 1–35

Workman, Leslie J. (ed.) *Medievalism in England* (Cambridge, 1992)

OBITUARIES

Beveridge, W. H. 'Professor Lilian Knowles 1870–1926', *Economica*, 6 (1926), 119–22

Chibnall, Marjorie 'Eleanora Mary Carus-Wilson, 1899–1977', *Proceedings of the British Academy*, 18 (1982), 503–20

Clapham, J. H. 'Eileen Power, 1889–1940', *Economica*, 7, 27 (1940), 355–9

Coulton, G. G. 'Memories of Eileen Power', *Cambridge Review*, 52 (1940), 28–9

Curran, M. B. 'Ellen Annette McArthur, 1862–1927', *Girton Review*, 75 (1927), 83–103

Gras, N. S. B., Neilson, N. and Thompson, J. W. 'Eileen Power', *Speculum*, 16 (1941), 381–2

Greville, J. A. S. 'C. K. Webster, 1886–1961', *LSE*, 51 (June 1976), 4–5

Harte, N. B. 'Julia de Lacy Mann, 1891–1985: a memoir', *Textile History*, 17 (1986), 3–6

Jamison, E. R. 'Memoir', in Levett *Studies in Manorial History*, pp. i–xix

Jones, M. G. 'Memories of Eileen Power', *Girton Review*, 114 (1940), 3–13

Levett, A. E. 'Sir Paul Vinogradoff', *Economic Journal*, 36 (1926), 310–17

Miller, Edward 'Michael Moissey Postan 1899–1981', *Proceedings of the British Academy*, 69 (1983), 543–57

'Sir Michael Moissey Postan, 1899–1981', *Economic History Review*, 30 (1982), iv–vi

Power, Eileen 'Professor Lilian Knowles', *Girton Review*, 72 (1926), 3–6

'Eileen Power', *Manchester Guardian*, 12 August 1940

'Eileen Power', *The Times*, 15 August 1940; 19 August 1940

Tawney, R. H. *Eileen Power*, address delivered at Golders Green Crematorium, 12 August 1940 (London, 1940)

'Eileen Power', *Economic History Review*, 10 (1940), 91–4

T. E. G. [T. E. Gregory] 'Lilian Knowles', *Economic Journal*, 36 (1926), 317–20

Webster, C. K. 'Eileen Power (1889–1940)', *The Economic Journal*, 50 (1940), 561–72

Wolffe, Philippe 'Eileen Power', *Annales d'histoire sociale*, 7 (1945), 127–8

NEWSPAPER ARTICLES AND REVIEWS

Bloch, Marc 'Review of Power and Postan, *Studies in English Trade in the Fifteenth Century*', *Annales d'histoire economique et sociale*, 6 (1934), 316–18

Cannadine, David 'Review of Skidelsky, R., *John Maynard Keynes*', *Observer*, 1 November 1992

Collini, Stefan 'Like family, like nation, review of Cannadine, D., *G. M. Trevelyan*', *Times Literary Supplement*, 16 October 1992, 3–4

'Early English trade: review of *Studies in English Trade in the Fifteenth Century*', *The Times Literary Supplement*, 1 June 1933

'English nunneries: review of *Medieval English Nunneries*', *The Times Literary Supplement*, 28 December 1922

Henri, P. 'Review of Alfons Dopsch, *Naturalwirtschaft und Geldwirtschaft in der Weltgeschichte* (Vienna, 1930)', *Economic History Review*, 4 (1930), 359–60

Lynd, S. 'New history for old: *Medieval People* by Eileen Power', *Time and Tide*, 5 December 1924, 1188–9

McIntyre, I. 'Finest flower of an autumnal civilisation', review of Skidelsky, *John Maynard Keynes*, *The Independent*, 14 November 1992, 29

Pares, Richard '*A Study of History* by Arnold J. Toynbee', *English Historical Review*, 71 (1956), 256–72

Postan, M. M. '*Medieval People*', *The Clare Market Review*, 5, 1 (1924), 27–8

'*A Study of History*. A review of Professor Toynbee's book', *The Sociological Review*, 281 (1936), repr. in Postan *Fact and Relevance*, pp. 144–53

Putnam, B. H. '*Medieval English Nunneries*', *American Historical Review*, 29 (1924), 538–9

Samuel, R. 'One in the eye', *The Times Educational Supplement*, 18 May 1990, 16

Tawney, R. H. 'Review of Marc Bloch', *Economic History Review*, 4, 2 (1933), 230–33

Index

Abram, Annie 10, 115
account rolls 119
Adams, Herbert Baxter 7
Adams, W. G. S. 163
Agathon 59
All-India Home Rule League 89
Amritsar massacre 89, 92, 93, 148
Angel, Norman 147
Anglo-American Historical Conference 166
Annales d'histoire économique et sociale 210–11, 251
Annales school 211, 251
Anstey, Vera Powell (1889–1976) 70, 157, 168
anthropology 5, 162, 165, 212
anti-Semitism 60, 61, 236, 240
Apostles 39
archaeology 208
Armstrong, Edward (1846–1928) 36–7, 65, 134
Ashley, W. J. 166
Ashton, T. S. 252
Atkinson, Mabel 66, 68
Austrian school of economics 165

BBC 224, 232–4
bankruptcy 18
Barker, Ernest (1874–1960) 224
Barnard College, USA 158, 172, 177, 178
Baron, Lily 82
Bateson, Mary (1865–1906) 6, 9–10, 115
Baynes, Norman H. 214
Beales, Hugh Lancelot A. (1889–1988) 144, 150, 157, 159, 160, 170, 183
Beard, M. G. 'Barbula' 38, 78, 153, 155n., 209
Bedier, Joseph 62
Beggs, Mary 234
Behrens, Betty 252
Benedictine rule 119, 121
Bennett, H. S. 85, 134, 250
Bennett, Judith 1n., 7n., 8n., 10n.
Benson, Stella (1892–1933) 174–5, 179
Berenson, Mary Pearsall Smith (formerly Mrs Frank Costelloe) 50, 51

Bergson, Henri (1859–1941) 58
Besant, Annie (1847–1933) 90, 93
Beveridge, William (later Lord) (1879–1963) 109, 146, 199
birth control 45n, 145
Black Death 7, 132
Bloch, Marc (1886–1944) 2, 14, 56n., 61, 62, 169, 198, 200, 208–17, 221, 249, 250, 252, 254, 260
Bognetti, G. P. 214, 215
Bosanquet, Bernard 224
Bowley, Sir Arthur L. (1869–1957) 144–5, 182
Brace, Donald 169, 185
Braudel, Fernand 251
Braudel, Paule 194
British Federation of University Women 135, 136n., 177, 178
Brittain, Vera 25–6, 28, 29, 40, 77–8, 80
Brogan, D. W. 163
Brooke, Z. N. 36, 207
Browning, Oscar 85–6
Bryn Mawr College, USA 7, 169, 177, 261
Bücher, Karl 119, 208, 211
Buer, Mabel Craven 11, 70, 168
Burma 97–9
Burns, Arthur 145
Burns, Eveline Richardson (1900–85) 144, 187
Bury, J. B. 8

Cadbury, Laurence 169, 252
Cam, Helen 49, 66, 112–13, 168, 196, 197, 240–1, 251
Cambridge University 8, 35, 38, 76, 77, 141
degrees for women 108–9, 140, 142
Camden Society 112
Canada 107
Cannadine, David 10, 12, 195, 248
Cannan, Edwin 145, 146, 182
Cantor, Norman 8n., 260–1
Cape, Jonathan 169, 252
Carpenter, Edward 91

285